Young People in Contemporary Ireland

Young People in Contemporary Ireland

Kevin Lalor, Áine de Róiste & Maurice Devlin

Gill & Macmillan

Gill & Macmillan Ltd
Hume Avenue
Park West
Dublin 12
with associated companies throughout the world
www.gillmacmillan.ie

978 07171 4211 8

Index compiled by Helen Litton
Print origination in Ireland by Carole Lynch

*The paper used in this book is made from the wood pulp
of managed forests. For every tree felled, at least one tree
is planted, thereby renewing natural resources.*

A CIP catalogue record for this book is available
from the British Library.

Contents

Foreword

The publication of *Young People in Contemporary Ireland* is both significant and welcome. It is significant in the scope and comprehensiveness of the volume and the fact that it is the first study on this scale of young people in Ireland. It is welcome in that it addresses the full range of issues relating to that period in the life cycle during which, as the authors say, 'we probably see more change, transition, upheaval and reorientation than at any other time in our lives', and it places these in the context of a rapidly changing society.

The book makes it clear that the experience of being young in Ireland today is profoundly different compared with only a few years ago. Most of our young people have no experience of forced migration or unemployment, have disposable incomes unimagined by many of us when we were teenagers, enjoy a consumer lifestyle and have extensive opportunities for travel we could only dream of. On the other hand, they have to deal with considerable pressures relating to education and work, increasingly both at the same time, and with the challenge of balancing participation in a consumer youth culture – which seems always to urge them to live for the moment – with the need to act responsibly and prepare for the future. Most of them cope with these pressures and challenges very well. The authors certainly show that the simple stereotype of 'teenagers in turmoil' does not accurately portray the lived reality for most young people in Ireland.

Interdisciplinarity is one of the strengths of *Young People in Contemporary Ireland* and an early chapter examines a wide range of perspectives, both psychological and sociological, on adolescence and youth. There are comprehensive chapters on young people in families, their social world and peer relationships. The chapter on health and well-being examines all aspects of young people's health, both physical and mental, and among other things looks at the ill effects of drug use and binge drinking. It confirms that Irish young people top the league of young binge drinkers in Europe, which of course is something they have learned from their elders, so the challenge in this respect is one for Irish society and culture as a whole. A fundamental change at the level of values and attitudes – another one of the areas explored in depth in this volume – is required.

In relation to education and employment, the authors lay down a challenge for government when they argue that even at a time of unprecedented economic success, 'Irish funding of education does not match our international counterparts'. They outline numerous areas where there is scope for considerable improvement, such as school completion and access to third-level education. Leisure provision is another area where there is a need for improvement. The authors highlight some of the most significant barriers to young people's participation in leisure activities and they also draw attention to the need for young people to have a say in the content and format of leisure provision to ensure that their needs and preferences can be addressed and their growing autonomy respected. Thankfully, this need has been recognised by the Office of the Minister for Children during the development of the recreation strategy for young people.

Chapter 9 on juvenile justice contains a full discussion of the Children Act 2001 and the more recent amending legislation. It is recognised that while some positive and promising steps have been taken, they have been overshadowed by retrograde ones, such as increasing the age of criminal responsibility to only 10 years for some serious crimes, instead of the 12 years originally provided for, and the introduction of ASBOs despite intensive campaigning by children's and young people's NGOs, including the National Youth Council of Ireland. The authors note that the management of youth justice in Ireland was highlighted as a concern by the UN Committee on the Rights of the Child on both occasions that Ireland has come before it and express the hope, which many of us will share, that there will be dramatic improvements in this area next time around.

A feature of *Young People in Contemporary Ireland* which will be particularly valuable to students and practitioners alike is its overview of the major types of service and policy that are designed specifically with young people in mind. It pays particular attention to youth work, which is appropriate given the significant recent developments in legislation and provision in this area and the increasing recognition being given to youth work's role in meeting young people's needs. Current youth work thinking places a strong emphasis on equality, inclusiveness and the valuing of diversity, and this is also very true of this book. Chapter 11 on marginalised and excluded young people highlights the fact that 'youth' is not a homogeneous group and that some young people, by virtue of their identities and/or circumstances, face additional challenges which mean they find it more difficult than others to participate in mainstream youth culture. The concluding chapter of the book also reinforces a message for which evidence appears throughout the text: despite the 'success story' of Ireland's recent years and the many positive changes in the lives of young people, social and economic inequalities persist – and in fact in some cases have worsened – meaning that the challenge of combating social exclusion and marginalisation remains as important as ever.

Young People in Contemporary Ireland reflects the depth and range of the authors' collective expertise as teachers and researchers, but it also draws on direct experience at the levels of policy and practice in relation to adolescence and youth, and this is a rare combination. It provides a comprehensive and up-to-date overview of research on all of the key issues impacting on young people in Ireland, which those who work with or on behalf of them, or aspire to do so, need to be aware of. It will be an indispensable resource for all of us who work with young people, or hope to do so, across a wide range of disciplines, professions and sectors. The authors are to be congratulated on their achievement.

Mary Cunningham
Director, National Youth Council of Ireland

Acknowledgments

The completion of this book was facilitated greatly by:

Library staff at DIT Mountjoy Square, CIT and NUI Maynooth, for whom no source was too obscure, particularly Ralph Murphy, Catherine Cooke, Noreen O' Neill and Caroline Williams.

Colleagues who commented on portions of the text or otherwise gave assistance; Claire Hamilton, Mairéad Seymour, Joan Dinneen, Moira Jenkins, John McCormick, Michael McAlinden, Brendan Bartley, Paula Mayock, Saoirse Nic Gabhainn, Caroline Smyth, Fran Bissett, Anna Gunning, David Treacy, Michael Barron, Johnny Sheehan, Mary Cunningham, Liam O'Dwyer and the Irish Youth Foundation, and the Applied Social Studies team at NUI Maynooth.

Marion O'Brien and Emma Farrell at Gill & Macmillan, who were helpful and efficient and applied just the right amount of pressure to meet deadlines.

Family members provided endless patience and encouragement throughout: Órla Reidy, Ciarán Lalor, Eoghan Lalor, Elizabeth Roche and Kieran Cooney.

To them all, we offer our thanks and gratitude. That the book is completed owes much to them. The omissions and imperfections are our own.

1

An Overview of Youth and Adolescence in Ireland

INTRODUCTION

Adolescence and youth is an inherently interesting time of life. It is a time of energy, dynamism and, perhaps most of all, potential. It can also be a time of uncertainty, awkwardness and a searching for one's niche in society. In this period of tremendous physical, cognitive, emotional and relational changes, the fundamental shift from child to adult takes place, and it becomes possible to reproduce and create one's own children. All of this happens between the ages of roughly 13 and 18. For most people, few other five-year periods in their lives will see such change, transition, upheaval and reorientation.

In the preface to his *Adolescence* (1904), G. Stanley Hall gives an eloquent (but, as we shall see, controversial) description of 'coming of age'; the turmoil, change and sheer potential:

> The social instincts undergo sudden unfoldment and the new life of love awakens. It is the age of sentiment and of religion, of rapid fluctuation of mood, and the world seems strange and new. Interest in adult life and vocations develops. Youth awakes to a new world and understands neither it nor himself. The whole future of life depends on how the new powers now given suddenly and in profusion are husbanded and directed. Character and personality are taking form, but everything is plastic, self-feeling and ambition are increased, and every trait and faculty is liable to exaggeration and excess (p. xv).

Naturally enough, change and variation are interesting to social scientists. As a period of rapid physical, emotional and psychological development, adolescence has long been a focus of study for developmental psychologists. The years of adolescence and early adulthood are also important years for students of social care, social work, education and youth work. Sociologists, too, have seen the period of 'youth' as a fascinating fault-line between the cultural and social norms of one generation and the next. The 'sociology of youth' is a recognised specialism within academic sociology. In contrast, few professors of sociology have built their careers on the behaviour and attitudes of people in their forties!

This book is primarily concerned with the 927,230 people in Ireland aged between 10 and 24 years, although as will be seen throughout this book, rigid age boundaries are neither possible nor advisable in the study of young people's lives. According to the latest available figures, 37 per cent of the population is under 25 years of age (CSO, 2003a). Given inward flows of immigration, it is likely that the figures for 20- to 24-year-olds have increased from the 328,334 recorded in 2002.

The purpose of this book is to provide a unified commentary and analysis of research, policy and practice relating to adolescents and young adults in Ireland for third-level students of psychology, sociology, social policy, social care, social science, social work, education, youth work and nursing. The text will also be of interest to a range of professionals working with young people, such as teachers, youth workers, psychologists, social workers, community workers and related professions. The text will draw on the authors' extensive lecturing and work experience in the fields of adolescence and youth work, and will be informed by their continuing research in areas such as adolescent attitudes and behaviours, youth crime and victimisation, recreation, media and youth work. We shall employ a theme-based approach, allowing for perspectives from multiple academic domains. Our goal is to provide a multidisciplinary approach that extends beyond the boundaries of any one academic discipline.

This chapter firstly considers definitions of 'adolescence' and 'youth'. Then, some popular conceptions of young people are examined; specifically, that adolescence is a period of 'storm and stress' and that young people are more inclined than others to be troublesome and deviant. Thirdly, the development of young people's rights and status in Ireland in recent years is examined. Finally, a brief outline of each of the following chapters is provided.

DEFINITIONS

Internationally, a 'child' is deemed to be a person younger than 18 years. This is the definition used in the UN Convention on the Rights of the Child, and many jurisdictions grant privileges of adulthood (such as voting) on the eighteenth birthday. In this sense, the term 'child' includes most of the adolescent years.

'Adolescence' is a less clearly defined period. It refers to the transition between childhood and adulthood. In pre-industrial societies, this period may be brief, ending when biological maturity brings adult status. In contemporary Western societies, adolescence is a much lengthier period and is often considered to be an 'invention' of industrial Western society.

'In many cultures ... girls were expected to marry once they became capable of bearing children. But as the Industrial Revolution brought new technology and a need for more schooling, recognition of adult status was delayed and the long transition period we called adolescence evolved' (Passer and Smith, 2001, p. 481).

Of course, we should not be too simplistic in our thinking here. The transition from child to adult varied from time to time and place to place.

Conger (1997) describes the twentieth century as the 'era of adolescence', an era that has evolved due to the social and economic changes arising from industrialisation and capitalism in Western Europe and the United States. Prior to the Industrial Revolution and widespread schooling, there was little opportunity for a 'youth culture' to emerge. However, increasing segregation of adolescents from adults, the growing complexity of work and the need for prolonged education facilitated the creation of adolescence as a distinct phase of life – not a child, but not an active, adult part of the workforce either. In such a way, adolescence became a distinct phase of life in between childhood and adulthood. Of course, all societies acknowledge a transition between childhood and adulthood. Modern, complex societies differ from earlier societies because the distinction between adolescents and adults is not demarcated by a single widely practised rite of passage; instead, the transition to adulthood is marked by protracted schooling or training and the (relative) delay in assuming adult roles such as work and parenthood.

After the eighteenth birthday, a further change in status occurs. Terms such as 'youth' and 'young person' can vary in meaning, but it not uncommon in research and policy terms for them to refer to under-25-year-olds. This is the threshold used in much of the research described in this book, and it is also the definition used in the Youth Work Act 2001 and the National Youth Work Development Plan (Department of Education and Science, 2003a). Of course, there is considerable variation in how youth is experienced. For example, while many 24-year-old Irish men are living at home, studying full time and financially dependent on their parents, others have been in full-time employment for many years and may be self-sufficient, married fathers.

'Youth' is a social construction and the normative experience for people in their late teens and early twenties has changed beyond all recognition in recent years. For instance, participation in further and higher education in Ireland has increased dramatically, as has progression to fourth-level education, all of which further postpones many young people's full-time engagement in the workforce. This has implications for home life, with many young people living with parents until their mid-twenties. In Ireland, this trend has been aggravated by the dramatic rise in house prices since the mid-1990s. Thus, particularly for those in the higher socio-economic groups, offspring are unlikely to obtain full autonomy and financial independence until their mid-twenties. In this sense, 'adolescence' (the transition from childhood to self-sufficient adulthood) has stretched from the teenage years to the mid-twenties, giving rise to the demographic jokingly referred to as 'kippers' (kids in parents' pockets eroding retirement savings). The 'blurriness' of the boundaries between child and adolescent, and youth and adult, is outlined in the National Youth Work Development Plan:

Social and cultural boundaries distinguishing youth from childhood on the one hand and adulthood on the other, which have never been rigidly fixed in any case, are being blurred further. Children are continuing to develop faster and earlier, in physical terms; and in the post-industrial age of information technology they often have readier access to certain types of knowledge than many adults, without necessarily having had the opportunity to develop the capacity for critical and responsible use of that knowledge. At the same time, the acquisition of full 'social adulthood' is in many cases being delayed as young people stay in the education system longer, or for financial reasons find it difficult to develop a sense of (or an objective state of) full autonomy or independence (Department of Education and Science, 2003a, p. 3).

SOME POPULAR PERCEPTIONS OF ADOLESCENCE AND YOUTH

Which of us has not been berated with 'When I was your age ...' or 'Young people these days ...'? A mainstay of the relationship between the generations seems to be a perception by the 'established' generation that the 'coming' generation is lacking in moral fibre, respect for their elders, work ethic and so on. Are young people really so different from their elders? Are Irish young people as bad as portrayed in the media?

A second popular perception of adolescents and youth is that they are, to a greater or lesser extent, grappling with internal turmoil, angst-ridden, riven by storm and stress. Is this true?

As they are mainstays of any examination of youth, we shall consider both of these popular perceptions in a little more detail.

Young People as 'Problematic'

As elsewhere in Europe, the academic community, policy-makers and the popular media in Ireland have tended to focus on the problematic aspects of young people and their lives: alcohol and drug use, early school leaving, early sexual behaviour, pregnancy, STDs, delinquency. Indeed, the origins of academic Youth Studies after the Second World War is characterised by a heavy focus on gangs, delinquency and troublesome youth. As noted by Skelton and Valentine (1988):

Adolescents began to be treated as a problem for society after the Second World War, during a period in which young men, in particular, were gaining cultural and economic independence from their family of origin. Academic study of 'youth' as a distinctive social category became established during the 1950s and 1960s in the United States and Britain. The history of academic research about youth cultures reflects and reinforces the public condemnation of working-class adolescents. Academic interest in teenagers was born within criminology, fuelled by moral panics concerning the nuisance value of young people on the urban streets of Western societies. Thus, the research into youth groups was marked by a preoccupation with delinquency and associated with the study of so-called 'condemned' and 'powerless' groups in society such as the working class, migrants and the criminal (Skelton and Valentine, 1988, p. 10).

This, of course, is partly a product of the age-old tension between the established and the upcoming generation, the former viewing the latter as troublesome, poorly disciplined and even dangerous. Sociologists have long highlighted the never-ending series of moral panics about young people and their behaviour, be they 'teddy boys', 'boot boys', punks, hippies or, more recently, goths (Cohen, 1973; Collins et al., 2000; Hall and Jefferson, 1975; Miles, 2000; Thompson, 1998).

There is nothing new in this. Indeed, Plato objected to various aspects of young people's behaviour. He advised against allowing the young to drink alcohol, for 'fire must not be poured on fire'. He also described young people as argumentative: 'in their delight at the first taste of wisdom, they would annoy everyone with their arguments.' Aristotle, too, found adolescents to be 'passionate, irascible and apt to be carried away by their impulses' (cited in Fox, 1977).

Devlin (2006) describes a process where four Irish morning newspapers were monitored for three separate months (March, July, November 2000) for articles featuring 'youths', 'teens', 'juvenile', 'minor' and related words. A total of 608 news items were identified, including 248 stories where the ages of the young people were explicitly given and were between 12 and 21 years. After a thematic analysis, these stories about young people were found to consist of 32 specific categories in seven main themes.

- Criminal and violent behaviour (32.7 per cent of stories): Murder, assault, theft and so on.
- Victimhood (31 per cent): Young people as victims of physical and sexual assault, or of accidental death or suicide.
- Vulnerability (20.2 per cent): Young people as vulnerable to health problems, inadequate services, homelessness.
- Problematic behaviour (5.2 per cent): Alcohol, drugs, sexuality.
- Good behaviour (8.9 per cent): Sporting, artistic, musical success, political commitment, environmental awareness.
- Attractiveness (1.2 per cent): Style, attractiveness or desirability of young people.
- Miscellaneous (0.8 per cent): General stories about demographics or youth as a category.

Thus, Devlin (2006) shows that almost 85 per cent of stories about young people feature them as perpetrators or victims of crime or as vulnerable in some way. 'In short, Irish news stories tend in the vast majority of cases to portray young people either as being a problem or as having problems' (Devlin, 2006, p. 47). There are interesting gender differences. For example, 44 per cent of the stories about young males focused on crime or deviance, compared to 15 per cent of stories about young females.

As part of the same study, Devlin (2006) conducted 10 focus groups with a total of 90 young people, primarily in their mid-teens. There was a strong consensus that media portrayals of young people were primarily negative and simplistic. As one respondent stated: 'It's all trouble, vandalism, joyriding, drinking, drugs, smoking. They never have any of the good stuff we do in it' (Devlin, 2006, p. 20).

Another very strong impression from these focus groups was teenagers' resentment that they were viewed suspiciously by adults when in groups in public places as potentially noisy and troublesome. This was particularly so in disadvantaged areas with few amenities and facilities. Respondents were asked about their relationships with teachers, the gardaí, youth workers and adults in shopping centres. The strong overall impression that young people have is that adults perceive them in a negative light and that many adults hold negative stereotypes of adolescents.

In contrast to the focus on 'youth problems', the more normative aspects of the lived experience of young people in Ireland have received little attention. A detailed case for a national longitudinal study was made in the Final Report of the Commission on the Family (Commission on the Family, 1998). Also, in their review of published academic work on adolescence, Hennessy and Hogan (2000) concluded with a call for a national longitudinal study that would address many of the gaps in our understanding of the experiences of Irish children and adolescents:

> The most notable absences from research in child psychology in Ireland are nationally representative longitudinal studies. With recent dramatic social changes, including legislation on divorce, a booming economy, increasing cultural and ethnic diversity and new legislation acknowledging children's rights, the need for such studies is now clear (Hennessey and Hogan, 2000, p. 115).

Although a longitudinal study is a commitment in the National Children's Strategy (and is now at an advanced planning stage), there remains considerable scope to widen our understanding of children's lives. It is important to examine the more day-to-day aspects of young people's lives, not least to counterbalance the impression of wild hedonism associated with young people in the popular media. A research report published by Foróige (1999) suggests that society has lost touch with the young and tends to categorise young people according to simplistic stereotypes, with an emphasis on sexual activity and drinking. It is suggested:

> Society needs to develop a view of the mass of youth as individual persons who are members of families – sons and daughters, brothers and sisters; people who are friends and confidants of others, people who are concerned with the present and worry and hope about the future; people who want to be involved in the community and play their part in the work of society; people who enjoy healthy fun and frolics appropriate to their age; people who ponder serious matters of great concern to themselves and their society; people who know the reality of pressure and stress; people who sometimes make mistakes and do what is wrong and people who need the guidance and leadership of adult society (Foróige, 1999, p. 19).

Storm and Stress: Is Adolescence an Unusually Difficult Period of Life?

The first formal academic study of adolescence is usually dated to G. Stanley Hall's 1904 *Adolescence*. This two-volume work became widely read and was reissued a number of times. Hall hoped that the book would establish a new field of scientific inquiry. This first delineation of the field was wide-ranging. In Volume One, he describes physical changes such as height, weight and proportions of body parts to the whole body. He also examined criminality, sexuality and the treatment of adolescence in literary sources. Volume Two is more focused on philosophical and pedagogical (educational) issues.

Hall described a period of 'storm and stress' as adolescents adjusted to their changing bodies and roles in adult society. Is this an accurate description of teenagers' experiences? Not really. Certainly, there appears to be an increase in mood swings and family conflict, arguments and bickering. It is also true that many adolescents occasionally feel self-conscious, socially awkward, shy and lonely (Larson and Richards, 1994). However, most young people feel close to their parents and value their opinions on major issues. A recent study in Co. Kildare (Lalor and Baird, 2006) asked a sample of 988 adolescents a range of lifestyle questions. When asked about their level of contentment and well-being, 68 per cent described themselves as 'very happy' or 'happy most of the time', 18 per cent were 'average: sometimes happy, sometimes sad' and only 6 per cent said they were 'sad a lot of the time' or 'very unhappy.'

Similar results have been found in international studies. Daniel Offer of the University of Chicago conducted a well-known cross-cultural study in 10 countries of adolescents' self-image in the 1980s (Offer et al., 1988). They surveyed 5,938 adolescents in 10 countries (Australia, Bangladesh, Hungary, Israel, Italy, Japan, Taiwan, Turkey, US, West Germany). A key finding was that adolescents around the world share many similarities. Offer et al. coined the term the 'universal adolescent' to describe somebody who is happy most of the time and enjoys life. At a social level, they are caring and enjoy being with others. They value work and school and enjoy doing a job well. They express positive feelings toward their families, and feel that both their parents are usually patient and satisfied with them most of the time. They can solve problems and feel positive about the future. Important differences based on age, gender and region were also found. They found, for example, greater self-confidence and openness to feedback in older teenagers:

> They feel secure about experiences that used to be frightening, such as sexual feelings and aggressive activities. The implication of these data is not that young teenagers are in the throes of tortured self-doubt and frightening lack of control of impulses. Instead, the implication is that the young are uncertain but are gradually finding their way; the older adolescent is more sure and is steadily reaching toward the maturity of adulthood (Offer et al., 1988, p. 119).

These research findings illustrate that the simple stereotype of the 'teenager in turmoil' does not accurately portray the lived reality for the majority of young people.

ADOLESCENCE AND YOUTH IN IRELAND: RECENT IMPROVEMENTS IN KNOWLEDGE, RIGHTS AND REPRESENTATION

A substantial body of knowledge about adolescence and youth has developed in recent years. For instance, Hennessy and Hogan (2000) reviewed all published work on developmental psychology in Ireland between 1975 and 2000, with 'adolescence' as a key search term. What is notable is the lack of published work on adolescence until the late 1980s. In the mid-1970s, only three published papers per year were produced, but this increased substantially to 23 per year in the mid-1990s. Similar growth rates are found in other academic disciplines, reflecting the increasing emphasis in Irish IHEs (institutes of higher education) on generating research papers and publishing internationally. Also, there has been increasing government funding to produce research reports (the so-called 'grey literature') on topics of public concern, both within academic departments and by external consultants. Acknowledging the lack of extensive research on which to base policy and resource decisions, a central goal of the National Children's Strategy is that 'children's lives will be better understood; their lives will benefit from evaluation, research and information on their needs, rights and the effectiveness of services' (Department of Health and Children, 2000).

IS IRELAND BECOMING MORE CHILD- AND YOUTH-CENTRED?

Service providers and policy-makers are increasingly open to listening to the views of young people. A significant process of recognition of children's rights has taken place internationally and this is reflected in developments in Ireland. Many commentators date this to the 1979 United Nation's Year of the Child and, 10 years later, the 1989 UN Convention on the Rights of the Child (a 'child' is defined as any person below 18 years). Unlike UN Declarations, the Convention becomes law in those countries that ratify it. Ireland ratified the UN Convention on the Rights of the Child in 1992, thus binding Ireland to its Articles in international law.

The UN Convention on the Rights of the Child is perhaps the most significant international event for children's rights ever. Essentially, it is an international Bill of Rights for children (Hamilton, 2005). The Convention operates on the principle that there are universally accepted pre-conditions for any child's harmonious and full development. The Convention is an unprecedented attempt to collect in one document the minimum rights of all children in the world. The Convention recognises that children have needs and human rights that extend far beyond basic concepts of protection: children are recognised as having a full range of civil, economic, social, cultural and political rights. Specifically, the Convention has 54 articles detailing the individual rights of any person under 18 years of age to develop to his or her full potential, free from hunger and want, neglect, exploitation or other abuses. Each child has the right to life; to a name and state; to a freedom from discrimination of any kind; to rest and to play; to an adequate standard of living; to health care; to education; and to protection from economic exploitation and work that may interfere with education or be harmful to health and well-being.

The view that children have rights of their own, rights that transcend the family setting, is a new idea. Unlike earlier statements of children's rights, such as the 1924 League of Nation's Declaration and the 1959 Declaration of the Rights of the Child, the 1989 Convention is liberating as well as protective. The Convention is unique in that it allows for the child's own wishes and opinions to be expressed and given careful consideration. As stated in Article 12: 'States Parties shall assure to the child who is capable of forming his or her own views the right to express those views freely in all the matters affecting the child, the views of the child being given due weight in accordance with the age and maturity of the child' (UN, 1991, p. 20).

The Convention is overseen by a process whereby each country is required to present a National Report to the UN Committee on the Rights of the Child in Geneva. This has had a real impact on policy in Ireland. For example, the UN Committee on the Rights of the Child recommended in 1998 that Ireland prepare a comprehensive National Strategy for Children. Previously, in 1997, the government indicated that it had no immediate plans to draft a National Children's Strategy. However, as noted by Hayes (2004): 'in October 1998 the Minister for Health and Children announced … that, in response to the UN Committee recommendations, his department was coordinating the production of a National Children's Strategy. An interdepartmental group was established in 1999 and the Strategy was published in November 2000' (Hayes, 2004, p. 52).

More recently, the Irish government submitted its Second Report for the United Nations Committee on the Rights of the Child in July 2005 (National Children's Office, 2005a). This report details the progress that has been made in the development of policies and services for children since the First Report (in 1996), including the launch of the National Children's Strategy, the establishment of the National Children's Office, the creation of the post of Minister for Children and the appointment of the Ombudsman for children. The Report is a useful and comprehensive overview of the situation of young people in Ireland. It describes the government's progress on children's issues and also highlights areas of concern, such as obesity, high levels of binge drinking and drug use and suicide, particularly among young men.

An alliance of NGOs working with children and young people (The Children's Rights Alliance) also submitted a 'shadow' report (*From Rhetoric to Rights*) which highlighted continuing areas of concern, such as 'the absence of mental health services … and the alarming incidence of alcohol misuse, drug abuse and suicide among children and teenagers' (Children's Rights Alliance, 2006, p. 3).

Representatives from the Children's Rights Alliance were also consulted by the National Children's Office in the preparation of Ireland's Second Report to the UN Committee on the Rights of the Child, and commented on early drafts of the Second Report (National Children's Office, 2005a, pp. 44–9).

Ireland's hearing at the UN Committee for the Rights of the Child took place in September 2006. The report of the Committee is on the UNCRC website (www.ohchr.org/english/bodies/crc/index.htm), as report CRC/C/IRL/CO/2. In its report, the Committee welcomed legislative and policy developments since Ireland's last hearing, including the Equal Status Act and the Education (Welfare) Act 2000; the Children Act 2001; the Ombudsman for Children Act 2002; the National Children's Strategy (2000); and the National Play Policy (2004) (UNCRC, 2006).

However, a number of areas were singled out for critical attention, such as the slow pace of the implementation of the Children Act 2001 which governs the administration of juvenile justice. This is a topic we shall look at in greater detail in Chapter 9. The Committee also expressed concern that the Ombudsman for Children is precluded from acting in investigations related to children in prisons or garda stations. The Committee was 'deeply concerned that corporal punishment within the family is still not prohibited by law' (p. 9). However, as noted by the government's submission (National Children's Office, 2005a), such a development is not a priority for Ireland. Another area of concern is the high level of alcohol consumption by adolescents and its apparent link to the increase in young male suicide, and the government is urged to implement 'a comprehensive strategy which should include awareness-raising, the prohibition of alcohol consumption by children and advertising that targets children' (p. 11).

THE NATIONAL CHILDREN'S STRATEGY

There are three national goals in the National Children's Strategy (Department of Health and Children, 2000):

- Goal 1: Children will have a voice in matters which affect them and their views will be given due weight in accordance with their age and maturity.
- Goal 2: Children's lives will be better understood; their lives will be benefit from evaluation, research and information on their needs, rights and the effectiveness of services.
- Goal 3: Children will receive quality supports and services to promote all aspects of their development.

The first goal of Ireland's National Children's Strategy (Department of Health and Children, 2000) echoes a key principle of the UN Convention on the Rights of the Child – that children will have a say in matters that affect them in accordance with their age and maturity. As noted in the National Youth Work Development Plan 2003–2007:

… put forward to achieve this goal are the establishment of a National Children's Parliament [Dáil na nÓg] and an Office of Ombudsman for Children. Additional measures under this goal will include a review of existing arrangements at local level, particularly with respect to County and City Development Boards to ensure that children's views are obtained in formulating and implementing their Economic, Social and Cultural Strategies (Department of Education and Science, 2003a, p. 7).

Thus, involving young people in discussions and policy-making is a central feature of important documents such as the UNCRC and the National Children's Strategy and is an important fundamental principle for policy-makers and service providers.

The importance of listening to children and young people is emphasised in the National Children's Strategy (Department of Health and Children, 2000), which clearly states the need to give children a voice in matters affecting them. In *Hearing Young Voices* (2002), Karen McAuley of the Children's Rights Alliance and Marian Brattman of the National Youth Council of Ireland argued that involving children requires more than merely paying lip service to the Strategy. Their work highlighted the need to involve children and young people in decisions about what constitutes 'consultation', and discussed the importance of using accessible language and providing the support that children need in order to become partners in policy formation; for example, 15 young people were consulted by the Eastern Health Board's *Forum on Youth Homelessness* and their views informed the Youth Homelessness Strategy (2001). Also, the National Economic and Social Forum talked with a group of early school leavers in 2001–2002 and fed their views into policy recommendations to government.

With a view to facilitating the involvement of children and young people, the Irish Society for the Prevention of Cruelty to Children (ISPCC) established a Children's Consultation Unit in 2002, supported by the National Children's Office, to provide support and training for professionals involved in consulting children and young people. In addition to training, the Children's Consultation Unit offers an event management service to organisations wishing to consult with children. It also offers training to schools on the establishment of school councils and has developed a Schools Council Training Pack.

Hayes (2004) further describes the trend towards inclusion of young people in policy or services development in Ireland:

A number of different associations have held forums to access children's views on different issues, including the Irish Society for the Prevention of Cruelty to Children (ISPCC), which hosts regional Children's Forums annually, and the National Youth Council of Ireland's youth parliament. In addition a number of local communities and partnerships have specific projects which give voice to children on issues of importance to them such as play space (Dublin North Inner City) and creativity in the classroom (Dublin Canal Community Partnership) (p. 49).

Hayes (2004) details the consultation process with children that was adopted for the development of the National Children's Strategy itself. Consultation with children took three forms:

- Publication of notice inviting children to make submissions on being a child in Ireland.
- Visits to 10 schools by the Minister of State for Children
- In-depth consultations with children conducted by 10 children's agencies. In total, submissions were received from 2,488 children.

The results of the consultation process were published by the National Children's Strategy in September 2000: 'The summaries received from the different consultations represent a diversity of issues of interest to children. They include such key themes as Play and Leisure, The Environment, Social Issues, Having a Say, The Right to a Good Life and Expectations for the Strategy' (Hayes, 2004, p. 54).

The Education Act 1998 contains provisions for the establishment of student councils in post-primary schools to represent students' views and give them a voice in the affairs of the school. By 2004, a majority of secondary schools had such student councils (561 out of 744). However, only a very few such student councils are represented on the school's board of management (National Children's Office, 2005b).

The National Children's Office (NCO) is a main 'driver' behind increasing and enhancing the participation of young people in civic society and policy-making. The NCO website (www.nco.ie) details a range of child and youth participation projects:

- Comhairle na nÓg.
- Dáil na nÓg.
- Dáil na bPáistí.
- The Student Council Working Group.
- Guidelines on participation by children and young people.
- Establishment of an NCO Child and Youth Forum.
- Supporting the Young Social Innovators Exhibition.
- Supporting RTÉ News2Day.
- Involving children and young people in the appointment of the Ombudsman for Children.
- Involving children and young people in the development of a code of children's advertising.
- Involving children and young people in the Children Conference on adolescent health and service planning.

In June 2005 the National Children's Office, the Children's Rights Alliance and the National Youth Council of Ireland published *Young Voices: Guidelines on How to Involve Children and Young People in Your Work*. This is a useful document for anyone working with children and young people. It outlines the importance of an inclusive approach to working with young people, describes principles of best practice and contains sections on ensuring quality outcomes, support systems, service planning and including young people on delegations.

The importance of involving young people in the youth work process is highlighted below:

> As a society we are not good at involving young people in decisions that impact on their lives such as education, housing, health, relationships, sex, parenthood or career, despite the knowledge that decisions are most effective if all the stakeholders are involved in the process. Youth work, through providing opportunities and support for young people can significantly support the democratisation of young people's lives and supports the development of active citizenship (National Youth Federation, 2003, p. 11).

A further initiative has been the National Youth Work Development Plan (Department of Education and Science, 2003a). This document outlines the recent economic, political, technological and cultural changes in Irish society and describes a vision of youth work to meet the needs of young people in contemporary Ireland.

In the area of research, it is increasingly recognised that conducting research on children's issues should include the direct attitudes, views and opinions of young people and sensitively tackle the methodological and ethical issues this raises. That is, research should be 'conducted *with* rather than *on* children' (Greene, 2006, p. 13). This approach has been strongly advocated by researchers at the Children's Research Centre, Trinity College Dublin (for example, Greene, 2006; Greene and Hogan, 2005; Hogan and Gilligan, 1998). Indeed, 'participation' has been the main buzzword in children's research over the last decade.

ENHANCING THE CONSTITUTIONAL STATUS OF CHILDREN

In November 2006, as this book was going to press, Taoiseach Bertie Ahern, TD announced a constitutional referendum to protect the rights of the child. The purpose is to tilt the balance of rights towards the child by way of a specific provision protecting their interests. Such a constitutional amendment would have implications in cases of abuse, fostering and medical care. For example, long-term foster parents find it very difficult to adopt the children in their care, due to the weight placed on the rights of the natural parent, even where s/he plays no part in the care of the child and the foster parent is, psychologically and emotionally, the 'real' parent. Also, there was a recent case where a parent sought to refuse a blood transfusion for her child on religious grounds, even though the medical advice was that it was necessary to save the child's life. In that instance, the transfusion went ahead, but a constitutional amendment would formally prioritise the protection of the child over the religious beliefs of parents.

The announcement was widely welcomed by children's rights groups and opposition politicians, but many commentators noted that such an initiative had been called for by the Kilkenny incest case investigation 13 years ago and by the Constitution Review group 10 years ago. Scheduled for March 2007, some commentators have noted the coincidence of such a 'feel-good' referendum being held just months before the general election scheduled for summer 2007. At the time of writing, it is too early to speculate how any amendment will be reconciled with the cherished protection of the family in the Constitution, so that the amendment is not perceived to be an intrusion by the state on the family's 'inalienable and imprescriptible rights, antecedent and superior to all positive law' (Article 41.1.1 of the Constitution).

OUTLINE OF THIS BOOK

The extant literature on adolescence and youth issues in Ireland is now sizeable and substantial and it is timely to provide an overview of our state of knowledge in a single volume. Throughout, our focus shall be on the experiences of contemporary youth. There are three primary reasons for this focus.

Firstly, an exhaustive analysis of all historical documentation on adolescents and youth in Ireland is beyond the scope of this text. Such a work would require a number of volumes, analysing texts stretching back 150 years. A historical work of this kind would provide interesting comparative material, but it is beyond the scope of this text.

Secondly, Ireland has seen considerable social and economic change since the early 1990s. Many commentators on contemporary youth in Ireland refer to the rapid social and economic change of recent years, such as the decline in emigration, increase in immigration, near disappearance of unemployment, legalisation of divorce, rise of mass higher education, globalisation and the rise in women's participation in the workforce (for example, O'Connor, 2005; Sweeney and Dunne, 2003). While social change is normal, it is certainly the case that such change has been dramatic in recent years. For anyone over the age of 35, it is sometimes hard to believe that there is a new generation, just a few years younger, who have no experience of emigration and unemployment; who have disposable incomes unimagined by any but the extremely wealthy in the 1980s; and who enjoy a consumer lifestyle, world travel, new cars and fine dining. Writing as recently as 1995, Forde concluded that Irish young people live 'in the worst of all possible worlds – unemployment, violence and hopelessness are everywhere' (Forde, 1995, p. 6). The experience of being young in Ireland today is profoundly different from what it was only a few years ago. While we will frequently refer back to trends over the last two decades and highlight the changes that have occurred, our primary interest is in the state of young people today.

Thirdly, this text is aimed towards students and professionals aspiring to work or actually working with young people: social workers, youth workers, teachers, nurses, psychologists, social care workers, doctors and so on. We hope that we can bring an overview of research on the issues impacting on young people that these professionals can apply to their day-to-day work with adolescents and young people in Ireland.

Where research is available, we shall also refer to findings from Northern Ireland. However, as different legislation, policies and structures exist in the two jurisdictions on the island, our examination of, for example, educational structures, the criminal justice system and youth work shall primarily be focused on Ireland.

Chapter 2 describes the main theoretical perspectives on adolescents and youth. As the philosopher Kurt Lewin noted, 'there is nothing so practical as a good theory.' Theories provide us with a framework, a set of explanations, with which to approach an object of study. This chapter looks at some of the central debates in the study of adolescence and outlines some key theoretical perspectives: biological, cognitive, socio-emotional, sociological, focal and ecological theories. Each theoretical perspective has its own contribution to helping us understand the behaviour of young people and their position and role in their families, communities and wider society.

Chapter 3 examines the literature on families in Ireland. The composition of households is described, primarily from census data. With regard to children and young people, this will show that the vast majority live together with both of their parents. However, with divorce available since 1997, small, but increasing, numbers of children will experience the separation or divorce of their parents. We shall examine some recent research findings on the effects this has on children. We shall also examine the issue of lone parents and the role of the father in Irish families (the relationship between fathers and their offspring has been little studied in Ireland). Finally, we shall examine research findings on policies that promote family well-being and also briefly consider the issue of the domestic division of labour.

Chapter 4 examines adolescents' social worlds and peer relationships. It looks at the types of groups young people form and the stages of peer-group development. The processes of peer pressure, peer acceptance, neglect, rejection and bullying are also examined. Adolescent friendships and romantic relationships are examined with a particular focus on two issues that resonate strongly for parents and professionals working with young people: 'loneliness' and 'sexuality'. A review of numerous recent studies on early sexual behaviour in Ireland shall be examined, along with related issues such as contraception use, early pregnancy, abortion and STIs. The particular challenges and issues facing young gay and lesbian people will also be examined.

In Chapter 5, we shall see that Irish young people experience very elevated levels of mental health problems, parasuicide and suicide. Also, Irish young people, relative to their European peers, use high levels of illegal drugs such as cannabis and have the highest levels of binge drinking in Europe. These are extremely serious societal problems, not only for the young people directly affected, but for their own children in the years to come. The issue of binge drinking first emerged in the mid-1990s.

Many of those people have now started families of their own. What habits and values are they passing on to the next generation? What mental health and social stability outcomes can we expect? There are also serious concerns about child and adolescent obesity. Chapter 5 shall also detail the results of recent surveys on the habits and lifestyles of Irish teenagers. These habits store up problems for later life: obesity, heart disease or diabetes.

The education and employment experiences of young people shall be examined in Chapter 6. A key developmental task for our target audience is the transition from secondary school to further or higher education and/or the workplace. The decisions taken during this period (age 18–25) will have a profound impact on later earning capacity and thus on socio-economic status and security. Larger numbers of teenagers are combining low-paid part-time work with studying. Is this a good or a bad thing? The further education sector has grown enormously, offering greater avenues and options for career progression. The 1990s saw a burgeoning of third- and fourth-level courses and the growing maturity and status of the IoT (Institute of Technology) education sector, as all third-level institutions orient themselves towards a more competitive environment with a smaller cohort of school leavers.

Chapter 7 examines young people's values, attitudes and beliefs in relation to politics, religion, sexual morality and social issues. Young people's lack of engagement with institutionalised politics, common with other European jurisdictions, is considered and we look at suggestions as to how this might be addressed. Attitudes to religion are also examined and we trace the growth of secularisation among young Irish people, while also noting that engagement with organised religion is still relatively higher than elsewhere in Europe. Attitudes to sexual relations and the trend towards more liberal values are also considered. Finally, we look at attitudes to a range of 'social issues' such as equality, social justice and development issues.

Chapter 8 describes the developmental functions of recreation and leisure for young people. Theories and research that have illuminated the role of free-time use in psychosocial development, mental and physical well-being, gender socialisation, deviance and resilience will be discussed. Gender differences in leisure pursuits are examined, as are changing trends in how free time is spent by young people. In particular, we look at common activities such as television viewing, playing computer games, reading, listening to music, shopping, hobbies and sport. Finally, Chapter 8 examines what factors constrain and facilitate Irish young people in their recreation and leisure.

The Children Act 2001 is the primary statutory instrument for dealing with 'troubled and troublesome' children. The issue of youth justice is complex. Juvenile offending combines both child welfare and criminal justice concerns and is the responsibility of three government sectors – justice, health and education. What is the reality of juvenile offending in Ireland? Is it increasing, decreasing or stable? Have we struck the right balance between child welfare, diversion programmes and custodial sentences? How do the Irish Youth Justice Service and the Children Court operate? These and related questions shall be addressed in Chapter 9.

Chapter 10 outlines some of the major types of services and policies relating to young people and, where relevant, summarises the legislation that applies. The origins and development of youth work in the late nineteenth century are outlined. The establishment of the City of Dublin Youth Service Board, initially as a response to youth unemployment in 1940s Dublin, is sketched. A brief account is given of the emergence of the major voluntary youth organisations, including Foróige, Youth Work Ireland and the National Youth Council of Ireland. The complex relationships between these organisations and their government funders are described, as is the consultation process that resulted in the Youth Work Act 2001. The structure and functions of the National Youth Work Advisory Committee are outlined, as are the main provisions of the National Youth Work Development Plan. An overview of the National Children's Strategy is provided and its progress to date is assessed. Chapter 10 also outlines the system of child care services in Ireland and concludes with a summary of recent developments in the field of child protection.

The focus of Chapter 11 is categories of young people who experience marginalisation and social exclusion and, as such, are of particular concern for social policy-makers and service providers. The situation of the following categories of young people are described: young people with disabilities, young Travellers, young separated asylum seekers, young people in care and leaving care, young homeless people and rural young people. In one way or another, and to a greater or lesser degree, they face additional challenges to those faced by other young people.

Finally, Chapter 12 briefly reviews the contents of the book and identifies a number of emerging trends and issues of relevance to young people in contemporary Ireland. These include the changing demographic profile whereby young people account for a diminishing proportion of the population but one which will for some time remain high by European standards. Due to a projected continuation of net inward migration, the multicultural nature of Irish society, which has already become much more pronounced in very recent years, will increase further. Diversity in the formation of families and households also looks set to increase, and issues of gender inequality, far from being resolved, are if anything becoming more complex. Socio-economic inequalities remain a challenge in policy terms and a blight on the lives of many young people and communities, and there is a persistent spatial dimension to such inequalities. An enormous increase in material resources, and its impact on an already increasingly globalised Irish youth culture, has introduced an increased element of risk, which needs to be managed by both young people and adults. Finally, the increasingly 'extended' nature of adolescence and youth is being accompanied by a much greater complexity and contingency, presenting both opportunities and challenges for young people negotiating their pathways towards adulthood.

RECOMMENDED READING

Sweeney, J., & Dunne, J. (2003). *Youth in a changing Ireland: A study for Foróige, the national youth development organisation*. Dublin: Foróige. Provides a good overview of the situation of young people, with reference to historical changes and trends identified in other countries.

2

Theoretical Perspectives on Youth and Adolescence

INTRODUCTION

This chapter presents the primary psychological and sociological perspectives on adolescence. Particular attention is paid to focal theory and ecological theory, both of which are broad models of how adolescence can be examined. This chapter also considers the principal developmental milestones of this period: puberty, cognitive development, socio-emotional development and identity formation.

Adolescence is a formative, transitional period from childhood to adulthood involving biological, cognitive and psychological changes that contribute to young people reappraising themselves and their relationships to their social worlds. It is a time of identity formation, individuation and major adjustment by young people to changes within themselves and in society in terms of altered expectations placed on them. As far back as 1904, Stanley Hall constructed the view of adolescence as a time of storm and stress, characterised by what Rutter and colleagues (1976) termed 'inner turmoil' (feelings of misery and self-depreciation). It is also seen as a period of heightened vulnerability to social and emotional problems, although most young people negotiate their adolescence successfully.

Adolescence 'is a phase of imminence that is not quite imminent enough, of emergent adult biology that is not completely coordinated with adult roles, of hopes that are not yet seasoned by contact with adult reality, and of peer culture and society that mimic those of adults but are without ambitions or responsibilities' (Modell and Goodman, 1990).

ADOLESCENCE AS A SOCIAL CONSTRUCT

In viewing adolescence as a distinct and unique stage of development, attention needs to be paid to its social construction, that is, the extent to which adolescence itself is a product of society as opposed to a young person's biological or psychological development. According to British psychiatrist Michael Rutter, adolescence

was not discovered in the sense that anyone studied the behaviour of young people and noted its distinctive character. Rather, the teenage years came to constitute an age period of interest and concern and it was decided that adolescence, in the psychosocial sense, should be a universal experience …

Adolescence is recognised and treated as a distinct stage of development because the coincidence of extended education and early sexual maturation have meant a prolonged phase of physical dependence; because many of the widely held psychological theories specify that adolescence should be different; because commercial interests demanded a youth culture; and because schools and colleges have ensured that large numbers of young people are kept together in an age-segregated social group. To that extent, psychosocial adolescence is created by society and has no necessary connection with the developmental process (1979, pp. 6–7).

Similarly, sociologists have contended that the 'othering' of young people and the 'category of youth' is deployed when young people are seen to no longer perform the proper modes of conduct of childhood. 'Youth' defines a moment of disturbance: a space in between childhood and adulthood. Anthropological research has also highlighted that in some societies, such as the Samoans of the South Pacific and the Dobuans of the Solomon Sea, puberty is largely unmarked. The growth of secondary education clearly has been a critical factor for the emergence of 'adolescence' as a social category and for the emergence of 'youth cultures' discussed later under sociological perspectives.

CENTRAL DEBATES

A number of questions have received a lot of attention in the study of adolescence:

- Is adolescence a clear, distinct, unique stage with changes indicative of discontinuity, or is development continuous, with little change from late childhood to adulthood? (continuity vs. discontinuity)
- To what extent are there changes in adolescence and to what degree are adjustment to these influenced by biological or socio-cultural factors (family, peers and society)? (nature vs. nurture)
- Is adolescence a stressful period or is it a relatively calm time, reflecting a smooth transition from childhood to adulthood? (storm and stress vs. smooth transition)
- To what extent do adolescents disconnect from their family and connect more to peers? (connection vs. disconnection)

Continuity vs. Discontinuity

This debate focuses on the extent to which adolescence is a distinct developmental stage, with clear start and end points (discontinuity) or a continuation of child development without abrupt changes at any age level (continuity). Sociologically, the concept of adolescence as a distinct stage with legal boundaries did not exist until the late 1800s/early 1900s in the developed world (McCauley et al., 1995).

The precise age associated with youth differs between cultures and many of the psychological or biological universals may be considered as socially relative.

Psychologically, Piagetian theory, and those theories of Erik Erikson and Peter Blos (outlined later), construe adolescence as a distinct stage with characteristic features and developments. Information-processing perspectives, on the other hand, see development as continuous with greater significance given to features, such as personality characteristics, which show stability and consistency.

Isolating adolescence as a distinct stage of development has been criticised by theorists who see development as continuous without linear stages. Applying stages to development also undermines a holistic view of the young person. From this standpoint, it is more useful to adopt a broader perspective in looking at any individual adolescent, taking into account the young person's past, present and future and the systems in which they live. Ecological and anthropological perspectives allow for this, construing adolescence more as 'a period of transition' than 'a distinct, universal developmental stage', where the young person is no longer considered a child but also not yet considered an adult.

Nature vs. Nurture

This debate centres on the extent to which biology (nature) or environment (nurture) influences the changes that arise in adolescence and how young people adjust to these. Many propose that the changes are primarily biologically determined, arising from increases in sex hormones and alterations in body (including brain) structure and function. Adjustment to such changes are dependent on genetic influences via temperament.

On the other hand, others contend that many of the changes young people experience arise primarily from social and cultural factors. According to this perspective, requirements and expectations laid down by a young person's culture are pivotal to understanding the changes young people experience and their adjustment to these. Even biological markers of adolescence, such as the menarche, change over time and across cultures.

However, most researchers see the reality as being a middle ground between nature and nurture, acknowledging the role of **both** biological **and** socio-cultural factors in understanding the changes young people experience and their adjustment to these.

Storm and Stress vs. Smooth Transition

Another point of debate is the extent to which adolescence is an undemanding, easy period or a time of turbulence and tribulation. As far back as the early 1900s, Hall (1904) argued that it was a time of upheaval and distress and over the years this perspective has resulted in the stereotypic perception of the adolescent as moody, distressed, conflictual and in need of help. Relating to this is the finding that suicide is one of the leading causes of death among teenagers (after accidents) worldwide

(Dusek, 1991). While statistics vary across studies regarding the prevalence and severity of teenage depression, adolescence has been proposed to be a time of heightened vulnerability for depression (discussed later in Chapter 5). Others, however, have argued that the 'storm and stress' of adolescence has been exaggerated and that the universality of adolescent distress and turmoil is questionable (Ebata and Moos, 1991). The research of Margaret Mead in Samoa has drawn attention to how cultural practices and values may make adolescence an easy period without the storm and stress (Samoa) or alternatively, a time of conflict and stress (Western world).

Connection vs. Disconnection

Much research has concentrated on adolescent disengagement from the family with greater peer engagement, contributing to individuation and identity development. Erikson (1968) spoke of the young person's need to achieve some physical and psychological distance from the family. Early adolescence has been reported to be the most strained period in adolescent-parent relationships, although such temporary perturbations in relations tend to be resolved by mid to late adolescence through individuation and a renegotiation of the family system. Nonetheless, the family continues to be a significant social context for the young person. Attachment relationships to parents do not weaken. Rather, they typically remain significant for development. In addition, the contrast between parental and peer influences in adolescence has been spoken of as 'a false dichotomy' in that there is often considerable overlap between parents and peers in socio-economic, ethnic, religious, educational and even geographical backgrounds (Janeway-Conger and Galambos, 1997).

Over and above these central debates, much attention in adolescent literature has centred on the developmental landmarks or 'tasks' of the adolescent years.

DEVELOPMENTAL TASKS OF ADOLESCENCE

As far back as the 1950s, Havighurst (1953) identified a number of developmental problems, issues or 'tasks' arising in different periods of life, which are still valid today (Kirchler et al., 1993). These tasks vary across cultures and individuals and originate from developmental maturation, social and cultural expectations as well as individual aspirations and values. If successfully coped with, these tasks contribute to happiness and increased likelihood of success with future tasks, while failure contributes to unhappiness, societal disapproval and difficulty with future tasks. Such tasks may not necessarily be difficult or problematic; rather, they may simply be new challenges to be coped with. In adolescence these tasks include (ibid):

- Acceptance of one's physical make-up and sex role (masculine/feminine) acquisition.
- Developing appropriate relations with peers and skills relating to social competence.

- Emotional independence of parents and other adults.
- Choice and preparation of a career and entering employment.
- Understanding and achieving socially responsible behaviour.
- Preparation for marriage and family life.
- Acquisition of values and an ethical system of beliefs that underlie behaviour, becoming an ideology.

How well these tasks are coped with depends on a variety of factors, such as personality characteristics and social support (Kirchler et al., 1993). To understand the tasks of adolescence, it is useful to consider these from the frameworks of the wider theoretical perspectives.

THEORETICAL PERSPECTIVES

Theories provide an organising framework useful in understanding young people's development and experience. Different theories enable us to look at adolescence from contrasting standpoints with different values of what is important or not in examining and understanding adolescent development. Theories and associated research inform us about what to expect in adolescent development and help us to answer questions such as: 'What are the key milestones of development in this period?', 'What helps or hinders this development?', 'What is "normal" or "abnormal"?' Most of all, by applying theory and research to practice, we can be guided in how best to work with young people in different contexts. The theoretical perspectives outlined in this chapter include:

- The biological perspective, which focuses on adolescent physical development.
- Cognitive psychological perspectives, including Piagetian theory, the information processing perspective and Kohlberg's moral developmental theory.
- Socio-emotional psychological perspectives, including the identity theories of Erikson and Marcia and the psychodynamic theories of Anna Freud and Peter Blos.
- Sociological perspectives, including generational, conflictual, transitional and constructivist viewpoints.
- Focal and ecological theories, which provide a more holistic perspective on adolescence.

It is critical to acknowledge that while theories allow for broad generalisations about adolescence and while there has been increasing globalisation of adolescence, the experience of adolescence itself is overwhelmingly contextually bound. Features of a young person's social context, such as family experience, cultural and ethnic background, religious beliefs as well as contemporary issues and the norms of the day, all contribute to a wide variability in how young people experience adolescence.

THE BIOLOGICAL PERSPECTIVE

From a biological perspective, puberty is central to understanding physical development in adolescence.

Puberty refers to the process through which young people achieve sexual maturity and consists of physiological (hormonal), physical (secondary sexual characteristics) and psychosocial (identity) development. Genetics undoubtedly underpin the onset of puberty and its associated hormonal changes and typically puberty is two years later for males than for females. Socio-cultural factors (including diet) also influence the onset of puberty.

For females, the menarche (first menstruation) is a key indicator of the onset of puberty. The average age of the menarche varies across cultures and has become earlier across most cultures over past centuries. In the 1800s the average age of the menarche was approximately 16 years, while it is approximately 12.5 years now. Recent Irish research also shows this falling age at menarche. Currently in Ireland, over one-third (42.5 per cent) of women (aged 18–24) had their menarche aged 12 or less and under half (44.2 per cent) had their menarche aged 13–14, while 13.3 per cent had theirs at aged 15 or older (Layte et al., 2006). Improvements in nutrition, living conditions, physical training and health care have contributed to this as well as to the timing of the first ejaculation in males. This usually happens a year or so after the onset of penile growth. This is experienced by most males in a positive way and discussed little with parents or peers. Menstruation, on the other hand, is often experienced in both positive and negative ways.

Only a quarter of girls tend to tell anyone other than their mothers about starting their periods, although other girls simultaneously experiencing it are also often told (Brooks-Gunn et al., 1986). Culturally, menstruation is often considered as dirty and something to be kept hidden. One term used to describe it is 'the curse'. Consequently, many young women perceive it as dirty and 'yucky' and associate it with feelings of embarrassment and a lack of cleanliness. Unpleasant side effects (cramps, headaches and mood changes) can also be linked with it and it can be a barrier to certain leisure activities, such as sport (Martin, 1996). As an indicator of physical growth, many girls though look forward to the menarche, perceiving it as a symbol of increased maturity. Reactions to it also depend on the degree of preparation, time of onset and whether girls feel 'left out' by menstruation starting late or, on the other hand, unprepared by it starting early (Brooks-Gunn and Ruble, 1983). In addition, many girls are afraid of being away from home when their periods begin and not having any pads or tampons with them (Martin, 1996).

Physical Changes

Even before puberty begins, a number of pertinent physical developments have occurred in both sexes. Testicular cell growth and secretion of male sex hormones begins in boys from approximately 11.5 years, while secretion of female hormones occurs in girls aged nine to 10. Body shape changes in puberty, particularly in terms of shoulder width relative to hip width. Shoulder width increases more in males, whereas hip width increases more in females. Height and weight accelerate in both sexes with puberty, though height is more linked to pre-pubertal growth than the pubertal growth spurt; the latter is linked more to an acceleration of trunk length (Janeway-Conger and Glambos, 1997).

Typical Male Maturation Sequence

- Testes and scrotum begin to increase in size.
- Pubic hair appears.
- Start of growth spurt; penis begins to enlarge.
- Voice deepens as larynx grows.
- Underarm and lip hair appears.
- Sperm production increases and nocturnal emission (ejaculation of semen during sleep) may occur.
- Growth spurt reaches peak; pubic hair becomes pigmented.
- Enlargement of prostate gland.
- Sperm production sufficient for fertility; growth rate decreases.
- Physical strength reaches a peak.

Janeway-Conger and Galambos (1997)

Typical Female Maturation Sequence

- Downy (non-pigmented) pubic hair appears.
- Elevation of breast ('bud stage') and rounding of hips begins with appearance of downy axillary (armpit) hair.
- Uterus, vagina, labia and clitoris increase in size.
- Pubic hair grows and becomes slightly pigmented.
- Further breast development; nipple pigmentation begins with increase in size of areola and slight pigmentation of axillary hair.
- Growth spurt reaches peak and then declines.
- Menarche (onset of menstruation) occurs.
- Pubic hair, axillary hair and breast development complete.
- Period of adolescent sterility ends with young woman now capable of conception (up to one year after menarche).

Janeway-Conger and Galambos (1997)

Brain Development

Several changes in brain development arise in adolescence, which may relate to enhanced thinking. In particular, research has centred on three areas of change:

- Brain growth spurts at puberty.
- The relative development of the cerebral hemispheres.
- The impact of the timing of puberty on spatial and other cognitive abilities.

Researchers have attempted to relate growth spurts to the Piagetian milestones of cognitive development and contended that the learning of more complex academic material should be left until late adolescence, when brain maturation is completed. However, this research has been heavily criticised, with many studies failing to support it (Keating, 1990).

Research on hemispherical development has proposed that adolescence is characterised by the development of frontal lobe connections, but again, this research still needs empirical support. Finally, while early or late maturation effects of puberty on cognitive abilities have been reported, these effects have been small and possibly due to other factors such as social influences (Keating, 1990).

More recently, research has focused on adolescent brain development in terms of emotion regulation, cognitive control and information processing abilities. Across adolescence, the brain shows an increasing volume of white to grey matter and both brain structure and function alter, particularly with respect to response inhibition, the perception and evaluation of risk and emotion regulation (Steinberg, 2005). Changes in arousal and motivation instigated by puberty precede the development of emotion regulation, resulting in a situation similar to that of 'switching on a car without yet having a skilled driver behind the wheel'.

Relating to this is cognitive or inhibitory control: attention and behaviour as controlled rather than impulsive. Using magnetic resonance imaging (MRI scans), researchers have proposed that young people appear to become more cognitively and emotionally controlled (regulated) over their own thoughts, feelings and behaviour, possibly due to brain maturation (as well as socialisation), but research is still new and unclear on this. Development of the prefrontal cortex, especially in terms of myelination, may contribute to cognitive control and to enhanced information processing, which is explored later in this chapter (ibid). Whether, and to what extent, these improvements in information processing are linked to aspects of pubertal maturation is not known.

Hormonal Changes and Primary Sexual Characteristics

The endocrine systems play a key role in puberty, particularly the gonadal, adrenal and hypothalmo-hypophyseal (hypothalamus and pituitary) systems. The sex hormones (chemical messengers) androgens (the 'male' hormones and primarily responsible for genital and pubic hair development) and oestrogens (the 'female' hormones and primarily responsible for breast development) are produced by both sexes, with males producing more androgens than oestrogens and vice versa for females. The flow of these hormones is controlled by the pituitary gland, which is in turn under the control of the hypothalmus in the brainstem (Petersen and Taylor,

1980). Hormone levels fluctuate with the menstrual cycle in females as well as with stress, food intake and physical activity, among other variables.

Interest in the extent to which pubertal hormones directly contribute to behaviour is a concern of behavioural endocrinology. One key focus is the relationship between testosterone and aggression. An increase in testosterone from 12 to 14 years is linked to a greater sex drive in males (manifested in nocturnal emissions and masturbation) (Susman and Dorn, 1991). While the relationship between sex hormones and sexual functioning is less clear cut, androgens appear to be significant in the female sex drive, evidenced in masturbation and thinking about sex (Udry et al., 1988). Such hormonal effects may occur in a regular or irregular (rapid bursts) manner.

The effects of hormonal changes upon behaviour tend to be stronger in males. 'The effects of hormones on male behaviour are much stronger than females because, as males mature, their androgen levels go up by a factor of 10 to 20 while, in females, androgen levels hardly double, with males and females starting from the same pre-pubertal levels. In males, the hormone levels may overwhelm the social controls' (Udry and Billy, 1987, p. 852). The greater rates of reckless behaviour in young men compared to young women are also associated with aggression-related hormonal changes, particularly the rise in testosterone and decline in serotonin (Arnett, 1996).

However, direct causal links between any given hormone and behaviour is nearly impossible to prove given the mediating roles of personality, learning, physical and social contextual factors in any behaviour produced.

Secondary Sexual Characteristics

Stages in genital, pubic hair and breast development have been documented and while they proceed in the same order for all young people, differences arise in how synchronous these changes are with each other. For example, a male may be at stage 2 of genital development and stage 5 of pubic hair development or the reverse. Axillary hair (underarm hair) and facial hair typically develop about two years after pubic hair and these continue to mature even after genital and pubic hair development is completed.

Change in quality (timbre) of the voice occurs in both sexes, and while a minor deepening of the voice arises in females, males experience a significant change in voice pitch late in adolescence. The sebaceous and apocrine sweat glands develop rapidly, and acne and other skin conditions are common, especially in males, due to pore enlargement and increased oiliness of the skin.

As young people focus on their bodily changes and appearance, they become more self-conscious and egocentric, which can result in negative feelings of low self-worth. If expectations about how one will look with puberty are not fulfilled, feelings of disappointment or anger may arise. This can be true as well for young people engaged in athletic or professional endeavours that require particular physical characteristics (e.g. ballet or horse-racing, which require a low weight, or basketball, which values height).

Gender Differences

In terms of feelings about puberty, young women feel ambivalent about leaving childhood and anxious about their new bodies, associating sexuality with danger and shame. As adult masculinity is strongly valued and not as negatively sexualised like adult femininity, puberty may thus be easier for males (Martin, 1996). With puberty, young women also experience more objectification of their bodies; others might comment on their weight, height or breasts, raising self-consciousness (Martin, 1996). Breast development is associated with a young woman's satisfaction with her body, while for a young man fitness, strength and the need to shave are more important (ibid).

On the other hand, for young males puberty is characterised by an eagerness for adulthood, with some uncertainty about their new bodies. Young males take pleasure in their change of voice and shaving although masturbation makes them feel unsure of themselves (Martin, 1996). Gender differences in how young people experience their body with puberty may arise from girls having less 'subjective knowledge' of their bodies than boys. According to Lerner (1976), from a young age boys are encouraged to have more interest in their genitals than girls, as shown in the fact that 'names' are often used for male but rarely for female genitalia (Ash, 1980).

Pubertal Timing

Pubertal onset is significant for two main reasons. Firstly, early or late onset may confer on the young person better or lower peer social status. Young men who mature early report receiving more warmth, acceptance and autonomy than their counterparts maturing on time or later (Silbereisen and Kracke, 1990). Secondly, the time of onset may lead to young people being more (late onset) or less (early onset) ready for pubertal changes. From this perspective, early maturation may interrupt development in late childhood, explaining why early maturing females and late maturing males are more at risk of adjustment problems. Early maturing males tend to have better self-esteem, to be more popular with peers and to have a better school life than their counterparts maturing on time or later (Brooks-Gunn and Reiter, 1990). This may be because greater value is attached to the physical features of masculinity linked to sexual development (strength, height, deep voice). In contrast, early maturing young women tend to have a poor body image, eating problems, greater conflict with family and teachers and tend to smoke, drink alcohol and engage in sexual intercourse earlier than their counterparts maturing on time or later. They can be drawn into heterosexual peer relationships before they are psychologically ready for them, often 'hanging out' with older-age cliques that encourage sexual and risky behaviour. By contrast, late-developing girls may feel left behind by their peers and look forward to the menarche and breast development. They worry about their femininity and want to leave childhood behind. Late physical maturity is also associated with feelings of inadequacy, poor self-image and adjustment difficulties, which persist into adulthood (Martin, 1996).

Clearly, the impact of an early or late onset of puberty is not straightforward, but dependent upon other factors, such as personality characteristics, cultural values and social support. An example of how timing with peers in pubertal events is significant for girls is illustrated by Martin's (1996) research. Young women spoke of friends hearing about another girl getting her first bra, running home and telling this to their mothers and then asking 'When can I get mine?' Others spoke of wanting to get their period if their friends had started because 'you want to be like your friends and you want to be noticed by the guys' (Martin, 1996, p. 25).

COGNITIVE PSYCHOLOGICAL PERSPECTIVES

Piaget's Theory of Cognitive Development

Looking at adolescence in terms of cognitive development, a lot of attention has been paid to enhanced flexibility and the logical-hypothetical nature of thinking (Piaget) and to the development of higher-order 'executive' functions (the information processing perspective). At about 12 years or thereabouts, children move into the final Piagetian stage of cognitive development: formal operations. This represents a qualitative shift in thinking from the more limited stage of concrete operations. While younger children may sometimes show aspects of formal operations thought, thinking now more routinely shows:

- Logical, hypothetical and abstract reasoning abilities (consideration about what might happen or what could have been).
- Recognition of knowledge being relative as opposed to absolute.
- Ability to see other perspectives, acknowledging more than one solution to a problem (Keating, 1990).

These developments or 'cognitive milestones' enable the young person to think about possibilities, alternatives and to envision idealised worlds. After thinking of one possible solution to a problem, they are less likely to immediately accept it as true, but rather are more likely to recognise the possibility of other solutions. In evaluating evidence for different arguments or explanations, the young person is now more likely to make comparisons between them, to test explanations against facts and to discard those that prove wrong. Reasoning is, however, heavily dependent upon familiarity with the content about which one is reasoning (Glaser, 1984).

Their enhanced reasoning ability can be seen in their improved ability in games like '20 Questions'. In this game the player who asks the fewest questions to find the answer wins. Adolescents are more likely than younger children to be strategic in their thinking, asking increasingly narrow categorical questions dependent on the previous answers. In assessing formal reasoning, Inhelder and Piaget (1958) used 15 different tasks divided into three areas:

- Combinatorial reasoning.
- Isolation of variables.
- Proportionality.

'Combinatorial reasoning' refers to the ability to combine prepositional statements expressing combinations of facts reflecting an underlying logical system. 'Isolation of variables' refers to the ability to separate the effects of different variables through the method of holding them all constant except one. This has been assessed by a pendulum task whereby young people had to estimate the effect of various factors (length of string, weight of object) on the period of a pendulum. Finally, 'proportionality' refers to the ability to deduce the rules regarding different influences, such as the effects of different proportions of different objects, for example weight and distance of objects on a balance beam on equilibrium.

Adolescent thinking also becomes more flexible and creative with thinking at the symbolic level of metaphor, the 'as if', the manifestly absurd and more frequent use of irony and sarcasm (Elkind, 1970).

Greater self-awareness and self-reflection is evident in metacognitive understanding (involving reflection on one's own thinking). Unlike younger children, the adolescent can take his or her own thought as an object and reason about it. They are more aware of their own memory capacities and limitations and use mnemonics to help them remember information. They are also more aware of having personality traits, which can be changed by conscious intent (Youniss and Smollar, 1985). Greater reflection on their own thinking is also shown in propositional thinking, the ability to attempt to logically reason out propositions such as:

- God loves humanity.
- Humanity experiences much suffering (wars, famines).

The apparent incompatibility of these may be tackled by trying to find ways to reconcile these or by questioning the validity of one or the other (Janeway-Conger and Galambos, 1997). They now think beyond the present and are influenced by their perceptions of their future, showing a greater time perspective than that of younger children (Keating, 1980; Weissbourd, 1995). They begin to think about their long-term future and what they will do with their lives, whereas younger children may only typically think about the coming year, their attention more focused on the short term, such as their next birthday.

Many have questioned the validity of Piaget's formal operations theory, in particular the identification of logic as the actual source of age-related changes in performance. The methodology of his research has also been criticised (Gelman and Baillargeon, 1983; Keating, 1990). The neglect of the powerful influences of individual differences (thinking styles, IQ), social (instruction), cultural (social values, the mass media) and contextual (presentation of material) factors has also been a constant criticism of his theory (Kuhn et al., 1988). Research with 12- to 15-year-olds has illuminated the positive impact of socio-contextual factors, which Piaget neglected; these include peer conflict and discussion on the understanding of scientific concepts (Howe et al., 1991). Studies have also failed to find evidence of the highly generalisable, content-independent formal logic, proposed by Piaget, in young people (Keating, 1990).

Others have argued that different competencies in thinking (logic, creativity, problem-solving) develop at different rates rather than 'all at once' in a generalised stage, as advocated by Piaget. In addition, many people never attain true formal operational thought because of limited ability or cultural limitations. Thus, such abilities may be better considered as 'potential accomplishments for most adolescents rather than typical everyday thinking' (Keating, 1990, p. 65).

Poor motivation, boredom, tiredness or emotional overinvolvement may also compromise the use of formal operational thought, for example behaving irrationally when trying to solve a problem rather than reasoning it out in a rational, logical manner (Janeway-Conger and Galambos, 1997). Other difficulties associated with cognitive development include disillusionment, frustration and unhappiness as young people see the discrepancy between 'what is' and 'what could be'.

MORAL DEVELOPMENT

Adolescence is also the time when young people come to question moral issues, values, rights and duties and what it means to be alive. Building on Piaget's theory, Kohlberg (1976) formulated a theory of moral development with six stages divided into three major levels: preconventional, conventional and post-conventional reasoning. Conventional reasoning is what characterises adolescent thinking. The changes across the stages are gradual, with some overlapping between the stages, reflecting the influence of general cognitive development spoken of earlier.

Preconventional Reasoning

- **Stage 1 Punishment-Obedience:** Behaviours are judged as good or bad dependent on their visible consequences. Behaviours that are punished are judged as bad and behaviours that are rewarded are judged as good. This is characteristic of children who show obedience to rules and authority to avoid punishment.
- **Stage 2 Instrumental hedonism:** Attention is now paid to fairness, reciprocity and equal sharing. This is characteristic of young adolescent thinking.

Conventional Reasoning

- **Stage 3 Good boy-Good girl:** Greater attention is now paid to societal needs and values over those of the individual. What is considered 'right' and normal by the majority takes precedence and heightened importance is given to 'being a good person in your own eyes and those of others' (Kohlberg, 1976, p. 34).

- **Stage 4 Authority maintenance:** A respect for authority, doing 'one's duty' and supporting the social order 'for its own sake' characterise this stage. Believing rules or laws should not be bent is also a feature of this stage. Many adolescents (and adults) do not advance beyond this stage (ibid).

Post-Conventional (Principled) Reasoning

- **Stage 5 Social contract:** A broader moral perspective at this point is used to evaluate society and recognition is given to various conflicting perspectives on moral issues such as abortion and euthanasia and other social concerns.
- **Stage 6: Universal principle:** This is the most advanced and least likely to be reached stage of moral thinking. There is an attempt to develop abstract ethical principles that are logical, consistent and comprehensive. A person now considers the 'right or wrong' of an action from different standpoints, acknowledging that what is right from one perspective may be wrong from another perspective and that attention needs to be given to various factors, such as intent.

Taken as a whole, this theory suggests that development in moral reasoning arises across adolescence, influencing how a young person thinks and evaluates actions as right or wrong. Research has supported this theory across a variety of cultures and has been further used to explore changes in adolescent political thinking.

There have been many criticisms of this theory, in particular methodological problems associated with the testing and scoring of the moral dilemmas used in the research. Others have argued that the sequence of stages is not invariant, as some people regress to less mature stages and that cultural differences exist, post-conventional moral reasoning being not as frequently used in less developed societies (Murphy and Gilligan, 1980). Kohlberg's theory is also criticised for reflecting male as opposed to female morality. For example, his failure to recognise that caring for others (indicative of female morality) can be as morally principled as abiding by a universal principle (Gilligan et al., 1990). However, his theory has provided a useful conceptual framework for the study of moral development.

The Information Processing Perspective

The information processing approach to adolescent cognitive development is not a general theory per se. Rather, it is more concerned with development in terms of the processes and mechanisms through which information is organised by mental processes and represented internally and manipulated by mental processes.

This perspective focuses on the enhanced development of 'executive functions'; these refer to 'high-level cognitive functions that enable people to plan, initiate and carry out goal-directed behaviour in an organised and thought-out way' (Hughes et al., 2004, p. 207). While low-level cognitive functions include the processing of sensory information, higher-level 'executive functions' include integration, planning, organisation and so forth. Enhanced executive functioning across adolescence may be due to an expanded enhanced attention span, greater automatisation of more basic cognitive processes (e.g. perception), increased information, rehearsal of information and the use of mnemonics. An important executive function is cognitive or inhibitory control (concentration and control of impulsivity). This is critical for sustained attention and concentration. Young people with ADHD show significantly poorer performance on inhibitory control reflected in their greater impulsivity, distractibility, reduced concentration span and poorer emotional regulation (Hughes et al., 2004).

Gender differences are also apparent in information processing. Consistent with international trends, Irish research has found young women and girls to show better verbal abilities than their male counterparts, who performed better on spatial abilities. These differences become more pronounced across adolescence (Lynn and Wilson, 1993).

SOCIO-EMOTIONAL PERSPECTIVES

Theories on socio-emotional development across adolescence have focused in particular on self-awareness, emotional regulation and identity formation. According to the American Psychological Association (2002, p. 17):

> being aware of and being able to label their feelings helps adolescents identify options and to do something constructive about them. Without this awareness, if the feelings become uncomfortable enough and the source is undefined, they may seek to numb their emotions with alcohol or other drugs, to overeat or to withdraw and become depressed. Adolescents who feel angry may take out their anger on others, hurting them or themselves instead of dealing with their anger in constructive ways if they are not aware of its source.

Greater self-awareness evolves though cognitive development and the young person's relationships and socio-cultural life. Cognitive development equips the young person with greater insight, reasoning and analytic skills (along with a tendency towards self-centredness, Jaffe, 1998) that they apply to their emotional life. Through their relationships and socio-cultural life, young people learn more about their own emotions and those of others, including how they are expressed, received and regulated; acceptable 'limits' (boundaries); antecedents and consequences and empathy.

Young people become more introspective and self-conscious, often forming an 'imaginary audience' (the feeling of being on a stage, all eyes on you), assuming others are preoccupied with their appearance and behaviour (characteristic of adolescent egocentrism). When the adolescent is self-critical, s/he is likely to anticipate that the audience will be similarly critical (Elkind, 1981; Lapsley et al., 1986). Complementing this are feelings of invulnerability and what has been called 'the personal fable', referring to the 'belief in one's personal uniqueness and indestructibility' (Lapsley et al. 1986, p. 800). This underpins common adolescent behaviours such as interests in fads and fashions and risk-taking, the latter in the belief that 'it can't happen to me'. Investigating a young person's personal fable and the thoughts they attribute to an imaginary audience can be useful in understanding a young person's behaviour.

Other related socio-emotional milestones of adolescence include achieving new and more mature relations with peers of both sexes, learning to resolve conflict constructively, forming an overall identity (including a masculine or feminine sex role) and achieving emotional independence of parents. Adolescence is a time of exploration and the building of commitments in interpersonal relationships in four domains: friendship, dating, sex roles and recreation. Such interpersonal explorations and commitments are important aspects of identity development (discussed later), serving as precursors to truly intimate relationships. For Erikson (1968), the identity crisis that occurs in adolescence needs to be resolved before a young person can move on to real intimacy. Steinberg, on the other hand, sees the two as developing in tandem. 'Close relationships are used as a safe context in which adolescents confront difficult questions of identity; yet at the same time, the development of an increasingly coherent and secure sense of self provides the foundation upon which adolescents build and strengthen intimate relationships with others' (Steinberg, 1993, p. 325).

While most people acquire a gender identity (awareness and acceptance of one's biological nature as male or female) in childhood, gender intensification across the adolescent years contributes to increased femininity and masculinity. Socialisation pressures to conform to traditional masculine and feminine sex roles influence this. Self-consciousness and concerns around self-esteem are particularly strong in early adolescence. Challenges to self-esteem are experienced in terms of altered body image, altered values and goals and new significant others against whom the young person rates themselves. Central to understanding self-esteem is the fact that young people compare themselves with their peers to discern their own self-worth or self-esteem. Research on young people's self-concept has identified five domains in which young people judge themselves: scholastic ability, athletic ability, social acceptance, behavioural conduct and physical appearance (Harter, 1985). How good a young person feels about her/himself relates to how they perceive themselves across these five domains.

George Herbert Mead (1934), from the 'symbolic interactionist' school of psychology, saw the self-concept as having two components: an 'I' and a 'me'. The 'I' is the 'self as subject', consisting of a basic capacity for awareness or 'experiencing', reflected in spontaneous, creative behaviour. It is the part of the self-concept that is unique. The 'me' is the 'self as object', consisting of what can be known about the self, such as physical features, values, reputation, behaviour, possessions, roles and social identity. It reflects the influence of others, what has been internalised. Relating to this is Cooley's (1902) concept of the 'looking-glass self'. This portrays the self as having three elements:

- Imagination of our appearance to others.
- Imagination of how others judge that appearance.
- Some sort of self feeling (for example, pride or shame).

These ideas emphasise how a young person's self-concept and feelings about themselves are intrinsically related to social experiences and how they think others think about them. According to Festinger (1954), people are driven to compare themselves to others to validate their opinions, abilities, sense of self and identity. This contributes to conformity, as people generally prefer to be like other people that are similar to them. People are more confident in their opinions, beliefs and attitudes if they are shared with similar others.

Across adolescence, young people interact with their peers in cliques and crowds and the significance of these (along with friendships) for a young person's development are explored in Chapter 4. The role of the family in young people's development is explored in Chapter 3.

One of the key features of adolescent socio-emotional development is identity formation.

THEORIES OF IDENTITY DEVELOPMENT

A number of theories of identity development have been formulated and the theories of Erikson, Marcia and Berzonsky will be studied here.

Erikson's Theory of Identity Development

Erik Erikson was a psychoanalytic theorist who formulated a psychosocial theory of identity. He saw identity formation as the hallmark of adolescence. During this stage, young people strive to establish a sense of self as distinct from and yet appreciated by loved ones, particularly one's parents. This theory emphasises the contribution of social life to identity formation. For Erikson (1968, p. 19), identity is a 'subjective sense of an invigorating sameness and continuity' with four components:

- A conscious sense of being a separate and unique individual.
- A feeling of inner sameness and continuity over time.
- A sense of 'wholeness' achieved through the synthesising functions of the ego.
- A sense of solidarity with the ideals of some group that in turn affirms a person's own identity.

The Origins of Identity

Erikson saw the origins of identity in the trusting relationship between the parent and the infant. The infant interjects (takes in) the parents' images and then identifies with them in childhood, taking on their values and interests. Following this in adolescence, the young person retains and rejects some of these childhood identifications and comes to form new identifications with peers and others (Erikson, 1968). The search for identity often might force a young person to reject and rebel against their parents. This frees her/himself from childhood identifications with their parents and from parental control or authority. Peers and other social contexts (school, work, leisure) also help to expand a young person's 'social worlds' and to find their own identity. By mid-adolescence (approximately 14 years), young people 'use possessions and clothes to construct and express identity and various "styles" allow young people to present particular identities and to ally themselves with, or differentiate themselves from, other young people' (Phoenix, 2005, p. 230). This quote highlights how the people from whom a young person disassociates is as important as who they associate with in terms of their status or 'street cred'.

Young people need to actively seek out their identity, moving beyond their childhood identifications, and for some this may not be resolved until early adulthood. This search is fraught with challenges to one's self-esteem, beliefs, values, opinions and attitudes. 'The young person, in order to experience wholeness, must feel a progressive continuity between that which he has come to be during the long years of childhood and that which he promises to become ... between that which he conceives himself to be and that which he perceives others to see in him and to expect of him' (Erikson, 1968, p. 87). The preservation of a sense of personal continuity over time – a sense of 'sameness of self' – a paramount concern in adolescence as it is challenged by physical changes, cognitive advances and altered socio-cultural expectations.

Identity as a Developmental Task of Adolescence

In his developmental theory, Erikson (1968) proposed that 'identity vs. identity confusion' is the developmental task of adolescence. Healthy resolution of identity formation leads to a clear sense of personal identity that joins the past, present and future into a strong and meaningful sense of self. Commitments, the determined adherence to a set of values, beliefs and goals are central to this.

Yet while retaining a sense of sameness and continuity is important for the young person, so is the need for distinctiveness and uniqueness achieved through experimentation, role-testing and exploration. It is also important that this is achieved with the support of significant others, such as parents and peers.

According to Erikson (1968, p. 130), 'in the social jungle of human existence there is no feeling of being alive without a sense of identity'. This is formed in adolescence when exploratory self-analysis and self-evaluation ideally culminate in a cohesive sense of self or identity that integrates gender, occupational, political and religious identities amongst others (ibid). Exploration and testing of alternative ideas, beliefs and behaviours is central to the creation and consolidation of such identities, as is dealing with potentially conflicting identities. Exploration refers to the extent to which a young person undertakes a search for values, beliefs and goals.

Inherent to this is experimentation with different social roles, plans and ideologies. Youniss and Smollar (1985) contend that adolescents develop a social sense of self as well as an individual sense of self. Peer group or 'crowd identities' act as public identities for young people, through which they are recognised and accepted by peers. In contemporary society, consumption behaviour, particularly of clothes and music, plays a key role in the construction of identities, helping to define their style, group membership and identity. Brand name goods are status symbols and help some people to express particular aspects of themselves (Phoenix, 2005). In contrast to adults, young people are more likely to read identities from bands on clothes and possessions than adults (Anderson, 2004). The role of consumption in adolescence is discussed further in Chapter 12.

Adolescence as a Moratorium

Young people need a psychological moratorium, a period of time without excessive responsibilities or obligations for optimal personal self-discovery (Erikson, 1968). Adolescents are

> sometimes morbidly, often curiously, preoccupied with what they appear to be in the eyes of others as compared with what they feel they are, and with the question of how to connect the roles and skills cultivated earlier with the ideal prototypes of the day. In their search for a new sense of continuity and sameness, which must now include sexual maturity, some adolescents have come to grips again with crises of earlier years before they can install lasting idols and ideals as guardians of a final identity. They need, above all, a moratorium for the integration of the identity elements (Erikson, 1968, p. 128).

This 'moratorium' refers to the suspension or deferral of some less primary issues or concerns to deal with what has become most significant to them: their identity.

Cognitive development is required for identity formation, as the young person needs to be able to conceptualise the 'self' in abstract terms. 'From among all possible and imaginable relations, [the adolescent] must make a series of ever-narrowing selections of personal, occupational, sexual and ideological commitments' (Erikson, 1968, p. 245). This leads them to form an integrated plurality of identities, a 'community of selves in constant conversation', identities which are discursive, influencing each other (Benson, 1994, p. 320).

Difficulties Experienced in Identity Formation

In the formation of such an identity, young people often experience identity confusion, an identity crisis manifested in confusion, mood swings, experimentation, impulsive and acting-out behaviour as well as poor coping skills (Bostik and Paulson, 2005). Problems with identity formation are reflected in identity confusion. This can be expressed in a number of ways:

- Firstly, fear of intimacy, as intimacy is perceived as compromising identity. This is manifested in an avoidance of close relationships or commitments via isolation or rigid, detached relationships. Trying to balance 'a need to trust in oneself and others' versus 'a naive, all too trusting commitment in others' is often expressed, paradoxically, in mistrust.
- Secondly, a poor sense of time (diffusion of time) with a reluctance to plan for the future. This may arise because anxiety is linked to change and consequently undertaking change is 'put on the long finger'; the young person stands back from taking on a change and from seeing events in a realistic time frame.
- Thirdly, diffusion of industry; preoccupation with a particular concern with an inability to concentrate on work or study. This reflects how 'caught up' young people become with a particular concern.
- Finally, negative identity, where a young person rejects the roles valued by his or her parents or community (ibid).

Another way that identity formation may be hindered is when it becomes prematurely foreclosed (fixed too early). This results in young people taking on the values and interests of others without having explored these fully for themselves. Young people with a prematurely foreclosed identity tend to be very conforming, basing their self-esteem largely on the recognition of others.

Given that Erikson developed this theory largely from work with young people with problems attending clinics, greater attention is understandably placed on how identity is problematic rather than how it is more usually, and positively, developed. A more positive perspective on identity formation recognises the beneficial role of specific interests, abilities, accomplishments, group memberships and social supports in building a young person's identity.

Others, such as Coleman (1980), contend that the majority of young people do not experience identity problems and that Erikson overstated the case for identity problems in adolescence. It may be that identity problems are more transitory rather than being enduring and long term.

Marcia's Theory of Identity Development

Another perspective on identity formation was proposed by Marcia (1980), who saw identity as achieved by a young person imagining possible future options including possible selves (thoughts and feelings about what one might become in the future). In measuring identity formation, Marcia (1980) used semi-structured interviews to investigate 'exploration', whether young people sought out knowledge and information leading to a personal choice; and 'commitment', young people's investment in a particular choice or orientation in their lives. Using these two dimensions, young people could then be categorised into four types, as follows:

- **Identity diffusion:** Characterised by no commitment or effort to make any commitments. In some cases young people try to make an effort but with no resultant commitment; in other cases no active exploration of possibilities is shown. Young people in this category tend to see their parents as indifferent or rejecting (low on commitment, low on exploration).

- **Foreclosure:** Characterised by a strong commitment but with little evidence of exploration or consideration of alternatives. Family beliefs and values, or those of significant others, are adopted with little questioning. Young people in this category tend to have very close relationships to their parents (high on commitment, low on exploration).

- **Moratorium:** Characterised by an identity crisis whereby a young person struggles with issues relating to choice in career, commitment or beliefs. It is essential for identity achievement. Moratorium and identity achievement are associated with conflict in family life (low on commitment, high on exploration).

- **Identity achievement:** On the resolution of crises linked to adolescence, young people are enabled to make a choice and commitment linked, for example, to some value or belief significant to their identity. Consideration of alternatives, self-insight and thoughtfulness are characteristic of such identity achievement (high on commitment, high on exploration).

Many now consider that shifts in these statuses represent normal, developmental change as opposed to purely being a typology of individual differences. Across the adolescent years, there is a rise in the number achieving identity achievement.

It is important to note that a young person may achieve identity in one area but not other areas. Areas of identity include political ideology (left wing, right wing), sex role orientation, religious beliefs and vocational (career) choice. Most young people demonstrate several identity statuses across these different areas at any one time. Thus, a young person's development is often differentiated, with identity achievement in one area but not in others.

One of these areas is sexual identity: how a person thinks of himself or herself as a sexual being, their own sexual attractiveness and what one finds sexually attractive in others. This is formed from a combination of gender identity, the roots of which are in childhood, sexual orientation (heterosexual, homosexual or bisexual), which is consolidated in adolescence, and social processes such as family, peers and culture. From this perspective, social processes shape sexual behaviour and identity with biology providing the 'machinery' and hormones the 'predisposition' to act sexually (Katchadourian, 1990).

Berzonsky's Theory of Identity Development

Berzonsky (1999) focused on how different socio-cognitive styles underlie differences in identity development, as a consequence of differences in information processing. Two cognitive dimensions – 'active/thorough vs. superficial information processing' and 'adherence to traditional opinions vs. open mindedness/liberal thinking' – underlie three different 'identity styles' (information style, normative style and diffuse/avoidant style).

Information Style

This is characteristic of young people who undertake exploration through searching and evaluating information relevant for their identity before making committed decisions. Adolescents with this style often revise aspects of their identity when faced with discrepant information about themselves. High levels of self-reflection, active information processing and an openness towards new information are evident in this style. It is associated with more adaptive coping, including problem-focused and social support-seeking strategies. Typically this style is the underlying style of the moratorium and achievement identity statuses (outlined earlier) (Soenens et al., 2005).

Normative Style

This style is characterised by a reliance on norms and expectations held by significant others. Young people with this style are closed to information that threatens the values and beliefs (typically conservative or traditional in nature) central to their identity. They show a strong need for structure and use of defence mechanisms that distort reality. This style is the underlying style of the foreclosure status (ibid).

Diffuse/Avoidant Style

This style is characterised by an avoidance of personal issues and identity-relevant decision-making and problem-solving. This leads to a very fragmented and disjointed identity. Identity is also often readily altered to suit changing social norms and mores with a lack of commitment to identity-relevant beliefs and values. This style is associated with less adaptive coping strategies, such as avoidance and emotional strategies (wishful thinking, fantasy), and is typical of late adolescents in the diffusion status (Soenens et al., 2005).

Criticisms of Identity Theories

A major criticism levelled at identity theories in general is that they are more preoccupied with the outcomes of exploration than with the process of identity formation in itself (Kerpelman et al., 1997). In recent years greater attention has focused on processes such as consumption behaviour. Consumption enables young people to use objects, music and clothes to project the image and meanings they want others to interpret about themselves, including their group identities. Others have questioned the validity of identity statuses for young people in low socio-economic groups, who typically do not have the luxury of an extended moratorium associated with third-level education. Others again have contended that identity theory is very male in perspective, emphasising vocation or career while undervaluing female values (empathy, caring for others).

GENDER AND SOCIAL-CULTURAL FACTORS

Gender and socio-cultural factors also influence the extent to which young people engage in identity exploration in different areas, such as education, vocation and family. Typically young women engage in greater family and education exploration than young males (Nurmi, Poole and Kalakoski, 1996).

The role of social context in identity has been emphasised by many theorists, such as Stryker (1987), who saw identity as embedded in social networks (such as family, friends, community or culture) of various salience or importance to a young person. Commitment to a particular identity is high if it is associated with relationships important to the young person. Research in Northern Ireland with a university student cohort highlighted how changes in social context, such as the move to third-level education, influence identity, with religious identity becoming more salient for young people (Cassidy and Trew, 2004). Reasons for this include university being a more heterogenous environment than religious segregated schools. Consequently, young people become more aware of their religious identity and it becomes more important to them (ibid). As noted by Waddell and Cairns (1991), it may be possible to feel or possess different social identities at different times or when faced with different choices between identities.

According to Egan and Nugent (1983, p. 195), 'it is understandable that Irish adolescents, who tend to see themselves as a minority culture within the larger Anglo-American culture, do not speak of politics, but turn to cultural and psychological matters in the hope of finding a unique identity for their homeland', a response they suggest 'is a feature of all groups threatened by cultural assimilation'. Research with young people in Northern Ireland also identified how social context is crucial in understanding young people's commitment to a group identity and ideology. Young men with greater experience of violence were more committed to their own socio-political group identity and ideology. They were typically alienated from any means of social control, resulting in a greater willingness to engage in and tolerate violent behaviour as a means of redressing a situation in which they felt themselves wronged or as a means of self-protection. Young men were seen to actively value and develop an identity that incorporates both a personal capacity for and tacit acceptance of violence, reproducing a form of masculinity in which violence is virtually compulsory (Muldoon and Wilson, 2001; Reilly et al., 2004).

PSYCHODYNAMIC THEORIES OF ADOLESCENCE

Understandably, with its emphasis on the biological basis of motivational drives, psychodynamic theory sees puberty as having a major bearing on behaviour and development.

Psychodynamic theory in relation to adolescence has centred on it as a time of increased instinctual urgency and anxiety, heightened conflict over impulse expression and emotional instability. Not only is there the appearance of conscious sexual urges at this time, but also unconscious experiences and primitive urges and feelings from earlier years. Much attention has been paid to the use of defence mechanisms against the heightened anxiety and unconscious conflict in adolescence. Defences against feelings of 'shame' and loss of pride are common for the young person and shyness is often symptomatic of this. Defence mechanisms feature prominently also because the young person's Oedipal feelings towards his/her parents (which were inhibited in the latency psychosexual stage) are reawakened with puberty, becoming a source of anxiety. According to Anna Freud (1958, p. 268), 'the reawakened pre-genital urges or – worse still – the newly acquired genital ones, are in danger of making contact with them, lending a new and threatening reality to fantasies which had seemed extinct but are merely under repression.' A revolution in the young person's primary attachments leads to altered ties to the parents due to the intensified sexualisation of parental affectional bonds reactivating Oedipal fantasies. This leads to defences being used against emotional ties to the parents, with the eventual reinvestment of primary sexual and affectional needs outside the family (Freud, 1958).

Other defence mechanisms used include the reversal of affection, from love to hate or from dependence to revolt, and the transference of affection from parents to others, including peers and repression (ibid).

Blos's Phase Theory of Adolescence

According to Blos (1972, p. 11), 'adolescence cannot take its normal course without regression'. Expressions of regression (in behaviour or fantasy) resembling the Oedipus or Electra complexes are to be expected (Haan, 1974). The sequential recapitulation of pre-Oedipal and Oedipal experiences feature in Peter Blos's (1962) phase theory of adolescence. This theory begins with the preadolescent psychosexual phase of latency. This is characterised by emotional quiescence, sexual inhibition and increased control by the ego and superego over the instinctual id. With the onset of puberty, an instinctual upsurge arises and a concomitant rise in the use of defence mechanisms (such as regression). These act to reduce the instinctual anxiety that accompanies sexual development. Castration anxiety reappears in the male with fear and envy of the female, while the female defends herself against a regressive pull toward the mother by a forceful move towards heterosexuality.

In the next phase, early adolescence, a move away from the parents towards the peers and close idealising of same-sex friendships arises. This move away from the parents and their values leads to a weakened superego and thus diminished self-control, possibly leading to delinquent behaviour. In the next phase, middle adolescence, a move towards opposite-sex peers arises with sexual development. A sense of mourning is experienced for the loss of the primary love objects (parents), who have become fallen idols. Increased narcissism, reflected in self-aggrandisement and self-absorption, are features of this phase.

In the next phase, late adolescence, sexual identity is established and a positive awareness and acceptance of the self contributes to identity resolution and self-esteem. The ego is strengthened and emotions become stabilised, leading to greater constancy in the personality.

The final phase proposed by Blos (1962) is post-adolescence. Tasks of late adolescence including the forging of intimate, sexual relationships are acted on. The young male must come to terms with his father image and the young woman with her mother image, each having a bearing on the young person's parenting in the future.

While psychodynamic theory has identified a number of interesting concepts with which to consider adolescence, scientific validation and assessment of these is lacking as a consequence of the unconscious nature of the material. Psychodynamic theories are impossible to test and consequently are described as 'non-falsifiable'. Overall, psychodynamic theories provide interesting and undoubtedly controversial ideas about adolescence. Such theories shift attention away from the social and conscious experience of adolescence to unconscious aspects and processes. While lacking in scientific credibility, they do offer a different standpoint from which to consider adolescence, which is drawn on by some professionals in therapeutic work with young people.

SOCIOLOGICAL THEORIES

We have already seen that while there are some overlaps between the usages of the terms 'adolescence' and 'youth', there are also some differences, both of denotation and connotation between these words and their variants. Consider, for instance, whether you think a typical adult would prefer to be described as 'adolescent' or 'youthful'! This is not to say that 'youth' always has positive connotations; far from it. 'Youth' in the public mind and in media usage is often associated with criminal and/or delinquent behaviour, and insofar as it relates to individuals ('a youth'), it almost exclusively refers to males. A key difference between the terms is that adolescence developed primarily as a psychological concept, while youth, which is much older both as a word and as an idea, is more commonly used within sociology. Sociology's principal concern is with the position of young people (or particular groups of young people) in society and their relation to key social institutions, rather than the processes of development they are going through as individuals. However, it is unnecessary and unwise, in attempting to understand the lives and experiences of young people, to focus only on one at the expense of the other, and throughout this book we attempt to take account of both. Moreover, many sociologists have drawn substantially on the insights of psychologists, and vice versa; and the disciplines share many key concepts and working methods. The overlap is particularly noticeable in the case of the first of the four sociological approaches summarised below. While not exhaustive or mutually exclusive, these cover the main perspectives within sociology on the position of young people in the social structure (Devlin, 2000). They are:

- Generational perspectives.
- Conflict perspectives.

- Transitional perspectives.
- Constructionist perspectives.

Generational Perspectives

Generational accounts of youth are those which accept that young people, by virtue of their age alone, are inherently different from children on the one hand and adults on the other; that these differences are in themselves of profound significance for individuals and for the broader society; and that they manifest themselves in a distinctive *youth culture* with its own roles, values and behaviour patterns. Generational accounts typically combine a functionalist sociology which sees youth culture, despite its apparent 'unruliness' and 'rebelliousness', as serving a number of 'important positive functions' both for young people and for society as a whole (Parsons 1972, p. 146) with a close adherence to the tenets of developmental psychology, for example the ideas of Erik Erikson presented earlier in this chapter. The positive functions of youth culture, even when it appears problematic or troublesome from many adults' point of view, include the fact that it encourages young people to be creative and innovative rather than unquestioningly accepting the values and norms of their elders, and such a willingness to innovate is vital if society is not to stagnate.

Paradoxically, however, another positive function of youth culture is that it is through the very same 'problematic' or 'troublesome' peer groups that young people learn to *conform*, and conformity is necessary for social stability. Most rebellious young people, the thinking goes, 'return to the fold' having had the chance to experiment and innovate.

Generational accounts of youth were predominant in sociology throughout Europe and the United States in the 1950s and 1960s. The most systematic treatment came from S.N. Eisenstadt in *From Generation to Generation* (1956). Starting from the position that 'age and age relations are among the most basic aspects of life and the determinants of human destiny' (1956, p. 26), Eisenstadt argued that youth is a stage of particular importance in modern industrial societies. This is because there is a pronounced structural gap between the family of origin within which children spend their early years and the economic and social system in which they must eventually take their place. The family has become concentrated on emotional and sexual (rather than economic) functions, so new institutions are necessary to manage the transition out of the family. These include education, youth services and the media. They also include youth culture itself, the key function of which relates to identity and autonomy:

> Youth's tendency to coalesce ... is rooted in the fact that participation in the family became insufficient for developing full identity or full social maturity, and that the roles learned in the family did not constitute an adequate basis for developing such identity and participation. In the youth groups the adolescent

seeks some framework for the development and crystallization of his identity, for the attainment of personal autonomy, and for his effective transition into the adult world (Eisenstadt, 1963, pp. 31–2).

Youth culture therefore has to be understood by reference to 'the process in which industrial society detaches children from their families and places them in/prepares them for the wider social system' (Frith, 1984, p. 20). It is clear from the emphasis on identity development and the use of the concept of adolescence itself that this perspective within sociology is very close to developmental psychology. While it no longer commands the dominant position it once did within sociology, it continues to influence much 'common sense' thinking about young people and youth culture, and indeed continues to be reflected in much social policy on youth. Much of the empirical material presented in the rest of the chapters of this book does in fact support the basic idea of generational distinctiveness, although it also suggests the need to take factors other than age and generation into account. This brings us to the second major set of sociological approaches to youth.

Conflict Perspectives

If generational perspectives reflect the assumptions of functionalism, the dominant paradigm in mainstream sociology for much of the twentieth century, then conflict perspectives reflect the influence of 'conflict theory' more broadly, which became prominent within sociology in the century's latter decades (and is usually contrasted with 'consensus theory'). This approach regards the view of young people outlined in the previous section as being based on an 'obsession with *age* as the most significant factor of social stratification' (Hall, Jefferson and Clarke, 1976, p. 17). By contrast, a conflict analysis rests on the basic assumption that the most significant features of the lives of individuals and groups are *systematically structured* by factors far more important than age.

> [I]f groups are positioned differently in the society by virtue of their class, race and sex, experience very different types of youth in their trajectory to adulthood (and to very different adulthoods at that), is it even true that youth can be definitively claimed as a stage of life? ... Youth as a single, homogeneous group does not exist (Hall, Jefferson and Clarke, 1976, p. 19).

The best-known and most influential work in this tradition emerged from the Centre for Contemporary Cultural Studies (CCCS) at the University of Birmingham in the 1970s, most notably the seminal volume *Resistance Through Rituals* (Hall and Jefferson 1975). Here, while factors such as gender and 'race' are acknowledged as important, the reading is essentially Marxist and pivotal significance is attributed to class: 'In modern societies, the most fundamental groups are the social classes, and the major cultural configurations will be, in a fundamental though often mediated way, "class cultures" (ibid, p. 13). From this perspective, young people's lives and lifestyles are worthy of study not as a uniform 'youth culture', but insofar as they provide examples of class-based youth *subcultures*. Young people may dress differently than their parents, may like different music, may 'hang out' together in different places, and yet:

> ... despite these differences, it is important to stress that, as sub-cultures, they continue to exist within and co-exist with, the more inclusive culture of the class from which they spring ... [T]hey belong to the same families, go to the same schools, work at the same jobs, live down the same 'mean streets' as their peers and parents (Hall and Jefferson, 1975, p. 14).

The title of *Resistance Through Rituals* actually captures its key point: that the subcultural activity of working-class young people is a form of resistance to their subordinate class position; but that this resistance, because 'ritualistic' and symbolic – largely taking the form of distinctive dress and body image, collective and expressive use of public space, argot (slang) 'style' – cannot offer a material solution to their oppression:

> There is no 'subcultural solution' to working-class youth unemployment, educational disadvantage, compulsory miseducation, dead-end jobs, the routinisation and specialisation of labour, low pay and the loss of skills ... When subcultures address the problematics of their class experience, they often do so in ways which reproduce the gaps and discrepancies between real negotiations and symbolically displaced 'resolutions' (Hall and Jefferson, 1975, p. 47).

The work of the CCCS, particularly in the early years, focused almost exclusively on young males and the key method was ethnography (participant observation). Subsequent work from a conflict perspective began to redress the gender balance (an influential early example was McRobbie and Nava, 1984) and moved beyond class to look at the subcultures of young people based on such shared experiences and identities as ethnicity, sexuality and disability (for example, Back, 1997; Blackburn, 1990; French and Swain, 1997). In all such cases, emphasis is placed on the fact that young people's experiences and opportunities are shaped by their position within systems of social inequality and cannot adequately be explained, or responded to, in terms of a neat developmental or generational model of adolescence and youth.

There have only been a few ethnographic studies of young people in Ireland. Richard Jenkins's *Lads, Citizens and Ordinary Kids* (1983) was a study of Protestant working-class youth in Belfast, placing the analytical and explanatory emphasis very much on class and – as its title suggests – on divisions within the working class in particular. It was roundly criticised by Bell (1990), who regarded it as 'somewhat perverse' to focus on the social class dimension in Northern Ireland in isolation from ethnic considerations and to ignore the 'all-embracing sectarian habitus' within which people in Northern Ireland, of whatever age, live their lives. Bell himself used a research strategy that combined an ethnography of a small group of Protestant teenagers involved in marching bands, an important element of Loyalist street culture, with survey research and secondary analysis of existing data on young people. He concluded that the cultural practices of Protestant working-class young people are 'best understood as an attempt to confront and overcome, at a symbolic level, the contradictions experienced in Loyalist parental culture' (Bell, 1990, p. 23). In the Republic, Gaetz's *Looking Out for the Lads* (1997) is based on an ethnographic study carried out in Cork. Again, class differences are highlighted, as are geographical divisions, and an account is given of the contrasting experiences of 'advantaged youth', 'mainstream youth' and 'the boys'. Fagan's study (1995) of the experiences of early school-leavers employs a post-structuralist and post-Marxist framework and seeks to play a concrete role in creating 'a cultural politics of early school leaving' and contributing to the development of a radical democracy in Ireland.

Transitional Perspectives

Transitional perspectives are not as clearly aligned with a particular macro-sociological world view as generational and conflict perspectives are (with consensus and conflict theory, respectively) and they are perhaps the most empirically orientated of all accounts of youth. They can be dated back at least several decades, and particularly to the concern throughout the EC (as it then was) in the 1970s and early 1980s with policy relating to youth unemployment and youth training, resulting in numerous studies focusing specifically on the 'transition from school to work' (TSW). More recently, however, transition research has had a broader focus exploring a *variety* of aspects of young people's progression into adulthood, and particularly the relationship between the two principal 'axes' of transition, the public and the private (Galland, 1995). In the transitional pattern that came to dominate the industrial era, the public and private transitions of young people – from education into employment and from living at home to living independently with a partner – were relatively predictable and unidirectional, and also relatively irreversible (in the sense that having left the education system for the workplace, people did not normally return to it; and having left the parental home to marry and set up an independent household, they did not go back). There were, of course, some differences in the experience of transition, both public and private, based on factors such as class and gender (young working-class people moving into the workplace earlier; young women much more likely to move out of the workplace and into home duties after a few years), but overall the framework was relatively stable and predictable, like two parallel lines along which young people made the public and private transitions into adulthood.

More recent accounts of youth transitions for the most part argue that the model just described was historically specific to industrial society and is increasingly being subverted as we move into a post-industrial era, in which transitions are much less unidirectional and much more contingent and reversible. In this context, not only the nature of youth but the nature of adulthood itself is changing: '"Transitions" that were previously linked to youth are frequently no longer the sole property of a particular age group. Backtracking, re-visiting, revising and the reversing of earlier decisions regarding lifestyle and content are a growing feature of life' (Jeffs and Smith, 1998/99, p. 54).

Much of the recent European research on youth transitions has had a comparative focus, contrasting the experiences of young people in different countries or exploring and describing different *regional* patterns of youth, northern and southern, eastern and western (Galland, 1995; Wallace and Kovatcheva, 1998; du Bois-Reymond and Chisholm, 2006). There is also a strong emphasis on the persistence of gender differences in traditions.

> Regardless of what individual girls and women may be able to negotiate and achieve for themselves in work and family life, the collective patterns of girls' and women's lives remain sharply different from those of boys and men. In this sense, European societies are remarkably similar, and have been for a very long time (Chisholm, 1995, p. 132).

Other ideas which have been influential on recent studies of youth transition have been those of Ulrich Beck (1992) on individualisation, risk and life as a 'biographical project'; and Anthony Giddens (1991) on modernity, identity and reflexivity. For Giddens, life transitions, including the transition from adolescent to adult, demand the exploration and construction of the self as part of a reflexive process of connecting personal and social change (1991, p. 33). However, while accepting that individualism is a prominent feature of contemporary culture and that young people in modern society are presented with much greater *choice* than before in respect of both their public and private lives, many writers are keen to stress that significant structural *constraints* remain and that the choices are by no means evenly divided across different social groups. Moreover, the 'choices' may be experienced by many young people as increased pressures or problems (Department of Education and Science, 2003a).

An important Irish study which draws on aspects of the transitional approach is Hannan and Ó Riain's *Pathways to Adulthood in Ireland: Causes and Consequences of Success and Failure in Transitions Amongst Irish Youth* (1993). Their report is based on intensive interviews with a national sample of school-leavers who were followed up and reinterviewed a number of times after they left school and entered the labour market in the mid to late 1980s. The authors note that 'the transition to adulthood is an important factor in the social and cultural reproduction of society' (p. 18) and set out to examine whether a singular 'normal' pattern (in both the statistical and normative sense) in the sequencing and means of attainment of adult status still exists in Ireland, having already acknowledged that such a pattern 'may have broken down in other European countries' (p. 2). In the event, they conclude that 'there is substantial support ... for a "normal" or majority pattern of integration into adult life which exists for over 90 per cent of young people at least up to age 22' (p. 223). Recalling the points made above about choices and constraints, the authors say that while 'youth may be a time of freedom and self-indulgence in some ways ... it is a highly structured and regulated experience and ... success or failure in early transitions ... affect the course of [young people's] adult lives in very important ways' (p. 237).

Constructionist Perspectives

Constructionist perspectives on the position of young people in society sometimes overlap with one or other of the perspectives outlined above, but they are distinctive in that their primary interest is in the ways in which the youth stage has been actively *constructed* by social and economic change during the industrial age. A clear early statement of this approach came from Peter Berger, who was a key figure in the development of the 'social constructionist' approach in sociology.

> The basic causal factor for youth today is industrial society and its institutional dynamics ... [T]he deepening of the division of labour, brought about by the Industrial Revolution ... separated the family (and thus childhood) from the process of modern production and administration. Modern youth is a further extension of the same process of institutional separation or differentiation ... [T]he Industrial Revolution has produced an institutional structure which 'allows room' for youth (Berger and Berger, 1976, pp. 240–241).

Coming from a rather different theoretical perspective, British sociologist Sheila Allen, who had a strong influence on much of the Marxist sub-cultural research carried out in the 1970s and after, took issue with the 'normative functionalist model most highly developed in the work of Talcott Parsons', and also with the 'crude empiricism' of other studies of youth. Allen argued instead that:

> It is not the relations between ages which explain change or stability in societies, but change in societies which explains relations between different ages ... Social adolescence, that is behaviour not appropriate for adults, can be created and for the past two hundred years societies in Western Europe have been creating adolescence (Allen, 1968, pp. 321, 324).

Part of this process of 'creation' was the emergence of professions concerned with young people's education, welfare and development (for example, teachers, youth workers, social workers and care workers), drawing on the theories and concepts developed within new disciplines such as psychology and sociology. A very full account of the emergence and institutionalisation of the key elements of adolescent psychology in the late nineteenth and early twentieth centuries is given by Hendrick (1990). Hendrick questions the widely accepted interpretation provided by Gillis (1974) to the effect that adolescence was 'discovered' (or 'invented') in public schools (that is, elite fee-paying schools) between 1870 and 1900 – that in effect it was a middle-class creation which was gradually 'democratised' to include the working class – and argues instead that the concept of adolescence was at first 'principally concerned with working-class youth' (1990, p. 84) and related to the emerging social problem of urbanism.

> The concept of adolescence as the social psychologists developed it and as other social scientists and educationalists adopted it was important for categorising knowledge of youth: it delineated reference points; it established norms; and, moreover, it facilitated a more precise age-structuring of the urban population at a time when commentators were eager to know as much as possible about what they regarded as the pathology of urbanism (Hendrick, 1990, p. 88).

Ultimately, concerns about working-class young males became concerns about adolescence and youth in general. As Griffin (1997, pp. 17–18) has suggested, 'one of the key features of academic (and non-academic) representations of youth is the widespread construction of youth in general, and specific groups of young people in particular, as "problems".' This problem status may involve being seen as the source of a particular focus of adult concern (such as football hooliganism) or being 'at risk' of getting into difficulty (for example 'teenage pregnancy'). The media play a pervasive role in the construction of 'problematic' negative stereotypes of young people, often with significant differences in the patterns of representation of young men and young women (Devlin, 2006).

An important constructionist analysis with a fully pan-European perspective is provided by Wallace and Kovatcheva (1998) in their study of 'the social construction of youth in Eastern and Western Europe'. In their account, youth was just one of a number of essentialist categories like 'race' and 'gender' which emerged and – at least for a time – became entrenched during modernity, when there was a 'need to divide people into strongly distinguished groups ... with the elaboration of theories to sustain and justify this division' (Wallace and Kovatcheva, 1998, p. 6). In particular, youth was the creation of state systems through which age became 'bureaucratically calibrated':

> Without a comprehensive state, such precise definitions of age would not have been possible ... [Y]outh was constructed as a social category, one destined for educational, legislative and other interventions. In addition, new scientific studies were developed to analyse this new category and thus provided the professional ideology for the new youth professionals. In those capitalist societies which developed earlier, this was done through pressure from voluntary organisations and individuals who constituted an active 'civil society'. In states which developed later under authoritarian control, this construction of youth took place more obviously as a product of state policy ... [In both cases] youth

held a key position as agents of the transformation of society ... (Wallace and Kovatcheva, 1998, p. 83).

Ultimately, Wallace and Kovatcheva argue that just as modernisation constructed youth as a social category, so too 'postmodernisation is deconstructing youth' (ibid., p. 209), an idea which clearly ties in with some of the current thinking on youth transitions outlined above. A further strand within constructionist approaches and one which also has links with some of the transitional studies discussed earlier is the concern with the ways in which young people individually and collectively construct their own identities, often using patterns of consumption to do so, a process which has been termed 'shopping for subjectivities' (Frost, 2003). Group boundaries – who belongs and does not belong – can be delineated through such consumption patterns. Of course, the choices young people make in this regard will be constrained by 'the versions of self available, often presented through advertising or branding and other visual mediums such as television and film' (Frost, 2003, p. 54). An increasingly important medium is the internet, through which young people (and older people) can participate in and construct web-based identities and sub-cultures. While new technologies have the potential to enhance and enrich personal and social development, they can also be used to harmful effect, so it is important that young people are supported and enabled to become 'critically aware' consumers and creators of these media resources (Department of Education and Science, 2003a).

FOCAL AND ECOLOGICAL THEORIES

While biological, psychological and sociological perspectives provide useful perspectives to explore and understand adolescence, each are constrained by their disciplinary boundaries. Focal and ecological theories, on the other hand, reflect an attempt to provide a broader, more all-inclusive approach to the study of adolescence.

Focal Theories

Coleman (1980) proposed that to accomplish the transition between childhood and adulthood, major psychological and social adjustments have to be made. The young person is an 'active agent' in these adjustments and thus in their own development. The notion of 'personal agency' and how young people pace themselves through adolescent transitions is central in this theory. Across adolescence, particular 'relational' issues come into focus sequentially at different ages and decline as the young person develops the psychosocial skills to resolve them. Usually teenagers cope with these issues or 'crises' one at a time. If a young person has to deal with more than one issue at once, they are more likely to encounter adjustment problems. Initially, concern about gender roles and relationships with the opposite sex peaks at 13 years and then declines afterwards. Acceptance by, or rejection from, peers peaks at about 15 years, while independence from parents peaks at 16 years and then declines (Coleman and Hendry, 1999). It is easier to deal with negotiating more independence from parents if a young person is not at the same time striving for better esteem within the peer group. In their words, 'most young people pace themselves through the adolescent transition. Most of them hold back on one issue while they are grappling with another. Most sense what they can and cannot cope with, and will, in the real sense of the term, be an active agent in their own development' (Coleman and Hendry, 1990, p. 205).

According to this theory, most young people do not experience major difficulties in adolescence because they cope by dealing with one relational issue at a time.

Research with young people in Belgium and other countries has supported this. According to Marcoen and Goosens (1999, pp. 65–80), 'The general pattern of peak ages for adolescents' interpersonal concerns provided support for the focal model. Negative feelings about being alone, relationships with parents, heterosexual relationships, small groups and rejection from large groups do not emerge all at once, but [rather young people] seem to deal with one issue at a time.'

While relational issues may 'overlap' at any point across adolescence, for most only one relational issue is prominent at any one point in time. However, those who have to deal with more than one issue being prominent at the same time are more likely to experience difficulties. This is illustrated in Figure 2.1, with each 'curve' representing a different relational issue or relationship. This theory thus offers a model of the relationship 'hurdles' of adolescence and of how the majority cope by dealing with one relational issue at a time. However, a minority do not cope because they have more than one relational issue prominent at the same point in time.

Figure 2.1 Coleman's focal theory model

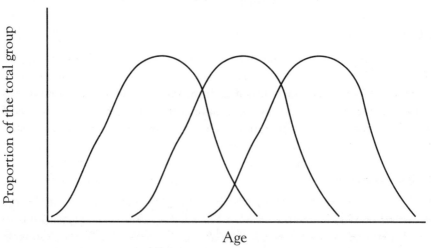

Proportion of the total group

Age

The amount of anxiety or difficulty in the various relational issues can be assessed by identifying the extent to which a young person's self-image does not match what s/he thinks others see them as, or expect of them, for example, if a young person thinks her parents see her as a child, yet she considers herself as an adult; or if she thinks she needs to be more outgoing to be liked by her peers.

But as a consequence of focal theory concentrating on the psychological transitions of adolescence, it neglects social and cultural factors. Socio-economic status and broader social and cultural factors such as religion and urban or rural background also influence how a young person copes with the teenage years. Family income, for example, may constrain or support a young person being given more independence (such as being supported to live away from home). In addition, social factors such as ease of employment or educational opportunities, family, friends and community may make adolescence more or less of a difficult period.

Ecological Theory

A useful theoretical framework for looking at adolescence holistically is the ecological model proposed by Bronfenbrenner (1979). As acknowledged by Valsiner (1993), each young person has his or her own 'personal culture' and 'collective (Irish) culture'. A developmental contextual perspective places the young person's development within a multi-layered social context, seeing development as the culmination of many direct and indirect influences (including culture), which either facilitate or impede an individual's development. Young people themselves act in and on their world and vice versa. In the widest sense, young people can be seen to be influenced by the time frame in which they live (chronosystem), general cultural and social structures (macrosystem), more immediate contextual factors which exert an impact via others (exosystem), immediate relationships (microsystems) and the relations between these (mesosystems).

The Chronosystem

This refers to the temporal or 'time' dimension of the model, recognising the impact of social change on the ecological systems mentioned above. Such change may take the form of changing laws or political institutions, technological development, economic recession or boom and social upheavals (disasters, pivotal historical events). The time frame or 'generation' in which a person lives frames the entire model.

The Macrosystem

This refers to cultural and social structures consisting of beliefs, values, attitudes and social institutions (including the school). The neighbourhood a young person lives in as well as any sub-culture they belong to also are considered to be macrosystemic influences on development. Other influences include expectations placed on young people across different social contexts, accepted norms (ways of behaving, ways of doing things) and social roles, experienced and responded to. Access to third-level education, further training and other means of social mobility are other features of this system. Culturally, young people are fed messages about what is expected of them that shape their experience of the world. If they feel unable to meet these expectations because of individual or social factors, they are more at risk for 'anomie' or marginalisation. At a broader level, the macrosystem includes cultural, social and global events such as war, poverty, racism and environmental influences, which impinge, perhaps in only a subtle way, on the young person.

Figure 2.2 Bronfenbrenner's ecological model

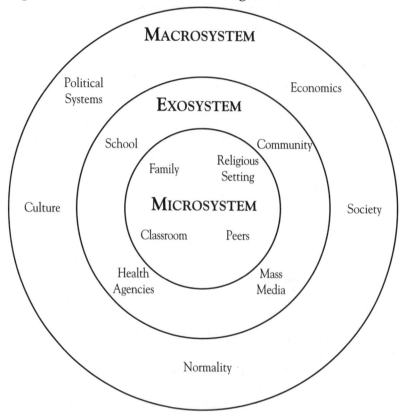

The Exosystem

This consists of institutions and contexts which, while not directly in contact with the young person, still indirectly influence the young person's quality of life. These include parental socio-economic status, the media and political and economic systems. The extent to which these provide support for the young person and his/her family is very important for the young person's quality of life (Greene, 1994). Government cutbacks in health services, for example, may negatively affect a young person's health.

The Mesosystem

This refers to the interrelationships between two or more microsystems, each of which contain the young person, such as relations between a young person's peers and family. Such relations may be harmonious or in conflict, possibly causing stress for the young person.

The Microsystem

This incorporates immediate contexts that include the young person, such as the family, friends, school, leisure or part-time work. Typically this includes a young person's relationships with family members, peers, teachers and other people in their life. Probably nearly all of the effects of the systems mentioned above are mediated through the young person's microsystems. These moderate and mediate (buffer) the effects of changes in the other systems, with some heightening and others minimising these effects. For example, the impact of parental separation may be heightened in a young person's relationships with other family members but minimised in their relations with their friends or peers in a sport they participate in.

Example

An example of this model as a whole can be seen in relation to young people's drinking in contemporary Irish society. This has become more of a prominent social concern across the media in recent years (exosystem influence), possibly due to changing social values in Ireland or due to young people having more money to spend on alcohol, reflective perhaps of the so-called 'Celtic Tiger' economic improvement (chronosystem influences). It has become less socially acceptable to serve young people alcohol as well as to drink and drive and to condone binge drinking across all age groups (macrosystem influences). However, while a young person's parents may not allow her or him to drink (microsystem influence), it may be normal for her or him to drink when with her/his friends (microsystem influence), placing a young person's family and peers at odds with each other (mesosystem influences).

The radio advert targeted at parents which raises the question 'does your drinking affect their thinking' illustrates how social forces at large via the media (exosystem) act to heighten parental awareness of the impact of their drinking on their children (microsystem).

This model helps in designing interventions with young people, whether at a one-to-one level (microsystem) or at the broader systemic levels of the community and culture. It also ensures attention is paid to what makes adolescence a unique as well as a shared experience for each individual. Sociologically, it is very useful in that it facilitates links to be made between social institutions, structures, changes and events and adolescent experience. Useful reading on this in an Irish context is Greene and Moane's (2000) article 'Growing Up Irish', referenced below.

CONCLUSION

This chapter began by examining some of the major points of debate about adolescence, including the extent to which it is a social construction. Some of the major theoretical perspectives were then explored, identifying the primary 'milestones' and features of the adolescent years from a physical, cognitive, moral, socio-emotional and sociological perspective were then explored. Each of these perspectives provides a framework with which to examine adolescence. Finally, focal and ecological theories were discussed as useful broader frames of reference with which to explore adolescence.

RECOMMENDED READING

Coleman, J.C., & Hendry, L. (1999). *The nature of adolescence*. London: Routledge.

Greene, S., & Moane, G. (2000). Growing up Irish: Changing children in a changing society. *Irish Journal of Psychology, 21*, 122–37.

Jackson, S., & Rodrigues–Tomé, H. (1993). *Adolescence and its social worlds*. Hove: Lawrence Erlbaum Associates.

Heaven, P.C. (2001) *The social psychology of adolescence*. London: Palgrave Macmillan.

3

Young People in Families

INTRODUCTION

The family is the primary socialising agent for young people. It is where we receive basic care such as food, warmth and shelter. The family also provides love, affection and acceptance and is central in shaping our views on right and wrong and acceptable behaviour. During the teenage years, peers and relationships with others outside the family become increasingly important and we shall examine these relationships later, in Chapter 4. However, parents, siblings and families remain central to the lives of adolescents and young people and it is this dynamic that we shall examine in this chapter.

An important source of research on families in Ireland is the Families Research Programme at the Department of Social and Family Affairs. A very useful review of various studies from the Families Research Programme was published recently (Cousins, 2006). It provides a summary of the main findings from 15 research projects conducted since 2000 on topics such as balancing work and family life, marital counselling, family policy, family formation, family well-being and children's experiences of parental separation. The focus of much family research tends to be on problematic issues. This is not surprising given the remit of government research agencies to devise social policy in response to need. Thus, there has tended to be an emphasis on research examining marital breakdown; the impact of separation and divorce on young people; lone parents; and absent fathers. Such family experiences can have considerable social policy implications and psychological consequences for young people and we shall examine the main research findings in this chapter. However, we must always remember that family breakdown and disruption is not the normative experience and that the majority of young people continue to live in a home with both their mother and father.

In this chapter we shall first examine census data on family form and household composition. We shall consider a number of the changing dynamics that are impacting on Irish families (and families in the developed world generally), specifically, the increased participation of women in the workforce, the falling birth rate, the fluctuating marriage rate, the increased numbers of children being born outside marriage and the increase in separation and divorce. We shall look at some recent research on the impact of parental separation or divorce on young people. Finally, we shall examine some selected aspects of families that have attracted considerable policy and research attention, namely, the one-parent family, fathers, family well-being and the domestic division of labour.

DEFINING THE FAMILY AND FAMILY COMPOSITION

Ireland's official stance on the family is found in Article 41.1.1 of the Constitution: 'The State recognises the Family as the natural primary and fundamental unit group of Society, and as a moral institution possessing inalienable and imprescriptible rights, antecedent and superior to all positive law.'

The family in the Constitution is based on marriage: 'The State pledges itself to guard with special care the institution of Marriage, on which the Family is founded, and to protect it against attack' (Article 41.3.1). However, there are numerous other types of families. The primary source of information on family forms and household composition is the Central Statistics Office (CSO, 2003a) (although a national census was conducted in 2006, the results are not available at the time of writing). The 2002 census reveals that there are 1,287,958 households nationwide, with an average of 2.94 people per household. Table 3.1 shows the make-up of private households, ranked by proportion of the total.

While the commonly perceived notion of a 'family' (husband and wife with one or more children) is the most frequently occurring type of household in the state, it only accounts for 35.9 per cent of all households. Thus, 'households' are composed of a much greater range of living arrangements than the traditional 'family'. As we can see, a large proportion of households (22 per cent) are made up of just one person, or one parent with one or more children (10.2 per cent). Perhaps surprisingly, given the amount of attention the issue receives, only 3.2 per cent of households consist of a cohabitating couple, and a further 2.1 per cent of households consist of a cohabitating couple with children.

The census also tells us what proportion of children are living with one or both parents, as we can see in Table 3.2. There are three primary conclusions to draw from this table. Firstly, the majority of Irish children (83.5–86.5 per cent) live with both parents. Secondly, there is an age effect on the numbers of children living with both parents (and, conversely, on the numbers living with a lone parent) – specifically, the younger the child, the more likely he or she is to be living with both parents. The differences are not very large, but we can see that 86.5 per cent of 0 to 4-year-olds live with both parents, compared to 83.5 per cent of 15- to 19-year-olds. Thirdly, this table shows the falling numbers of children in the more recent age cohorts (from 285,729 15–19-year-olds to 250,735 for 0 to 4-year-olds).

Table 3.1 Composition of private households

	No. of private households	As a % of total private households
Husband and wife with children (of any age)	462,283	35.9
One person	277,573	22
Husband and wife	169,668	13.2
Lone mother with children (of any age)	111,878	8.7
Non-family households containing no related persons	53,019	4.11
Husband and wife with children (of any age) and other persons	41,819	3.24
Cohabiting couple	41,751	3.2
Non-family households containing related persons	38,681	3
Cohabiting couple with children (of any age)	27,188	2.1
Lone father with children (of any age)	19,313	1.5
Lone mother with children (of any age) and other persons	15,785	1.22
Husband and wife with other persons	11,138	0.86
Cohabiting couple with other persons	6,027	0.46
Two family units with or without other persons	5,685	0.44
Lone father with children (of any age) and other persons	3,658	0.28
Cohabiting couple with children (of any age) and other persons	2,445	0.18
Three or more family units with or without other persons	47	0.0036
Total private households	1,287,958	100%

Source: CSO, 2003a

Table 3.2 Children living with one or both parents, by age

	Number (%) of 0–4 years	Number (%) of 5–9 years	Number (%) of 10–14 years	Number (%) of 15–19 years
Children enumerated with both parents	216,777 (86.5%)	213,949 (85.07%)	232,182 (84.4%)	238,567 (83.5%)
Children enumerated with a lone parent	33,958 (13.5%)	37,528 (14.93%)	42,890 (15.6%)	47162 (16.5%)
Total	250,735	251,477	275,072	285,729

Source: Extracted from CSO, 2003a, Table 33

Further insights to the composition of Irish families are provided by surveys by McKeown, Pratschke and Haase (2003) and Lalor and Baird (2006). McKeown et al. (2003) conducted a nationwide survey of a representative sample of 1,500 households which had at least one child below age 18. They categorised households into four main types:

1. Two parents (married)   66%
2. Two parents (cohabiting)   8%
3. One parent (never married, not in a relationship)   9%
4. One parent (separated, not in a relationship)   7%
    Other   10%

'Other' includes remarried parents, cohabiting parents following separation, divorce or widowhood, and single parents in a non-cohabiting relationship.

A slightly different make-up was reported in a survey of 988 secondary school pupils and Youthreach participants in Co. Kildare. Respondents were asked to describe the marital status of their parents. The majority (82 per cent) reported that their parents were living together (married or unmarried) (compared to 74 per cent in the McKeown et al. study). Thirteen per cent indicated that their parents were separated or divorced. The remaining 5 per cent lived in homes with a widowed parent (3 per cent) or a different domestic arrangement (2 per cent) (Lalor and Baird, 2006).

Thus, the main conclusion we can draw is that families (and households) in Ireland are quite varied in their make-up.

Nixon, Greene and Hogan (2006) conducted focus groups with a sample of 99 children and young people (nine to 16 years) regarding their views on what constitutes a family. They were presented with five vignettes briefly describing (a) a childless couple, (b) a married couple with a child, (c) an unmarried couple with a child, (d) a divorced (resident) parent and child, and (e) a non-resident parent and child. They were asked to consider if each constituted 'a family'.

Not all of the participants responded to each of the categories, so the 'N' is not 99 in each case. The childless couple were considered a 'family' by about two-thirds of respondents. For those who did not consider them a family, the absence of children was an important factor. All respondents considered the married couple with a child to be a family. The unmarried couple with a child were considered to be a family by over 80 per cent of respondents and the divorced mother living with her daughter were considered a family by over 90 per cent of respondents. Finally, about 80 per cent considered the father and his daughter, who lived separately, to be a family. Clearly, these young people recognise a variety of family forms. The researchers concluded:

> they conceptualised 'family' in an inclusive and flexible way. While many of the children conceived marriage, children and co-residence as important components of a family, their concept of a family did not rest solely upon such

structural features. Rather, the way in which family members loved and cared for each other emerged as the key factor in defining a 'family'. The importance of marriage was highlighted by a small number of the children in their discussion of divorce and unmarried cohabiting parents. The lack of stability and sense of impermanence that these situations may generate were highlighted. This suggests that the concept of the traditional nuclear family of two parents biologically related to and living with their children remains important, at least to some children. The presence of children also appeared to be fundamental for defining a group as a family' (Nixon, Greene and Hogan, 2006, pp. 85–6).

FAMILIES ARE CHANGING

This diversity in family make-up is greater than it was in the past. That is to say, the profile of the 'typical' Irish family has been changing in recent years (but perhaps not as dramatically as some commentators suggest). The main changes include:

- Increased participation of women in the workforce.
- A falling birth rate.
- A fluctuating marriage rate.
- Increased numbers of children being born outside marriage.
- Increases in separation and divorce.

Thus, a family form common a generation ago (a married man and woman living together with four children) has become a rare household indeed (such households make up only 41,741 out of the total of 1,287,958 (or 3.2 per cent). Let's examine each of these changes in a little more detail.

Increased Participation of Women in the Workforce

The 'traditional' model of man as sole breadwinner and woman in the home was still the reality for approximately 50 per cent of Irish families in 2001 (McKeown, 2001a). However, the numbers of double-income families are increasing as women's participation in the workforce increases. The EU has a target (called the Lisbon target) of 60 per cent of women in the workforce by 2010. Women's participation in the workforce is highest amongst younger women – 75.6 per cent of 25- to 34-year-old Irish women are in paid employment (www.worklifebalance.ie).

Men and women have different degrees of engagement with the labour force. Women are more likely to have part-time jobs, to avail of job-sharing schemes and to work fewer hours. Women also earn less than men, reflecting their greater involvement in lower-skilled, part-time jobs. Referring to figures for 2002, the Irish Congress of Trade Unions noted that nearly one-third of women worked for less than 30 hours per week, compared to just 6 per cent of men (www.ictu.ie).

The increase in dual-income families has brought about considerable economic and social change to Irish couples and their children. This expansion of women in the labour force has been credited with contributing significantly to economic growth in recent times. It has also resulted in a considerable increase in child care services.

Increasing numbers of mothers working outside the home bring increased income and provide a richer source of role models of gender roles, particularly for daughters. Morgan and Grube (1987) detailed some of the perceived benefits to adolescents of their mothers working outside the home. They studied the sex role attitudes of a sample of over 2,000 Dublin adolescents and found that both the sons and daughters of women working outside the home had less stereotyped beliefs about sex role behaviour. Also, there was no significant difference in 'self-image', 'relationship with mother' or 'anti-social behaviour' between those adolescents whose mothers worked in the home and those whose mothers worked outside the home. Indeed, the only difference the researchers did find was that the children of working mothers had significantly higher academic aspirations, that is, they rated more highly the likelihood that they would go on to higher education. The researchers speculate that this may simply be because two-income families are in a better financial position to send children to college.

A Falling Birth Rate

Another major change in Irish families is that they are getting smaller. By 2002, Irish fertility fell to 1.6 (below replacement level). However, while family sizes have been falling, the numbers of births has actually been increasing for the last decade. In 1996, 50,655 babies were born and this figure has been steadily rising, to 61,517 in 2003. In other words, the numbers of families is increasing (by over 30 per cent since 1981), but these families are having fewer children. Inward migration flows will ensure continued population growth for the foreseeable future.

The falling birth rate means that Irish children and adolescents are less likely to have older siblings, who can act as role models, and younger siblings, who can foster experiences of care and guardianship that are potentially so empowering for young people to feel.

Interestingly, although Irish birth rates have fallen considerably in recent years, they are still the highest in the EU25. For example, in 2004 Ireland had 15.2 live births per 1,000 inhabitants, compared to 12 in the UK and 8.6 in Germany (Eurostat, 2006).

A Fluctuating Marriage Rate

As we can see from the figures below, marriage rates in Ireland have tended to fluctuate up and down.

1974	7.4 per 1,000 people
1993	4.4 per 1,000 people
1996	4.5 per 1,000 people
2003	5.1 per 1,000 people

The rate of 4.4 per 1,000 people in 1993 was the lowest in 100 years, presumably tied to economic factors (high cost and high emigration of young people of marriage age). The figure of 5.1 per 1,000 people in 2003 is relatively high by EU standards. The highest marriage rate in 2004 was in Cyprus (7.2) and Denmark (7); the lowest rates were in Slovenia (3.3) and Belgium (4.1) (Eurostat, 2006).

Marriage is also occurring later in life. The average age for brides and grooms in 1977 was 24 and 25 years, respectively. In 1993, it had increased to 26 and 28 years, respectively (Ireland, 1998). This postponement of marriage is a feature of numerous other European countries, more noticeable in northern Europe (particularly Scandinavia) than in southern European countries.

Increased Numbers of Children Being Born Outside Marriage

A further, quite dramatic, change in family form is that more children are being born outside marriage (or 'wedlock', to use a more archaic term). In 1980, 5 per cent of births occurred outside marriage. In 2003, there were 61,517 births and 19,313 (31.4 per cent) of these were outside marriage – this represents a dramatic change. The numbers of babies born outside marriage varies enormously in the EU25, from 58 per cent in Estonia in 2004, to 3 per cent in Cyprus (Eurostat, 2006). The Irish proportion (31.4 per cent) is very close to the EU25 average of 31.6 per cent (Eurostat, 2006).

Historically, children born outside marriage had limited rights or claims on their father's wealth. Such children were considered 'illegitimate', which by today's norms seems a harsh and archaic way to view a child (who, after all, had no say in who his/her mother or father were!). However, the Status of Children Act 1987 in effect abolished the concept of illegitimacy (Kennedy, 2001) and ensured children born outside marriage were afforded the same legal standing as other children.

Of course, many children born outside marriage are born into secure, loving families whose parents may marry in the future. However, the marriage rate of this group is not known. From a child welfare point of view, the less important statistic is the number of children born outside marriage. In terms of psychological and emotional well-being of children, the more important statistic is the number of children living with both of their parents (whether married or unmarried).

INCREASES IN SEPARATION AND DIVORCE

In the year divorce was first available in Ireland (1997), 95 divorces were granted. In 2003, 2,970 divorces were granted, and this increased to 3,347 in 2004 (an increase of 12.7 per cent on the previous year). The numbers of divorced persons in Ireland trebled between 1996 and 2002 (from 9,800 to 35,100). The number of separated (including divorced) persons increased from 87,800 in 1996 to 133,800 in 2002 (National Children's Office, 2005a).

That said, Ireland continues to have the lowest divorce rate in the EU. In 2003, Ireland had 0.7 divorces per 1,000 inhabitants, compared to 3.2 in the Czech Republic and Lithuania (Eurostat, 2006).

As the legalisation of divorce has been one of the most significant (and controversial) changes for Irish families in the last decade, we shall examine the implications in some detail below.

Separation and Divorce

After a referendum in November 1995, the Family Law (Divorce) Act 1996 was passed (after an appeal to the Supreme Court was unsuccessful) and came into operation in February 1997 when, for the first time, divorce became available to couples in Ireland (who had lived apart for four of the previous five years).

What impact does separation and divorce have on children as they mature? The longitudinal studies to answer this question have not yet been conducted in Ireland. However, we can look to research from the United States, long a high-divorce society. Booth (1999) notes an inter-generational effect whereby the children of divorce families are more likely to divorce themselves and, indeed, their own children are likely to experience similar effects. He concludes that 'unless the divorce rate declines, we can expect the same high levels of personal disorganisation in generations to come' (Booth, 1999, cited in McKeown, 2001a).

It remains to be seen whether Ireland will see the very high divorce rates that occur in the US, the UK and in some northern European countries. Sweeney and Dunne (2003) describe this as one of the 'the great imponderables for those concerned with the Irish family today' (p. 20).

There are certain factors that may minimise the divorce rates in Ireland. For example, the dominant religion, Catholicism, prohibits divorce. Ireland is also characterised by other socio-demographic factors associated with lower divorce rates – high home ownership rates, rural populations, late marriage age and (relative) cultural homogeneity.

What is clear, however, is that there will be further increases in the numbers of children and young people who experience parental separation and divorce. State and voluntary child and family services must prepare themselves for this predictable eventuality. As separation and divorce become more prevalent in Ireland, all those working with children and young people must develop an appreciation of the effects of parental separation on children.

The Impact of Parental Separation on Children

The issue of what effect parental separation or divorce has on children and young people has received some research attention, particularly by researchers in the Children's Research Centre at Trinity College Dublin (Greene, 1995; Halpenny, 2004; Hogan et al., 2002).

Hogan, Halpenny and Greene (2002) examined 60 children aged 8 to 17 years who had experienced parental separation in the previous five years. They divided the sample into 'younger children' (8–12 years) and 'older children' (13–17 years). For the purposes of this book, we are interested in the experiences of the 'older children'. They found that children differed considerably in their reactions to parental separation and that 'it is not possible to conclude that separation is either a "positive" or "negative" experience for children' (p. x). Hogan et al. (2002) found that the most common initial reaction to discovering that parents were to separate was 'shock', a feeling of unreality. Sadness was expressed by 38 per cent of the sample. Other common reactions were relief (43 per cent), but also anger (47 per cent), confusion (40 per cent), embarrassment (37 per cent) and loneliness (42 per cent). Thus, children and young people report a spectrum of emotions on learning of their parents' separation, primarily negative.

The separation led to a change of address for 27 per cent of the sample, although younger children were more likely (37 per cent) than older adolescents (17 per cent) to experience a change of address. In almost all cases (93 per cent) the mother remained the resident parent. For most of the respondents, there was no change to their daily care arrangements. Their mothers had prepared their meals, washed their clothes, brought them to school, and they continued to do so. Older adolescent respondents noticed the additional strain this put of their mothers and were keen to help out around the house more.

Interestingly, contact with the non-resident parent occurred with weekly regularity for 68 per cent of children. Only 10 per cent had no contact at all with their non-resident parent. The authors note that these contact levels are higher than those found in UK and US studies. For example, Dunn et al. (2004, cited in Halpenny, 2004) found that only 33 per cent of children in the UK had weekly contact with non-resident parents. Bradshaw and Miller (1991) found that 40 per cent of non-resident fathers in the UK had lost all contact with their children five years after divorce. Perhaps the small size of Ireland facilitates greater contact. Halpenny (2004) speculates it may be due to the strong tradition of family influence and experience in Irish society. Whatever the reason, it is a positive finding in the otherwise fairly fraught area that is family breakdown.

The primary finding of the Hogan et al. study (2002) is that there is no single, simple experience of parental separation. Children experienced both positive and negative reactions; they were able to avail of a range of supports from parents, extended family, school, formal support services and peers. That said, there were common experiences. Shock at the announcement was widespread, even where parents had had prolonged conflict. Also, sadness at the division of the family was widespread. However, not all felt regret, and relief was also experienced, typically as the separation resulted in a reduction of household fighting and conflict.

They also found that many of the children had a range of worries:

Children worried initially about loss of contact with the non-resident parent, and some had on-going concerns about the implications of the separation for the future of the family. Some feared further loss, particularly when contact with non-resident parents was problematic ... A number of children worried about a parent's welfare, and this inhibited children from sharing their anxieties with these parents (p. 99).

Thus, parental separation has a considerable impact on young people and requires significant adjustment, such as living with only one parent (usually mother) and the loss of day-to-day contact with the other (usually father). Indeed, satisfaction with post-separation residence and visiting arrangements was a key factor in helping children cope.

Hogan et al. (2002) further note that divorce occurs within a social context. Thus, the impact of parental separation on a child may be modified by public attitudes, values and ideologies. With increasing numbers of young people experiencing parental separation, it can plausibly be argued that fewer children and adolescents will feel unique, different or 'weird' as a result of their parents' split.

Halpenny (2004) further examined some of the sample from the Hogan et al. (2002) study. She gathered detailed information on the experiences of 40 children (aged eight to 17) who had experienced parental separation and interviewed the same children again two years later (now aged 10 to 19 years) regarding their perceptions of closeness and security. That is, she examined how children's relationships with their parents alter after separation. Halpenny (2004) found that the children she interviewed could be divided into a number of categories:

- First, those children who were successfully navigating the breakdown in their parents' relationship and who were succeeding in maintaining feelings of closeness and security with both of their parents.
- A second category (approximately 20 per cent of the sample) was struggling to resolve problems with one parent, typically the non-resident parent, and a further 20 per cent had effectively 'pared down to one relationship'.
- A third category described feelings of being caught in the middle of hostile parental relations. Not surprisingly, children exposed to such hostile conflicts found it difficult to maintain feelings of closeness and security.

A key finding was that, for children, feelings of closeness and security depend on day-to-day 'opportunities and experiences of intimacy and familiarity' (p. 211) and that the children are more likely to report such experiences with their 'present parent', as opposed to their 'absent parent'. The implication of this finding is that absent parents who wish to maintain close relations with their children must optimise the frequency and consistency of contact and interaction in everyday activities. 'Regular and repeated interaction and interchange were represented as fostering ease of communication and greater awareness of what was happening in each other's lives' (Halpenny, 2004, p. 213).

Caveat to Research Findings on the Impact of Parental Separation on Children

Both of the studies described above (Halpenny, 2004; Hogan et al., 2002) shared the same sample of children and young people. It is important to note that the sample was not a random selection of young people who have experienced parental separation. Parental consent was required and it is possible that this consent was more likely to be forthcoming in certain circumstances, specifically, where parents deemed children to be coping well, and in a position to talk to unknown researchers about their feelings. Also, 75 per cent of the children in these studies were engaged with counselling services (this is how they were accessed). We cannot assume that children engaged with counselling services are representative of children experiencing parental separation. For these reasons, we must be cautions about generalising the findings. That said, these studies represent a rare insight into the feelings of a sample of Irish children and young people whose parents have separated.

Parental Access to Children Post-Divorce or Separation

A frequent complaint of post-separation fathers is that the courts do not take their fathering role seriously and that access granted to their children tends to be over-delineated. The reality for the 'Saturday dads' is that their interactions with their children must be carefully planned, with the result that they can feel artificial and, frequently, strained. It is difficult to manage spontaneous, natural interactions when your time together is restricted to 2 p.m. to 6 p.m., regardless of the weather or the mood you or your children are in. Poorer fathers, who do not have suitable accommodation with cooking facilities or private transport, are forced to spend their access time in public spaces. The strained, artificial nature of a father's access to his children after separation is expressed by a respondent in Corcoran's (2005) study of 'absent' fathers:

> 'I am always aware of time, your whole life it becomes a series of appointments. Other people can be with their children ... this wonderful flexibility is what I have lost. I have to fit everything into these two nights. I have to live this whole life of fitting everything into times and watching the clock' (p. 147).

Step-Parents

As an inevitable consequence of the increase in separation and divorce, we will see an increase in step-parents (and 'step-boyfriends' or 'girlfriends') in Ireland in the years to come. Such families cannot be seen as a homogenous group, as they vary from the stable and long term, to the more fleeting. McKeown (2001a) considers the impact of step-parents on the well-being of children. Again, the Irish data is not available and he turns to UK and US studies, which show that the formation of stepfamilies usually increases family income and thus improves children's standard of living. On the other hand, contact with non-resident biological fathers is likely to decrease once a stepfather is present. Also, relationships with the new father figure are often fraught, particularly for adolescents. Many children view the stepfather as an outsider, reject the stepfather's attempts to exert authority and are jealous of the emotional bond between stepfather and the mother (Hetherington and Clingempeel, 1992, cited in McKeown, 2001a, p. 40). Of course, stepfamilies have the potential to be secure, loving family homes. McKeown concludes: 'Overall, the evidence on stepfathers, and stepfamilies generally, suggests that they are likely to be more vulnerable than conventional two-parent families, particularly in terms of relational well-being and its associated benefits' (2001a, p. 41).

In one of the few empirical studies on fatherhood in Ireland, Ferguson and Hogan (2004) interviewed a sample of 'vulnerable' fathers (those engaged with social services). They found similar variability in terms of delivering family social work services to step-parents (usually stepfathers). On the one hand, social workers may exclude stepfathers as another passing casual acquaintance or transient lover of the mother and children they consider to be their main client. On the other hand, 'some stepfathers were recognised as being a huge resource for the family to an extent where children were either not taken into care, or were returned to mothers and their new partners because of the stability and care the latter now offered the family' (pp. 15–16).

THE LONE-PARENT FAMILY

As noted in the Final Report of the Commission on the Family (Commission on the Family, 1998), lone-parent families are not a new phenomenon: 'it is only during the 20th century that the death of a parent or spouse at a young age has ceased to be a common event' (p. 97). As we saw in Table 3.1, there are 111,878 'lone mother with children' and 19,313 'lone father with children' households in the country. Lone-parent families are composed of three main groups:

- Parents whose spouse has died.
- Parents who have separated/divorced.
- Parent who never married.

One-parent families are 'heavily concentrated in lower socio-economic strata' (McKeown et al., 2003, p. 24). Not surprisingly, as social class is significantly related to educational attainment, the education level of one-parent families is significantly lower than two-parent families.

Note that McKeown (2001b) describes the limitations of the term 'one-parent family' as 'strictly speaking, it is a misnomer to speak of one- or two-parent families since every child has two parents irrespective of whether they are married, separated, single, cohabiting or living apart; in this sense, there are no one-parent families – only one- and two-parent households' (p. 4).

Lone mothers, in particular, have received considerable attention and there has been much debate about the effects of social welfare payments to them. Introduced in 1997, the One-Parent Family Payment is the main income support for those lone parents who do not have adequate income to support themselves. In 2006, this payment was a maximum of €165.80 per week, and €19.30 for each 'qualified child'. It is a condition of the payment that the parent lives alone (that is, without a partner), known as the 'cohabitation rule'. This has led to criticisms that it may serve to ensure that children are not provided with the opportunity of living with a (generally, male) role model and that it contributes to the erosion of the family and the marginalisation of men. Corcoran (2005) studied a sample of young, disadvantaged, never-married fathers in Dublin and found that:

> In cases where cohabitation occurs the residency of the father is often denied and evidence of his presence in the home is hidden. This leads to a distortion of the relationship between the mother and the father and the father and his children (p. 140).

As Ferguson and Hogan (2004) put it, 'the social welfare system creates a financial benefit for mothers to claim lone-parent family benefit and for fathers' names not to be put on the birth certificate, in effect for them not to be seen to officially exist' (p. 12). This concern was also raised by the Final Report of the Commission on the Family: 'The Commission is concerned that the tax or social policies should contain no unnecessary obstacles in establishing a stable relationship and providing joint parenthood to children, but recognises that no system which has a support conditional upon lone parenthood can avoid some financial incentive to lone parenthood and an obstacle to the formation of a stable relationship' (Commission on the Family, 1998, p. 101). That said, the Commission found that income support is essential for lone-parent families and that it must 'continue to be an essential priority for State policy in relation to families' (p. 102).

FATHERS

Although previously quite neglected in family studies research in Ireland, fathers have been the focus of some attention by researchers (primarily men) in recent years (Corcoran, 2005; Ferguson and Hogan, 2004; Kiely, 2001; McKeown, 2001a). However, it remains the case that there is little empirical data on fathers and their interactions and relationships with their offspring in Ireland. For instance, the authors are aware of no published work on how Irish adolescents and young people interact with their fathers. In this section, we shall examine the main findings of recent studies, which have primarily focussed on disadvantaged fathers.

Ferguson and Hogan (2004) studied 'vulnerable fathers', those whose families are engaged with social services and family support agencies. They interviewed 24 such vulnerable fathers and a selection of their partners, children and the professionals involved in their particular case with a view to developing a 'father-inclusive framework' for family policy and practice. They report a pattern of fathers being excluded by service providers, particularly social workers, sometimes on the basis of their perceived intimidating appearance (tattoos, bulked-up physiques, skin heads); that is, they may be 'framed as dangerous and unfit to care' (p. 16). In general, they found that social workers were not well-equipped to deal with the men or fathers attached (sometimes very loosely) to the women and children with whom they worked. 'The net effect is that social workers in general do not "know" men, have little confidence around them, and often fear having meaningful discussions with them. They also lack skills in discussing fatherhood with men and strategies to divert attention and responsibility for child care away from the mother' (p. 9). McKeown (2001a) notes a similar trend: 'services often accept the lack of involvement of men without question and often unwittingly promote it by failing to collect information – from fathers or mothers – about the role of the father in the family thereby rendering men invisible in the family support system, (p. 42). Buckley (1998) also makes a similar point in her paper on the 'filtering out' of fathers in child protection social work.

Although not explicitly raised by Ferguson and Hogan (both male social workers), there is a gendered element to the social work services they describe. Social work, social care work and family support work are overwhelmingly female professions and while of course these professionals are trained to communicate with a wide range of people – men and women – there may be instances where gender (and class) pose obstacles to communication.

Young, Disadvantaged Fathers

Corcoran's (2005) study of absent fathers is a rare instance of empirical work on fathering. In noting the dearth of previous work, she states, 'Young mothers are more likely to be involved in formal and informal community networks. There are many more services directed at them, and for that reason, they are frequently more accessible for the purpose of carrying out research' (p. 135). If previously married fathers are somewhat shadowy figures in studies of lone parents, absent non-married fathers are invisible. Not being married, they do not have the same legal status as their previously married counterparts. It is this group of unmarried, absent fathers that are the focus of Corcoran's study. Unlike older absent fathers (who were typically married or in long-term relationships), these men were typically young, from disadvantaged backgrounds and had become fathers as a result of a casual or non-committed relationship.

> Among the young men from the North Dublin suburb there appeared to be a high degree of sexual promiscuity characterised by transient relationships, one-night stands, and several men going out with the same girl at once. On the subject of taking responsibility for sexual activity most of the young men

felt that taking precautions was a matter for the young women (Corcoran, 2005, p. 139).

Not surprisingly, such casual approaches to sexual intercourse, often after alcohol has been consumed, together with ignorance of the reproductive cycle, have previously been noted on studies of young single mothers. The picture that emerges from Corcoran's (2005) study is one of immature, impotent young fathers unable to deal with the economic and relationship responsibilities consequent to fathering a child. As Corcoran notes, similar studies in the UK have found that, in these circumstances, the role of fatherhood is reconfigured to 'emphasise emotional support and guidance over economic responsibility' (p. 142). For very young fathers, even this level of input was beyond them:

> Several younger fathers – that is, fathers in their late teens or early twenties, reported feelings of alienation in relation to the mothers of their children ... Respondents felt that their girlfriends or former girlfriends had changed after the birth of the child and they had great difficulty communicating with them ... They felt they had to tiptoe around the young women, that arguments would start over the smallest thing, and that the only way to survive the storm was to keep their mouths shut and try to diffuse the situation at all costs ... In almost all cases, the mother of the child was perceived to have all the control in the relationship, a fact that created feelings of anger and fear as well as undermining the role of the father in his attempts to co-parent (Corcoran, 2005, pp. 142–3).

Therefore, fatherhood for the unemployed or poorly paid and poorly educated young men in Corcoran's study was not about 'creating and sharing a family home', but it was about 'occasional child care by them or their parents, providing some financial support if possible, and buying gifts for their child' (Corcoran, 2005, p. 151).

Corcoran (2005) paints a bleak picture of fathers' experiences after they have separated from the mother of the children, whether they are previously married, older, affluent men, or young, never-married, poorer adolescents or young men:

> The majority of fathers in the study, whether previously married or not, reported that they had experienced negative feeling states as a result of their current situations including susceptibility to depressive disorders, repressed feelings of anger or suicidal tendencies. Nevertheless, almost all shared sense of commitment to their children and to embodying a fathering role, even in the face of institutional, social and economic barriers (p. 150).

McKeown (2001b) notes that unmarried fathers in Ireland are not always placed on their children's birth certificates, which is contrary to Article 7 of the UN Convention on the Rights of the Child, which states: 'The child shall be registered immediately after birth and shall have the right from birth to a name, the right to acquire a nationality and, as far as possible, the right to know and be cared for by his or her parents.' He cites research from the Department of Social, Community and Family Affairs that suggests 20 per cent of children born to unmarried parents do not have a father on their birth certificate.

FAMILY WELL-BEING

'All happy families are alike but an unhappy family is unhappy after its own fashion.' – opening sentence of Leo Tolstoy's novel, *Anna Karenin*.

What is a happy family? Why are some happier and better places to grow up than others? McKeown, Pratschke and Haase (2003) were concerned with what makes a family happy and what factors influence family well-being. They carried out in-depth interviews with four different family types – two-parent married families, two-parent cohabiting families, one-parent single families (never married) and one-parent separated families. Their key research question was whether family well-being varied systematically across family types. They used a wide range of psychometric instruments to measure well-being of parents and children and they found that 'the particular type of family in which one is living has little or no impact on well-being, with the exception of one-parent single families where mothers tend to have lower levels of psychological well-being than other parents' (2003, p. 6).

This is intuitively valid – there is no reason a family should be less happy simply based on whether or not parents are married. So, what factors do affect family well-being? An important factor they found was the personality characteristics of parents. Those with 'negative emotionality' (feeling distressed, upset, guilty, scared, irritable, ashamed, nervous, jittery, afraid) had lower levels of well-being. On the other hand, traits of 'psychological independence' (feelings of self-reliance, independence, assertiveness, ambition) enhance family well-being.

The quality of mother-child relationships was also found to be an important determinant of physical and psychological well-being for parents. Not surprisingly, the nature of a couple's relationship also had an important impact of family well-being: 'the well-being of men and women was heavily influenced by the quality of the couple relationship and the ability to satisfactorily resolve conflicts and arguments' (McKeown et al., 2003, p. 7).

They also studied the well-being of children in their sample (all aged 11 to 16 years). They found that there were four main factors which influence young people's well-being. Firstly, if the child perceives there to be unresolved conflicts, this leads to a major reduction in their life satisfaction. These conflicts include progress at school, drinking, smoking, drugs, household work, pocket money and how it is spent, boyfriends or girlfriends and going to church. Conflict on any or all of these issues has a strong impact on a young person's general sense of life satisfaction. Secondly, a helpful, supportive and encouraging mother, skilled in resolving conflicts with her partner, is important for her offspring's well-being. Thirdly, having a supportive father and fourthly, family income, whereby 'children tend to show fewer signs of psychological disturbance as family income rises' (p. 9). As we noted earlier, they found no significant variation in children's well-being based on family type, 'indicating that the parents' marital status and the presence of one or two parents in the household do not, of themselves, affect the child's well-being' (p. 9).

Table 3.3 Principles of good practice in Child and Family Services

Management principles	Intervention principles
A range of services is available, targeted at different levels of need, within a framework of prevention.	The service is 'whole child' focused.
	The service is accessible and attractive – it should be user-friendly, local and unfussy.
Services have clear objectives and a management and organisational culture that facilitates their achievement – management should be open and nurturing.	Services are integrated – they respond to the changing developmental needs of children and their families in a cohesive way, avoiding the fragmented experience of the 'multi-agency family'.
The service has a culture of learning and development – it should evaluate its efficacy, innovate and be open to learning from others.	The service is responsive to need and effective – there should be a clear logic for the chosen intervention.
The service measures outcomes – it should regularly ask, 'Does this work?'	The service works in a way that is collaborative and strengthening – parents and families should be involved as active partners for change, not as passive recipients of 'expertise'.
The service has adequate resources to meet its objectives and offers value for money.	
The service has a commitment to effective partnership practice – consulting and communicating with families, service users and relevant stakeholders.	The service is culturally competent – it should reflect the cultural values and traditions of families.
Services provide good staff development and support – staff should feel empowered, trusted and valued.	Staff are interested and able – they are most effective if seen as friendly, helpful, down-to-earth, easy to talk to.

Source: Summarised from Department of Health and Children, no date

The Department of Health and Children carried out a review of good practice in working with children and families. Conducted by researchers in the Child and Family Research and Policy Unit at NUI Galway in 2003, this report gathered together instances of good practices from Health Boards nationwide. The report does not claim to be the definitive compilation of good practice with children, young people and their families. Rather, it is a compilation of strategies, projects and interventions that are thought by service providers to be useful and successful, from which other service providers could learn. The researchers summarised some 'general principles of best practices' based on their examination of a total of 26 projects nationwide, including early years projects, parenting initiatives, youth projects and after-care services for young people leaving residential care. These 'principles of good practice' are reproduced in Table 3.3 and offer a benchmark against which child and family service providers can evaluate their service provision.

DOMESTIC DIVISION OF LABOUR

In one of the very few Irish studies on the domestic division of labour, Kiely (1995) reports the results of a survey conducted in the late 1980s, whereby 513 urban mothers were surveyed regarding their attitudes to work and family roles. Paradoxically, therefore, one of the only pieces of research on the domestic work of fathers in Ireland comes from the perspectives of mothers. The researchers found that 81 per cent of the sample agreed that husbands and wives should share housework equally. However, this rarely occurred in practice. Across a range of household tasks, mothers bear the main responsibility (with the exception of household repairs).

Table 3.4 Distribution of household and child care tasks in Irish households, n = 513

	Father only (%)	Mother only (%)	Both (%)	Other* (%)
Breakfast	16	51	15	18
Dishes	5	48	17	30
Shopping	5	69	22	4
Ironing	1	78	5	16
Hoovering	6	52	19	23
Repairs	76	10	9	5
Putting to bed	12	43	42	3
Homework	23	43	30	4
Discipline	16	26	58	0.4
School meetings	3	53	43	1

Source: Kiely, 1995
* 'Other' includes children, other family members and outside help

What variables influence men's share of household tasks? No significant differences were noted based on social class. However, older men (mid-forties up) were less likely to engage in household and child care tasks than younger men, suggesting a generational factor (Kiely, 1995). Generally, the higher the educational level of parents, the greater participation of fathers. Kiely suggests that more 'traditional' definitions of family roles may be a feature in households with lower levels of educational attainment. However, this increase in the father's role where both parents have a third-level education may be a product of both parents being engaged in paid employment. In summary, Kiely concludes:

> What emerges from these findings is that the mothers are clearly the managers. They manage the internal affairs of the family. They take care of the children, do the household tasks and make most of the decisions. The father, on the other hand, appears to do very little around the house except household repairs, play with the children, decide on what TV programme to watch, and are unlikely to change this low level of participation unless their wives become sick or go to hospital (1995, p. 154).

Irish men are not unusual and Kiely observes that this household task inequity is common across Europe (and, indeed, the world). It is important to note that this data is 20 years old and that these figures reflect the situation as perceived by the *female* interviewees. With increased numbers of women working outside the home, the distribution of household tasks may have become more equitable since this data was collected. However, anecdotal evidence suggests women continue to bear considerably more responsibility for all matters relating to the household and the care or management of children.

THE COMMISSION ON THE FAMILY

We conclude this chapter by noting the work of the Commission on the Family. The Commission was established by the government in 1995 to review policy and service provision, and it reported in 1998 (Commission on the Family, 1998). Although almost a decade has passed since its publication, and although Irish society has been through a period of rapid change in this time, the Final Report of the Commission on the Family is still a useful document, as it provides a thorough overview of family services, child care, lone parenting, marriage, family mediation and fathering. It details a range of recommendations to the state for the provision of effective family policy and services (Commission on the Family, 1998). The report also summarised the 536 submissions it received, giving an insight into the issues that concerned members of the public throughout the state. In its report, the Commission on the Family proposes six principles that should underpin the development of family policy:

1. The family unit is a fundamental unit providing stability and well-being in society.
2. The unique and essential family function is that of caring for and nurturing all its members.
3. Continuity and stability are major requirements in family relationships.
4. An equality of well-being is recognised between individual family members.

5. Family membership confers rights, duties and responsibilities.
6. A diversity of family forms and relationships should be recognised.

(Commission on the Family, 1998)

As we can see, there is no attempt to restrict the concept of family to married couples with children, as per the Constitution.

CONCLUSION

The family is a young person's most important source of security, love, belonging and identity. Notwithstanding the process of individuation and independence from the family that occurs throughout the adolescent years, families remain central to the social worlds of most people throughout their entire lives. In common with other European countries, the Irish family has experienced considerable change in recent times, including the increased participation of women in the workplace, a falling birth rate, a fluctuating marriage rate, increased numbers of children being born outside marriage and the increase in divorce. This represents a considerable shift from the 'traditional' conception of a family and social services professionals must recognise the many varying forms of families that now exist and their potential to provide the security, love, belonging and identity mentioned above.

RECOMMENDED READING

Commission on the Family. (1998). *Strengthening families for life: Final report of the Commission on the Family to the Minister for Social, Community and Family Affairs.* Dublin: Stationery Office.

Cousins, M. (2006). *Family research in Ireland: A review of the studies published under the first phase of the Families Research Programme.* Dublin: Family Support Agency.

Hogan, D., Halpenny, A., & Greene, S. (2002). *Children's experiences of parental separation.* Dublin: Children's Research Centre, TCD.

McKeown, K., & Sweeney, J. (2001). *Family well-being and family policy. A review of research on benefits and costs.* Dublin: Government Publications.

4

Peers, Relationships and Sexuality

INTRODUCTION

This chapter examines young people's social worlds and their peer relationships, including types of peer group, friendships and romantic relationships. Peer influence in terms of peer pressure, including bullying, as well as peer acceptance, neglect and rejection are discussed.

Particular attention is paid to 'loneliness' and 'sexuality', two features of young people's relationships that resonate strongly for professionals working with young people.

MOVING BEYOND THE FAMILY

During adolescence, more importance is placed on peer approval, views and advice and more time is spent with peers in contrast to parents and family (Fuligni and Eccles, 1993). This represents a move towards greater independence and autonomy. Adolescent autonomy-seeking reduces emotional dependence on the parents and frees young people to explore other relationships, develop their independence and their identity. The importance of non-parental adults also tends to increase because of the young person's need to differentiate themselves from their parents. However, young people still perceive their parents as the most important people in their lives and family support and attachment to parents remain important for adolescent development (Lee and Bell, 2003).

Coleman (1961), amongst others, spoke of the presence of a distinct 'youth culture' alienating young people from their parents. Such a youth culture, according to Coleman (1961), is characterised by three key factors differentiating it from adult culture:

- Aspirations that focus on pleasure over useful career choices.
- Peer popularity criteria which were not valuable in the eyes of adults (such as being 'cool').
- An opposing value system to parents.

Research on these factors is, however, inconclusive and has failed to support the notion of a distinct monolithic youth culture. Instead, it is now seen as more useful to consider young people as belonging to a multiplicity of youth cultures in various forms which are dynamic, varying over time and social contexts such as school and leisure contexts.

Adolescent Social Worlds

Across the adolescent years, young people become more aware of and involved in their wider social environment, beyond their family and school. They experience a broadening of their life experience and an expansion of involvement in different spheres of social life. For a sizeable number of young people, late adolescence involves a move away from home, to work or to study at third level. Differing perceptions of leaving home are common in young people (loss of security, excitement, fear, emancipation) and their parents (conflict reduction, empty-nest syndrome, loss, relief).

Movement within a wider geographical and social environment leads to a greater diversity in social activity. More social contexts are presented for meeting new people and undertaking new activities, including employment and further study. Some of these social contexts or 'social worlds' (Jackson and Rodreiguez-Tomé, 1993) may be quite separate to each other. For example, the social worlds of a young person's peers and part-time work may be very different and have little in common with each other in terms of values, norms and activities. The family social worlds of young people may have little contact with their peer social worlds or their leisure social worlds and so forth. The breadth, importance and stability of these social worlds varies for each young person.

Conflicting demands and values may arise between these social worlds, contributing to difficulties for the young person. What a young person's parents value may differ from what their peers value. What the peers want or expect may clash with the expectations of the young person's sports club. Disruption in one social world can impact on another. For example, change in family circumstances, such as parental separation, may disrupt a young person's continued involvement in music or sport. On the other hand, such involvement may help them to cope with the parental separation. Involvement in a variety of social worlds enhances a young person's resilience or ability to cope with disruption and difficulties in another social world.

Expanding social worlds also enable young people to build-up their 'social capital'. This refers to the flow of information and the sharing of values and norms that act to restrict or foster the actions of people who interact in the community's social structures (schools, health services) (Coleman, 1988). The young person's social networks (family, friends, neighbours, relatives) are part of his or her social capital. Overall social capital serves a number of functions (Coleman, 1988), including:

- The provision of social support.
- Exposure to a wider array of interaction patterns and breadth of knowledge of 'normal life'.
- Easier social adjustment within and outside of the family.

PEER GROUPS

Across the adolescent years, more time is spent with peers and greater attention is given to peers relative to parents for companionship, support, advice and as models of behaviour (Hendry et al., 1993). Groups give a sense of belonging and a sense of who you are.

Irish research, part of the international Health Behaviour of School-Aged Children (HBSC) study, found that over 60 per cent of Irish 10- to 18-year-olds report positive relationships (in terms of enjoyment, support and acceptance) with their classmates. However, this drops with age, with 15- to 17-year-olds reporting less positive relationships than their younger counterparts. Positive peer relationships are associated with better physical and mental health and a lesser probability of smoking and drunkenness. Consequently, the 40 per cent of the sample who did not report positive relationships are at risk for health problems, an obvious matter of concern (Kelleher, et al., 2003).

In their peer group, young people share interests, values and 'norms'. A group of young people may share a strong interest, for example, in sport, which may then become a focus of their social world. They may attach a greater value to activities associated with health and fitness and this may be reflected in their identity, in how they spend their time, what they wear, how they see themselves and how others see them. This identification with a group of similar peers is positive in terms of providing a sense of belonging, facilitating identity formation and providing social support. Excessive involvement, though, in any such 'social world' may be detrimental, inhibiting development in other social worlds (Kirchler et al., 1993).

A major concern for adolescents is 'fitting in' with their peers. Young people have to deal with the contradictions between their developing individuality, their wanting to 'fit in' with peers and their fear of 'sticking out'. Peer groups set the styles and norms for those who are attracted to identifying with their values and exert pressure towards conformity (Hendry et al., 2002). Once a young person becomes popular with his or her peers, s/he no longer has to try so hard to fit in and can express more individual identities in terms of styles and interests without fear of exclusion (Phoenix, 2005).

Bonds with peers form the basis for future attachments during adulthood, and peer friendship and acceptance serve to enhance resilience. Groups and friendships are also favourable because they enhance a young person's involvement in activities, conflict resolution and relationship management skills. Time spent with 'troubled' peers may sometimes contribute to a young person being exposed to 'deviant' behaviour, leading, perhaps, to delinquency or substance abuse.

Peers also act as a reference group, enabling young people to consider themselves relative to others similar to them in age and, usually, in interests. They provide support in identity formation and a forum for group membership through which the young person strikes a balance between individuality and conformity.

Types of Groups

A young person's groups may act as 'membership groups' (cliques or crowds an adolescent belongs to and identifies with) or reference groups (the groups the young person judges themselves with and uses as a guidepost for values, aspirations and so forth). For many young people, these are both the same; their membership group acts also as their reference group. More specifically, peer groups in adolescence can be classified into different types, according to Bradford-Brown (1990):

- Peer friendships or relationships that involve two individuals.
- Formal peer groups (structured: initiated and controlled by adults).
- Informal peer groups (transitory and casual).
- Cliques (small, relatively intimate, cohesive groups).
- Crowds (large groups of shared interests/reputations/statuses).

All of these have different dynamics or features of functioning and serve different functions (social support, compatible interests, fun, identity) for the young person. Each of these will now be discussed with the exception of peer friendships, which are discussed in detail later in this chapter.

Informal and Formal Groups

Informal peer groups tend to be casual and transitory in nature, often initiated and controlled by young people themselves. They may often be part of the development of cliques or friendships. In contrast, formal groups are more structured and enduring. Examples of these include youth clubs or groups and scouts and guides which play a significant role in young people's lives, particularly in early adolescence (Connor, 2003; de Róiste and Dinneen, 2005).

Participation in such formal clubs and groups enhances an individual's 'social capital', socio-emotional development, social skills and relationships. This is discussed further in Chapter 8.

Cliques

Cliques have been subdivided into activity cliques (developed from shared activity involvement) or friendship cliques (developed from the spontaneous, free choice of young people). As Thurlow (2002, p. 246) recognised, 'peer groups and cliques are almost always held together by shared interests, tastes, activities and/or hobbies'. While clique norms develop within the group, crowd norms are imposed from others, reflecting the stereotypic image (nerds, geeks, arty) that peers have of crowd members (Brown et al., 1990). Critical to the cohesion of the clique is its exclusionary nature. Young people know that who they associate with affects their own status in the clique. Who they do not associate with is thus as important as who they associate with. As noted by Erikson (1959, p. 92), young people 'may be remarkably clannish, intolerant, and cruel in their exclusion of others who are different ... in petty aspects of dress and gesture arbitrarily selected as the signs of an in-grouper or out-grouper'. This is particularly salient in early to mid-adolescence, but by late adolescence young people are less rigid in their exclusions and more tolerant of individual differences.

Female cliques tend to be more 'tight-knit', more intimate, enduring and closed to outsiders than male cliques. Socio-economic status and possibly consumption behaviour are very significant in determining clique and crowd membership and in particular female cliques. Male cliques, on the other hand, tend to be more democratic and flexible (Janeway-Conger and Galambos, 1997). 'Being a member of a clique in adolescence', according to Weissbourd (1995, p. 84), 'is a significant predictor of adolescent emotional well-being and ability to handle stress'. Belonging to a clique is particularly important in early adolescence but then diminishes with greater individual autonomy. Roles within a clique vary from being a leader or being on the periphery (a 'hanger-on' or 'wannabe').

Crowds

Crowds are 'categories of individuals based on personality dispositions as well as on typical activity patterns' and can form quite spontaneously (Bradford-Brown, 1990, p. 180). Crowds may be comprised of several cliques and are characteristic of middle adolescence (14–16 years), arising out of a need for heterosexual contact (Dunphy, 1963). Crowds are identifiable by their reputations and membership of crowds happens through stereotyping by others. Being a member of a crowd is indicative of 'who you are' in the eyes of your peers. Social activities and contexts and delinquent behaviour (drinking, smoking, fighting) mark crowds out from each other as well as subtle yet distinctive markers (hairstyle, dress, accent, behaviour), all of which create an 'us' and 'them'.

As noted by Hendry and colleagues (2002, p. 372):

> When young people gather in various social settings, they see other crowds as somehow "different" in style of dress and behaviour, and at times threatening to give rise to 'trouble'. These variations appear to be associated with factors such as hedonism (smoking and drinking), 'trouble' (wanting to appear 'hard'), transformation (leisure as fun) or boredom ... this creates a growing ground for conflict, as the different crowds are unable to avoid each other in the limited public 'spaces' available.

Other crowd labels include 'lonely' and 'withdrawn', which may be more manifested in the eyes of others rather than forming coherent groups per se.

Research in America (Brown et al., 1990) has highlighted that adolescent crowds are often based on ethnic distinctions (rappers (African-Americans), Asians, Hispanics, etc.) with the remainder being reputation based (nerds, populars, jocks or athletes and so forth). A standard set of crowds has been proposed by Bradford Brown (1990) as constant in peer cultures, including: jocks (sporty crowd), populars, brains, delinquents or alienated youth and nerds. Such crowd labels may, however, be just stereotypical categories. Many young people are aware of their membership of a crowd but want to belong to another crowd (their reference group). Others float among crowds varying their membership and identity and often belonging to more than one crowd at any point in time. Across adolescence, a steady decline occurs in the importance attached to belonging to a crowd with a simultaneous rise in concern about how crowd membership may stifle self-expression and individuality. This is understandable given the growth in individual autonomy across the adolescent years.

STAGES OF PEER-GROUP DEVELOPMENT

A number of stages of group development in the adolescent years are visible (Dunphy, 1990):

- Same-sex isolated cliques (stage 1).
- Same-sex cliques engage in heterosexual interaction (stage 2).
- Formation of heterosexual clique with retention of same-sex clique (stage 3).
- Same-sex cliques reorganise into heterosexual cliques (stage 4).
- Disintegration of crowd, couples form (stage 5).

In early adolescence, same-sex cliques predominate. With opposite-sex peer interaction, larger crowds come to be formed. Conformity and concerns about peer acceptance are especially strong at this time, along with a preoccupation about how their peers see them. In order to gain acceptance and to conform, young people may engage in activities in which they would not normally engage, such as various risky behaviours, including alcohol consumption. Initial tentative heterosexual relationships or 'dyads' then develop within the crowd and this is followed by the stage of fully heterosexual cliques with more intimate heterosexual dyads. Same-sex cliques continue to be maintained throughout this. Following this, mixed-sex cliques emerge through which young people begin to form heterosexual relationships. Whether the same applies to the formation of homosexual relationships is not known. Across these stages, conformity lessens and a greater tolerance of individual differences evolves in the young person, reflecting enhanced social cognition.

PEER PRESSURE

Peer pressure is a particular focus of concern for professionals working with young people. Peer pressure can exert a powerful effect on a young person's behaviour, health and quality of life. Types of peer pressure including bullying as well as the processes of peer acceptance, neglect and rejection will now be discussed.

To belong to a crowd, young people tend to conform to peer norms and values. The pressure to conform may be explicit or implicit, awareness of it varying across individuals. Peer pressure can be defined as pressure from peers to 'do something or to keep from doing something else, no matter if you personally want to or not' (Clasen and Brown, 1985, p. 458). Peer pressure communicates group norms, maintains loyalties amongst group members and appears strongest in mid-adolescence (15–16 years). What these norms are vary across groups and over time. Peer pressure may create a conflict between what the young person believes and what many of his or her friends are doing. Worries about social acceptance are thus an understandable feature of this time. Three categories of peer pressure have been identified by Brown and colleagues (1986):

- **Peer social activities**: Spending time with friends, going to parties, gigs and events, pursuing opposite-sex relationships.
- **Misconduct:** Drug and alcohol use, sexual intercourse, petty thefts, vandalism, minor delinquent activities.
- **Conformity to peer norms**: Dress, grooming and appearance, musical preferences, involvement in school, academic matters, extra-curricular activities.

Others have described peer pressure in terms of the types of power that peers hold (French and Raven, 1959). These include:

- **Coercive power**: Ability to punish for non-compliance with a suggestion or command. This power may be overt but more often is subtle through ridicule and strong teasing (slagging).
- **Reward power**: Ability to confer rewards such as praise, status or enhanced esteem.
- **Referent power**: This is where a young person admires another and wants to be like them. No pressure may be exerted and no interaction may even take place, yet the referent still influences in terms of, for example, style and conduct.

Peer pressure may also be described as 'normative' – pressure to conform to the positive expectations of others – or 'informational' – the pressure to accept information from others as real (Deutsch and Gerard, 1955). Berndt (2002), on the other hand, used the concept of 'interactional' influence, proposing that young people are influenced most by friends who provide support and avoid conflict. Modelling and reinforcement also play a role, but it is important to note that *type* of influence varies depending on the group, the behaviour and the social context. In general, young people are less easily influenced to engage in anti-social (than social) behaviour and perceive more pressure towards self-enhancing activities (peer socialisation, school or leisure achievement) (Clasen and Brown, 1987).

Overall, in understanding peer pressure, recognition needs to be given to the fact that it is only *one* influence in any given context. Family features, individual differences, group dynamics and what the pressure itself is directed towards all contribute to the degree of pressure perceived and the influence it exerts. The less a young person identifies with a group, the less s/he will be influenced or pressurised by them (Emler and Reicher, 1995). The influence of a friend is stronger than that of a same-aged peer. Friends are more likely to be influential if the friendship is stable, reciprocal and exclusive. Closeness in friendship determines how influential the friend is. Best friends are particularly influential in the maintenance of drug use, smoking and drinking. Irish research has shown that when a young person's best friend is engaged in such behaviours, the young person him or herself is more likely to continue doing it too (Morgan and Grube, 1991).

However, young people often act out of their own inclinations, independently of friends, family or others. Some theorists argue that peer pressure is more myth than reality and used to explain young people's risky behaviour rather than explaining this as a consciously chosen action on the part of young people to attain more social power (Ungar, 2000).

Peer Acceptance, Neglect and Rejection

'Those of us who knew the pain
Of valentines that never came
And those whose names were never called
When choosing sides for basketball'

(Janis Ian, 'At Seventeen')

Peer pressure can also be seen by the peer group accepting, neglecting or rejecting a young person. Some adolescents are very popular and liked by many of their peers. Others are hardly noticed and some are not accepted and are ostracised or picked on by their peers.

A high value is placed on being popular during adolescence. Popular, accepted adolescents are typically lively, cheerful, physically attractive, interesting and good-natured. They generally have a good sense of humour, are not very anxious and usually have a reasonable level of self-esteem. They are seen as liking others and as being tolerant, flexible and sympathetic. They show good social skills, are able to make others feel involved and know peer group norms and values. Physical attractiveness, socio-economic status, intelligence and sport (especially for males) or leisure are other factors that influence peer acceptance and popularity. By contrast, young people who are neglected (neither liked nor disliked) tend to be low in self-esteem, nervous and ill at ease. They may often avoid or withdraw from social interactions and are more likely to experience feelings of loneliness (ibid), discussed later in this chapter.

Young people who are rejected (actively disliked) are more likely to be inconsiderate, aggressive, self-centred and attention-seekers. They often display poor social skills, being tactless, disruptive and unwilling to participate in the give and take of social interaction. It is strongly associated with loneliness and adjustment difficulties in later years (Janeway-Conger and Galambos, 1997). Rejected young people are also described as either aggressive-rejected (aggressive and disruptive) or submissive-rejected (unassertive, social withdrawal). Both are prone to teasing and bullying, with the former tending to overreact to it and the latter responding by withdrawing even more (Heaven, 2001). Rejected young people appear to be disliked wherever they are, whereas neglected young people often make a new start by changing their social context (school, community).

With respect to both rejected and neglected young people, a 'vicious cycle' may arise. Neglected adolescents may give up making friends or make little effort, thinking 'what's the point'. A rejected adolescent may react more extremely to episodes of rejection, to give the impression 'they don't care', leading others to dislike them even more.

BULLYING

Bullying has been defined as (Olweus, 1993):

- An imbalance of strength (physical and/or psychological).
- A deliberate intention to hurt another with little if any provocation.
- Repeated negative actions against another person.

It can take a variety of different forms, including name-calling, being picked on, teased, being hit and pushed around, being made fun of or being ostracised. It has insidious effects by contributing to a tense and unpleasant climate for young people as well as direct effects on adjustment and mental health. Understandably, peer bullying is a key determinant of adolescent quality of life and is known to be a factor in loneliness, depression, self-harm, poor perceptions of self-worth and suicide (Wilkins-Shurmer et al., 2003).

According to the Irish Society for the Prevention of Cruelty to Children (ISPCC, 2006, www.ispcc.ie), bullying is an ongoing concern for young people and has always been one of the main reasons behind calls made to Childline. In 2005, 4.7 per cent of calls answered by Childline were concerns about bullying and the ISPCC amongst others has highlighted new forms of bullying involving the use of mobile phones, e-bullying and the internet, where the bully may be unknown to the victim (ibid).

The Health Behaviour of School-Aged Children (HBSC) study with approximately 1,500 young people from each of the 35 participating countries found that over one-third (34 per cent) report being bullied at least once in the previous couple of months and that the rate of bullying reported decreases across the adolescent years (Currie et al., 2003). Figures for bullying experienced (in the past few months) for Irish 11-, 13- and 15-year-olds and the HBSC averages in Table 4.1 illustrate this.

Table 4.1 Early teens' experiences of bullying

	11-year-olds	13-year-olds	15-year-olds
Irish females	30.5%	22.7%	18.2%
Irish males	29.8%	32.1%	23.1%
HBSC female average	35.2%	33.8%	25.3%
HBSC male average	39.9%	37.7%	28.5%

This finding of approximately one-third of a sample reporting bullying is in agreement with other Irish research (Mills et al., 2004).

From the HBSC data it is clear that teenage males tend to report more bullying than their female counterparts. They also report more physical fighting, with well over one-third (39 per cent) of young males in the HBSC study reporting involvement in at least one physical fight in the previous year. Like bullying, this also declines with age.

In early adolescence (by age 13), bullying rates increase from late childhood, possibly because of factors such as school transitions and puberty, especially for boys, where hormonal changes have been linked, albeit contentiously, to a rise in aggressiveness. Of particular concern is the 11 to 14 per cent of young people who experience frequent bullying and fighting. They are more likely to experience the greatest negative effects and are most in need of intervention.

Research with Irish school-going adolescents has indicated that bullying tends to peak at 14 years of age and that 15 per cent were bullied in their current school term (James et al., 2003; O'Moore et al., 1997). One in 50 young people are bullied on a weekly basis, and the incidence peaks in the second year of secondary school (approximate age 14 years). Verbal bullying (name-calling, rumour spreading) was the most common form reported (55 per cent), followed by physical (25 per cent) and psychological bullying (14 per cent), including exclusion (O'Moore, Kirkham and Smith, 1997).

International research shows that bullying diminishes and becomes less physical and more indirect or relational (spreading rumours, ostracism) with age (Smith et al., 1999). This drop arises despite the fact that older adolescents have a broader, more inclusive definition of bullying, recognising a broader variety of forms of bullying. It is probably due to more effective responses to bullying by young people, as how a victim deals with an incident is critical to his/her future risk of being bullied (Kochenderfer and Ladd, 1997).

Looking at bullying from the victim's perspective, regardless of its frequency, feelings of anger, frustration, anxiety, depression and suicidal ideation are common (Mills et al., 2004). Victims of bullying also tend to have low self-esteem, to be anxious and are often socially isolated. Those who are excluded or who have had rumours spread about them report significant anxiety and sadness (James et al., 2003).

Many young people are also reluctant to tell others about being bullied and this reluctance increases with age. Of 1,660 victims of bullying in one study of 7,400 Irish post-primary school-age young people, 84 per cent stated that they had not told their teachers and 66 per cent did not tell anyone at home (O'Moore and Minton, 2003).

Bullies, on the other hand, tend to be more extroverted and 'tough-minded', less socially competent and lower in esteem than other children, although sometimes their self-esteem is high. Many claim they don't know why they bully their peers and often they have also been victims of bullying themselves (bully/victims). While popular, their popularity within a crowd is often only superficial due to the pressure they exert as opposed to being liked or admired (Merten, 1996). Research varies as to whether or not bullies themselves report more negative feelings, depression and other peer difficulties than their peers.

Clearly, bullying is a significant concern for young people, especially in the early adolescent years. It affects young people's quality of life and health and well-being. Programmes such as the Relationships and Sexual Education programme and more specific anti-bullying initiatives along with support services such as those offered by the ISPCC are currently in place to reduce bullying and support victims. However, as noted by the Children's Rights Alliance (2006), there is no strategy to combat bullying outside school, yet nearly one-fifth of young people in Co. Kildare report being affected by bullying 'a little bit' outside of their schools or CTC or Youthreach centres (Lalor and Baird, 2006).

FRIENDSHIPS

'A best friend to me is someone you can have fun with and you can also be serious about personal things, about girls, what you're going to do with your life or whatever ... A best friend is someone who is not going to make fun of you just because you do something stupid or put you down if you make a mistake. If you're afraid of something or someone they'll give you confidence' (13-year-old boy cited in Bell, 1988, p. 64).

Friendships are intimate, loyal, honest and open relationships. They are intrinsically satisfying as they offer companionship, emotional support, a sense of belonging, enjoyment and stimulation. They revolve around shared interests, beliefs, values and leisure activities. Friendship is determined by the strength of mutual liking, the amount of time spent together and its duration. Friendships play a key role in a young person's development by providing a 'safe' environment for reciprocal personal exploration and identity development. They provide information, offer feedback, act as an ally and confidant and facilitate social skills such as conflict management and negotiation. They afford young people opportunities to discuss ambitions, doubts, worries, hopes, fears and daily experiences with similar same-aged peers without the fear of scorn, mockery, mistrust or rejection.

Findings from the Health Behaviour of School Children study reveal that the vast bulk (over 88.9 per cent) of Irish young people has three or more friends, placing them in the top two (in terms of number of friendships) of all the participating European countries. Over one-third (35 per cent) of Irish female 15-year-olds and 43 per cent of Irish male 15-year-olds spend time with their friends after school four or more days per week (Currie et al., 2003). This is about the European average and may be lower than other countries, possibly because of living further away, more time spent on homework or due to different after-school arrangements. Interestingly, electronic communication by e-mailing or telephone tends to increase with age and probably enhances networking within friendship groups (ibid).

Good friendships at school lead to a more enjoyable experience of school life and of other social worlds where friends are present. On the other hand, not having good friends in a leisure activity, for example, is known to be a reason for not joining that activity or a reason for dropping out of it (de Róiste and Dinneen, 2005).

Close friends differ to other friends in terms of intimacy, loyalty, reciprocity (shared disclosure) and stability. Close friendships are a key source of social support, helping the adolescent to deal with feelings and problems, interpret romantic experiences and act as a sounding-board for changing beliefs and ideas. They bolster confidence and self-esteem, as friends value each other despite knowing each other's foibles, insecurities and problems. Satisfying and supportive friendships are positively associated with self-esteem, emotional adjustment, social skills and peer popularity (Hartup and Stevens, 1999). Typically the number of close friends is highest in early adolescence at about four to six and declines thereafter. Quality of close friendships (stability, reciprocity, trust, loyalty and support) is more important then number of close friends. While there is a move towards more heterosexual partnerships in the latter years of adolescence, close friends remain more likely to be of the same sex across adolescence (Hendry et al., 1993). For most of adolescence, same-sex friendships are seen as more supportive than opposite-sex ones, although by late adolescence the latter are nearly the same (Lempers and Clark-Lempers, 1993).

Falling out with friends can be a significant source of distress for young people. A shared history and intimacy is lost and many feel awkward and unsure how to behave now with the person who they were friendly with. Feelings of betrayal, loss, hurt and anger may be felt and these feelings may be intensified if the 'falling out' is under the eyes of the peer group. Untrustworthy behaviour is the main cause of serious conflict between close friends, reflecting the critical role of trust. This is understandable in that sharing personal, private information and feelings is compromised if an adolescent feels s/he cannot trust his or her friend with what they disclose (Youniss and Smollar, 1985).

Friendship Formation

Friendships are usually forged between young people from a similar socio-economic background and locality and with similar intelligence, interests, adjustment, attitudes and behaviours. Young people of both sexes value the same qualities in a friend: loyalty, frankness and trustworthiness (Claes, 1992). In contrast to friendships in general, close friendships develop by choice and mutual preferences for certain characteristics and shared interests or activities.

Much research on adolescent friendships has focused on behavioural similarity (homophily) between friends (Kiesner et al., 2004). Friends tend to be similar on sports, music and hobbies. Interestingly, adolescent friends tend to become more similar on a growing number of traits if the friendship is reciprocated and enduring. Research has even highlighted how having anti-social friends is associated with anti-social behaviour (Kiesner et al., 2004). However, a friendship between opposites occurs when a young person finds in this friend something they feel is desirable but is lacking in the self. Similarity between friends may have more to do with the way adolescent social worlds (school, leisure) are structured, providing more opportunities for interaction with others who are alike in certain respects (academic ability, leisure interests, home location). Overall, similarities between friends can be seen to be due to a number of processes and conditions (Jaffe, 1998):

- **Socio-demographic conditions:** Young people from a similar background come into proximity with each other more.
- **Differential selection:** Young people seek out as friends others that are similar to them.
- **Contagion:** Friends do things together that they would not do on their own.
- **Mutual socialisation:** Similarity arises between friends because of interaction between them.
- **Selective elimination:** Non-conforming peers leave the friendship group voluntarily or are pressured out.

A key influence on a young person's friendships in adolescence is their attachment to their parents. Young people with insecure attachments tend to be more hostile and anxious and less close in their peer relationships than those with secure attachments (Zimmerman, 2004). This highlights the role of a young person's relationship history, in particular the impact of their relationship with their significant others, upon their current relationships. Bowlby's concept of the 'internal working model', outlined in his attachment theory, has been used to help explain how people carry forward their relationship experiences onto new relationships.

From a contrasting viewpoint, some theorists contend that the role of adolescent friendships has been overstated, that friendships are 'managed' in a pragmatic way as opposed to being extremely precious relationships (Brooks, 2002). From this perspective, friendships are not as salient for identity formation and individuation as others would suggest. This remains a topic for debate within sociological circles.

Gender and Age Differences

Gender differences are also evident in friendships with young females reporting more numerous, deeper and interdependent friendships than young males. This is in agreement with other research that shows females are more emotionally invested in relationships than males. Male friendships, on the other hand, are characterised by shared interests and leisure activities (Youniss and Smollar, 1985).

Patterns of friendships change across the teenage years. Across adolescence, friendships become less superficial, developing in mutual understanding, emotional investment and a sense of shared identity. Trust, loyalty, reciprocity and mutual respect increase and by late adolescence friendships are characterised by greater space and support for individuality and independence. While friendships vary in degree of self-disclosure, intimacy and self-disclosure become defining features of close friendships.

Table 4.2 Friendship features across adolescence

Early Adolescence	Late Adolescence
Mostly same-sex cliques	Mostly heterosexual cliques
Same-sex dyads	Same-sex and heterosexual dyads
Peer acceptance concerns and conformity high	Conformity low; greater tolerance for individual differences
High number of close friends	Lower number of close friends
Friendships often superficial	Friendships more intimate, trusting and supportive

Loneliness

When a young person is dissatisfied with his or her friendships and relationships, when these don't meet the needs of that young person, he or she may feel lonely. The adolescent years are a particularly acute time for loneliness because of all the transitions being experienced. Developments in the peer group (outlined earlier), greater psychological separation from the parents, increased peer orientation, greater self-reflection as well as any changes in school or other social worlds contribute to this. In adolescence, 'self-definition is achieved, paradoxically by group membership'. If social integration is hampered, however, the distress of being 'left out' or not feeling 'a sense of peer belonging' may be acute, leading to loneliness (Tanner, 1973, p. 147).

Hartog (1981, p. 19) described adolescence as 'the loneliest developmental period' when questions relating to core issues of development, such as identity, are addressed. 'Aloneness', solitude and the capacity to be alone are also part of healthy development, representing individuation and emotional development (Buchholz, 1997).

Loneliness has been defined by Rook (1984, p. 1391) as 'an enduring condition of emotional distress that arises when a person feels estranged from, misunderstood, or rejected by others and/or lacks appropriate social partners for desired activities, particularly activities that provide a sense of social integration and opportunities for emotional intimacy'. In studying loneliness, many researchers examine loneliness within particular relationships (loneliness in parental relationships, loneliness in peer relationships) as opposed to just examining loneliness in a more general sense (Goosens and Marcoen, 1999). Simply measuring the number of social relationships a young person has is inadequate as a measure of loneliness, as loneliness intrinsically depends on how the young person appraises these. This appraisal is in turn influenced by a wide variety of factors, such as mood, sex, age, cultural norms, social comparison and so on.

Several factors aggravate adolescent loneliness, including the greater likelihood of being misunderstood at this time, individualistic cultures (which emphasise independence and individualism) and the experience of being discounted in conversations. Interestingly, psychotherapists see many of the symptoms of loneliness as originating from a re-experiencing of the anxiety produced by the fear of abandonment in childhood (Tanner, 1973).

Loneliness is more of a concern for younger adolescents. This may be because in early adolescence there is an increased orientation towards, and dependency on, peers and concerns about peer acceptance peak at this time (Kloep, 1999). Cultural features of this time, such as social expectations and the transition from primary to second-level education, may also contribute to greater loneliness in younger adolescents.

A study with 665 Irish children and young people aged 10 to 13 years found that slightly over a third of the sample reported some feelings of loneliness and social dissatisfaction. Approximately 13 per cent of the sample reported 'sometimes' or 'often' feeling lonely at school. Over a third indicated that they only 'sometimes' found it easy to make new friends or to be good at working with other children in school. In addition, if those who responded 'sometimes' are included, over a quarter responded that 'children in school did not like them', they 'found it hard to get other children to like them' and 'felt left out of things at school' (de Róiste, 2000).

Past research has reported that loneliness in adolescent-parent relationships tends to *increase* with age, probably due to a renegotiation of family roles and an emotional distancing from parents. However, loneliness in adolescent-peer relationships tends to *decrease* with age as a consequence of increased intimacy in peer relationships (Brage, Meredith and Woodward, 1993). Research, though, with over 1,000 Irish adolescents found that both parent- and peer-related loneliness peak in early adolescence and then decrease (de Róiste, 2000). This is probably because in early adolescence a trade-off occurs between parental closeness and increased peer orientation, particularly where parental power and restrictiveness are perceived as high (Fuligni and Eccles, 1993). Additionally, across adolescence young people feel more positive about being 'alone' and thus are less likely to feel lonely (Goosens and Marcoen, 1999). This is consistent with the belief that a person's capacity to engage in periods of solitude is a sign of emotional maturity.

Romantic Relationships

I learned the truth at seventeen
That love was meant for beauty queens.

(Janis Ian, 'At Seventeen')

Janice Ian's lyrics evoke the angst that many young people experience about their physical appearance and attractiveness to the opposite sex. Romantic relationships emerge during early to mid-adolescence, offering opportunities for developing interpersonal skills (empathy, pro-social behaviour), intimacy and identity. These relationships are a means of socialisation, entertainment, status enhancement and courtship. Young adolescents tend to get involved in romantic relationships for recreation, intimacy and status, placing greater importance on superficial features (appearance and image) and the approval of others than older adolescents. Older adolescents place more emphasis on intimacy, companionship and socialisation. They are more concerned with the future orientation of partners (what they plan to do with their life) (Zani, 1993).

Are teenage dreams so hard to beat?
Every time she walks down the street.
Another girl in the neighbourhood.
I wish she was mine, she looks so good.
I wanna hold her, wanna hold her tight.
Get teenage kicks right through the night

(The Undertones, 'Teenage Kicks')

Overall, romantic relationships serve a number of functions for young people:

- Companionship and social support.
- Recreation and fun.
- Socialisation: Learning relationship skills.
- Status enhancement: Means of improving social status by seeing someone considered as highly desirable.
- Self-esteem: The attention and liking of admirers, enhanced status and feeling good about oneself because of the interest of an opposite-sex peer.
- Sexual experimentation.
- Identity formation and individuation: As noted by Erikson (1968, p. 132), 'To a considerable extent adolescent love is an attempt to arrive at a definition of one's identity by projecting one's diffused self-image on another and seeing it thus reflected and gradually clarified.'

- Intimacy: Erikson (1968, p. 263) defined intimacy as 'the capacity to commit to concrete affiliations and partnerships and to develop the ethical strength to abide by such commitments even though they may call for significant sacrifices and compromises'. Typically it refers to emotional closeness, honesty, empathy, mutual disclosure and trust. Intimacy is argued to play an important role in adolescent identity formation and emotional growth through the opportunities it affords for self-exploration and self-reflection and the experience of relating closely to another person.

In early adolescence, a member of the peer group often helps 'set up' their friend with another person, which prevents any potential embarrassment in the event of rejection. Research with Irish early school-leavers found that early ventures into romantic relationships tend to be short-lived, with only a very small number reporting a past relationship lasting over one year (Mayock and Byrne, 2004). 'Going out' with someone is clearly differentiated from just 'meeting' (or in rural settings, 'going off with') someone. Meetings are usually just casually getting to know someone, often in a group context, and are transitory in nature. They allow for opportunities for sexual experimentation without any future commitments, which is mutually understood. Sometimes they may develop into romantic relationships. By mid to late adolescence, young people rely less on peers to arrange their romantic liaisons with young men by age 15–16, generally wanting to take the responsibility for initiating romantic relationships (ibid).

Anxiety and the fear of rejection and humiliation are clearly associated with asking someone out and alcohol and drugs are often used to reduce inhibitions. Only a very small number of Irish young men are asked out by young women. However, young women are not passive in initiating romantic relationships, as they use many signs and gestures to signal interest to young men (ibid).

Pressure to have a boy or girlfriend is rarely direct. Instead it is more commonly exerted in terms of personal feelings of alienation or exclusion from the social life of romantically involved peers. In fact, during early to mid-adolescence, having a boy or girlfriend and its associated conferred status seems more important than the romantic relationship itself. It also seems to be stronger in females than males (Mayock and Byrne, 2004).

Gender Differences

Gender differences are evident in young people's romantic relationships. In considering potential partners, young men are more interested in physical appearance and the sexual activity of such partners, whereas young women place greater importance on personality and behavioural traits (Zani, 1993). In the early stages of a relationship, young men are more oriented toward sexual-impulse gratification, are more permissive and expect physical intimacy sooner than young women. Young women, on the other hand, relate sexual intimacy to love, emotional intimacy and commitment. At later stages, though, this gender difference diminishes (Roche, 1986).

Teenage girls also appear to be more concerned with forming intimate relationships of an exclusive nature, whereas teenage boys try more to reconcile the formation of a steady couple and belonging to a group (Zani, 1993). Same-sex friendships may, however, suffer with the onset of romantic relationships as priority (in terms of time and intimacy) is given to the latter. Adolescent females may romanticise their boyfriend's position by perceiving unprotected sexual intercourse as an affirmation of love and commitment to the relationship. In relation to this, research in Northern Ireland found that 'being in love' was the main reason cited for having sex by nearly a third of young females compared to only 14 per cent of young males (Schubotz et al., 2003).

Along with such gender differences, a number of other difficulties are faced by young people in their romantic relationships:

- Prematurely exclusive relationships may lead to a premature identity formation, undermining the realisation of a young person's full potential with a variety of people.
- Emotional involvement may occur without sufficient emotional maturity in young people.
- The break-up of romantic relationships may be associated with a loss of self-esteem (particularly when the break-up involves rejection, loss of face or loss to a rival), depression and grief (Mathas et al., 1985).

SEX AND SEXUALITY

Sexuality is a broad, holistic concept encompassing biology (the anatomy, physiology and biochemistry of the sexual response system), sexual orientation (heterosexual, homosexual, bisexual) and identity. Central to understanding sexuality is how a person thinks and feels, their personality. How they relate to others, how they receive and express intimacy and how comfortable they are with different expressions of sexuality all affect it. A person's social context, social 'norms', how they were reared, the values and beliefs they hold as well as their sexual experience are other critical factors to understanding any person's sexuality.

Psychologically, sexual behaviour in adolescence serves a variety of functions, including the enhancement of physical and emotional pleasure; as a means of coping with negative experience; to attain intimacy with another person; and to gain esteem and to avoid the censure of others (Cooper et al., 1998).

Erotic fantasies are common in the adolescent years, serving as a means of sexual arousal and as a substitute for sexual needs. They are associated with masturbation, which acts as a sexual outlet. Masturbation can be particularly problematic when associated with feelings of guilt and anxiety. Young men in contrast to young women report a greater frequency of masturbation, though this may be because of a greater willingness of males to report it (Katchadourian, 1990).

Figure 4.1 Components of sexuality

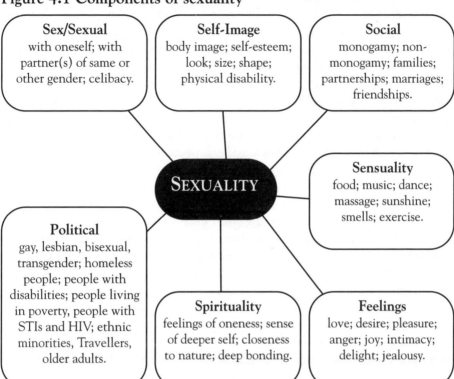

Sociologically, attitudes towards sex can be grouped into four categories encompassing the dualisms between 'good vs. evil' and 'spirit vs. matter' (Malesevic, 2003):

- Sex as 'demonic', where sex is seen as holding a 'demonic' power of destruction (destruction of self and others). This relates to some religious perspectives that associate sex (outside marriage) with sin and evil.
- Sex as divine, where sex is seen as profound, mystical and celestial. This links in with liberal perspectives of sex as a pleasurable and joyful experience.
- Sex as casual, where sex is viewed as a commodity like any other, without any profound, symbolic meaning. This has been linked to the dualistic perception of sex as public or private with sex being more casual the more it is in the public arena.
- Sex as nuisance, where sexual intercourse is itself of value but everything that goes with it, the foreplay, the after-play, the hassles and gratitude, become a burden, 'a nuisance'.

Using this theoretical framework, Malesevic's (2003) survey with over 300 Galway students found a generally liberal view of sexuality in young people, although attitudes were also influenced by religious traditionalism and by peers. Overall the majority did not link sex to the creation of life and over three-quarters disagreed that young people should not engage in sex. Over 80 per cent felt contraception was the responsibility of both partners. Almost one-third (31.9 per cent) thought that abstinence and marital fidelity were the only true protection against HIV/AIDS. In addition, more than one in five felt guilty about masturbation. These ambivalent attitudes suggest Irish young people's thoughts on sexuality are not clear cut and straightforward. Rather they are complex, liberal in some ways, yet traditional in other respects and open to socio-cultural influences. This is corroborated by research in Northern Ireland, which found 'conflicting perceptions – negative as well as positive attitudes to sexuality' were common in young people (Schubotz et al., 2003, pp. 22–3).

Much attention has been paid to the influence of social and cultural context on the sexuality of young people. In the past in many countries, young women were often considered ready for sexual activity not long after the menarche and then married off. Young men, on the other hand, were seen to need sexual experience once pubescent (Dehne and Riedner, 2001). The onset of sexual maturity makes adolescent sexuality a particular concern in many countries, including Ireland. Parental fears about exploitation, peer pressure, unwanted pregnancy and sexually transmitted infections (STIs) are common in this time period. Open, frequent and comforting communication between parents and their adolescent children has continually been shown to be of critical importance, contributing to delayed sexual onset and, when sexually active, to improved use of contraceptives and fewer sexual partners (Crosby et al., 2002).

Gender socialisation around sexuality is also evident through parents sending different signals about sex to their sons (more messages about being sexual predators and about protecting themselves against unwanted side effects) as compared to their daughters (messages about abstinence and chastity) (McShane, 2004).

More recent sociological research has focused on media representations of sexuality. Generally these reflect a liberal ideology but a tendency by the media to sensationalise adolescent sexuality is also evident. Adolescent sexuality is often portrayed as problematic and as a 'spectacle', thereby contributing to the construction and maintenance of the 'problem' of young people's sexuality (Devlin, 2003).

It is worth noting that many see the fields of sociology and psychology as adopting a moral, judgmental perspective, focusing on considering adolescent sexual activity as a deviant or risk behaviour, with little attention paid to the normality of it (Dehne and Riedner, 2001).

The age of consent in Ireland is 17 years of age for male/female, male/male and female/female sexual intercourse. The law as to the criminal penalties that can be imposed where consensual sexual intercourse occurs with a child under the age of 17 have recently been changed. Sexual intercourse without consent, regardless of age, is rape.

Up until 2006 it was an offence for any person to have unlawful carnal knowledge (sexual intercourse outside of marriage) of a girl under 17 years of age, with penalties varying dependent on whether the girl was aged under or over 15 years. This provision in the Criminal Law Act 1935 excluded any defence of reasonable mistake, and on 23 May 2006 the Supreme Court found this aspect of the 1935 Act to be unconstitutional. The Criminal Law (Sexual Offences) Act 2006 was introduced to remedy this lacuna by introducing a defence of honest mistake, as well as the following changes:

- Defilement of a child under 15 years being extended for the protection of both genders (previously only men could be prosecuted for unlawful carnal knowledge, though women could be charged with sexual assault).
- The consent of the DPP being required for proceedings against a child under 17 years.
- Underage 'consent' being deemed inadmissible as a defence for carnal knowledge of children under the age of 15. (The introduction of this provision as a 'change' in the law suggests consent was a defence under the old law. However, this is not so, as under the 1935 Act children under the age of 15 were deemed incapable of giving consent.)
- No proceedings to be taken where a defendant is aged not more than two years older than the child under the age of 17 with whom s/he has engaged or attempted to engage in a sexual act.

However, debate remains over the interpretation of sections of the Act, particularly regarding the criminal liability of underage boys and girls. In particular, argument has arisen over whether the provisions of the Act are perpetuating the gender discrimination evident under the old law. This discrimination remains a feature of the new law as, although adult men and women are now treated in the same way, Section 5 provides that underage girls cannot be prosecuted. On this point, the **Advice of the Ombudsman for Children**, dated 1 June 2006, is informative. The announcement by the Minister for Children on 21 June 2006 that the government would consult with teenagers as to what they think the age of consent should be is yet to produce any tangible result.

It is important to note that use of the age of legal consent appears *not* to be used as a benchmark by young people (Mayock and Byrne, 2004).

When Do Young People Have Sexual Intercourse for the First Time?

Sexual activity in all its general forms is very common for Irish young people across the adolescent years. As noted by Hyde and Howlett (2004, p. 10), 'non-penetrative sexual activities such as masturbation and oral sex appear to be very commonly practiced'. However, the prevalence of different forms of sexual activity in Irish teenagers is not accurately known. Research into this topic is hindered by the sensitive nature of the topic as well as by concerns about such research influencing young people and by the difficulty of obtaining valid results.

One question that has received a lot of attention is age at first sexual intercourse. First sexual intercourse is very significant as a 'rite of passage' for young people. Up until 2006 it was an offence for any person to have unlawful carnal knowledge (sexual intercourse outside of marriage) of a girl under 17 years of age, with penalties varying dependent upon whether the girl was aged under or over 15 years. This was high relative to other countries, with 14 being the age in some countries, but complexities in law make it difficult to compare the law between different countries.

Age at first sexual intercourse has become younger over recent decades. Quite a number of Irish young people have had sexual intercourse by the age of 16. From 15 to 17 years of age, over a third of Irish young men and over a quarter of Irish young women are sexually active (Dunne and Seery, 1997; MacHale and Newell, 1997). An AIDS Alliance study in Cork reported that just under a third (30 per cent) of females and nearly half (45 per cent) of males aged 15 to 17 are sexually active (Dunne and Seery, 1997).

More recently, Mayock and Byrne (2004) reported that the mean age of first sexual intercourse was 13.5 years, usually with a partner their same age or, for young women, older than themselves. The male average (12.9 years) was younger than the female average (14.4 years) and there was no urban-rural difference. This was based on a small sample of 41 early school-leavers (the mean age was 14.5 years). In this sample first sexual intercourse was almost always unplanned and usually took place in the context of a one-night stand situation.

In contrast, with a larger and broader sample of Irish 18- to 24-year-olds (n=1,667), Layte and colleagues (2006) reported the average age of first vaginal intercourse to be 16.9 years for males and 17.4 for females. Nearly one-third (31 per cent) of the 18- to 24-year-old males and over one-fifth (22 per cent) of females of the same age sampled had their first vaginal intercourse before the age of 17. This proportion has risen strikingly over past decades (ibid).

With a sample of over 2,700 young people in Galway, aged 16 on average, over a fifth (21 per cent) had experienced sexual intercourse (mean age of first intercourse was 15.5 years) and a fifth reported regular sexual intercourse (MacHale and Newell, 1997). An age-related increase in sexual intercourse was evident; 17 per cent of 16-year-olds had sexual intercourse compared to 21 per cent of 18-year-olds (ibid).

Northern Irish research with over a thousand 14- to 25-year-olds indicated that over half were sexually active, and of these, half reported their first sexual intercourse occurring by age 16. Young men reported having sex about a year earlier than young women (Rolston et al., 2004; Schubotz et al., 2003). These findings are consistent with international research.

Overall, young men are one and half to two times more likely then young women to report sexual experiences before age 16. In addition, young people from urban areas are significantly more likely to report having had sexual experiences before age 16 than those from rural areas (Lalor et al., 2003).

Turning to the reasons for having sex for the first time, the most common reason given by Northern Irish young people was that it was *not* planned, reasoned out or clearly decided upon; rather it was a 'spur of the moment' decision (45 per cent of males and 30 per cent of females). Other less common reasons included 'going along with my partner's wishes'; 'being drunk' or, for a small minority, as a consequence of being on drugs at the time (10 per cent of males; 4.5 per cent of females) (Schubotz et al., 2003).

Young women tend be more dissatisfied at having had their first sexual intercourse when they did, feeling they had sex too early (61 per cent) or that they did not want it at all (12 per cent). In contrast, nearly two-thirds of young men (62 per cent) felt they had sex at the right time although those who had it before age 16 were less likely to report feeling this way (Schubotz et al., 2003).

In general, as noted by Mayock and Byrne (2004, p. 75):

> having sex for the first time did not appear to occur at a point when young people no longer felt 'too young' or 'too afraid' to have sexual intercourse. Rather it happened 'out of the blue' with a recent romantic partner, often in the context of a one-night stand. While for young men first sex emerged as a significant marker through which they 'certified' their gender (Holland et al., 1996), the experience was not depicted by young women as a momentous occasion and, for many, it was disappointing or distressing.

In terms of the influence of religious affiliation, research in Northern Ireland indicated that religious affiliation influenced timing of first sexual intercourse. Just over a third (37 per cent) of Catholics reported sex before age 16, compared to nearly two-thirds (62 per cent) of Protestants, 58 per cent of atheists and 54 per cent of those of other religions (Rolston et al., 2004).

While early sexual activity has little association with income group, research in other countries has found that young people who have greater motivation to achieve and who have better access to educational opportunities are more motivated to delay sexual activity and childbearing (Trent and Crowder, 1997).

A health concern associated with sexual activity is contraception. While condom use, and to a lesser extent, other forms of contraception are common for regular sexual intercourse, this does not apply to first intercourse.

Over half of a sample of early school-leavers report not using a condom or any form of contraception at the time of first sex (Mayock and Byrne, 2004). Other research found that close to three-quarters (72 per cent) of Irish adolescents report using contraception at first intercourse, and usage after this, while high, is inconsistent (Dunne and Seery, 1997). Recent Irish research has found that 88 per cent of men and 94 per cent of women aged 18–24 used contraception at first vaginal intercourse (Layte et al., 2006). However, the younger the adolescent at first intercourse, the less likely contraception is to be used. This may reflect concerns about age of consent and confidentiality as well as a reluctance to plan ahead for fear of being labelled promiscuous. Alcohol intake has also been identified as compromising the use of contraception along with embarrassment when purchasing contraception, fear of side effects, drug use, indifference and the sporadic or unplanned nature of sexual activity (Fullerton, 2004).

What Are the 'Norms' of Sexual Activity in Adolescence?

Table 4.3 Key features of adolescent sexual activity

Early age at first sexual intercourse, compared to previous decades (discussed above).

Peer influence plays a key role in information provision and the initiation of sexual activity.

Young men and women differ significantly in how they think about sexual behaviour.

Contraception is used inconsistently.

The number of teenage pregnancies has risen from the 1970s to 2000*.

* The number of teenage pregnancies per 1,000 females aged 15–19 has ranged from 17.04 in 1970 to 25.66 in 2001, with a recent rise from 1996 to 2001 (McGrath et al., 2005). The teenage fertility rate refers to the number of live births per 1,000 females aged 15–19 (excl. abortions and miscarriages). This has slightly declined in Ireland from 22.4 in 1973 to 18.8 in 2003 (McGrath et al., 2005). Like Belguim and the Netherlands, this is amongst the lowest in the EU.

There are four primary sources from which young people obtain knowledge and understanding about sex and relationships: peers, the media, schools and parents (Burtney, 2000). Most Irish young people do not discuss sex with their parents (Hyde and Howlett, 2004). Yet most Irish parents report having spoken to their 12- to 18-year-old children about sexual matters (Ruddle et al., 2004) and research by McShane (2004) found that the majority of their Irish 15- to 24-year-old sample (especially females) who had had sex claimed their parents were fully aware of this. This implies that sexuality is no longer something that is hidden away from parents.

Hyde and Howlett (2004) carried out focus groups with a sample of 226 Irish young people drawn from 10 schools and their research provides an informative snapshot of teenage sexuality in the early years of the twenty-first century. While the sample of this study is restricted and contentious in its generalisability, it does afford us a valuable and rich insight into discourses and trends in Irish teenage sexuality in the early twenty-first century.

Peer influence was a factor in the initiation of sexual activity. Group norms were found to be influential with young people engaging in sexual activity to feel a sense of belonging to a peer group. Research with Irish early school-leavers found that a small number of young women reported sexual violence or coercion, and several others reported subtle or overt pressure to have sex at some stage (Mayock and Byrne, 2004). Linked to this is the view reported by some young people that virginity is a 'stigma' to be removed, irrespective of whether or not an individual is in a committed relationship (Hyde and Howlett, 2004). In addition, young men experience pressure from the male peer group to display sexual knowledge and experience through 'performance stories' of sexual conquest (Mayock and Byrne, 2004).

Striking gender differences are evident between young Irish men and women (Hyde and Howlett, 2004). Young women are more likely than young men to associate sex with being in a relationship and see it as related to the emotional side of the relationship. Young men, on the other hand, tend to consider sexual intercourse as acceptable, to varying degrees, irrespective of whether or not they are in a relationship. They put greater emphasis on their sexual drive and experience anxiety in relation to sexual performance more so than young women. Young women are also thought to bear the responsibility for maintaining the 'sexual boundaries' of any relationship and for them enjoying sex is linked to pleasing men sexually rather than satisfying their own desires. Such a 'double standard' of sexual behaviour that encourages young men to be predatory, knowledgeable and sexually active but disapproves of young women engaging in multiple sexual relationships and/or in certain types of sexual activity was also highlighted by Mayock and Byrne (2004).

In the past, young women were traditionally more dependent and less proactive in sexual matters than young men (Heaven et al., 1992). Traditional sex roles encouraging males to be active and females passive in dating and sexual practices may account for this.

While condom use appears common, it seems to be used inconsistently. Young women do not carry them for fear of being labelled a 'slut' and typically most young people feel that young men are responsible for obtaining and carrying condoms (Mayock and Byrne, 2004). Reasons given by young men for not using condoms include added stress and decreased sensitivity. Other reasons cited by both sexes for not using condoms include the spontaneity of sex, alcohol intoxication, feelings of invulnerability to pregnancy and STIs (Hyde and Howlett, 2004, pp. 9–10). More young people are concerned about pregnancy than STIs as an outcome of sexual activity and many showed a lack of knowledge about STIs. Availability of condoms through vending machines has removed the barrier of embarrassment of buying these. Research with Irish students indicates that nearly half (47 per cent) of 18- to 21-year-olds obtained condoms from vending machines (Duggan, 2000). However, in contrast to those over 18, the prevalence of vending machines in the environments of teenagers tends to be low. Concerns about the provision of condom machines in schools leading to a rise in sexual activity appear to be misplaced, as no increase in sexual activity or pregnancy has been found (Kirby, 2001 cited in Fulerton, 2004).

What Are the Difficulties Faced by Adolescents with Respect to Sex and Sexuality?

A wide array of difficulties are faced by young people with respect to sexuality. It may be used as a 'quick fix' with little planning or thought about it. Irish research, for example, found little discussion between young people before sexual activity as to 'how far things would go' (Hyde and Howlett, 2004). Being pressured to have sex, rape, STIs or an unwanted pregnancy may occur. Finally, confusion around sexual orientation may arise across the adolescent years.

One of the risks of adolescent sexual activity is that it can become a 'quick fix', a means of expressing or satisfying emotional or interpersonal needs which have little to do with sex and may interfere with personal growth. Sexual activity is often a symptom of extreme dependence rather than independence and thus can become the fulfilment of dependency needs.

For young people, sex may be used as a means of gaining affection, of enhancing self-esteem or sex-role identity, of venting anger or frustration or as an escape from boredom or loneliness (ibid). While sexual activity may temporarily ease uncomfortable or confusing emotions, the build-up of a hunger for the immediate gratification of the sexual 'quick fix' means that hypersexuality may result, with sexual and non-sexual needs only being partially satisfied. Consequently, the adolescent may be perceived as attention-seeking, troublesome or promiscuous and non-sexual motives may continue to drive their sexual behaviour (White and DeBlassie, 1992).

Teenage Pregnancy and Fertility

The number of teenage pregnancies per 1,000 females aged 15–19 in Ireland has ranged from 17.04 in 1970 to 25.66 in 2001, with a recent rise from 1996 to 2001 (McGrath et al., 2005). The teenage fertility rate refers to the number of live births per 1,000 females aged 15–19 (excluding abortions and miscarriages). This has slightly declined in Ireland from 22.4 in 1973 to 18.8 in 2003 (McGrath et al., 2005). This is in the context of a European-wide trend of an increase in the fertility of older women in the 30- to 34-year-old age group (ibid). The birth rate for the under 20-year-old age group in Ireland is 19.31 per 1,000, placing Ireland in the top 10 of developed countries for births in the 15- to 19-year-old age group (Fullerton, 2004). While parenthood is one consequence of teenage conception, miscarriage, perinatal loss, adoption and abortion are other possibilities. Teenagers have a higher risk of adverse health and obstetric outcomes than older women, although this may be more a function of social deprivation and lifestyle features (poor diet, smoking and alcohol use during pregnancy) than physical immaturity (Olausson et al., 2001).

Abortion is more likely for teenagers than for older women. While conception is *less* likely to result in abortion in Ireland than in other countries, statistics indicate that of 93 conceptions among young women aged under 16, over a quarter went to the UK for a termination in 2000 (Fullerton, 2004). Overall it is *estimated* that approximately 22.4 per cent of pregnancies to Irish young women aged under 20 end in abortion (McGrath et al., 2005).

In relation to adoption, the adoption rate has experienced a dramatic decline since the 1970s. In 1976 there were 1,006 non-relative adoptions in Ireland and by

2002 this figure had dropped to 99 (McGrath et al., 2005). While no data is available by age group, it can be surmised that this trend applies to teenagers as well as older women.

SEXUAL ORIENTATION

With sexual maturity, masculinity and femininity are renegotiated, and as sexual and gender identity are interlinked, experimentation in sexual orientation is common in adolescence. Linked to the consolidation of one's gender identity, established in childhood, is sex-role identity, formation of a sexual identity (an awareness of self as a sexual being and of one's sexual orientation).

Sexuality, like gender, is a social construction and as such different meanings have been attached to various sexualities. Sociologists and social psychologists have emphasised how sexual orientation is learned in conjunction with masculinity or femininity. Many theorists contend that homosexual experience is a part of normal sexual experimentation and development, with very little association between adolescent homosexual experience and self-identification as a homosexual adult (Glasser, 1977). According to this perspective, it is only possible to be labelled 'gay' or 'lesbian' after adolescence, as confusion and indecision over sexual desires and orientation are an understandable feature of adolescence. However, research with adult homosexuals has found that most can trace their sexual orientation back to adolescence (Bell et al., 1981). American research some years ago suggested that very few young people label themselves as homosexual, most only beginning to label themselves as gay or lesbian around 19 years of age and tending to only disclose it to others in early adulthood (23–28 years) (Remafedi, 1987). However, there has been considerable cultural change in the intervening years, both in America and in Ireland. Recent research among a sample of 362 LGBT (lesbian, gay, bisexual and transgender) young people in Northern Ireland (Carolan and Redmond, 2003) found that in response to the question 'what age were you when you realised you were gay, lesbian or bisexual?', 40 per cent responded 10 to 13 years and a further 37 per cent said 14 to 17 years. The average age of 'realising' for young men was 12 and the average age for young women was 13. In both cases, the point at which they were prepared to tell someone else came, on average, five years later (17 and 18, respectively).

Garnets and Kimmel (1991) proposed a series of developmental milestones (with approximate age ranges) for homosexual identity development:

- **12–16 years:** Initial awareness of same-gender affectional-erotic feelings.
- **14–20 years:** Initial same-gender experience (earlier for gays than lesbians).
- **Early adulthood 20–25 years:** Self-identification as lesbian or gay.
- **Mid to late twenties:** Formation of a positive gay or lesbian identity.

The 'exotic becomes erotic' (EBE) theory of sexual orientation emphasises the role of early childhood experiences in the formation of sexual orientation (heterosexual as well as homosexual orientation). According to Baumeister (2001), young children feeling different to their same-sex or opposite-sex peers in early to middle childhood leads them to view whichever gender they perceive to be different as exotic. This sex then comes to have emotional and sexual associations for the growing child with puberty. However, this theory lacks widespread research support and does not adequately explain why so many young girls who are tomboys and see feminine girls as more different or 'exotic' to them than boys do not become lesbian, as this theory would suggest.

Others, such as Goggin (1995), have proposed four stages of homosexual identity development:

- **Stage 1: Sensitisation:** Awareness of being different from others of the same gender.
- **Stage 2: Identity confusion:** An altered awareness of the self, sexual arousal with those of the same gender, a sense of stigma around homosexuality and inaccurate information about homosexuality.
- **Stage 3: Identity assumption:** Taking up the identity of being homosexual and disclosure of this to others, at least close friends.
- **Stage 4: Commitment:** The individual can now make a commitment to an intimate relationship with someone of the same gender.

However, as with all 'stage theories' of development, caution needs to be exercised regarding the sequence and generalisability of such stages to any individual. Individual, socio-cultural and contextual factors, as reflected in ecological theory (see Chapter 2), all have a bearing on any aspect of human development.

Despite greater openness in discourse, little is known about the prevalence of homosexuality and homosexual behaviour in Irish adolescents. Looking at Irish adults, 4 per cent of men and over 1 per cent of women report ever having same-sex genital contact and in general, younger adults are more likely to report homosexual and bisexual identity as well as some level of same-sex attraction (Layte et al., 2006). Research in Northern Ireland found that 2 per cent of young men and 1.4 per cent of young women sampled expressed exclusively homosexual feelings, but 11 per cent and 13 per cent, respectively, reported being at least once sexually attracted to someone of the same sex (Schubotz et al., 2003).

Drawing on personal narratives from four gay Irish men, Ryan (2003) highlighted how social forces (such as the Church and education) have shaped the Irish homosexual experience. Over recent years great change has taken place in Irish sexual attitudes and practices with changes in discourses (dominant ideas and understandings) from a Catholic perspective to one involving concepts such as pleasures, diversity, preferences and choices (O'Toole, 2005). This can also be seen with respect to discourses on sex education in Ireland. Inglis (1998) identified four of these: traditional, progressive, liberal and radical, which reflect differences in values on adolescent sexual education. As noted by Lalor and colleagues (2003,

p. 122), 'much debate on adolescent sexual behaviour is informed by beliefs in how young people should, or should not, behave. Young people's actual behaviour can be sidelined in such value-laden debates (and pronouncements)'.

A survey undertaken by the Gay and Lesbian Equality Network in conjunction with NEXUS Research Cooperative (1995) with 159 adults in 1993 indicated that nearly half (49 per cent) had become aware of their sexuality before reaching 15 years of age; a further 20 per cent realised they were gay or lesbian by 19 years. However, only over one-third (38 per cent) had revealed this to their family by the age of 20.

Coming Out and the Problems Facing LGBT Young People

'Coming out' refers to the process by which lesbian, gay, bisexual and transgender (LGBT) people openly declare their sexual identity, to themselves and to others. In general, the younger a person is when they 'come out', the better his or her self-esteem (Savin-Williams and Rodriguez, 1993). Coming out requires a lot of courage and is a difficult process. Many LGBT people prefer to stay in the closet due to social pressures and homophobia. Many fear being judged, excluded or rejected by their family. Avoidance, often by involvement in opposite-sex relationships, is another possible response by LGBT young people. Although contemporary culture shows greater acceptance of different sexual orientations, parents and relatives may respond in very different ways to the revelation that their son or daughter is gay or lesbian. Verbal harassment, physical violence, feelings of shame, embarrassment and denial often occur.

Over two-thirds of the sample in the GLEN/NEXUS (1995) study, described earlier, reported difficulties in coming out to their families, such as the risk of rejection, breakdown in family relationships and the sequelae of being forced to leave home. Almost a third had experienced homelessness. Interviews highlighted that while they were not asked directly to leave home, the atmosphere became so difficult they felt they had to leave. The first reaction of many parents is to try to hide their child's sexual orientation from relatives and others, thereby removing a source of social support and adding further difficulties to their child's coming out.

While coming out to friends tended to be less problematic than to family, the survey indicated that 'the reaction of friends included embarrassment and, in many cases, fear that others would presume that they were also lesbian or gay if they were to continue their friendship' (GLEN/NEXUS, 1995, p. 37).

Many reported problems at school because they felt they did not fit in or due to fear of harassment or violence because of their sexuality. For some people this appears to have impaired their educational achievement, as they left school early to avoid further harassment. Isolation and difficulty, especially in rural areas, in meeting other lesbian or gay people was another striking finding. Even in large cities, meeting other lesbians and gays can be problematic, as some people dislike going to gay or lesbian pubs and clubs for fear of being seen. Consequently, many gay and lesbian people move to Dublin for greater anonymity, though this can be costly (ibid).

A quarter had been subjected to violent attacks and many had experienced discrimination and harassment at work. Many of the sample also reported signs of psychological distress, particularly those affected by poverty. Such distress is understandable given the prevalence of harassment reported by this sample. Two-fifths (41 per cent) of the sample had been threatened with violence, a quarter (25 per cent) had been physically assaulted while the vast majority (81 per cent) said the possibility of anti-gay harassment affected their behaviour (ibid).

Northern Irish research by Schubotz and colleagues (2003, p. 17) included the following illuminating accounts from young homosexual people.

I identify myself as being male homosexual and come from a homophobic family. My family would find it very difficult in coming to terms with my sexual orientation (male, 19 years old).

I didn't know I was attracted to women until it just happened. When it did, I didn't tell anyone for fear they would reject me and treat me differently. I felt that I had let my family down and I didn't come out for about four years (female, 25 years old).

In other research in Northern Ireland by Lourdes (2003, p. 16), LGBT young people spoke of how 'it is very hard to tell them [parents] that you are gay. Once you tell them, they think that you are confused and try to talk you out of it.' This research also drew attention to how coming out is a process affecting the family as a whole, beyond the young LGBT person himself or herself. Northern Irish society was perceived as not being conducive to coming out. LGBT young people spoke of this being 'a political and religious thing ... people have strict ideas around sexuality' (Lourdes, 2003, p. 17).

Being bullied and feelings of marginalisation, isolation and unhappiness are common in gay youth. Many gay and lesbian young people also report feeling obliged to pretend they are heterosexual and engage in strong teasing (slagging) and 'queer bashing' to avoid self-revelation. In Northern Ireland, common forms of harassment reported by LGBT people include verbal abuse, being followed on foot, subjected to graffiti and offensive phone calls. In addition, over half of those sampled, particularly males, had experienced homophobic violence (Jarman and Tennant, 2003).

Isolation and stigmatisation experienced by gay youth in a dominant heterosexual culture may explain their greater risk (than non-gay youth) for behavioural problems, substance abuse and unsafe sex (Faulkner and Cranston, 1998). Marginalisation and a sense of isolation appear to be even greater amongst young lesbians and bisexual women (Lourdes, 2003). This 'invisibility' of lesbians and bisexual women has been emphasised in the report by the International Lesbian and Gay Association (2000). Worryingly, suicide rates for young lesbians, gay men and bisexuals tend to be higher than average for young people (ibid).

From a survey with twenty-six 16- to 25-year-old LGBT Irish youth in 2003,

MacManus (2004) found that the majority (73 per cent) reported a wide range of problems in school, including discrimination, bullying and alienation. Homophobia appeared to be widespread in the school system and under half (42 per cent) of the sample felt that homophobia (negative and/or fearful attitudes about homosexuality or homosexuals) hampered their studies, with some reporting skipping school to avoid bullying. One-fifth left school early, citing negating reactions to their sexual orientation as one of the main reasons why they left (ibid; see also Pobal, 2006).

Many of the difficulties faced by LGBT young people are due to homophobia and heterosexism (an underlying belief that heterosexuality is the natural, normal, acceptable or superior form of sexuality). Homophobia is very widespread, especially among males (Lynch and Lodge, 2002). Such homophobia originates in a lack of understanding and anxiety about homosexuality. A lack of opportunity to discuss it in a non-threatening and open way that diffuses fear and nurtures understanding contributes to this. For many, homophobia is still a 'respectable and acceptable' prejudice and its widespread prevalence hinders young people coming out as lesbian, gay and bisexual (Jarman and Tennant, 2003). While some young LGBT people deal well with difficulties, others show fear of being 'found out', denial, shame, isolation, self-harm and suicidal ideation or behaviour (Burtney and Duffy, 2004). Internalised homophobia may be related to this. This refers to 'the fear and self-hate of one's own homosexuality or bisexuality that occurs for many gay and lesbian individuals who have learned negative ideas about homosexuality throughout childhood' (Lourdes, 2003, pp. 17–18).

SEX EDUCATION

Sexual health education involves recognising a young person's personal, family, religious and social values in decision-making about sexual behaviour. Sexual health education enables young people to develop the knowledge, motivation and behavioural skills needed to enhance sexual health and to avoid sexual health-related problems. Sexual education programmes in other countries have reported a number of results, including a delayed initiation of intercourse, a reduction in number of sexual partners, fewer feelings of coercion and a drop in teen pregnancy rate (Fullerton, 2004).

According to the Sex Education Forum (1992), sexual health education should encourage the exploration of values and moral issues, consideration of sexuality and personal relationships and the development of communication and decision-making skills. It should foster self-esteem, self-awareness, a sense of moral responsibility and the skills to avoid and resist sexual exploitation.

Ideally it should start early, before puberty and before young people have developed established patterns of behaviour. It should be sustained throughout adolescence, with each 'module' of sex education building on previous modules.

Any sex education also needs to be age appropriate and cognisant of cultural and contextual factors that have a bearing on the young people it is targeted at.

In 2004, the National Youth Council of Ireland identified the components of an effective sexual health education and related curriculum topics, presented in Figures 4.2 and 4.3. These need to be adapted to suit the needs of any particular group of young people and could incorporate a variety of methodologies, such as role play, case studies and creative methods. A detailed account of planning, implementing and evaluating a sexual health education programme with young people is presented in the 2004 NYCI report, *Sense and Sexuality* (NYCI, 2004a).

Sex education may act as an agent of social control, legitimising a model of sexual behaviour embedded in the context of a Christian marriage and negate behaviour deviant of this. Sex education is always likely to be value-laden and used to influence, directly or indirectly, the sexuality of young people (Schubotz et al., 2003). Positive and negative attitudes to sexuality are common in young people (Schubotz et al., 2003). 'Apart from the media, parents, school peers and feelings of socio-religious belonging also encourage often conflicting and ambiguous or contrasting feelings, which result in pressures and challenges, (ibid, p. 21).

In addition, gender differences are evident in the experience of sex education. According to Schubotz and colleagues (2003, p. 21), 'males are less likely to receive sex education in school or are less likely to remember it, which is just as detrimental'. Northern Irish research found that while young people were dissatisfied with the sex education they received at school, the majority still felt that school was the safest place for them to learn about sex (ibid).

However, most Irish parents report having spoken to their 12- to 18-year-old children about sexual matters. Most also feel confident as sex educators of their own children though would welcome support in this such as booklets, parent meetings in the school or community and classes or training (Ruddle et al., 2004).

Effective sex education, according to Coleman and Hendry (1999), involves five features:

- A curriculum that extends beyond biology to include the dilemmas and contradictions inherent in sexual behaviour and relationship skills.
- The inclusion of sexual issues pertinent to minority groups, including ethnic minorities and those who are gay, lesbian, bisexual and transsexual youth.
- Recognition that young people vary in their level of knowledge about sexuality.
- A curriculum that is not prescriptive and is without moral messages about what is right or wrong.
- Clear, reasonable goals.

Figure 4.2 Learning outcomes of a sexual health education programme

Acquisition of knowledge:
- Information relevant to personal sexual health.
- Understanding of individual and cultural differences in attitudes and beliefs about sexual health.
- Information about ways to achieve/maintain sexual health.

Sexual health enhancement:
- Positive self-image and self-worth as an aspect of acceptance of one's own sexuality;.
- Integration of sexuality into mutually satisfying relationships.
- Attainment and maintenance of sexual and reproductive health.

Development of motivation/ personal insight:
- Acceptance of one's own sexuality.
- Development of positive attitudes towards sexual health – promoting behaviours.
- Critical consciousness-raising about sexual health issues.

SEXUAL HEALTH BEHAVIOURS

Development of skills that support sexual health:
- Ability to formulate age-appropriate sexual health goals.
- Ability to carry out sexual health-promoting behaviours for each of these goals.
- Ability to evaluate and modify one's sexual health goals as necessary.

Creation of an environment conducive to sexual health:
- Developing personal awareness of environmental influences on sexual health.
- Acquiring skills needed to identify and influence the social practices/ policies/structures that affect sexual health.

Prevention of sexual health problems:
- Prevention of unintended/crisis pregnancy.
- Prevention of STIs, including HIV/AIDS.
- Prevention of sexual harassment/exploitation/abuse.

Source: National Youth Council of Ireland (2004a).

Figure 4.3 Components of a sexual health education programme

1. Self-Esteem and Self-Awareness
Recognising my uniqueness; Building on my strengths; Developing my self confidence; Body image and self worth.

2. Communications & Assertiveness
Expressing myself; Learning to listen; Passive, assertive and aggressive communication; Dealing with conflict; Negotiation skills.

3. Relationships
Respecting myself and others; Types of relationship – family, friendships, boy/girl sexual, future permanent relationships; Friendship skills; Relationship skills.

8. Personal Safety
Looking after myself – physically, socially, mentally, emotionally and spiritually; Identifying risks to myself and to others in relation to sexual risk-taking, substance use, bullying and violence; Strategies for self-protection; Child protection considerations.

KEY COMPONENTS:
Knowledge; Skills; Motivation and Personal Insight; Supportive Environments

Sexual Health Enhancement and Prevention of Sexual Health Problems

4. Body Awareness – Body Care
Knowing my body; Body parts – male/female; Human life cycle; Growth and development; Body changes and puberty; The reproductive system; Menstruation; Health and hygiene; Valuing my body – nutrition, physical activity, substances; Physical ability/disability.

7. Sexual Health
Exploiting sexuality; Sexual body changes and human reproduction; Contraception; STIs and HIV/AIDS; Respect and commitment within sexual relationships; Pregnancy and birth; Teenage pregnancy/crisis pregnancy; Parental responsibilities; Responsible sexual behaviour; Information, advice and support services; Legal considerations, e.g. age of consent, etc.

6. Influences & Decision-Making
Identifying and understanding influences, e.g. peers, family, media, stereotypes, gender, religion, culture, substances; Factors influencing decision-making; Recognising options and making health choices; Decision-making skills; Asking for information and help.

5. Emotional Health
Recognising feelings; Respecting my feelings and the feelings of others; Coping with feelings – anger, loss, jealousy; Feeling relating to power, gender, disability, race, ethnicity, sexual orientation, spirituality.

Source: National Youth Council of Ireland (2004a).

Relationships and Sexuality Education Programme

The Department of Education's Relationships and Sexuality Education programme (RSE) was initiated in 1997. This is part of the broader 'Social, Personal and Health Education' programme. Despite considerable opposition, the RSE programme became a designated part of the national curriculum. Many teachers and parents felt sex education of their children was solely a parental responsibility. While the Catholic Church felt that sex education was primarily the responsibility of the parents, they acknowledged that most parents needed the help and support of teachers and schools. However, the Catholic Church contended that it was of critical importance that any sex education provided was grounded firmly in the context of Catholic moral teaching. The *gap* between the traditional discourse about sexuality advocated by the Catholic Church and the progressive perspective of the State is at the centre of the implementation of the RSE programme in schools.

The local adaptation of the RSE programme has resulted in the provision of relationship and sexuality education being patchy, with schools varying significantly in the RSE programme that they provide and the messages communicated (Inglis, 1998). Research with young people in Kildare found that while almost 80 per cent have received classes on RSE, only one-third found them 'very helpful' (Lalor and Baird, 2006). An early evaluation of the RSE programme also identified that in over a quarter of schools there was no RSE programme of any kind with a tendency for less provision in boys' than girls' schools. While there was strong support among teachers for the principles of RSE, they overwhelmingly identified the 'overcrowded curriculum' as the chief barrier to the actual implementation of the programme (Morgan, 2000a).

Consequently, 'what was proposed as a progressive discourse, could, in some schools, be turned back into a traditional discourse through:

• The teaching materials and resources adopted
• The language, concepts and terms employed to talk about sexuality
• The teaching methods used (Inglis, 1998, pp. 68–9).

Inglis (1998) highlighted how the RSE programme attempts to assist young people to deal with the ambivalent messages of traditionalism and liberalism on sexuality in Ireland today.

> The RSE programme aims to help young people to stay safe, happy and comfortable in the middle of the road, somewhere between chastity and sexual activity. In concentrating on developing self-esteem, the programme tries to teach children to be confident, mature and responsible in their social relationships. The message, in other words, is that when it comes to travelling the road of sexuality, they are in the driving seat of a car, which can bring as much pain as pleasure and happiness. The approach of the RSE programme may be the only sensible way forward. The

only problem is who is best able to teach these young people ... (Inglis, 1998, p. 176).

Inglis (1998) reported that young people prefer to be taught the RSE programme in small groups by someone a little older and more experienced than themselves, someone they could identify with and who would empathise with them and understand the social world in which they live. If this person were to be a teacher, they would prefer if they did not know the teacher and that s/he did not know them.

Research published in 2007 reported that two-thirds of schools surveyed felt RSE implementation levels have improved since it was introduced in the 1990s. Approximately 81 per cent of schools reported teaching RSE in first and second year, and 11 per cent of schools reported not teaching RSE. Overall a decline was found in RSE teaching during third year, followed by a very low rate of RSE taught in the senior cycle. Arising from this, the authors recommended the introduction of SPHE/RHE at senior cycle (Mayock, Kitching & Morgan, 2007).

CONCLUSION

This chapter began by examining adolescent social worlds and peer relationships. Types of peer group and the stages of peer group development were outlined, followed by a discussion of peer pressure in terms of bullying as well as peer acceptance, rejection and neglect. Adolescent friendships and romantic relationships were then considered and a cause for concern, adolescent loneliness, was examined. Finally, adolescent sexuality was discussed in terms of norms and the issues faced by young people with respect to their emerging sexuality and sexual orientation.

RECOMMENDED READING

Coleman, J.C., & Hendry, L. (1999). *The nature of adolescence*. London: Routledge.
Hyde, A., & Howlett, E. (2004). *Understanding teenage sexuality in Ireland*. Dublin: Crisis Pregnancy Agency.
Inglis, T. (1998). *Lessons in Irish sexuality*. Dublin: UCD Press.
Jackson, S., & Rodrigues–Tomé, H. (1993). *Adolescence and its social worlds*. Hove: Lawrence Erlbaum Associates.
Miles, S. (2000). *Youth lifestyles in a changing world*. Buckingham: Open University Press.

5

Health and Well-Being

INTRODUCTION

This chapter explores health as a concept, physical and mental. The primary health challenges faced by young people relating to physical activity, diet, substance use, sexual health and mental health are discussed. With respect to mental health, particular attention is paid to body image, depression, self-harm and suicide. Protective and support factors for young people's mental health are discussed and this chapter concludes by looking at health promotion, with special consideration given to sexual and mental health.

HEALTH

Health has been defined as 'the extent to which an individual or group is able, on the one hand, to realise aspirations and satisfy needs, and on the other hand, to change or cope with the environment. From this perspective health is seen as a resource for everyday life, not the objective of living; it is a positive concept emphasising social and personal resources, as well as physical capacities' (WHO, 1984).

This holistic definition construes health as more than just physical health. It is not just the absence of disease but the presence of positive health. It recognises the multiplicity of factors that influence health and portrays health as a means to an end rather than an end in itself, incorporating need fulfilment, personal growth and development, and adaptability to change. Physical, social, mental, emotional, sexual and spiritual needs all interact in a young person's social context (Naidoo and Wills, 1994). This is illustrated on the next page.

Determinants of health can be seen as layers of influence (Dahlgren and Whitehead, 1991), including:

- Personal behaviour and lifestyle (diet, exercise, smoking).
- Support and influence within communities which can sustain or damage health (ethnic group, peer and family group).
- Living and working conditions and access to facilities and services (geographical location).

- Economic, cultural and environmental conditions, such as standards of living or the labour market (socio-economic status, housing) (see Fig. 5.2).

Figure 5.1 Promoting health with young people

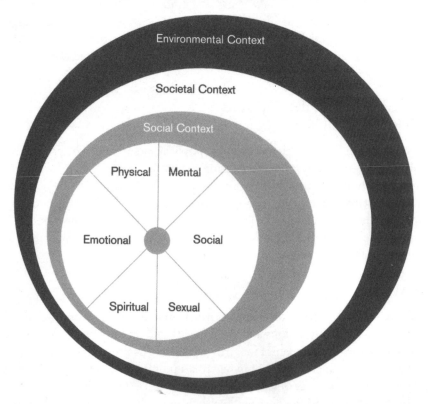

The significance of socio-economic status (SES) for adolescent health cannot be over-emphasised, as illustrated by the Health Behaviours in School-Aged Children Survey (HBSC). This was undertaken in 2002 (following a previous study in 1998) across 30 countries (including the USA and Canada), with approximately 1,500 young people from each of the 11-, 13- and 15-year-old age groups in participating countries. The Irish data was collected by the Centre for Health Promotion Studies at NUI Galway.

The HBSC study found SES to be consistently related to adolescent health across most HBSC countries, with young people from higher socio-economic groups reporting better health and higher levels of physical activity (Currie et al., 2003).

However, other research reveals the relationship between socio-economic status and health in adolescence to be not so straightforward and rather influenced by many personal and socio-cultural factors (Friel et al., 1999; Kelleher et al., 2003). In childhood and adolescence, behaviour that compromises, maintains or promotes health is predictive of morbidity, health service use and, indirectly, educational involvement and social development. Factors that place young people at risk for adverse health include poor mental health, being out of the home or in care, intellectual disabilities, psychological or behavioural problems, families with problems such as abuse or substance misuse, criminal problems, living in geographically isolated areas and being in a minority (ethnic, sexual orientation) (Department of Health and Children, 1999).

Before discussing adolescent health behaviour, including risky health behaviour, such as excessive drinking or smoking, it is useful to consider adolescent risk-taking from a broader perspective.

Figure 5.2 Health determinants

Source: Dahlgren and Whitehead, 1991.

Risk-Taking

Risk-taking is considered to be normal in adolescence, placing young people at risk for social, psychological and health problems (Arnett, 1999). Adolescence is characterised by experimentation that, while developmentally appropriate and socially adaptive for most, may be harmful to others. Sensation-seeking, experimentation and egocentrism, amongst other factors, make risky behaviour more likely during adolescence than other developmental periods, with the form that it takes dependent upon socio-cultural environment and individual characteristics. A young person's own inclinations as well as what is 'normally done' by peers contribute to what risky behaviour is more or less probable. For some young people this may mean skateboarding down a busy road, shoplifting, sex without contraception, smoking, drug use and so forth.

Typically, risky behaviour refers to an action that entails some chance of loss and tends to be high in novelty and intensity of sensation. What is defined as a 'risky behaviour' is socially and culturally constructed. What may be risky in one era or culture may not be so at other times or in other cultures. Equally, what is risky to some may be a rational means of pleasure, escapism, garnering status, self-esteem enhancement, sensation-seeking or a combination of these to others.

In their review of research studies on adolescent risky behaviour, Furby and Beyth-Marom (1992) summarised a number of key points:

- Young people may not be fully aware or informed of risks associated with their behaviours, underestimating risks and seeing themselves as invulnerable.
- Sensation-seeking, challenge and fulfilment may underpin much risky behaviour in adolescence and crucially, risk-avoidance behaviours may threaten well-being much more than risky behaviour itself. In relation to this, risky behaviour may be a source of stress relief
- Young people may not be able to resist peer pressure to engage in risky behaviour.
- Risky behaviour may be a rational choice for young people.

Differences in values, decision-making and risk perception may arise between young people and adults. Associated with this is the tendency for young people to focus more on the *potential gain* over the *potential loss* associated with risky behaviour.

However, research support for these points is inconclusive. Even if young people are more likely to engage in risky behaviour, a case can be made for this being developmentally advantageous in terms of challenge, fulfilment, facilitating transition to adulthood and enhancing self-esteem (Furby and Beyth-Marcom, 1992).

A range of sociological and psychological theories have attempted to explain adolescent risk behaviour. Some emphasise personality features and the need for excitement and pleasure (Arnett and Balle-Jensen, 1993). Others emphasise the role of the peer group in terms of peer pressure, group solidarity, conformity and peer status in risk behaviours. Other theories again construe risk behaviour as a form of gaining entry into the adult world and of identification with adult behaviour.

Finally, sociological attention has also focused on risky behaviour as a form of 'social resistance' through which traditional norms are challenged (Wearing et al., 1994). This relates to the view that the very labelling of behaviour as 'risky' may be a means of political or social control. Why society is so concerned with adolescent risk-taking over the greater risk-taking prevalent in adulthood is unclear. Little evidence exists that young people actually seek out or are willing to accept greater risks than adults.

HEALTH BEHAVIOURS

A range of key health challenges in adolescence will now be explored. Demographic information will be presented as well as the benefits and harm associated with such behaviours. The behaviours chosen reflect policy concerns, representing what are seen as the health behaviours of most concern in the adolescent years in Ireland.

Physical Activity

The increasing number of Irish young people, particularly girls and young women, that do not participate in sufficient physical activity has received a lot of attention over recent years (Kelleher et al., 2003).

The internationally recognised recommendation is that young people participate in physical activity for at least an hour per day in order to maintain healthy body weight and to reduce the risk of developing cardiovascular disease, diabetes, some cancers, osteoporosis, obesity and other non-communicable diseases later in life (National Heart Alliance, 2001). The evidence for the health benefits from regular physical activity is overwhelming and undisputed. Regular physical activity is second only to diet in the prevention and treatment of overweight and obesity (Nieman, 1998). Regular physical activity is also associated with self-worth, self-esteem and reduced incidence of depression (ibid). Physically active young people are also *more* likely to be physically active as adults (Sallis et al., 1992).

The Take PART (Physical Activity Research for Teenagers) study found that 65 per cent of Irish young people are *not* regularly active (involved in moderate or vigorous physical activity for at least an hour for four days a week). Obese teenagers are more than twice as likely to have sedentary leisure habits compared to normal or overweight young people, and teenage girls in particular are significantly *less* likely to be physically active (Woods et al., 2004).

The National Health and Lifestyle Surveys 1998 and 2002 asked children (aged 9–17) to recall the frequency with which they exercised, outside of school, so much that 'they got out of breath or sweated'. Overall, figures for 1998 showed 53 per cent of children exercising four or more times per week, dropping to 48 per cent in 2002. In 1998, 5 per cent of boys and 7 per cent of girls were exercising less often than once per week. These figures had risen to 8 per cent of boys and 14 per cent of girls by 2002 (Kelleher et al., 2003). Yet in the HBSC study, Irish 11- to 15-year-olds reported high rates of weekly physical activity, in contrast to many other participating countries (Currie et al., 2003).

Consistent with international research, these rates decline with age (especially for girls), an issue discussed further in Chapter 8. Across all the countries, boys were more likely to meet recommended physical activity guidelines than girls (ibid).

From all of this it is clear that inadequate physical activity is a concern for Irish young people, at least adolescent girls. Cultural changes in terms of transportation to and from school and the greater choices and popularity of sedentary home-based leisure, outlined in Chapter 8, undoubtedly contribute to this.

Table 5.1 Mean number of days with physical activity for 1 hour or more (typical week)

Age group	11	13	15
Irish females	4.6	4.3	3.4
Irish males	5.0	5.1	4.4
HBSC female average	3.8	3.5	3.2
HBSC male average	4.3	4.2	3.9

HEALTHY EATING

The adolescent years are important for physical growth and as the physiological need for nutrients escalates, a balanced diet becomes especially critical. Increased obesity has led to greater attention on adolescent diet and eating behaviour. In 1990 the Irish National Nutrition Survey indicated that 1.9 per cent of young people aged 12 to 15 were significantly overweight (Irish Nutrition and Dietetic Institute, 1990). In 2000, this rate had trebled, with levels of overweight and obesity in Irish adolescent girls in particular being higher than the international average (Griffin et al., 2004).

In Irish second-level students, approximately one in five are obese or overweight. One in 20 Irish children are obese, with one in five being overweight (Fahey et al., 2005). In a Cork-based study, 15.5 per cent of parents of eight-year-old children described their child as 'fat' or 'very fat' (Foley-Nolan et al., 2005). This is worrying given that research shows that about half of obese children become obese adults and 80 per cent of obese adolescents continue to be obese in adulthood. As well as the health risks of obesity (such as diabetes, cardiovascular disease, hypertension), obese young people experience ridicule, bullying and prejudice more than their average-weight counterparts. Obese adolescent girls are *less* likely to hang out with friends, and *more* likely to report emotional problems, hopelessness and suicide attempts than their average-weight counterparts. Obese adolescent boys are also *less* likely to hang out with friends, and *more* likely to report emotional problems and to quit school (Falkner et al, 2001).

Patterns of eating are critical to this. High-fat energy-dense 'obesogenic' diets (high-fat, high-sugar and high-salt foods) and sedentary lifestyles have caused an elevation in the prevalence of obesity, while cultural factors have led to image consciousness and dieting. The combination of such a high-sugar, low-fibre diet in conjunction with a sedentary lifestyle is central to adolescent obesity. However, the relationship between physical activity and obesity is not robust, possibly because measures fail to capture real variations in energy expenditure or because of other factors such as diet.

Research for the HBSC study highlighted that fruit and vegetable consumption is relatively low and decreases with age in young people. A clear gender difference is evident, with boys eating less fruit and vegetables than girls. Over half (51 per cent) of Irish 10- to 17-year-olds eat sweets, over a third (37 per cent) drink fizzy drinks, over a quarter (27 per cent) eat crisps, 12 per cent eat chips and 7 per cent eat hamburgers at least once daily. Irish 15-year-olds eat the most sweets on a daily basis (56 per cent female; 52 per cent male) compared to young people in 34 other countries (including the UK and USA). Overall, about one-third of young people eat sweets every day (29.5 per cent of females; 28.1 per cent of males), indicating a high consumption pattern (Currie et al., 2003).

Another key HBSC finding is the frequency with which breakfasts are skipped, an unhealthy eating habit that has become normative in youth culture. A high number of teenage girls across countries in the HBSC study skip breakfast (15-year-old HBSC average of 48.3 per cent of girls compared to 36 per cent of boys). Skipping breakfast is known to lead to fatigue, concentration and learning difficulties. General well-being can also be compromised by a poor diet. An unbalanced or inadequate diet can lead to feelings of fatigue or lethargy and caffeine and sugary substances can affect moods and energy cycles. Changes in eating habits may reflect a shift away from parental control towards increased autonomy, as one means of expressing independence or defiance is through eating behaviour.

Cultural factors such as the availability, range and price of foods available, the advertising of high-calorie foods, peer norms and cultural pressures to have a so-called 'ideal body image' all influence adolescent eating behaviour. Other influential factors include the high frequency of children and young people being driven to school, increased mechanisation and insufficient amenities for physical activity.

Research with 3,436 young people across the island of Ireland found that young people generally prefer 'tasty' but 'unhealthy' foods. They have a very basic knowledge of their own diet, relating health of diet to particular food items as opposed to overall pattern of consumption (Trew et al., 2006). As anticipated, older adolescents have a greater knowledge of nutrition than their younger counterparts. In general, nutritional knowledge *per se* was not found to be associated with dietary practices, implying that dietary education may not be the best way to improve healthy eating in young people. Young men tend to eat a poorer diet than young women, and pay less attention to healthy eating issues in both print and broadcast media. However, for young men weight control and nutrition awareness are associated, whereas for young women weight control is more often at the expense of nutrition. This reflects different concerns young men and women have with respect to body image, a topic discussed later in this chapter. Young people from lower socio-economic groups also report a poorer diet, reflecting that health of diet is not evenly distributed across the population (ibid).

Four barriers to healthy eating have been identified by Stevenson and colleagues (2006) from focus groups undertaken with young people in Ireland and Northern Ireland.

- **Physical and psychological reinforcement of eating behaviour**: This refers to what is rewarding and punishing about eating or not eating particular foods. For example, the taste of a particular food may be a stronger reason (more rewarding) for why someone chooses to eat one food over another rather than its nutrient value.

- **Perceptions of food and eating behaviour**: This refers to how a person perceives and thinks about food and eating behaviours. Adolescent thinking about food tends to be polarised into categorising foods and eating as 'good' or 'bad' rather than seeing food and eating holistically in terms of nutrient or 'dietary' balance. In addition they appeared quite resistant to challenges about their food likes and dislikes.
- **Perceptions of contradictory food-related social pressures**: This refers to contradictory and inconsistent messages received and the acknowledgement that fast food, while unhealthy, is desirable. Conflicting pressures towards eating unhealthily and against obesity result in a focus on weight rather than on health as the motivating factor in dietary choice.
- **Perceptions of the concept of healthy eating**: In general young people associate healthy eating with weight control and see attention to diet as only a means to an end rather than important in itself. Healthy eating is typically seen as an unnatural, unpleasant short-term activity undertaken to avoid the stigma of obesity or to enhance attractiveness.

While the number of Irish young people (especially girls) following weight-reducing diets has increased since 1998 (Kelleher et al., 2003), healthy eating programmes addressing these barriers are needed.

Eating Disorders

While younger children are at risk, eating disorders usually emerge during adolescence. They are more common in females, reflecting the impact of the cultural value placed on thinness for female beauty. Anorexia nervosa is an eating disorder most likely to occur after the pubertal growth spurt. Bulimia is another eating disorder most likely to arise in late adolescence or early adulthood, characterised by binge eating followed by vomiting, laxative abuse or exercise-induced weight loss to prevent food absorption. Both are associated with other mental health problems, such as depression and obsessive-compulsive disorder. Irish research has estimated that 0.5 per cent of young people aged 12–19 have anorexia nervosa, 2 per cent bulimia nervosa and 4–5 per cent partial presentations of these (Irish College of Psychiatrists, 2005).

A review of anorexia in Ireland from 1977–1995 found a psychiatric hospital admissions rate for anorexia of 1.64 per 100,000. When general hospital admissions are included as well, the rate rose to 4.8 per 100,000. Over 90 per cent of admissions were female, mostly aged 15 to 24, which is in accordance with international trends. While the admissions rate dropped from 1977–1985, this was due, to a degree, to fewer admissions because of community treatment programmes. Worryingly, more recent data points to anorexia appearing at an earlier age (7–8 years) (Department of Health and Children, 2006).

SUBSTANCE USE

This section will examine three forms of substance use (and abuse) that are of particular concern in young people in contemporary Ireland: alcohol consumption, smoking and illicit substance use.

Alcohol

The teenage years are characterised by greater experimentation with alcohol and heightened high-risk drinking patterns, such as drunkenness and binge drinking (consuming five or more drinks in a row on a single drinking occasion for males and four drinks for females, although other definitions may vary from this). For many young people, alcohol may represent a privilege of adulthood, helping them to feel older and more autonomous. Through drinking alcohol a young person may feel more confident, brave, sociable and relieved from stress. It may be a way to fit in with peers, to seem more attractive to the opposite sex, to fulfil expectations and to experiment with the unknown.

Irish adults have the highest alcohol consumption per drinker and the highest level of binge drinking relative to other European countries (Ramstedt and Hope, 2004). According to O'Connell and colleagues (2003, p. 110), 'The worryingly high levels of alcohol use and alcohol-related harm in Ireland tells us that Irish society can no longer hold its drink.' Irish young people aged 16 or older are among the highest alcohol abusers in Europe in terms of binge drinking and drunkenness. The Lifestyle and Coping Survey (Sullivan et al., 2004), with over 3,800 15- to 17- year-olds in the Irish Southern Health Board region, indicated that over two-thirds had at least one drink weekly, with drinkers typically consuming up to five drinks weekly. Young males drink more than females, and while over a third (36 per cent) had never been 'really drunk' in the past year, 17 per cent said they had been 'really drunk' more than 10 times, with little gender difference in this.

Other Irish research in 2002 found that over two-thirds (71.3 per cent) of the 1,426 adolescents sampled had consumed alcohol, and this had changed little (72.5 per cent) compared to similar research in 1997. Over half reported being regular drinkers, with a slightly greater proportion of females than males (51.9 per cent) being regular drinkers. A clear rise is evident in binge drinking and drunkenness since 1997. Over half the sample (56.3 per cent) reported being drunk 10 or more times by age 17 and overall the percentage of drinkers having 10 or more drinks doubled from 3.5 per cent in 1997 to 6.9 per cent in 2002. The authors concluded that adolescent alcohol use has become a major social and health problem (Flanagan et al., 2003).

However, from 1998 to 2002, the HBSC study reported a decrease in the number of children aged under 15 years experimenting with and consuming alcohol, though no reported change in the drinking patterns of those aged 15 up. In 2002 among the 12- to 14-year-olds, 16 per cent of boys and 12 per cent of girls were current drinkers in comparison to 1998, when 26 per cent of boys and 17 per cent of girls were current drinkers. However, in the 15- to 17-year-old age group, about half of the boys and girls were regular drinkers and drunkenness was also prevalent (60 per cent boys; 56 per cent girls) (Kelleher et al., 2003).

All of these studies highlight how binge drinking has become a 'normal' behaviour for Irish adolescents.

In attempting to understand youth drinking, it is important to recognise four key influences associated with youth drinking (Baer, 2002):

1. **Family history and parental behaviour**: This includes genetics, parents' drinking patterns and parenting skills.
2. **Personality**: In particular, the traits of impulsivity/disinhibition, extroversion/ sociability and neuroticism/emotionality.
3. **Drinking motives, alcohol expectancies and perceived norms**: Drinking as an escape/relief, social reasons, attitudes towards drinking and social norms.
4. **Social affiliation**: Social drinking norms and habits.

Drinking is very much a social activity and young people may be subjected to pressure on their drinking, leading to unhealthy drinking patterns. Drinking can be a competitive and instrumental activity (to gain acceptance, status) rather than a purely social activity.

Attitudes towards drinking and the impact of social and cultural factors have received a lot of attention in the literature on youth drinking.

Attitudes towards Drinking

To fully understand drinking behaviour, it is important to consider young people's attitudes towards drinking.

One study, with a sample of 57 young people (aged 15–19) drawn from inner-city Dublin, identified heavy sessional outdoor drinking as a significant social activity (Mayock, 2004). The principal reason given by young people in this sample for drinking was to get drunk 'to get a buzz'. In a follow-up three years later, the vast majority had established regular drinking patterns by age 18 and practically all reported increased frequency and intensity of alcohol consumption. These developments were closely related to the transition from school (or training) to the workforce and increased attendance at city-centre pubs and clubs (Mayock, 2004, p. 128).

According to Mayock (2004), Irish and British research over recent decades highlights greater experimentation with alcohol and a rise in 'high-risk' drinking behaviour, such as binge drinking and drunkenness, in both youth and young adults. Another rising trend is towards an alcohol-based polydrug behavioural repertoire. This refers to the mixing of alcohol with other psychoactive substances such as ecstasy, cannabis and cocaine. The generalisability of these findings for young people across Ireland is, however, contentious.

Other research found that having generally positive thoughts about binge drinking is the main determinant of binge drinking in adolescent males who tend *not* to consider it as risky and see the adverse consequences of it as acceptable (Dempster et al., 2005). Consequently, tackling attitudes about binge drinking needs to be considered when designing interventions to reduce adolescent binge drinking.

Youth Drinking Culture

Social and cultural factors are also crucial to understanding youth drinking. Much sociological attention has focused on 'wet' and 'dry' cultures and how cultural factors contribute to increased youth drinking. Factors identified include increased affluence, the relative decline in alcohol taxes and increased availability of alcohol. According to the Department of Health and Children's Strategic Task Force on Alcohol (2002b), these all contribute to the sharp growth in alcohol consumption in Ireland. Alcohol advertising also plays a role. Younger teenagers are more susceptible to alcohol advertising 'given that they perceive the advertising messages as saying that alcohol can help them have fun, make friends and become popular and those that don't drink are missing out' (Dring and Hope, 2001, p. 7).

Transformations within the alcohol market have also altered youth drinking culture. These include the diversification of the alcohol market with the introduction of 'designer drinks' and 'alcopops'; the mixing of non-alcoholic mixer drinks containing legal stimulants such as caffeine; the advertising of alcohol as lifestyle markers, associating it with pleasure, fun, being 'cool' and 'attractive'; and the expansion of the pub culture to include 'super pubs' and club bars more appealing to young drinkers, which 'encourage excess rather than moderation' (Mayock, 2004, p. 124).

Consideration of the adverse effects of excess alcohol consumption in young people highlights why it is a key policy concern.

Adverse Effects

Alcohol is estimated to cause one in four of all deaths of young men aged 15 to 29 years in Europe. The majority of these deaths result from injuries (unintentional and intentional). For young men, alcohol contributes to nearly half of all deaths from motor vehicle accidents, over one-third of poisonings, drownings, homicide and falls and in one-fifth of suicides. For young women aged 15 to 29 years, alcohol contributes to about one in three of all deaths from poisonings, drownings and homicide, and one in five deaths from motor vehicle accidents and falls. Other adverse health consequences include destructive behaviour, risk of assault, aggressiveness, mood swings, academic underachievement, unprotected sex and delinquency. It is also a contributory factor in self-harm (intentional and unintentional) and suicide, the leading cause of death in Irish males aged 15 to 35 years (Hutchison et al., 1998; Skegg, 2005).

The Strategic Task Force on Alcohol (STFA) (2004) made a number of recommendations on reducing alcohol-related problems in adolescence, including a significant reduction in the exposure of alcohol marketing to children and young people; greater regulation in the availability of alcohol; the promotion of alcohol-free sporting environments; health education; and improved support services. Alcohol-free alternatives such as youth cafés were recommended by STFA (2004) as important for consideration.

Smoking

Like alcohol consumption, smoking is another risky behaviour, which is a 'rite of passage' for young people. A young person may smoke simply to 'try it out', to 'fit in' with a peer group, to feel 'cool' or better about themselves and the image they project or as an act of defiance or resistance to authority.

In the 1980s Grube and Morgan (1986) found over two-thirds (67 per cent) of Irish 13- to 17-year-olds had smoked and nearly a quarter (24 per cent) were regular smokers. In 2002 research that was part of the HBSC study found that 41 per cent of Irish young people had smoked a cigarette, 19 per cent (17 per cent male; 20 per cent female) of whom were current smokers. This was less than previous years. Typically rates of young people reporting *ever* having smoked increase with age and are lower than the international average.

Comparing research with Irish young people in 1997 to similar research in 2002, Flanagan and colleagues (2003) found:

- A decline in the number of regular smokers from 40.7 per cent in 1997 to 18.2 per cent in 2002.
- A decline in the number of male regular smokers from 29.7 per cent in 1997 to 16 per cent in 2002.
- A rise in the number of female regular smokers from 21.6 per cent in 1997 to 32.2 per cent in 2002.
- A rise in the number of cigarettes smoked by regular smokers.

Over 83 per cent of the regular smokers reported buying their cigarettes themselves despite the fact that it is illegal to sell cigarettes to those aged under 18.

Over recent years the rate of adolescent smoking has dropped, although the numbers of young women smoking have increased. Smoking now seems to have become more normative for young Irish women but less so for young Irish men. Irish young women now have higher rates of lifetime and current smoking than young men, which is consistent with international research (HSE, 2003).

By the age of 15 young women outnumber young men internationally as having smoked (Currie et al., 2003).

Research by the Office of Tobacco Control (2006) revealed that 16 per cent of Irish 12- to 17-year-olds smoke and that the average number of cigarettes smoked by young people was around 10 per day. Most opted for packs of 10 cigarettes and 77 per cent indicated that they would be 'fairly or very unlikely to continue smoking' if the price of cigarettes doubled. Most also saw the prospect of having to purchase a pack of 20 as a disincentive to purchasing cigarettes.

The report identified that 23 per cent of young smokers sourced their first cigarettes from shops and an overwhelming 92 per cent of young people report not being asked for identification the last time they purchased cigarettes.

Another study found that while over half of the Irish teenagers surveyed did not smoke and nearly one-fifth had given up, more young women than men smoked and more of them were heavy smokers (50 cigarettes or more per day) (Sullivan et al., 2004).

Age at onset of first smoking influences future regularity of smoking. The Irish average age for having the first cigarette is 12 years, consistent with international data (Currie et al., 2003). The earlier a person tries smoking, the higher the risk of becoming a regular smoker and the more difficult it is to quit (National Centre for Tobacco-Free Kids, 2002 in HSE, 2003). The longer the onset of smoking is delayed, the less likely a person is to become addicted.

Overall, these studies show that while the numbers of young people smoking is still a concern, the rate of teenage smoking is dropping. The rise in the number of young women smoking, though, is a serious worry and may be related to body image and weight management, as smoking is perceived by many to be an appetite suppressant. The fact that young people who are regular smokers are now smoking *more* cigarettes is another concern (Currie et al., 2003), along with the apparent ease with which young people can purchase cigarettes in Ireland (often using the excuse that the purchase was for parents) (Hanrahan, 2002). Economic improvement with the 'Celtic Tiger' may mean young people have more money to spend on cigarettes. Even though young people may use older friends and siblings to purchase cigarettes, the enforcement of legislation on the sale of cigarettes to young people seems to be of limited effect.

Influential Factors

As with alcohol consumption, many factors influence whether or not young people try out smoking or become regular smokers.

A variety of theories have been applied to adolescent smoking behaviour. The theory of reasoned action identifies the role of perceived beliefs about others (a young person's beliefs about what others would think about their smoking) and the perceived social consequences of smoking (higher status, attractiveness, or 'street cred' or the opposite). Building on this theory, Morgan and Grube (1994) identified two key normative influences on adolescent smoking behaviour:

- **Behavioural norms:** Beliefs about the extent to which significant others engage in smoking themselves.
- **Perceived approval:** Beliefs about the extent to which parents or peers may approve or disapprove of the smoking behaviour.

A young person is more likely to smoke if people they hold in esteem smoke and if they see it as acceptable, 'cool' or advantageous.

Social-learning theory emphasises the role of observational learning and the modelling of smoking behaviour by significant others. According to this theory, young people smoke because they see others smoking in their environment and view the consequences of smoking as favourable. Seeing others you know smoke normalises the behaviour. It is thus understandable why a young person smokes if exposed to family or friends who smoke. In terms of perceived positive consequences, these may include smoking being seen as 'adult-like', 'cool' or 'sociable' behaviour. However, this theory seems better able to explain smoking maintenance than smoking initiation (Hoffman et al., 2006).

According to problem-behaviour theory, smoking is one of a number of high-risk 'deviant' behaviours such as illicit drug use and delinquency. From this perspective, the combination of a young person's personality (such as rebelliousness) and environment (peers who smoke) contributes to such behaviour. Consequently it is understandable why other risky behaviours are associated with smoking in adolescence and vice versa.

Other theories emphasise the role of smoking as a coping adaptation, a way of dealing with stress and the role of external influences, such as conformity and subcultural identity (ibid).

From all of these theories it is clear that there is no single cause of smoking in adolescence, rather it depends on a mixture of factors within any one young person's socio-cultural context. These theories can also be applied to adolescent drinking and illicit substance use.

Adverse Features

Smoking causes approximately 90 per cent of lung cancer deaths, 25 per cent of deaths from heart disease and approximately 75 per cent of deaths from bronchitis and emphysema (ASH, 2001). Young people are aware of the health sequelae of smoking although they underestimate their severity and tend to focus on the perceived immediate attractions of smoking (attracting members of the opposite sex, coping with stress and weight control or loss) rather than the long-term effects (Verduykt, 2002).

A number of anti-smoking health programmes and initiatives have been put in place over recent decades, which are contributing to smoking becoming a less socially acceptable behaviour. Advertising bans, the prohibition of smoking in public buildings, high taxation on cigarettes and anti-smoking advertising campaigns have added to this. How effective these will be with young people, and with girls in particular, is unclear.

Illicit Drug Use

Drugs are the most important social issue to be faced in contemporary Ireland according to Irish young people (National Youth Council of Ireland, 2000). Ireland currently has one of the most 'drug-experienced' youth populations in the EU

(European Monitoring Centre for Drugs and Drug Addiction, 2003). Encountering (and often taking) drugs, alcohol or smoking may be considered a 'rite of passage' for adolescents today. As noted by Sweeney and Dunne (2003, p. 10), 'it is difficult for parents and teachers to grasp the extent to which handling situations where drugs are introduced and used constitutes a veritable rite of passage, an almost unavoidable defining moment for the Irish teenager today.'

Illicit drug use has become more normal for young people in Ireland today. It is no longer an extreme form of deviance but is associated with other problem behaviours such as anti-social behaviour and truancy. Parker, Aldridge and Measham (2005) in the UK contend that certain drugs (cannabis, amphetamines, LSD and nitrates) have become 'normalised' in adolescence. Normalisation, however, does not mean that these drugs have become 'normally used' by young people. Rather it means a drug has become less deviant, less 'on the margins' of deviant activity. According to Parker and colleagues (2005), normalisation is characterised by particular criteria, including ease of drug availability; frequency of drug trying; recreational patterns of drug use; and young people being 'drug-wise' (knowledgeable on drug use and misuse and safety measures). Heroin and cocaine are drugs that do not fulfil these criteria in contemporary Ireland.

In attempting to understand adolescent drug use, it is important to consider factors such as risk-taking, identity formation, peer influence and the socio-cultural context of drug use. As with alcohol consumption or smoking, taking drugs may represent a way to assert identity, to rebel against others or the 'establishment', to fit in with others, to appear 'cool' or 'attractive' to others or simply just to 'try it out'. Nearly one-fifth of Irish young people report using drugs or alcohol to cope with 'feeling down' (Lalor and Baird, 2006). The role of cultural factors in teenage drug use also cannot be ignored. Paramilitary group involvement and the impact of ceasefires on drug trafficking and supply, for example, contributed to an escalation in substance use in young people in Northern Ireland (Higgins et al., 2004).

Generally, problem drug use is associated with areas of socio-economic disadvantage and poor facilities (at least for some drugs such as heroin), though general drug use is common across the range of socio-economic and urban or rural communities. In the rural mid-west of Ireland, over one-third (39.4) of young people have used an illicit drug, with 15.4 per cent reporting being current users, representing a rise in the region over recent years. Cannabis and solvents or inhalants (aerosols and glue) were the most common drugs used (Health Services Executive, 2003).

In 2002, Irish research compared to a similar study in 1997 found:

- An increased rate of young people having taken an illicit drug (41.2 per cent in 2002; 34.9 per cent in 1997).
- A diminished gender difference since 1997, with young men and women now similar in illicit drug use.
- A rise in the proportion of teenagers using drugs regularly (15.1 per cent in 2002; 11.9 per cent in 1997).

- 'Discos' and 'on the street' are the most common places where drugs are offered.
- Regular smokers and regular drinkers are more likely to be offered, to have taken and to be regular users of drugs.
- Cannabis (12.5 per cent), glue or solvents (2.5 per cent) and ecstasy (1.3 per cent) to be the most common drugs used.
- The most common reason for taking drugs to be because 'the people they hang around with do it' (58.6 per cent), followed by 'just to try it out' (52.4 per cent).
- Overall, no relationship is present between social class and illicit drug use (Flanagan et al., 2003).

On the other hand, in the Lifestyle and Coping survey over a third of young men (37.4 per cent) and over a quarter of young women (27 per cent) had taken an illegal drug in the past year and marijuana was the most commonly used illegal drug. Ecstasy, heroin and speed were some of the other drugs mentioned (Sullivan et al., 2004).

Lower rates of drug use have been reported in other research. In the HBSC study over a quarter (25.5 per cent) of Irish 15-year-old males, in contrast to 14.4 per cent of females, used cannabis in the past 12 months. While the male rate was slightly higher than the average HBSC 15-year-old male (21.7 per cent), the Irish female rate was slightly lower than the average HBSC female 15-year-old rate (16 per cent) (Kelleher et al., 2003).

Trends in Drug Use

Trends in drug use vary across time, age and location. Solvents are used more by younger adolescents, while cannabis, ecstasy and LSD are used more by older adolescents (Flanagan et al., 2003). In general, short-term, experimental use of inhalants is common, at least in certain areas of the country.

Research undertaken by the Kilbarrack Coast Community Programme in 2004 with young people found cannabis to be the most used illicit drug, particularly by older teenagers. More than one-third had used cannabis at some point and over one-fifth (20 per cent) had used it in the past month. Interestingly, the rate of current cannabis use by young people was only slightly lower than the rate of current tobacco use (25 per cent). Slightly more young men than women were users. Small numbers reported ever using ecstasy (4 per cent), LSD (under 3 per cent), prescription drugs (8 per cent), cocaine (6 per cent) or heroin (under 1 per cent).

In terms of age when drugs are first tried, research in inner-city Dublin identified 13.2 years as the average age of onset for drug users in general and 12.4 years for problem drug users. Most young people were introduced to drugs by a close friend or peer, and all, from an early age, had a high degree of exposure to drugs in their local environment (Mayock, 2000).

Rates of illicit drug use amongst Irish young people have visibly increased and now young women appear to be nearly as likely to use drugs as young men. While the most common drugs used vary over time and location, a general trend is evident in terms of solvents in early adolescence and cannabis, ecstasy and other drugs in older adolescence. Drug use is clearly associated with drinking and smoking and is strongly anchored in the peer group. In addition, it is strongly concentrated in areas with high social adversity, that is, areas, very often inner city, with public housing and socio-economic disadvantage (Fahey, 1999). Recent Irish research, though, has drawn attention to the ready availability of drugs, including heroin, beyond inner cities, to young people in the Midlands (McElwee and Monaghan, 2005).

Reasons for Taking Drugs

The most common reason for taking drugs is peer influence. Most young people take drugs because 'the people they hang around with do it' (Flanagan et al., 2003 p. 5). The most common reasons found by other research include 'to see what it was like' (64 per cent), 'their friends do it' (63 per cent) or 'to act cool' (54 per cent) (Kilbarrack Coast Community Project, 2004). Other research has highlighted that the time-distorting properties of some drugs are part of their attraction; they make time go slower (Abbott-Chapman, 2000). Generally, young people who use drugs have friends who use the same drugs and are considerably less likely to have friends who don't use drugs. Many of the theories outlined in the discussion on smoking have also been applied to drug use, particularly problem-behaviour theory, construing drug use as a form of rebelliousness and deviance. However, among Irish adolescents, unlike their American counterparts, drug use seems relatively independent of a general tendency towards deviance (Grube and Morgan, 1990).

Others contend that adolescent drug abuse is a progression from problems in childhood, resulting in attention being focused on factors placing children at risk for drug abuse. These include low self-esteem; academic failure; sensation-seeking; poverty; family conflict; and alienation. Risk indices are used to assess the combined influence of risk factors and protective factors, the latter serving to inhibit, reduce or buffer the probability of drug use or abuse. Irish research suggests that the number of risk factors experienced is an important predictor of the level of substance use a person engages in, especially peer-related factors such as peer substance use (Brinkley et al., 2003). Peers, though, seem to be more important for the initiation of substance use, while family- and social-related factors appear more important for increased drug involvement (ibid).

Examining drug use as a risky behaviour, Paula Mayock (2005) explored how young people in Dublin (from 1998–2001) rationalise their history of drug use. This research illuminated the 'habituation' or normalisation of such risk-taking behaviour in a particular social group. The majority of drug takers were initially daily cannabis smokers, but by 2001 these young people had sampled at least five drugs and a large number had become cocaine users. In their stories or 'scripts' of drug taking, social aspects of drug taking were predominant, including self-indulgence, pleasure and the recognition that risk-taking was intrinsic to the psychoactive 'hit'. In the words of one drug taker, 'Oh, don't get me wrong I think ecstasy is really dangerous myself, you know what I mean? But sometimes it's the risk that gets you' (Mayock, 2005, p. 355).

The narratives illuminated the 'normality' rather than the 'deviancy' of drug taking, emphasising social and recreational aspects and the 'situationally appropriate nature of socialising on drugs' (ibid). Young people differentiated between recreational and compulsive drug use, reflecting different lifestyle choices. The picture painted of recreational drug taking was that it was a positive part of life, conferring social and personal rewards such as status, social expression and style. It did not detract from their world of work and other responsibilities. Drug users did not portray themselves as helpless victims but rather as people who exercised choice and control over their drug use.

However, the interviews simultaneously illuminated the influence of *social context and constrained choice* on drug use over the adolescent years (ibid). The transition to intravenous drug use, for example, 'arose out of the need to feel normal under mounting financial pressure' (ibid p. 360). Extending drug use was not seen as a significant added risk by these young people. In making the transition to new drugs, 'prior sensitivities to danger and potential harm subsided and were replaced by feelings of relative invulnerability. These shifts transpired, often gradually, through immersion in drug scenes, often with experienced colleagues or mentors. In this way, new definitions of "normal" risk were introduced and learned casually through participation' (Mayock, 2005, p. 357).

For young people who initially were not drug takers, hanging out with drug users altered how they thought about drugs, leading many to modify their previous anti-drug stance. Young drug takers take risks while simultaneously attempting to reduce harm; for example, sipping water while taking ecstasy and staggering drug use over a night out. Risk socialisation in the drug-taking peer group such as passing on advice also acted to reduce harm. Overall Mayock's (2005) research showed that risky behaviour, in the form of drug use, was not undertaken purely for the benefit of risk, but rather more for social and individual factors. Socialisation played a key role in 'normalising' the risk and constrained choice and opportunities appeared to contribute to a greater likelihood of drug use. Decision-making on risk in terms of drug use was rarely based on expert warnings, but rather on ongoing social and personal experience.

Adverse Effects

Illicit drug use is associated with a wide breadth of adverse physical, psychological and social outcomes. Cardiac or respiratory failure, permanent organ damage, cancer, impaired cognition and neurological damage are some of the harmful consequences of taking heroin, cannabis, cocaine and inhalants. Drug use often occurs with other psychological problems, such as conduct disorder, attention deficit hyperactivity disorder (ADHD) and depression. In addition, early onset of drug use is associated with serious and more enduring patterns of use in later years (Fergusson and Horwood, 1997).

Prevention Programmes

Two conceptual positions underpin drug education or prevention programmes. At one end is the primary prevention 'total abstinence' approach. This is based on encouraging young people to 'say no' to drugs, education on the effects of drugs and fostering skills to bolster self-image and resist peer pressure. To be more effective, such programmes also need to focus on resistance to social pressures, ideally by using same-aged peer leaders as teachers of the programme. The schools-based Relationships and Sex Education programme addresses aspects of these. Fostering self-esteem alone, though, seems to have little effect in reducing smoking or other unhealthy risk behaviours.

At the opposite end are 'harm-reduction' programmes. These aim to limit the health and social risks associated with drug use, accepting that drug offers will happen and that drug use is likely to happen (Mayock, 2000). A slow shift towards the latter position is now evident, particularly with young people who have already experimented with drugs. Many such programmes now use a peer-led approach, involving drug-experienced young people as leaders of the programme. As leaders they may be easier to relate to, to learn from as a model and may be less judgmental than adults or professionals (Shiner and Newburn, 1996).

In Ireland, programmes are in place with a harm-reduction perspective targeted at youth at risk in their local context. However, according to Mayock (2005), such programmes need to focus more on the 'risk environments' that create vulnerability to risky drug-use practices, recognising the role of social and cultural factors on drug use and what is construed as risky (ibid). Early intervention is needed with young people living in areas where drug use is concentrated, particularly with young people there who are already marginalised and vulnerable, such as poor school attendees. Such programmes also need to tackle drug use according to the meaning and role it has for young people in the area.

Some people argue for legislative changes for the decriminalisation of cannabis and marijuana, contending that this would reduce the criminal risk associated with drug use. While cannabis use is illegal in most countries, this has little bearing on the growing number of young people internationally who perceive it as normal and part of their peer group culture (Nic Gabhainn in Currie et al., 2003). However, the extent to which legalisation of particular drugs would reduce the risk and harm associated with drug use in general is seriously contentious. Additionally, regardless of the relative risks of various drugs, all drug use should be regarded as potentially problematic. Others argue for stronger social controls, such as policing. They point to the ease with which young people can obtain illicit drugs as reflecting the inadequacy of social controls on drug trafficking and distribution (Hibbell et al., 2000).

SEXUAL HEALTH

According to the World Health Organisation (1984 in National Youth Council of Ireland, 2004a) sexual health is 'the integration of the physical, emotional, intellectual and social aspects of sexual being, in ways that are enriching and that enhance personality, communication and love'. It requires a 'positive and respectful approach to sexuality and sexual relationships as well as the possibility of having pleasurable and safe sexual experiences, free from coercion, discrimination and violence' (National Youth Council of Ireland, 2004a, p. 14).

Table 5.2 Sexual Health

Integral to sexual health is:

- Knowledge about the body and how it works.
- Feeling good and comfortable about one's body.
- Being able to express oneself as one chooses.
- Being able to negotiate safe sex.
- Being able to have enjoyable friendships with both sexes.
- Being able to discuss sexual (inc. health) concerns with professionals.
- Being able to challenge norms and beliefs about how males and females should behave with each other.

Source: NYCI (2004a).

Central to sexual health is safe sex and an awareness of and ability to seek help for sexually transmitted infections (STIs).

Sexually Transmitted Infections

Diagnoses of STIs in Ireland have risen dramatically over recent decades (2,228 in 1989 to 8,869 in 2000 to 11,153 in 2003). Anogenital warts, chlamydia trachomatis and non-specific urethritis are the three most common (in that order) for Irish young people aged under 19 in 2003. In 2003, 11 per cent of notified cases of STIs were aged under 19 years, highlighting the significance of sexual health as a health concern for young people. Greater public awareness, testing and attendance at STI clinics undoubtedly contributed to this, although the number of cases of gonorrhoea and chlamydia notified are underrepresented due to their asymptomatic nature.

Chlamydia, a bacterial STI, is of particular concern as approximately 50 per cent of females and 70 per cent of males show *no* symptoms but, if left untreated, it can result in infertility (Fullerton, 2004). For this reason it is called the 'silent epidemic'. Risk factors for chlamydia include more than one sexual partner in the past six months, more than eight lifetime sexual partners and/or current symptoms (dysuria or discharge) (Health Services Executive, 2003).

In addressing adolescent sexual health, as well as greater information on STIs, a number of other factors need to be considered. Alcohol- or drug-induced loss of inhibition is a significant factor in sexual risk-taking. Health promotion and sexual education thus need to warn how alcohol or drugs affect judgment, including the use of contraception for safe sex (Fullerton, 2004). Assertiveness and behavioural change in the context of relationships and sexuality is also needed, as many young people who are informed on STIs still engage in high-risk sexual behaviour (MacHale and Newell, 1997). A more liberal social climate towards sexuality with greater openness about sexuality is also protective.

Figure 5.3 An ideal sexual health service for young people

An Ideal Sexual Health Service for Young People

- Games and activities on offer
- Informality and absence of appointment system
- Accessible drop-in centre
- Generic name
- Provide advice on a range of issues
- Friendly, non-judgmental staff – male and female
- Address concerns about confidentiality
- Free contraceptives
- Short waiting times
- Low-cost or free service
- Promoting the service through helpline/ website posters/ leaflets, booklets
- Flexible opening hours – weekends and evenings

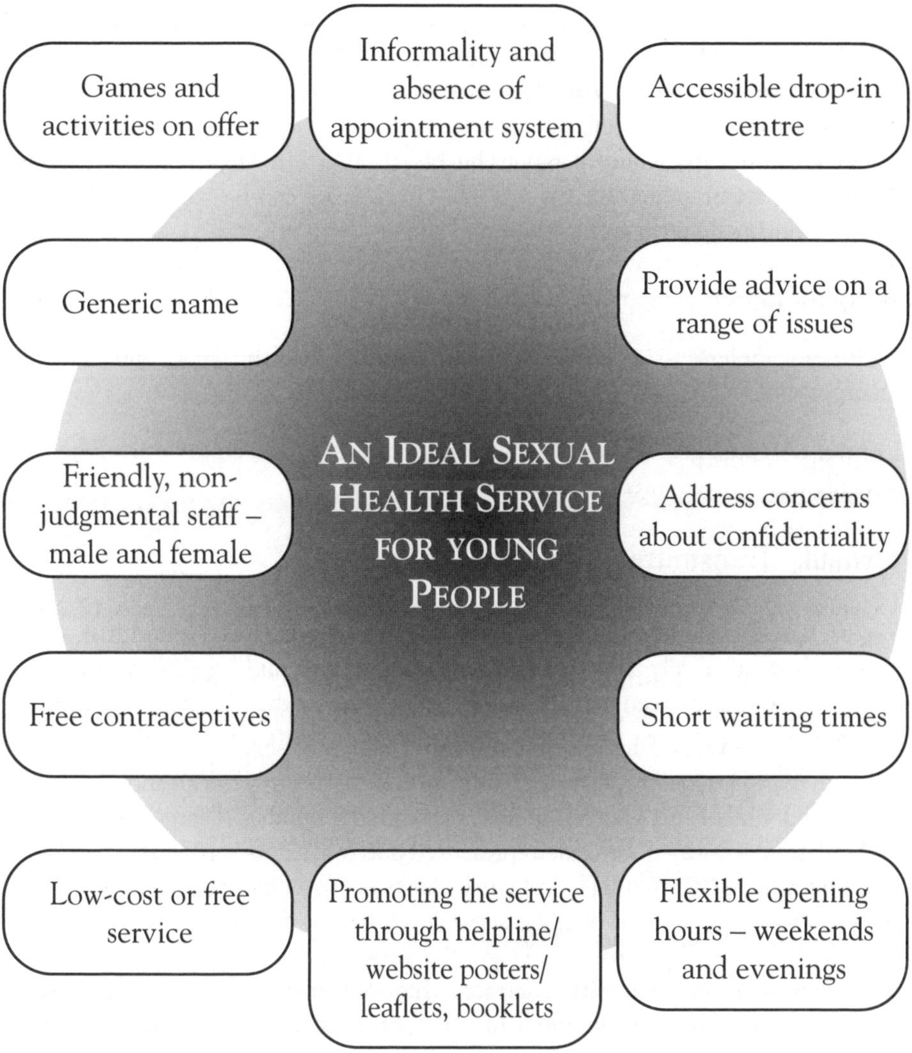

Source: North Western Area Health Board (2004a).

Looking at contraception use and *use* of sexual health services, the three As – awareness, availability and accessibility – are critical in understanding usage rates for any population group.

- **Awareness:** Knowledge of sexual health services, different types of contraception and their use and the overall importance and need for contraception use. Many young people may not know what to do if a pill is missed or if they experience medical complications.
- **Availability:** Prevalence of sexual health services (geographical convenience), degree of choice offered on contraception and ease of use.
- **Accessibility:** Ease of access to sexual health services, opening times and approachability of staff. Ease of access to different forms of contraception, cost and location of vending machines or pharmacies are also relevant here. Contraceptive services tend to be more effective when in youth-oriented clinics.

From research with young people, the North Western Health Board (2004a) outlined an 'ideal' sexual health service. This service can be seen to address the three As outlined above and is illustrated above.

Well-Being

Well-being refers to general, everyday mental health. It is multifaceted, incorporating:

- Absence of distress.
- Happiness.
- Life satisfaction.
- Health.

Research undertaken for the HBSC study (Kelleher et al., 2003) found Irish young people show relatively high levels of self-rated health and happiness. Well over three-quarters (86 per cent) of 10- to 17-year-olds report their health as being 'good' or 'excellent' and 88 per cent report being 'very' or 'quite happy' with their lives. Gender differences are present, with young females less likely than young males to report being 'very happy' and to report their health as being 'excellent'. This difference between the sexes increases with age as females report a decline in health and happiness across age.

Factors which Compromise Well-Being

In attempting to uncover what compromises well-being in young people, research has investigated the problems and difficulties that young people encounter, their sources of anxiety and worry.

Problems with schoolwork (34.8 per cent), difficulties with parents (28.7 per cent) and/or friends (26.1 per cent) and a family illness or accident (17.8 per cent) are the most common problems in young people (Sullivan et al., 2004). Young women are more likely to report schoolwork problems, relationship difficulties with friends, boyfriends and parents and to be affected by their parents' arguments.

In 2006, research by Lalor and Baird (2006) found 'failing exams' and 'being bored/having nothing to do' to be the most common concerns experienced by young people in Kildare. Unhappiness with physical appearance, boy or girlfriend problems and not feeling part of a group were also widespread concerns. Almost one-third worry about their parents or guardians not getting on; 17 per cent worry about parental or guardian separation or divorce; 13 per cent worry about a parent's or guardian's drink problem; and 11 per cent worry about a parent's or guardian's mental health (ibid). The impact of parental or guardian issues on young people's mental health clearly should not be neglected.

Of 1,422 Leaving Certificate pupils in County Kerry, over two-thirds (66 per cent), especially females, understandably identified the Leaving Certificate exams as being a source of considerable stress for fear of doing badly. After this, career choice (46 per cent), being criticised or mocked (35 per cent), bullying (35 per cent), feeling unattractive (33 per cent; especially females), being ignored (32 per cent; especially females) and strained parental relationships (31 per cent) were the more prominent concerns. Other frequent concerns included peer rejection, boy or girlfriend relationships, alcoholism in the family and family problems such as poor communication and lack of finance (Kerry Mental Health Association, 2001). Overall, this study concluded that the majority of young people report coping 'fairly well' with the stress in their lives. However, a sizeable minority (6.4 per cent) report extreme levels of stress and 4.4 per cent feel they can't cope. Inappropriate coping strategies such as alcohol or drug abuse, feelings of hopelessness and self-derision and low social involvement, all of which contribute to depression, were associated more with the latter group. Gender differences are again very prominent, with young females more stressed than young males, consistent with international research trends.

Sexuality is another issue that influences a young person's well-being, with concerns regarding sexual orientation and pressure to be sexually active potentially compromising well-being (National Youth Council of Ireland, 2004b). The particular problems faced by young people who are gay, lesbian or bisexual have already been discussed in Chapter 4.

In Northern Ireland, research suggests that political conflict does not necessarily, in a general way, impact negatively on well-being. While the Troubles have been associated with behavioural adjustment difficulties and externalising behaviours, commitment to a group ideology may act as a buffer, contributing to resilience (Muldoon et al., 2000). On the other hand, such an ideological commitment may increase young people's engagement with the conflict, leading to more polarised and intransigent attitudes, which in turn sustain the conflict at a societal level (Muldoon, 2001).

Another way to assess young people's problems is by analysing reasons young people give for making calls to helplines. The ISPCC annual report for 2006 (www.ispcc.ie), for example, indicated that out of 203,593 calls answered by Childline in 2005, the following problems were the most common concerns of the calls:

- Sexual issues 9.2 per cent.
- Pregnancy 4.7 per cent.
- Bullying 4.7 per cent.
- Physical abuse 3.7 per cent.
- Boy/girlfriend problems 2.9 per cent.
- Relationships with parents 2.8 per cent.
- Sexual abuse 2.6 per cent.
- Relationships with friends 2 per cent.

It should be noted that these percentages are low given the high number of calls that were simply contact calls or calls reflecting a combination of reasons.

As these only represent the concerns of young people who have made a call to this helpline, it is questionable how representative these problems are of young people as a whole. However, many of these problems do feature prominently in research studies previously discussed.

Factors which Enhance Well-Being

In trying to discover, in practical terms, what boosts the well-being of young people, many studies have examined what makes young people feel happy and good about their lives. Happiness and health are associated with physical participation in life, with happiness in particular linked with spending time with friends, taking part in life and with a sense of belonging within families and communities. Unhappiness, on the other hand, is particularly associated with relationship difficulties (O'Higgins, 2002). Gender differences occur, with teenage girls reporting relationships having a greater impact on their health and happiness than teenage boys. The latter were also more likely than teenage girls to attach more importance to future plans and a sense of anticipation of life events to come (ibid).

Using an innovative approach with Irish children and young people, Nic Gabhainn and Sixsmith (2005) explored well-being, as part of the development of children's well-being indictors under the National Children's Strategy (Department of Health and Children, 2000). Participants were asked to take photographs of anything that contributed to their well-being. In classifying these photographs, they identified what children and young people see as contributing to their well-being, outlined below, in order of rank.

Other factors that were mentioned frequently included 'environment or places', 'houses or bedroom' and 'food' and 'money or jobs' and 'role models' from follow-on focus groups. Overall a broad variety of factors contributed to making young people 'feel good', but the primacy of interpersonal relationships with family and friends stood out. This is consistent with international research that identified the ability 'to get on with others' as intrinsic to young people's well-being.

In agreement with these findings, the National Youth Health Programme (2004) identified protective factors that enhance a young person's resilience (maintenance of well-being in the presence of adversity). These include individual factors such as self-esteem, an easy temperament, leisure interests and intelligence; family factors such as a supportive, stable family; social factors such as a sense of belonging, friends, a pro-social peer group and opportunities for recognition; life events such as good physical health and economic security; and community factors such as an attachment to community networks, a strong cultural identity and ethnic pride, access to support services and cultural norms against violence.

Bolstering these factors is a significant way to enhance the young people's well-being and overall mental health. The SPHE/RSE programme as well as the programmes and services offered by youth clubs and groups and sporting and cultural organisations represent ways in which this is carried out.

Table 5.3 Factors contributing to well-being

	Teenage girls	Teenage boys
1.	friends	friends
2.	family	TV/video-games
3.	pets/animals	sports/teams
4.	sports/teams	music
5.	music	pets/animals

Source: Nic Gabhainn and Sixsmith (2005).

Self-Esteem

Self-esteem is integral to well-being. Self-esteem is affected by any developmental transition and adolescence especially is a time when self-esteem is quite vulnerable. Physical, emotional and mental changes of this period contribute to this, along with mourning for the passing of childhood. In Irish young people, males and younger adolescents report higher self-esteem. Only a very small proportion of young people show 'very low' or 'very high' self-esteem. More modest reporting by young women, though, may explain the gender difference, although this is not definitive. As found elsewhere, social class appears to have no striking bearing on young people's self-esteem (Nic Gabhainn and Mullan, 2003).

Enhancing personal awareness, self-acceptance, relationship skills and self-confidence are all ways of building self-esteem. While some research has contended that enhancing adolescent self-esteem is a means of protecting against involvement in so-called health risk behaviours, recent Irish research found little support for this in relation to smoking, alcohol consumption and cannabis use (Mullan and NicGabhainn, 2002). The authors concluded that low self-esteem is too simple an explanation for why young people engage in smoking, drinking or drug use. 'Efforts need to move beyond a focus on the individual and on self-esteem as a type of inoculation, toward a focus on the "meaning" of different health behaviours to young people and the social environment within which this is constructed' (ibid, p. 34).

Body Image

Body image and self-esteem are seen as synonymous in terms of their importance in shaping how young people feel about themselves, with body image influencing self-esteem and vice versa. For teenagers, being popular is related to appearance and image. Three key variables influence the young person's emotional evaluation of, and adaptation to, her or his changing physique:

- The evaluations, reactions and impressions of others.
- Personality variables such as self-esteem.
- Socio-cultural factors such as cultural standards of attractiveness (Petersen and Taylor, 1980).

In general, young males evaluate their growing body more in terms of body efficiency and physical ability.

Young women, on the other hand, evaluate themselves more in terms of physical attractiveness and the reactions of others. In comparison to young men, they are more dissatisfied with their bodies, wanting to be thinner (even more so than healthier) and more influenced by the media (Trew et al., 2006).

Girls from a young age are exposed to highly valued cultural ideals of the female body. With adolescence, the desire to change their looks to be in more in keeping with these ideals contributes to reduced self-esteem, dieting and eating disorders. Some theorists argue that the contemporary ideal of female beauty as slender or thin (sometimes a 'prepubertal' look) has contributed to a devaluation of the typical mature female body. This ideal of a tall and thin figure is realistically normal for only a minority of women, yet many young and adult women feel pressurised to attain this figure.

The HBSC study revealed that dissatisfaction with body weight is common in young people, especially young women, and increases over adolescence (Currie et al., 2003). Critical to this is their *perception* of being overweight and dissatisfaction with body size, rather than their *actual* weight, as a reason for teenage female dieting and weight control behaviour (ibid). From the HBSC study, nearly a quarter of Irish 15-year-old females (23.5 per cent) and 5.5 per cent of their male counterparts engage in dieting and weight-control behaviour such as exercising to lose weight. These statistics are similar to the international average reported for the 35 participating countries (ibid).

In 2005 another Irish study with 2,260 12- to 18-year-olds found that over 65 per cent reported being happy with the way they look. However, significant gender differences were evident, with over three-quarters (77 per cent) of the males but only just over half (53 per cent) of the females being happy with their looks (de Róiste and Dinneen, 2005). There is a positive change across the adolescent years in male body image, with 78.4 per cent of 12-year-old males being happy with the way they look compared to 85 per cent of 17-year-olds. On the other hand, for females a negative trend is evident: 62.1 per cent of 12-year-old girls being happy with the way they look compared to only 54.7 per cent of 17-year-olds (ibid). Again, this is in agreement with international trends.

Given this trend it is understandable that dieting and weight control are more prevalent in adolescence, especially in young women. Many Irish young people eat a restricted diet based on low-fat foods in the bid to become thin. Such low-fat diets are often short on essential fatty acids and the fat necessary for brain and nervous system development. Nutritional needs increase across the adolescent years although there is wide variation across individuals. The relationship between body image and dieting may be also linked to 'a refusal to grow up', a rejection of femininity or a reaction to criticism or ridicule. Dieting in turn can make young women dislike themselves and their bodies more because they often fail at it.

Irish adolescent health practices are often motivated, at least in part, by self-presentation or 'image' concerns.

Body image and ideal body size in particular can act as strong motivators for girls and young women to exercise, especially in late adolescence. However, others may experience this in the opposite way, with their body image acting as a barrier to their engagement in various forms of recreation (Hendry et al., 1993). A North Western Health Board study illuminated the complexity of this issue, particularly in relation to girls and young women: 'You need confidence to go out and do activity, so that you're not worried about what people are thinking of you and how you are going to look. You think to yourself "I can't wear that until I lose some weight", but you won't lose it if you don't do any activity' (North Western Health Board, 2004b, p. 14). Interestingly, in relation to this young women very dissatisfied with their bodies are more likely to exercise in private settings and are less likely to play team sports (Kowalski et al., 2000). Encouragement to engage in individual, less public exercise such as walking or exercising to a video or DVD thus may be beneficial.

In terms of maintaining and improving body image and self-esteem, Ikeda and Naworkski (1992) identified four key conditions:

- **A sense of connectiveness:** Enabling young people to forge strong links and feel secure to the people and places around them.
- **A sense of uniqueness:** Reinforcing a young person's unique qualities, identifying how important they are to the person and to others around them. The objective of this is to reduce the experiences of feeling 'odd' and 'not fitting in' with others.
- **A sense of power:** Assisting and empowering young people to make choices and decisions and to take responsibility for their actions. This in turn reduces feelings of powerlessness and vulnerability.
- **A sense of role models:** Role models represent the standards and values young people aspire to and help a young person to make sense of the world. Positive

role models who do not have the ideal body image encourage young people to feel better about their own body image.

MENTAL HEALTH

While there are many different definitions of mental health, most recognise that it is more than just the absence of disorder. Rather, it encompasses concepts such as well-being, personal autonomy and the ability to realise one's potential in life. It is inherently contextual, influenced not just by physical health, but also by the social and cultural environment.

Mental health is an integral component of health through which a person realises his or her own cognitive, emotional and relational abilities. Mental health in children and young people has been defined by the (British) Health Advisory Service (1995) as:

- A capacity to enter into and sustain mutually satisfying personal relationships.
- A continuing progression of psychological development.
- An ability to play and learn so that attainments are appropriate for age and intellectual level.
- A developing moral sense of right and wrong, not necessarily present when psychological distress or maladaptive behaviour is appropriate, given a child or young person's age or context.

This definition recognises that mental health is multifaceted and inextricably linked with development within a social context. It recognises how development may be hindered and relationships disturbed when mental health problems are experienced. Examples of mental health or 'psychological' problems in adolescents include eating disorders, anxiety disorders, addictions, depression, deliberate self-harm and suicide.

Given the number of changes and transitions young people experience across adolescence, many would argue that it is understandable if mental health problems become more pronounced at this time. However, the majority of Irish young people do **not** have mental health problems, but a minority do show signs of depression (20 per cent) or anxiety (26 per cent), particularly teenage girls (Sullivan et al., 2004). Eating disorders, self-harm and body dysmorphic disorder all peak in adolescence and all are more prevalent in females (House et al., 1999). Similarly, other research estimates that over one-fifth of Irish young people, slightly more young women than men, have a psychological problem in the clinical range. Nearly twice as many young women than men report thoughts about suicide (Lawlor and James, 2000). This gender difference in mental health problems is consistently found. In general, females are more likely to show psychological problems first in adolescence, whereas males who display problems tend to have already shown them in childhood (Petersen et al., 1993).

In 2003, 15.6 per cent of young people had a psychiatric disorder and nearly one-fifth (19 per cent) of Irish young people were identified as 'at risk' of having a psychiatric disorder, with unhealthy family functioning being one key contributory factor (Fitzpatrick et al., 2003).

Some young people are more at risk than others for mental health problems in adolescence. These include young people in care, homeless, working in prostitution, living in poverty, with family problems or abuse, living in isolated areas or those who have had a crisis pregnancy at an early age. Young people with psychological or behavioural problems, young people from a minority and young people with learning and physical disabilities are also at greater risk.

Three of the primary mental health concerns of adolescence will now be explored: depression, self-harm and suicide.

Depression

Across adolescence, a rise occurs in depressive feelings and depressive disorder (as well as attempted and completed suicide), especially in young women. One in 10 adolescents experience a major depression at some stage, characterised by negativity and a reduced capacity to study, work or engage in leisure or social relationships (AWARE, 2000). It is associated with a variety of other problems, including substance use, self-harm and suicide.

Depression can be considered (Petersen et al., 1993) as a:

- **Depressed mood:** Feeling 'down in the dumps' or sad for a transitory period of time.
- **Depressed syndrome:** Part of a larger problem involving other experiences such as loneliness, anxiety or guilt.
- **Clinical depression:** A diagnosed condition involving a combination of symptoms, such as depressed mood or irritable mood, feelings of lethargy and fatigue, sleeping problems, psychomotor agitation, feelings of worthlessness or excessive guilt, suicidal ideation and poor concentration and decision-making ability.

Prevalence

American research suggests that 4 per cent of 12- to 17- year-olds and 9 per cent of 18-year-olds experience depression, making it one of the most prevalent mental health disorders (Weissman et al., 1999). The Lifestyle and Coping Survey (Sullivan et al., 2004) found that the vast majority of young people are not depressed (80 per cent) or anxious (74 per cent), with only 20 per cent showing signs of possible depression, especially teenage girls. When faced with a serious personal problem, these young people talk to friends or family members.

Age and Gender Differences

Across the 11- to 14-year-old age range, young females showed an increasingly higher rate of depression than males. Depression is also expressed differently by each sex, with males showing more 'externalising' (behavioural) symptoms, such as conduct problems, and females showing more 'internalising' (emotional) symptoms, such as low self-esteem and anxiety (Donnelly, 1995). Typically, in early adolescence, depression is associated with not looking forward to things (feelings of hopelessness), feelings of boredom, somatic (physical) complaints and having bad dreams. In contrast, by mid- to late adolescence, depression is associated with isolation from the peer group, lethargy and poor self-assertiveness (Kashani et al., 1989).

Causation

The causes of depression are multiple and varied. Hormonal factors, genetics, socio-cultural features, stress and cognitive development are all factors that contribute to depression. One particular social factor that contributes to depression, suicidal behaviour and referral to psychiatric services is bullying, discussed earlier in Chapter 4.

Sociologists have focused on alienation (involving feelings of estrangement, social isolation, powerlessness, meaninglessness and normlessness) as central to depression, substance use, suicidal behaviour and deviance. Alienation has its roots in social structures and processes and relates, in part, to Durkheim's concept of 'anomie' (a state of society characterised by a deterioration in norms and in the bonds among different social systems such as the family and school) (Lacourse et al., 2003).

Self-Harm

Self-harm is not an illness, rather it refers to a wide range of behaviour, including self-poisoning or injury, self-mutilation (including self-cutting), overdosing and attempted hanging. It is seen by some as a means of averting suicide, a morbid form of self-help and as addictive (Favazzo, 1998). As opposed to self-harm arising from recklessness, deliberate self-harm (DSH) refers to behaviour where there is an *intention* to self-harm.

The scale below presents behaviours beginning with forms of (non-deliberate) self-harm, followed by reactions to emotional pain and then ranging into attempted suicide (parasuicide) and suicide. Behaviour can be seen to range in degree of lethalness from low to high (Skegg, 2005):

- Deliberate recklessness.
- Stopping medication or starving with intent to cause harm.
- Self-hitting and battery.
- Self-injury with tissue damage (including gouging, scratching, self-biting).
- Self-cutting and burning.
- Overdosing.
- Poisoning.
- Hanging, shooting, drowning and other forms of suicide.

Parasuicide is where there is suicidal intent and overdosing is one of its commonest forms. Two-thirds of all parasuicides in the mid-west in Ireland in 2003, for example, involved an overdose of medication (males 55 per cent; females 74.5 per cent) (Health Services Executive, 2003).

Prevalence

Irish research estimates that 1 per cent of 12- to 19-year-olds display self-harm (Irish College of Psychiatrists, 2005). However, out of a sample of 3,830 Irish 15- to 17-year-olds from the Southern Health Board region, 9.1 per cent showed DSH (Sullivan et al., 2004). As with many statistics on health issues, these numbers may be an underestimation, as young people may engage in self-harm without coming to the attention of the health services.

Age and Gender Differences

Deliberate self-harm is rare before puberty but becomes more common in adolescence. In 2003, the rate of DSH was 241 per 100,000 in women and 177 per 100,000 in men. These rates are higher in particular age groups for each sex: 15–19 years in females and 20–24 years in males (National Suicide Research Foundation, 2004). Using a survey with Irish 15- to 17-year-olds, research found a history of DSH in 9.1 per cent of the young people sampled (Arensman et al., 2006). Both DSH and parasuicide are more common in young women, with young women being *three* times more likely to harm themselves than young men, particularly by cutting and overdose. Young men, on the other hand, use a wider variety of methods of self-harm and are more likely to be under the influence of alcohol or an illicit drug. While alcohol as the primary method of deliberate self-harm is rare, it is involved in nearly half (49 per cent) of all male episodes of self-harm and 39 per cent of female episodes (National Suicide Research Foundation, 2003). Gender differences may also be due to factors related to gender as opposed to gender *per se*, such as a higher prevalence of depressive feelings, disordered eating and romantic involvement in young women (Skegg, 2005). DSH is, however, more dangerous in males as it is more likely to lead to suicide (Skegg, 2005; Sullivan et al., 2004). Repetition of DSH is common in about half of Irish teenagers who present at hospitals and is associated with depressive symptoms and knowing of friends who had engaged in DSH (Arensman et al., 2006).

Profile

Bolger and colleagues (2004, p. 83), based on their Irish research, concluded that 'young people presenting to A&E departments with DSH tend, as a group, to be disadvantaged from a number of perspectives. They tend to be from socio-economically deprived backgrounds, with high levels of unemployment, previous mental health problems and previous DSH.'

Risk factors for self-harm include:

- Female gender.
- Socio-economic disadvantage.
- A homosexual or bisexual orientation.
- Interpersonal difficulties with few people to turn to for help.
- Low levels of serotonin.
- Adverse childhood experiences, including bullying and abuse.
- Impulsivity.
- Schoolwork difficulties.
- Poor problem-solving.
- Depression.
- Psychiatric disorder.
- Substance abuse.
- Alcohol consumption.
- Knowing someone that self-harms.

(Evans et al., 2005; Sullivan et al., 2004)

The media is also an influence through observational learning and the 'normalising' of such behaviour.

Reasons for Self-Harm

The primary reasons for self-harm include escape, depression, generating feelings in place of emptiness, wanting to punish oneself as well as social functions. It can be both internally and socially reinforcing as it acts to reduce tension and regulate mood. Reasons can also be seen in terms of:

- **Inner motives**: To gain relief from a terrible state of mind, to escape from a situation or from unbearable anguish, to punish oneself and not being able to think of an alternative and to die (suicidal intent).
- **Outer motives**: To seek help, to show desperation to others, as a response to conflict with others, to influence someone.

Additionally, both inner and outer motives are present in reasons such as getting back at others, making others feel guilty and wanting to die (Skegg, 2005). However, self-harm is often impulsive, undertaken by the young person without knowing why they did it, frequently in response to a situational event such as a relationship breakdown. Unconscious factors such as feelings of abandonment, guilt, ambivalence or desperation and rage towards others or the self may contribute to self-harm, with outer scars being symbolic of internal ones (Hendin, 1991).

Irish research found the two most common motives were 'I wanted relief from a terrible situation' (78.9 per cent) and 'I wanted to die' (60.9 per cent). Males are more likely than females to report reasons such as 'wanting to frighten someone' and 'wanting to find out if someone really loved them' as motives (Sullivan et al., 2004). Other Irish research by Bolger and colleagues (2004, p. 81) highlighted the following reasons: '(I was) feeling really low for weeks. My college course was getting on top of me and I was in debt, I never had money to do anything. I was thinking about suicide for a few weeks.' Another spoke of her reason as relating to the death of a friend through illness. 'I missed him so much ... I just wanted to be with him. I didn't really think about dying, I just thought I'd wake up with him [her friend].' Other reasons cited including a recent alleged sexual assault, worsening epilepsy seizures and the death of a friend though suicide.

A myriad of reasons underlie self-harm and socio-cultural factors also need to be considered. Rates of self-harm vary across countries, with higher rates reported in northern than southern Europe and in some indigenous people of colonised countries (Schmidtke et al., 1996). Overall, no one explanation underpins a young person's self-harm as a mix of intentions as well as contextual factors influence any one person who self-harms.

Treatment

Typically Irish young people who have self-harmed report a friend to be the most common source of help sought both before and after engaging in self-harm. Family members are the next source of help. A minority seek help initially from the medical services, though only small numbers present to the health or social services prior to or as a result of their self-harm (Sullivan et al., 2004).

Supports to prevent and reduce self-harm include:

- Provision of school-based counselling.
- Provision of greater information about mental health anti-bullying programmes.
- Greater recreational opportunities.
- Greater involvement of young people in decision-making about their lives (Sullivan et al., 2004).

Having someone to talk to in a crisis is critical. This is 'often a family member or friend, but for those for whom this was not possible, a service ... [that is] informal, accessible, available on a 24 hour basis, and staffed by people with experience of mental health disorders, including alcohol and drug problems [is needed]' (Bolger et al., 2004, p. 83).

In intervening to treat and reduce self-harm, it is important for professionals to consider the harm incident using 'the four Ps' (Skegg, 2005):

- **Predisposing (risk) factors**: Family discord, abuse, psychiatric problems.
- **Precipitating factors**: A row with a girlfriend or boyfriend, bullying, loss of a loved one.

- **Perpetuating factors**: Poor family communication, hopelessness, alexithymia (difficulty putting feelings into words).
- **Protective factors**: Good family and friend relationships, a capacity to bounce back from setbacks, an optimistic outlook.

In treating self-harm, anti-depressant medication is one approach used, although its effectiveness on its own is debatable. Psychotherapy, cognitive behavioural therapy involving problem-focused strategies and systemic family therapy have been found to be beneficial. However, young people, especially males, are hard to engage in treatment and such therapies depend on commitment to be effective (Fortune and Hawton, 2005).

Suicidal Behaviour

Suicidal behaviour refers to the spectrum of activities related to suicide, including suicidal ideation (thinking), self-harm and suicide attempts. Suicide rates consistently increase from childhood to adolescence, perhaps because of greater incidence of psychopathology (especially mood disorders) in young people, enhanced cognitive abilities and less supervision from parents (Bridge et al., 2006). Youth suicide increased over the twentieth century both in Europe and the USA (OECD, 2002). It consistently features as one of the top three causes of adolescent death, accounting for 30 per cent of deaths in 15- to 24-year-olds (Carr, 2002). In Ireland, youth suicide is the fifth highest in the European Union at 15.7 per 100,000 of 15- to 24-year-olds. This rate is higher again in 20- and 30-year-olds. It is more common in young men and Ireland has a very high national male-female ratio for suicide of 4.5:1 (Health Services Executive et al., 2005). About one-third of suicides in Ireland are preceded by parasuicide (attempted suicide). One in five people who engage in parasuicide repeat within six months and overall those who engage in parasuicide are approximately 20 times more likely to kill themselves (Health Services Executive, 2003). While some parasuicides are genuine suicide attempts, others are undertaken to change a person's circumstances.

Suicidal Ideation

Suicidal ideation occurs throughout childhood and adolescence and is especially common in 15- to 17-year-olds. Thoughts of suicide and acts of self-harm are common across all Irish young people and not just those attending mental health services (Rowley et al., 2001). According to one study, 6 per cent of Irish young people thought of suicide frequently and 17 per cent thought about it occasionally (Lawlor and James, 2000).

Prevalence has also been estimated to range from 15 to 25 per cent, varying in severity from thoughts of death and passive ideation to specific suicidal ideation with intent or plan (the prevalence of the latter being approximately 2–6 per cent) (Grunbaum et al., 2004).

Theories of Suicide

Several theories have been formulated to help explain why people commit suicide. These range from seeing suicide as having its origins in biological, psychological or sociological factors or a mixture of these. These are discussed in detail in any textbooks on suicide. Books by Kelleher (1996), *Suicide and the Irish*, and Smyth, MacLachlan and Clare's (2003) book, *Cultivating Suicide? Destruction of Self in a Changing Ireland*, explore suicide in an Irish context.

Prevalence

Suicide rates in Ireland doubled in the 1980s and 1990s, a time period when Irish society experienced significant transition. The strong association between the rate of Irish suicide and Irish economic growth from 1981 to 2000 is presented in figure 5.4. In considering this, it is important to note that it is purely a 'relationship' between the two variables. It does not show that economic growth 'causes' a rise in suicide rate. The association is stronger for Irish males then females. Reasons proposed for this include increased secularisation, alterations in gender roles (along with a shift of female identity into more traditional male domains), the diminution and isolation of fatherhood, the rise in male alcohol consumption and a relative lack of emotional expressiveness (Smyth et al., 2003).

Greater urbanisation and changes in legislation took place in Ireland across the 1980s and 1990s with the decriminalisation of suicide in 1993 and the introduction of divorce in 1997. Social institutions such as the Church, the family and the agricultural economy were undermined and challenged by more individualised, secular and economically developed values. The impact of the 'time-space' compression brought about on a global scale by information technologies and telecommunications are still unknown.

According to Abbott-Chapman (2000), in a rapidly changing world the usual problems young people face in making life choices and developing autonomy are exacerbated. The tensions between their struggle for autonomy and control with the constraints of social structures create feelings of powerlessness and alienation. Greater choice and opportunities have meant fewer certainties in life, which may exacerbate the pressure young people feel in making a choice. In addition, the pressure of insatiable consumerism and cultural globalisation erodes a young person's sense of individual human significance, undermining their perception of social structures, resulting in apathy. The focus on individual choices in contemporary society may lead young people to see their own crises as individual problems or failures, rather than the consequences of structural processes in society. Difficulty in finding a personal meaning in the contemporary 'Celtic Tiger' culture has been contended by Smyth and colleagues (2003) to contribute to a sense of hopelessness in some Irish young people, particularly males. Increased consumerism is inherent to this, as 'who we are (the very core self of being) has come to be determined by what we can buy and own' (Smyth et al., 2003, p. 59).

Figure 5.4 Rates of economic change and suicide

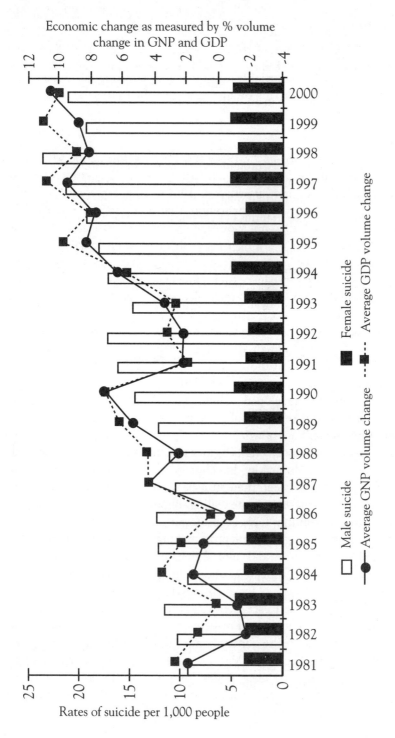

The need for young people to 'make space' in their day, to have a 'moratorium' or 'time out' in individual and collective safe havens in which to reflect and recollect was emphasised by Abbott-Chapman (2000), amongst others. Such safe havens refer to states of mind, time just *being* rather than *doing*, such as hanging out with friends or family.

While all of these represent social features that may contribute to suicide risk within any given society, it is also important to consider the factors that may put an individual at risk for suicide.

Risk Factors

A history of victimisation is a very prominent risk factor for any individual young person. This includes bullying and poor social relations where the young person may have felt helpless and hopeless in their relationships and belonging to a peer group. The peer group plays a key role in terms of peer rejection, neglect and low levels of friendship support. Attachment insecurity is another risk factor, with attachment figures, usually the parents, being perceived as being unavailable and unsupportive (Espito et al., 2003). Another key risk factor is a poor coping style with stress. Disengagement is more common as a coping style in suicidal youth characterised by problem avoidance, social withdrawal, wishful thinking and avoidance of negative emotions (Votta and Manion, 2004).

Table 5.4 Risk factors for suicide in young people

- Poor self-concept.
- A history of victimisation (bullying and rejection).
- Attachment insecurity.
- Poor coping style, feelings of hopelessness and hostility.
- Poor social support.
- A lack of a sense of belonging to a community or group.
- Loss (of role status, relationships, physical capabilities).

Source: Rutter and Behrendt (2004).

Based on an extensive literature review, life events such as interpersonal difficulties, illness, familial disruption and loss were identified by Smyth and MacLachlan (2004) as common precursors to suicide. Loss of role status is considered a risk factor. Smyth (2000) highlighted the role of 'role status'. This is a particular issue for Irish youth today and loss of role status is reflected in the inability to get a girlfriend or boyfriend, having no money and being unemployed, which were considered as being 'acceptable' reasons for taking one's life by suicide. Loss in general was one of the most pervasive themes, encompassing:

- Loss of role status (loss or absence of boyfriend or girlfriend, job and money).
- Loss of nurturing bonds or intimate relations (as a result of sexual and/or emotional abuse or loss of a fundamental relationship with a parent).
- Loss of physical capabilities, resulting from medical conditions or illness (ibid).

The significance of suicidal behaviour as a problem for young people in contemporary Ireland cannot be overemphasised. A multi-agency approach aimed at enhancing young people's ability to cope, promoting their mental health, well-being and sense of belonging, as well as their sources of support and use of these is clearly needed.

MENTAL HEALTH SERVICES

Mental health prevention is concerned with promoting well-being for all. The objective is the enhancement of potential via building psychological strength and resilience rather than on reducing disorders. This is in keeping with a goal of the National Children's Strategy (Department of Health and Children, 2000) that children will be supported to enjoy the optimum physical, mental and emotional well-being.

As 16- to 17-year-olds are *not* currently within the remit of the child and adolescent psychiatric services but rather treated within the adult setting, the need for specialised services for this age group has been emphasised by the Irish College of Psychiatrists (2005) amongst others. Such services should work in partnership with young people, listening to their needs, as well as with key stakeholders, such as families, schools and youth organisations, as outlined in the Adolescent Health Strategy (National Conjoint Child Health Committee, 2001). A Vision for Change: Report of the Executive Group on Mental Health Policy (2006) suggests a number of initiatives to develop the mental health services, which include:

- Each mental health catchment area of 300,000 having six multidisciplinary community mental health teams (CMHTs) for children and adolescents up to 18 years of age.
- Each HSE region having specialist teams dealing with child and adolescent problems such as eating disorders.

HEALTH PROMOTION

Promoting good health is not just about curtailing unhealthy behaviour. It is also about encouraging healthy lifestyles. During adolescence, lifestyles are established which affect health, thus the adolescent years are seen as a particularly valuable period for health promotion initiatives (WHO, 2005). Health promotion has been defined as 'the process of enabling people to increase control over, and to improve, their health' (WHO, Ottawa Charter, 1986). Five areas of action were identified by the WHO for health promotion:

- Building public health policies.
- Reorienting the health services.
- Creating supportive environments.
- Strengthening community actions.
- Developing personal skills.

Central to health promotion for young people is awareness building about how much they have control over their own health and how different lifestyle choices impact on their health across the short and long term. Attitudes towards health vary according to whether a person believes that they have control over their own health or whether they believe that health is more related to chance and this influences health-related behaviour and risk-taking. Most young people, though, have a positive sense of control over their own health, recognising that they can influence their health by their lifestyle (Hendry et al., 1993). Health promotion initiatives can assist them to become more informed and skilled in decision-making about their health and provide support so that healthier choices become the easier option. The Health Promoting Schools Initiative as well as the Social and Personal Health Education module are examples of health promotion programmes targeted at young people in Ireland today.

The need for mental health promotion cannot be overemphasised. Approximately one-third of Irish young people report not having enough information about suicide awareness, gay/lesbian/bisexual issues, mental health issues and divorce or separation (Lalor and Baird, 2006).

Mental health promotion, according to Hodgson and Abbasi (1995) means a variety of different things, such as the treatment of mental illness and increasing people's ability to overcome frustration, stress, problems, enhancement of resilience and resourcefulness. It refers to measures maximising mental health and well-being across three levels (Friedli, 1999):

- Strengthening individuals by building resilience via interventions promoting self-esteem and coping. Common training programmes offered in youth settings include assertiveness, conflict management, problem-solving, stress, sexual health and family issues.
- Strengthening communities or environments by fostering social inclusion and participation, social support, networking and a sense of integration.
- Reducing structural barriers to mental health by measures tackling inequalities and discrimination and promoting access to education, employment, services and support (National Youth Council of Ireland, 2004b).

Social support is strongly linked to young people's mental health and well-being, helping a person to see though their difficulties and that they are not on their own in times of need. However, young people may be slow to ask for help and support given that one of the main 'tasks' of adolescence is the attainment of autonomy.

Social support provides a realistic appraisal of events and offers solutions, help and guidance. Irish young people report plentiful sources of support. Parents are a key source of support, highlighting the significance of working with parents of adolescents and the potential of extended family in mental health promotion. While one in five young people do not nominate a close friend as a source of support and even though young people change friends over the time, friends are still frequently chosen and rated highly as sources of support. In contrast, although regularly nominated, siblings appear to be the poorest sources of support (Dolan, 2005). A clear gender difference is prevalent in young people's use of social support. Young men are less likely to seek help with their problems from friends, relatives or professionals (Lalor and Baird, 2006). Availability of support services thus needs to be stressed for young men even more than for young women.

Mental health programmes aimed at young people such as the SPHE (Social, Personal and Health Education) schools module, Mind Out, Mental Health Matters, the transition-year Personal Development Programme and the National Public Speaking Project have all reported positive results in terms of increased levels of understanding of mental health issues and services (Hastings et al., 2004). Mind Out, developed for Irish 15- to 18-year-olds, has 13 curriculum sessions, most of which are interactive and activity-based with time for reflection and discussion, running over two years (Byrne et al., 2005). It aims to help young people identify coping strategies and rational thinking skills, to raise awareness of personal feelings and sources of support and to explore attitudes towards mental health issues and seeking help. Evaluation of this programme highlighted that young people showed an enhanced ability to seek constructive help if distressed and greater compassion towards distressed peers. It was well received by both young people and teachers alike, which is seen as important for its effectiveness. However, it had a greater appeal for girls than for boys (Byrne et al., 2005).

Mental health interventions with young people need to adopt an ecological approach, aiming to positively influence the adolescent's environment as well as adolescents as individuals. The Adolescent Health Strategy (National Conjoint Health Committee, 2001) recommended this, calling for a life skills or SPHE strategy that is holistic, broad in content with the aim of building resilience and maintaining a healthy lifestyle. Experiential and adventure programmes such as the Outward Bound movement (based on the philosophy of Kurt Hahn), attempt to encourage and facilitate the development of life skills in innovative and engaging ways. Communication skills, co-operation, capacity to trust and to take responsibility, decision-making and problem-solving are central to many of these. Such programmes have been used internationally in a variety of settings such as schools, remand and treatment facilities. Many colleges in continental Europe now have an outdoor adventure-based induction programme to help students in a class group get to know each other, forge friendships and a positive class ethos.

Finally, it is important to note that health promotion as a public health strategy is not without its critics. Sociologically, it has been criticised from a number of standpoints. Some critics contend that locating health problems in individual lifestyle behaviours fails to address the material conditions of people's lives. Others construe the surveillance role of health promotion as being a form of social control, while others see health promotion practices as a dominant form of paternalism. These critiques have drawn attention to a number of dilemmas inherent in health promotion, such as the tension between individual responsibility and freedom of choice (Hyde, Lohan and McDonnell, 2004).

CONCLUSION

A striking conclusion from this chapter is the extent to which health problems of young people in Ireland today are a serious concern. The primary health challenges of adolescence include inadequate physical activity, poor diet, substance use and sexual health. These were explored with consideration given to patterns, features and contributing factors. Attention was also paid to Irish initiatives tackling these.

The primary mental health problems of adolescence, body image, depression, self-harm and suicide were also examined and support factors discussed.

In attempting to understand adolescent health problems and behaviour, risk-taking as well as psychological and sociological perspectives were drawn upon in this chapter.

RECOMMENDED READING

Heaven, P.C.L. (1996). *Adolescent health: The role of individual differences*. London: Routledge.

Inglis, T. (1998). *Lessons in Irish sexuality*. Dublin: UCD Press.

Kelleher, M. J. (2005). *Suicide and the Irish*. Cork: Mercier Press.

Mayock, P. (2000). *Choosers or losers? Influences on young people's choices about drugs in inner city Dublin*. Dublin: Children's Research Centre, TCD.

McShane, I. (2004). The youth of Ireland. In M. MacLachlan (Ed.), *Binge drinking and youth culture: Alternative perspectives* (pp. 103–112). Dublin: Liffey Press.

National Youth Council of Ireland. (2004a). *Sense & sexuality: A support pack for addressing the issue of sexual health with young people in youth work settings*. Dublin: NYCI.

Plummer, D. (2006). *Helping adolescents and adults to build self-esteem: a photocopiable resource book*. Gateshead: Athenium Press.

Smyth, C., MacLachlan, M., & Clare, A. (2003). *Cultivating suicide? Destruction of self in a changing Ireland*. Dublin: Liffey Press.

6

Education and Employment

INTRODUCTION

For all young people, the transition from school to work or further study (or both) is a primary developmental task. The transition to paid employment and independence from parents is a major landmark on the transition to adulthood. This chapter will examine the second- and third-level education system in Ireland. It will look at the factors that influence academic outcome in second level (such as school quality), the impact of part-time work and issues of equality. It will also examine the research pertaining to co-education (mixed-sex schools) and early school leaving. The second part of this chapter shall examine the transition from secondary school; the advent of mass higher education and the transition to full-time employment.

The primary challenge in coming to grips with the issue of education and transitions to the workplace in Ireland is the sheer volume of source material. Education, assessment, completion rates, early school leaving, higher education, apprenticeships, training, national skill needs and a plethora of related topics have all been researched in depth, reflecting the centrality of education and training in Irish society and its perceived importance in driving economic development. In this chapter, the main findings from the key texts and reports are presented. We are primarily concerned with young people's experiences of education and training and their progression to employment. This period of transition in young people's lives is the main focus of the 'transitional perspective' described in Chapter 2, a sociological theoretical perspective which is concerned with how the transition to adulthood contributes to the social and cultural reproduction of society.

EDUCATION AND ECONOMIC DEVELOPMENT

The increased investment in second- and third-level education by successive governments from the mid-1960s has been identified by many commentators as an important ingredient in Ireland's dramatic economic development since the mid-1990s (for example, Haughton, 1998; Nolan, O'Connell and Whelan, 2000; White, 2001). A widespread belief in the transformative potential of education has been a central plank of Irish social policy since the mid-1960s. The economic boom years of the 1990s are regularly attributed, at least in part, to a large and well-educated youth population. Writing in 2000, MacSharry and White remark:

> Over the past three decades the continuing investment in education made by successive governments has laid the long-term foundation for part of the economic success we now enjoy … The educated Irish workforce has become one of the primary reasons why the country has become such a favoured industrial location for foreign investment (p. 26).

Of course, there were other important factors in stimulating economic growth, such as foreign direct investment, a low corporate tax rate, EU regional development funding, use of the English language, social partnership and a large pool of skilled emigrants ready to return home. That said, there is no denying the importance of a highly educated workforce. We have certainly come a long way from the views of Michael Heffernan, TD, who responded to the School Attendance Act 1926 (which made attendance at primary school compulsory) by calling for 'more relaxed requirements to apply to the children of agricultural labourers, so that elementary education for the poor should not interfere with the higher priority of cheap labour for … farmers' (Lee, 1989, p. 131).

However, it is important to balance the rhetoric about valuing the education system and building a knowledge-based society with cold comparisons with other developed counties. The fact is, Ireland provides one of the lower levels of public funding of education in the OECD – in terms of expenditure per student, Ireland ranked twentieth out of 33 countries in 2003 (OECD, 2006). Whereas Ireland spent $6,000 (adjusted for purchasing power parity, ppp) per student across primary, secondary and tertiary education in 2003, Switzerland and the United States spent $12,000 and Norway spent $10,000 (OECD, 2006).

In terms of proportion of GDP in 2003 spent on education, Ireland spent the third lowest amount out of 31 countries. Specifically, Ireland spent approximately 4.5 per cent of GDP on education in 2003, compared to 8.5 per cent in Israel, 8 per cent in Iceland and 7 per cent in Denmark. Of 33 countries, only Greece and Turkey spent less of their national wealth on education in 2003 (OECD, 2006).

As we shall see later in this chapter, the Irish education system has much to commend it, but there is significant room for improvement on many fronts.

The National Qualifications Authority of Ireland and Levels of Learning

Before examining the second-level, post-Leaving Certificate level and higher education systems in Ireland, let us look at attempts in recent years to create a national unified system for understanding all learning awards, from the most basic all the way to the highest (the doctorate). This work is largely the responsibility of the National Qualifications Authority of Ireland (NQAI), which was established in

2001 by the Qualifications (Education and Training) Act 1999. Its primary function is to establish a national framework of qualifications based on standards of knowledge, skill or competence to be acquired by learners. In this way, all learners will have clearly understood competencies linked to a clearly understood 'level of learning' and this will promote and facilitate access, transfer and progression throughout the span of education and training provision nationally.

Figure 6.1 Diagram of the 10 levels of learning

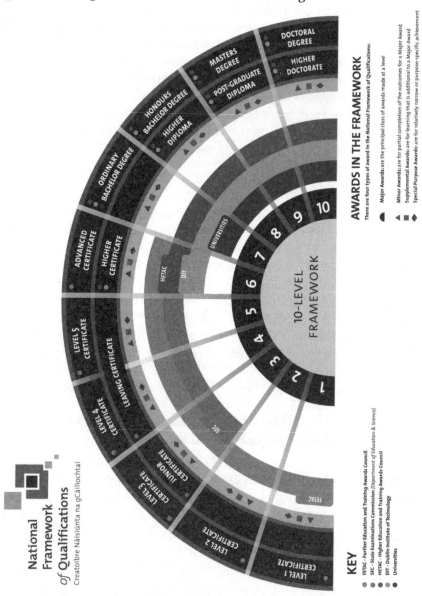

Source: National Qualifications Authority of Ireland.

The Authority is not an awarding body itself. Instead, it works closely with the various awarding bodies, such as HETAC (Higher Education and Training Awards Council) (which makes awards primarily in the Institute of Technology sector, excluding the Dublin Institute of Technology [DIT]), DIT (which makes it own awards), FETAC (Further Education and Training Awards Council) (which makes awards primarily in the Post-Leaving Certificate sector) and the universities.

As we can see in Figure 6.1, a number of bodies can accredit awards from Levels 6 (Higher Certificate) to 10 (PhD). This classification of awards is still in progress and, ultimately, all awards made within the State will be included in the national framework of qualifications, including the awards made by the universities, Dublin Institute of Technology, other Institutes of Technology, CERT, private third-level colleges, other third-level institutions, Teagasc, Bord Iascaigh Mhara and community and voluntary groups. This standardisation of awards is part of a wider European effort to improve comparability of educational awards across the European Union, which presently has a bewildering array of structures and systems for academic awards.

Secondary Schooling

Universal secondary education is relatively recent in Ireland. Only in the mid-1960s, with the publication of *Investment in Education* (Department of Education, 1965), did free post-primary education become available (from the academic year 1967–68). In addition, free school transport was provided in rural areas. This report highlighted Irish people's very limited access to secondary education. For example, in 1961 only 10 per cent of 15- to 19-year-olds from 'semi-skilled or unskilled' backgrounds were in full-time education (compared to half of the 15- to 19-year-old children of professional and skilled workers) (MacSharry and White, 2000). The *Investment in Education* report also highlighted the 'limitations of the educational system in producing the trained workforce necessary for economic growth' (Smyth and Hannan, 2000, p. 111). From such an extremely low base, there commenced a dramatic growth in access to second- and, later, third-level education.

HOW DOES THE IRISH SECOND-LEVEL EDUCATION SYSTEM COMPARE INTERNATIONALLY?

There is a pride in Ireland's perceived reputation as a land of 'saints and scholars' and in its literary figures. The general public consensus is that the education system is sound and the quality of its graduates compares well internationally. Is this the case? Tovey and Share (2003) note that Irish adolescents perform well in international comparisons; for example, a 2002 UNICEF report on educational effectiveness internationally placed Ireland fifth for teenage literacy (the highest placed of the EU countries) and well ahead of Germany, the US and the UK in maths (UNICEF, 2002, cited in Tovey and Share, 2003).

The academic performance of Irish 15-year-olds relative to international counterparts is measured in the regular PISA surveys (Programme for International Student Assessment). The most recent results are reported in a summary by the Educational Research Centre (2004). Students from 30 OECD (Organisation for Economic Cooperation and Development) and 11 non-OECD countries were surveyed. Results were scaled to have an OECD mean of 500 points. Irish students scored 502.8 on the combined mathematics scale, putting Ireland midway at twentieth place out of 40 countries. For reading literacy, Ireland's score of 515.5 is significantly above the OECD mean of 494.2, ranking Irish students seventh out of 40 for reading literacy (Educational Research Centre, 2004). However, 11 per cent of the Irish sample were scored at or below Level 1 literacy (associated with basic reading skills such as retrieval of information from a simple text), indicating that a sizeable minority of 15-year-olds have considerable literacy difficulties. However, this is still better than the OECD average, where 19.7 per cent of 15-year-olds are at or below Level 1 literacy. In science, Irish students were ranked sixteenth out of 40 countries.

In spite of these respectable, sometimes good, performances of Irish students relative to their international counterparts, the Irish education system has two major areas of significant weakness that we should note here. The first is that of literacy in the general population and the second is that of school retention. With regard to adult literacy, a 22-country survey of adult literacy published by the OECD found that 22.6 per cent of Irish people aged 16 to 65 were at the lowest level of literacy. According to the OECD survey (2000), this was similar to levels found in the US (20.7 per cent) and the UK (21.8 per cent) but considerably higher than Germany (14.4 per cent), the Netherlands (10.5 per cent) and Sweden (7.5 per cent).

The second major area of weakness in the Irish secondary school sector is the high level of non-completion of second-level education. As we shall see later in this chapter, approximately 20 per cent of students leave each year without completing the Leaving Certificate. What's more, this figure has not improved over the last twenty years, despite dozens of initiatives. The school completion rate seems 'stuck' at about 80 per cent. The 1997 National Anti-Poverty Strategy had a target of a 90 per cent senior-cycle school retention rate (Department of Social and Family Affairs, 1997). This target has not been achieved. The more recent National Action Plan against Poverty and Social Exclusion, 2003–2005 (Office for Social Inclusion, no date), however, has dropped the specific target of 90 per cent school completion. Instead, it seeks to 'continue to improve educational retention rates and attainment levels, especially for those who are less well off; to continue to address the issue of early school leaving and to further expand opportunities for lifelong learning' (Office for Social Inclusion, nd, p. 5).

DO ALL IRISH YOUNG PEOPLE BENEFIT EQUALLY FROM THEIR SECONDARY SCHOOLING?

Platitudes from government, teacher's unions and other groups with vested interests about the quality of Irish education should not blind us to the importance of comparisons with other developed countries, as noted above. The fact is Ireland has one of the highest rates of functional illiteracy in Europe and a persistent problem with early school leaving.

However, alongside the poor literacy levels and the low retention rates, we have the apparent paradox of Ireland's relatively good showing in internationally standardised tests of student performance. So, what does this tell us? On the one hand, Irish secondary students compare favourably with their international counterparts and, on the other hand, Ireland has high rates of functional illiteracy and school drop-out.

It would appear that the secondary school system in Ireland serves the majority of students well, but that it is less effective at catering for students with greater than normal learning or social needs. Also, it would appear that some schools are carrying more than their fair share of students with higher than normal learning or social needs. This can concentrate 'high-demand' students in particular schools, to the disadvantage of such pupils, their classmates and teachers. This process is well described by Sweeney and Dunne (2003):

> Internationally, policies to reduce school underachievement tend to take one of two general routes: those that change the system for everyone, and those that target the 'at risk' populations. The majority of parents have invested in making the current system work on their children's behalf and will not welcome mainstream restructuring motivated by the needs of an under-achieving minority. Not surprisingly, Ireland has increasingly been adopting the second route, ie, moving from pursuing equal educational 'opportunity' to combating educational 'disadvantage'. Ironically, targeting schools as disadvantaged makes them more visible as schools with particular problems, which parents, in a position to do so, are wise to avoid. The pupil intake of these schools, then, becomes more skewed and the challenge facing them greater. A further disincentive problem can then arise in these schools. Individual teenagers being experienced as disruptive may stand to benefit (and society certainly does) if the school manages to retain them, but the school itself and the classroom teachers may see only the downsides to doing so; they may be more influenced by the negative impact the uncooperative young person is having on the morale and schooling of the majority (p. 26).

The concern, of course, is that the entire secondary school system is geared towards those progressing to third level, with other students being offered an education that has little real meaning to their lives. Such students will find it difficult to 'see the point' of it all. It also makes it more likely for their educational experiences to be negative, marked by failure. What is the purpose of education? Is our second-level system overly focused on producing college entrants and thereby creating the impression that, with hard work, all students are capable of achieving at third level and progressing to well-paid jobs in the professions? Unless we want a nation exclusively populated by doctors and lawyers, this is nonsense. In the words of Sweeney and Dunne, 'education should enable every person to enhance their knowledge and skills to the best of their ability and enable them to experience satisfaction by carrying out fairly remunerated jobs that genuinely need to be done' (2003, p. 30). Wickham (1998), too, argues that Ireland's education system is too academic, with insufficient links to technology and industry.

A persistent feature of the Irish second-level system over many decades is that pupils from poorer backgrounds do less well academically (Clancy, 1982; Department of Education, 1965). They are thus less likely to progress to third-level education and to obtain higher-paid jobs. This perpetuates the unequal spread of wealth in Irish society. This state of affairs is offensive to our sense of meritocracy, where hard work, discipline and ability will bring academic and socio-economic rewards, regardless of one's social class. That is to say, an unequal school system has the effect of perpetuating the status quo by providing an unfair advantage to those who are better off in society. In other words, children born into different strata in society are not participating on a level educational 'playing field'. That said, even the concept of meritocracy is problematic. As Drudy and Lynch say, 'it is a logical and social fallacy to suggest that anyone who has talent and makes the effort can attain merit when the meritorious occupations or position are simply not available in large enough numbers even for those who are technically eligible to occupy them' (1993, p. 33).

Why do poorer children do less well in school? This is not a pattern unique to Ireland but is common throughout Europe. Drudy and Lynch (1993) summarise the explanations to be found in the international literature. The first explanation is attitudes and culture in poorer and working-class areas and families. The general argument here is that poorer families have different value systems and academic aspirations compared to the middle classes. A key variable, it is suggested, is a belief in one's ability to shape the future, as opposed to a more fatalistic belief that the future will 'just happen', more characteristic in families with little wealth, control or power over their circumstances. Craft (1974, cited in Drudy and Lynch, 1993) studied children in a Dublin working-class suburb and found that parents who were 'future-oriented' were more likely to have children who stayed on at school.

A second family of explanations are 'cultural deprivation' theories, expounded by psychologists in the US in the 1970s. Here, it is held that working-class families hold values that are not compatible with middle-class values and that their children are therefore less 'educable'. Another common explanation, based on the work of Douglas in the UK (1964, cited in Drudy and Lynch, 1993) is that parents of working-class children show less interest in their child's teachers, school and schooling than their middle-class counterparts. However, simple non-attendance at parent-teacher meetings may not indicate lack of interest. Rather, perhaps the parents of working-class children themselves had negative experiences of schooling and their non-attendance may be due to lack of confidence and lack of knowledge as to the purpose of such meetings. Drudy and Lynch (1993) suggest that an obvious, but less appreciated, reason may be simple poverty. There are considerable costs to second- and third-level education and the pull of paid employment may be too great for some to delay.

Explanations that focus on the individual young person and his or her social class, family, attitudes or community are said to be using an individualist or deficit model. That is, they target children being failed by the system rather than seek to bring about radical institutional reform (Smyth and Hannan, 2000). Structuralist models, on the other hand, seek to explain the process of early school leaving 'within the institutional or structural context of the school itself and focuses on issues such as streaming; availability of teaching and other resources; disciplinary regime etc.' (O'Shea and Williams, 2001, p. 49). The reality is that each young person leaves school early for his or her own unique reasons and 'the ultimate determinant of early school drop-outs is undoubtedly a complex, multi-dimensional mix of numerous aspects of both the individualist and structuralist theories' (O'Shea and Williams, 2001, p. 1). Taking a firm structuralist position, Lynch suggests that inequality in schooling is perpetuated by researchers and policy-makers:

> There has been a tendency in educational research to explain social-class differences in education by pathologising working-class culture and lifestyle. A cultural deficit model of educational inequality has been normalised in much of educational thinking. This implies that the reason low-income working-class groups (school leavers and adults) are not well represented in the non-compulsory education sector is because they have socially and culturally problematic backgrounds (Lynch, 1998, pp. 343–4).

Of course, any radical or structural reform would be fiercely resisted by the powerful classes, for whom the school system is the best way to ensure children can occupy powerful and well-paid positions in the workforce.

Initiatives to Address Education Inequality

There are a large number of initiatives to combat educational inequality and non-school completion. The Department of Education and Science (2003b) lists more than 60 initiatives designed to tackle educational disadvantage. The most recent approach is the DEIS (Delivering Equality of Opportunity in Schools) initiative (Department of Education and Science, 2005). Its aim is to strategically target initiatives that are known to work at children in disadvantaged communities from pre-school (aged three years) all the way through to the end of second level (age 18 years). DEIS is designed to be a co-ordinated plan that will incorporate elements of previous initiatives that have proven successful (such as the Early Start Programme and the School Completion Programme). The priority issues identified in the DEIS initiative are:

- Improving access to early education and the important academic skills it fosters.
- Improving literacy and numeracy standards (so as to facilitate children's further progress in the education system).
- Improving the involvement of parents and communities.
- Supporting school attendance and progression.
- Recognising the need to recruit well-qualified teachers to schools in areas of disadvantage.
- Enhanced monitoring and evaluation of initiatives.

(Department of Education and Science, 2005)

In short, the DEIS initiative is an attempt to pull together effective features of the plethora of previous pilot initiatives and to target them in a unified, co-ordinated way at pupils in the most disadvantaged areas. It is too early to judge the efficacy of this approach, but improving school completion rates (stuck at approximately 80–82 per cent for decades) would be a considerable achievement.

The creation of new routes to the Leaving Certificate – the Leaving Certificate Vocational Programme (LCVP) and the Leaving Certificate Applied Programme (LCA) – was an attempt to cater for students who were not served by the traditional Leaving Certificate. The LCVP and the LCA, however, are not widely seen as equivalent in prestige to the Leaving Certificate as they are not recognised for access to third-level colleges. The LCA is vocationally oriented; students spend a minimum of 55 per cent of their time on vocational preparation in areas such as horticulture and tourism, and a minimum of 30 per cent on general education (Clancy, 2005). It was introduced in 1995 to cater for those whose needs were not being accommodated in the traditional academic Leaving Certificate. Although introduced as a reform, Smyth and Hannan (2000) note that, paradoxically, it may have the effect of perpetuating disparities and inequalities, at least in so far as access to third level is concerned.

GENDER ROLE SOCIALISATION IN SCHOOLS

Lynch and Lodge (2002) have studied the Irish compulsory education system and examined the ways in which schools contribute to equality and inequality. They are particularly interested in how power relations operate in schools:

Schools are major players in the determination of patterns of inequality in society … Their role as producers and disseminators of cultural products has also meant that they play a powerful role in determining the order of cultural relations in society, and in elevating and denigrating different cultural forms (pp. 5–6).

Lynch and Lodge contrast the control and surveillance of dress and appearance in girls' schools compared to boys'. In single-sex girls' schools, control over uniforms, make-up and jewellery is a widely practised form of control, whereas monitoring and surveillance of dress and demeanour is not as pervasive in the boys' schools in their study.

Ryan (1997) studied how gender roles are created and maintained by school social relations, specifically, the regulation of girls through the concept of 'reputation'. Girls deemed to be 'loose' were branded 'tarts', 'sluts', 'slags' and so on. Conversely, girls deemed to have insufficient interest in boys were labelled 'frigid', 'lesbian', tight' and so on. The challenge for secondary-school girls in conforming to social norms, primarily policed by their peers, was that they:

> had to be seen to be attractive and interested in sex, but not so interested that they would appear 'easy'. On the other hand, they could not afford to appear too uninterested in sex and boys, for fear of being labelled 'frigid', 'stuck up' or 'lesbian' (Ryan, 1997, p. 29).

Coeducation: Better For Boys or Girls?

The principal source on the effects of co-education in Ireland is the ESRI (Economic and Social Research Institute) study *Coeducation and Gender Equality: Exam Performance and Personal Development* (Hannan et al., 1996).

Co-education (the education of boys and girls together) is a relatively recent practice and has its origins in the 'comprehensive' education programmes provided in numerous European countries from the 1950s. By providing schooling comprehensively (to boys and girls from all sectors of society) it was thought that this would reduce social inequalities in educational outcomes, facilitating society-wide growth in human capital and facilitating gender equality by 'providing a more natural social setting for adolescent development' (Hannan et al., 1996, p. 1). Numerous studies in Europe, the US and internationally have produced mixed results as to the effects of co-education. Persistent anecdotal evidence suggests that girls perform better in all-girl schools, where they benefit from female role models in senior staff positions and receive more teacher attention (Hannan et al., 1996). What is the experience for Irish adolescents? The Hannan et al. study was initiated by the Department of Education to determine if co-education has a detrimental effect on girls' academic attainment and personal and social development. The primary findings from this study are also published in Smyth and Hannan (1997).

More than 10,000 Junior Certificate and Leaving Certificate students from a nationally representative sample of 116 schools were surveyed. The focus was on girls' educational outcomes. This was measured by studying examination performance. It is important to note, however, that simply comparing Leaving Certificate results for girls in single-sex versus co-educational settings will not yield useful results. This is because there are numerous other intervening variables that determine academic attainment, for example, social class and prior academic ability. Single-sex schools tend to be more selective in their intake, resulting in a disproportionate number of working-class and lower-ability students being concentrated in co-educational schools, particularly vocational schools. For instance, lower-ability students make up 31 per cent of students in vocational schools, compared to 10 per cent in boys' secondary schools (Smyth and Hannan, 1997, p. 14). Thus, it would be meaningless to compare the Leaving Certificate results for girls in a co-educational vocational school and in a neighbouring single-sex secondary school with a strong academic record and restrictive intake, and attribute the differences solely to the mix, or otherwise, of pupils' genders. Thus, prior academic ability and social class need to be taken into account in determining whether girls are disadvantaged by co-education.

The ESRI researchers found that a number of factors determined girls' exam performance. Firstly, consider family and social background. Overall, girls from higher social classes perform better than girls from lower social backgrounds. Indeed, social background accounts for 42.8 per cent of the variance in Leaving Certificate results (Hannan et al., 1996).

Prior academic ability (before entering second level) also contributes significantly to eventual Leaving Certificate results (and may also determine whether a pupil is admitted to the more selective secondary schools, which tend to be single-sex). Over 30 per cent of the variance between schools and pupils in the Leaving Certificate results is due to prior academic attainment.

So, when social class and prior academic ability are combined, these two factors account for 74 per cent of the variance in academic attainment. Does it matter if girls are in a single-sex or a co-educational schooling environment? The researchers used advanced multi-level modelling statistical techniques to control for the other factors described above. They found that:

Coeducation has very little impact on Junior Certificate performance, when differences in social background, ability and school organisation are taken into account. Most of the differences in average exam performance between coed and single-sex schools are, in fact, due to differences in the social background and ability of their student intakes. In contrast, coeducation explains less than one per cent of the variance between schools in overall exam results (Smyth and Hannan, 1997, p. 18).

Thus, the impact of co-education on girls' academic attainment is very small. Interestingly, the impact is strongest (although still very weak) on lower-ability pupils. Co-education has little impact on middle- and higher-ability pupils. The same pattern occurs at the Leaving Certificate level, where the impact of co-education is even smaller than at the Junior Certificate level (it accounts for only 0.2 per cent of variance in Leaving Certificate results).

EARLY SCHOOL-LEAVERS

Early school leaving is defined as leaving school before the minimum statutory age, which is 16. However, given the importance of completing the Leaving Certificate for obtaining access to further and higher education and employment, those who leave school without the Leaving Certificate are frequently thought of as 'early school-leavers'.

As we noted earlier in this chapter, the school completion rate has remained fairly constant, at around 82 per cent, for some years now, despite changes to the curriculum, introduction of the alternative Leaving Certificate Programmes (the Leaving Certificate Applied Programme and the Leaving Certificate Vocational Programme) and increased funding of 'out of school' alternatives such as Youthreach and Community Training Workshops. For a developed country that aspires to become a leading 'knowledge-based economy' (and which is competing with many other countries with similar aspirations), it is a matter of concern that almost 20 per cent of secondary school students do not complete the Leaving Certificate examination.

The creation of the National Education Welfare Board (NEWB) in 2000 sought to address the issue of early school leaving by focusing on absenteeism, a common precursor to dropping out of school. The Board is charged with ensuring that every child either attends a school or otherwise receives an education. In particular, the NEWB has a key role in following up on children who are not attending school regularly. It does this through the work of the more than 70 Educational Welfare Officers who work in communities throughout the country.

Since the inception of the Education (Welfare) Act 2000, schools are obliged to submit a report to the NEWB on levels of school attendance. Key findings from this nationwide data show that secondary-school students, on average, miss 14 days in the school year. In the most disadvantaged areas, the average absence is 21 days for each student (National Education Welfare Board, 2006). Parents or guardians are responsible for ensuring that children in their care attend school. If they fail to do so, they are breaking the law and may be prosecuted. The NEWB took its first school attendance case to court in March 2006. By June 2006, the parents of 19 children had appeared in court and School Attendance Notices were issued by the NEWB to the parents or guardians of a further 80 children (*Irish Independent*, June 22, 2006). In July 2006, the first fines were handed down since the enactment of the Education (Welfare) Act 2000. Five Limerick couples were fined €400 each as their children dropped out of school after primary level. All five couples were members of the Traveller community, where school attendance often declines sharply at second level (*Irish Examiner*, July 12 2006). For parents or guardians convicted, the law allows the courts to impose a fine of up to €635 or up to one month's imprisonment, or both.

Boys are considerably more likely to leave school early than girls. For example, while 2.6 per cent of girls left school with no qualifications in 1998, 4.4 per cent of boys did so. Similarly, while 11.2 per cent of girls in 1998 left after the Junior

Certificate, 19.3 per cent of boys did so. This has been a persistent pattern over the course of the School Leavers' Surveys since they commenced in 1980. These surveys are conducted regularly by the ESRI and we shall examine recent findings later in this chapter.

In 2001, the ESRI conducted a survey of attitudes towards early school-leavers (defined as those who left school after the Junior Certificate or earlier) by employers (O'Shea and Williams, 2001). A total of 934 firms out of 2,526 contacted completed a questionnaire. A clear pattern of limited opportunities emerges. Most of the private sector employers surveyed (70 per cent) had never employed an early school-leaver. A further 9 per cent had done so at some point in the past, but not in the previous two years. Those firms who did take on early school-leavers generally did so in unskilled or semi-skilled areas, such as general labouring, general operatives, sales and bar or restaurant work. On a positive note, the vast majority (89 per cent) of firms that took on early school-leavers felt that they had the opportunity to expand their responsibilities and advance within the company. They also had positive views of their honesty, reliability, timekeeping and ability to fit in. However, about a quarter of firms employing early school-leavers rated them poorly in terms of initiative. They were also rated poorly in general numeracy and literacy skills and computer skills.

In Ireland, and throughout most developed countries, as you would expect, early school-leavers are considerably more likely to be unemployed. In 2003, 8 per cent of 25 to 29-year-olds without a Leaving Certificate were unemployed, compared to 3 per cent of college graduates. This pattern is found in most western European countries. Notable exceptions include Denmark and Italy, where, surprisingly, graduates are *more likely* to be unemployed, and not in education, than early school-leavers (OECD, 2005).

DOES IT MATTER WHICH SECONDARY SCHOOL YOU GO TO?

As any parent will tell you, schools vary significantly in the academic performance and social/personal development of their pupils. In educational research, this is known as the 'school effect'.

The issue of school effects in the Irish context was examined by Emer Smyth of the ESRI in *Do Schools Differ?* (1999). She makes the important point that schools can mediate only a certain amount of student outcome. A meta-analysis of a number of international studies found that 'schools account for 19 per cent of overall achievement differences among pupils, a figure which is reduced to 8 per cent when adjustment is made for pupil differences' (Scheerens and Bosker, 1997 cited in Smyth, 1999, p. 3). So, of course, family and social background and prior ability have a significant impact on academic attainment.

Smyth (1999) examined data from 10,000 pupils in a sample of 116 nationally representative second-level schools. Performance on the Junior Certificate examination results did vary between schools. As previously discussed, external factors had an important impact on outcomes (girls, middle-class pupils and those with highly educated parents did better). However, there were noticeable 'school effects' also. 'Streaming' had significant negative effects, particularly on those in the lower streams, perhaps due to lower expectations of pupils by their teachers. The culture of discipline in the school also had an effect:

> a 'strict but fair' school climate appears to be optimal for pupil performance; pupils tend to do worse where there school is too 'easy-going', where pupil misbehaviour disrupts their learning time, or where they feel teachers are not interested in them or are constantly 'giving out' to them (Smyth, 1999, p. 60).

Also, students had better results in the Junior Certificate where teachers expect them to stay on in full-time education. Similar factors were found to influence outcome at the Leaving Certificate examination. It is useful to quote at length from Smyth's (1999) overall conclusion as to what makes a secondary school effective:

> More academically effective schools tend to be more flexible in relation to choice of subjects and subject levels, delaying a final decision in order to maximise the number of pupils taking higher level subjects. These schools tend to have a more orderly learning environment with lower levels of misbehaviour, apparently a consequence of a consistent approach to school discipline. In addition, teachers in more effective schools tend to have higher expectations of their pupils along with more positive perceptions of both pupils and parents. There tend to be more supportive relations among management and staff in the more effective schools (pp. 213–14).

Smyth (1999) repeatedly stresses the positive outcomes where pupils experience a sense of involvement in the school, for example, through school prefect systems, pupil councils and extra-curricular activities. Students reporting a sense of involvement in school do better academically and are less likely to drop out.

Also, the nature of teacher-pupil interaction is important. Pupils do better when they receive positive feedback from their teachers. In addition, 'positive pupil-teacher interaction is … associated with enhanced developmental outcomes, including lower stress levels, more positive self-image and greater sense of control among pupils' (ibid., pp. 223–4).

Both in Ireland and internationally, research into school effects has provided an impetus for the provision of school assessment with a view to school improvement. As historically 'closed' institutions, this has been quite controversial. In Ireland, 'whole school inspections' have been implemented since 2003–04, with the results displayed on the Department of Education and Science website since February 2006. Naturally enough, schools and teachers have been keen to avoid a crude and narrow 'league table' approach which does not capture the personal development of their pupils or the extra-curricular cultural and sporting activities they provide. They also argue that league tables do not reflect the significant variations between schools in student background and ability at intake. On the other hand, the Department of Education and Science, and the various parent groups, have sought mechanisms to identify, and rectify, the 'school effects' known to impact on students' academic and personal outcomes, such as school management and staffing, facilities, disciplinary climate, absenteeism, pupil retention and homework.

Thus, we have entered an era of greater accountability and transparency regarding the performance of our second-level schools.

How does your college department rate?

External inspections of courses and departments have become a feature of the third-level landscape also. The Irish Universities Quality Board was established in 2002. It is funded by the Higher Education Authority and each of the seven universities. Its role is to identify best practice internationally, issue quality guidelines on issues such as PhD supervision and the organisation of student support services and to conduct external reviews of university departments. It has already conducted dozens of departmental reviews in all seven universities, which are available online at www.iuqb.ie. These reports are admirable in the forthright evaluations they provide on the performance of staff in individual university departments.

The Dublin Institute of Technology is responsible for making its own awards and for quality assurance of courses. This is principally done by way of five-yearly reviews where a panel of internal and external academics review all aspects of a given course, which are then published online, at www.dit.ie/DIT/registrar/qualityassurance/reports-responses.html.

For most of the other IoTs, quality assurance is overseen by HETAC. At the time of writing, they do not make programmatic reviews public, but plan to do so in the near future. Certain IoTs have what is called 'delegated authority' to manage their own quality assurance procedures (for example, Waterford Institute of Technology and Cork Institute of Technology). Neither of these colleges publish programmatic reviews on their websites, but plan to in the near future.

When evaluating a large and complex organisation such as a school or college department, sophisticated and subtle evaluation methods are required to identify the strengths and weaknesses in the context of the staffing and funding resources available. It is meaningless to speak of a 'good' or a 'bad' school. A school may vary in its performance from year to year; also, whereas it may excel in one area or subject, performance may be much lower in another area. In the same way, a college may have a world-class reputation based on the research work of a small number of staff.

However, a first-year student who is not exposed to these staff may have a far from world-class learning experience.

PARTICIPATION IN PART-TIME EMPLOYMENT: DOES IT MATTER?

Commentary on part-time work by secondary school students tends to be concerned about the possible negative impact on students' studies. However, part-time work has many positive features. It provides a source of independent income and consequent saving and budgeting skills, and it can lead to feelings of pride and independence.

The Dublin Employment Pact undertook research to determine whether students' part-time work is detrimental to their studies (Morgan, 2000b). A total of 1,097 students from 16 schools in Dublin were surveyed, of which eight schools are in the Disadvantaged Areas Scheme. Overall, Morgan (2000b) found that students were overwhelmingly positive about their part-time work; it gave strong feelings of independence, enhanced chances of getting work after leaving school and helped them to learn new things and meet interesting people. However, 45 per cent agreed that working meant they had less time for homework, 46 per cent felt it likely they would be tired at school and 36 per cent believed they would have little time for games and hobbies (Morgan, 2000b, p. 7). Substantial levels of part-time work were reported. For example, one-sixth of students (16.7 per cent) reported working 20 hours or more per week. This increased to almost one-fifth of students (18.7 per cent) in disadvantaged schools. Interestingly, only 5 per cent of the sample reported using their earnings to contribute to the family. For most, their earnings went on entertainment, holidays, clothes or shoes and alcohol. This suggests a pattern whereby a significant minority of secondary school students (particularly in disadvantaged areas) are undertaking excessive part-time work, even in the Leaving Certificate year, for non-essential, luxury expenditure.

The somewhat confusingly titled *2004 Annual School Leavers' Survey of 2002–2003 Leavers* (Gorby et al., 2006) contains information on part-time work by secondary school students. In 2002–2003, just over half (53 per cent) of school leavers participated in part-time work while at school. This is a reduction from 58 per cent in 2002 (Gorby et al., 2006). While only a minority of pupils in first, second and third year work while in school, 77 per cent of fifth years and 59 per cent of sixth years were engaged in some paid employment. Social class differences do not appear until the more time-intensive jobs (15 hours or more per week). While one-third of school pupils from a professional background are engaged in high-intensity part-time jobs, 55 per cent of pupils from an 'unemployed' background work more than 15 hours per week. Interestingly, there was no clear pattern between part-time working and examination performance. That is, whether or not a pupil was engaged in part-time work had no bearing on final results. However, this survey did not analyse school results by *intensity* of part-time work. While the occasional night babysitting or Saturday afternoon cutting grass is unlikely to interfere with one's

Leaving Certificate studies, the same cannot be said of 15 hours per week in the local supermarket.

The legislation that governs the employment of young people under age 18 is the Protection of Young Persons (Employment) Act 1996. The Act stipulates that those under age 16 may not be employed in a full-time job. They may be employed during the school holidays or, during term time, in a part-time (maximum of eight hours per week) capacity. There are also restrictions on night-time work, so, for example, those aged less than 16 years may not be required to work after 8:00 p.m. Similarly, 16- and 17-year-olds may not be employed after 10:00 p.m.

WHAT DO IRISH SCHOOL-LEAVERS PROGRESS TO?

The most important source of data about what young people do after leaving school is the *School Leavers' Survey*, conducted regularly by the Economic and Social Research Institute (ESRI). The *2004 Annual School Leavers' Survey of 2002/2003 Leavers* (Gorby et al., 2006) provides a fascinating insight into the economic status of school-leavers, categorised by educational attainment, gender and social class.

Figure 6.2 Percentage of school-leavers progressing to further studies, by father's socio-economic background

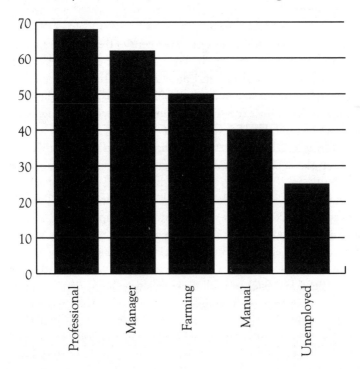

Source: O'Shea and Williams (2001); Gorby et al. (2006).

For the 2002–2003 survey, the most recent available report, a sample of 2,970 school leavers was interviewed 12 to 18 months after leaving school. Overall, 50 per cent of school-leavers were in the labour market, 45 per cent were studying, 4 per cent were unavailable for work and 2 per cent had emigrated.

This survey has been conducted most years since 1980, so it allows long-term trends to be observed. Over this period, there has been a dramatic increase in those progressing to further studies (from 20 per cent in 1980 to 45 per cent in 2004). Females are significantly more likely to proceed to further study; in 2004, 49 per cent did so, compared to 40 per cent of males. Why is this? Firstly, females are considerably more likely to complete second level. In 2004, 85 per cent of the female cohort completed the Leaving Certificate, compared to 79 per cent of males. Secondly, females are more likely to achieve higher marks in almost all subject areas at second level. Thirdly, females display lower levels of behavioural problems that interfere with the demands of schooling. This pattern is international – in most OECD countries, females are more likely to complete upper secondary education than males, a reversal of the historical pattern (OECD, 2005).

Figure 6.3 Percentage of secondary school students leaving with no qualifications, after the junior cycle and after the senior cycle

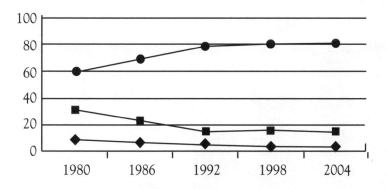

Source: O'Shea and Williams (2001); Gorby et al. (2006).

Social class is also an important determinant of one's second-level attainment. The father's socio-economic background is correlated to school completion and progression to further studies. In 2004, 69 per cent of a sample of school leavers from a professional background proceeded to 'further study', compared with just 26 per cent of those with unemployed fathers (Gorby et al., 2006).

In an analysis of the social backgrounds of college entrants in 2004, O'Connell et al. (2006) developed a social-class inequality index, a 'measure of the differential probability of being admitted to higher education as a member of the higher social classes compared to a member of the lower social classes' (p. 118). Nationally, the former are 1.6 times more likely than the latter to enter higher education (a fall from the social-class inequality level of 1.98 reported in an earlier 2001 report).

The School Leavers' Survey allows us to track school completion trends since 1980. Over this period, there has been a rise in those who completed the Leaving Certificate and a decline in those who left school with no qualifications. For instance, in 1980, 9 per cent of students left secondary school with no qualifications, 31 per cent left after the junior cycle, and 60 per cent completed to Leaving Certificate. In 2004, 4 per cent left with no qualifications, 15 per cent left after the junior cycle (Intermediate Certificate) and 82 per cent completed the Leaving Certificate.

These figures are encouraging and are moving in the right direction. However, many educational researchers have noted that the numbers of those completing the Leaving Certificate has been 'stuck' at between 79 to 82 per cent since the early 1990s. Table 6.1 below summarises the class-gender impact on secondary-school completion.

Table 6.1 Secondary level of education attained by socio-economic background (2004)

	Male				Female			
	No Quals	Junior Cert	Leaving Cert	Total (Col%)	No Quals	Junior Cert	Leaving Cert	Total (Col%)
Farmer/ agriculture	2.0	14.3	83.7	12.6	2.3	3.7	94.1	11.1
Higher-level professional	0.6	8.1	91.2	10.3	1.0	11.4	87.6	10.3
Employer/ manager	2.1	10.1	87.7	10.2	1.4	7.4	91.2	11.7
Intermediate non-manual	3.4	16.2	80.4	20.4	2.6	9.9	87.5	18.1
Skilled/semi-skilled manual	3.3	19.5	77.2	34.0	1.7	11.4	86.9	34.3
Unemployed	13.4	26.9	59.7	6.0	15.6	23.5	60.9	5.6
Other/ unknown	12.7	32.0	55.3	6.4	11.2	22.8	66.1	9.1
Total	4.0	17.3	78.7	100	3.5	11.5	85.0	100.0
Est. no. in category	1341	5833	26557	33731	1178	3930	29022	34130

Source: Gorby et al. (2006).

As we can see, in all social classes except 'higher-level professionals', girls are more likely to complete the Leaving Certificate. The difference is most marked amongst those with a farming or agricultural background, where 94 per cent of females complete the Leaving Certificate compared to 84 per cent of males, suggesting that a proportion of boys leave school early to commence farm work.

Also, both males and females from higher social classes are considerably more likely to complete the Leaving Certificate. Thus, for example, 91 per cent of males from a higher-level professional background complete the Leaving Certificate, compared to only 60 per cent of those from an unemployed background.

It is clear from many ESRI research reports that educational level is important in securing access to the labour market. As common sense would suggest, the findings show that those with no qualifications experience longer periods of unemployment. That is, education is highly predictive of labour market outcomes. However, *even controlling for educational attainment*, those from higher social classes obtain higher quality and better-paid jobs on their entry to the labour market. Smyth and Hannan (2000) suggest factors 'such as the role of informal networks in providing employment information and easing access to jobs, and "social capital" (status-linked personal characteristics, such as self-confidence, self-presentation, accent, etc.) may explain the continuing influence of familial statuses on early employment' (p. 124). This is rather disheartening for those with a belief in education as 'the great leveller'.

FURTHER EDUCATION

A relatively new aspect of the education scene in Ireland is the dramatic growth in the further education (FE) sector, largely delivered through Post Leaving Certificate (PLC) colleges. Over a thousand courses are offered in a wide range of vocational fields such as child care, horticulture, journalism, marketing, computers and fashion design and there are currently approximately 30,000 students in 220 schools and colleges nationwide.

Midway between second- and third-level education, further education courses offer options for further studies for those who do not wish to progress to third level, or who have failed to acquire sufficient points in the Leaving Certificate to enter a higher education programme. It also provides for those returning to education after a break or those seeking to acquire new skills or to avail of 'second chance education'. In some cases FE courses offer 'bridges' to specific higher education courses, primarily in the Institute of Technology sector.

In 2003, 21 per cent of female and 10 per cent of male school-leavers enrolled in a PLC course (Gorby, McCoy and Watson, 2006). This gender disequilibrium may be partly a product of the programmes on offer, many of which are in areas that traditionally provide employment overwhelmingly to women, such as hairdressing, child care, interior design, secretarial studies and beauty therapy. That said, there is a range of other courses that might be considered attractive primarily to men, such as boat building and security systems. A more detailed analysis of course take-up by gender would be required to explain this gender imbalance.

Further education students are drawn from across the socio-economic sector, as measured by the father's occupation, but there are class-based differences. For example, 9.7 per cent of children from 'higher-level professional' backgrounds progress to a PLC course, compared to 16.9 per cent of those from 'skilled/semi-skilled/manual' backgrounds and 19.5 per cent of those whose fathers are unemployed (Gorby, McCoy and Watson, 2006).

Broadly speaking, FETAC (Further Education and Training Awards Council) accredits awards in the PLC sector, which were previously awarded by a host of bodies, Irish and British; for example, the Business and Technology Education Council (BTEC) and City and Guilds of London. This sometimes created problems in progression to higher education courses in the universities and Institutes of Technology in Ireland. Now, at least in theory, all awards in Ireland can be placed on one of the 10 NQAI levels, as described at the beginning of this chapter, thus facilitating progression to the next level.

There has been criticism that the further education sector has not received sufficient funding and structural development relative to the higher education (HE) sector. The Progressive Democrat TD, Liz O' Donnell, recently described the FE sector as the 'Cinderella' of the education system. The Teachers' Union of Ireland (TUI), in particular, have criticised the Department of Education and Science for failing to implement the recommendations in the *Report of the Steering Group to the PLC Review Established by the Department of Education and Science* (Department of Education and Science, 2002a), also known as the McIver Report. This report recommended a significant increase in resourcing to bring the FE sector in line with comparable systems in Europe. It specifically recommended enhanced management structures, an increase in support staff, a reduction in teaching load and an improvement in library, computer, canteen, laboratory and sporting facilities. However, the Department of Finance has expressed reservations regarding the costs of pay increases, capital expenditure and the potential for overlaps between the Further Education and the Institute of Technology sectors.

HIGHER EDUCATION

Traditionally, Ireland has operated a binary system of higher education. Until relatively recently, five universities offered courses at honours degree and post-graduate level (levels 8, 9 and 10 as shown in Figure 6.1). Trinity College, the University of Dublin, was established in 1592. St. Patrick's College Maynooth, established as a seminary in 1795, became a recognised college of the National University of Ireland (NUI) in 1909. University College Cork (UCC) and University College Galway (UCG) were both established as Queens Colleges in 1849 and University College Dublin (UCD) was established in 1854, all three becoming constituent colleges of the NUI on its establishment in 1908. In 1997, these three colleges and the recognised college at Maynooth (but not the seminary, which remains a separate institution) became autonomous universities within a reconstituted confederal National University of Ireland. More recently, two additional universities were created. The University of Limerick and Dublin City University evolved from National Institutes of Higher Education in 1989.

Since the late 1960s, numerous Regional Technical Colleges (now Institutes of Technology) were established to provide sub-degree programmes, primarily at two-year certificate and three-year diploma level (now known as Higher Certificate, Level 6 and BA [Ordinary], Level 7, see Figure 6.1). The focus was on skills-based vocational and technical training in areas such as business, engineering, electronics, science and food technology, but also from an early stage containing elements of music, art, languages, media studies, social science and child care. The history of Irish higher education, from medieval times to the twenty-first century, is perhaps most comprehensively described in White (2001).

Irish higher education has grown from a small, elite system based on five universities with only 18,000 students in 1964 to a much larger and dynamic mass higher education system, with 20 or more public and private providers serving a population of more than 140,000 students in 2004. The range of courses available to college entrants is significantly greater than it had been up until the late 1980s. Increasing access to higher education is a strategic goal of most recent Irish governments, as the upskilling of the population is considered necessary in order to compete with other regions for foreign direct investment in growth industries such as computers and pharmaceuticals. This dramatic growth in higher education is not unique to Ireland and similar patterns can be seen in other developed countries.

Structurally, the biggest change underway at the moment is the result of a government decision to expand the responsibility of the Higher Education Authority (HEA) from the universities to the colleges of education, the Dublin Institute of Technology and ultimately all other Institutes of Technology to create a unified administrative structure (Clancy, 2005). While this may not have a seismic impact on students in the lecture halls, it will give greater autonomy to the non-university HE providers and remove them from the day-to-day control of the Department of Education and Science.

Mass Third-Level Education

In all cases, higher education providers are competing for a decreasing pool of school-leavers. However, the proportion of these school-leavers progressing to higher education is increasing with the result that the beginning of the twenty-first century has seen a considerable vibrancy enter the higher education sector in Ireland, with greater choices and options for students, and more (long overdue) routes of access, progression and transfer. The elitist, moribund higher education system of previous decades has been left behind as Ireland strives to make further education and higher education available to as many people as possible.

There is a good chance you are reading this book as part of your third-level studies. Forty years ago in Ireland, you would have been a member of a tiny minority of school-leavers to go for further study. If Catholic, you probably would not have entered Trinity College Dublin, but instead would have chosen University College Cork, University College Dublin, University College Galway or St. Patrick's College Maynooth. Courses were primarily confined to arts, science, classics, medicine and law. Alternatively, if male, you might have 'gone for the priesthood' in one of the many seminaries around the country. The Regional Technical Colleges did not exist and the PLC sector would not become a serious presence on the scene for 30 years.

Figure 6.4 Admission rates to higher education, as a proportion of the 17–19 years age cohort

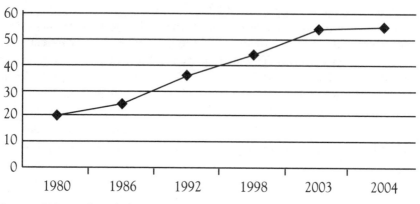

Source: O'Connell et al. (2006, p. 94).

Today, approximately 55 per cent of school-leavers go on to third level, either to one of the seven universities, 14 Institutes of Technology, teacher training college or one of the private colleges, primarily in Dublin, such as Griffith College, Portobello College and the Dublin Business College. The most up-to-date figures show that in 2004, 36,051 students entered higher education for the first time, which represents 55 per cent of school-leavers. Of these new entrants, 47 per cent enrolled in universities, 42 per cent in IoTs, 4.5 per cent in colleges of education and 6.4 per cent in other colleges (O'Connell et al., 2006). Furthermore, approximately 30,000 school leavers enrol on PLC courses, at the so-called 'second and a half' level. In 40 years, the third-level landscape has changed considerably, from 20,698 students in 1965–66 to 143,271 in 2003–04.

Differences in New College Entrants by College Type

O'Connell et al. (2006) conducted a postal survey of new entrants based on data provided by the Central Applications Office. A total of 34,682 questionnaires were distributed and 14,571 (or 42 per cent) were returned. Although low, this is not an unusual response rate for a postal survey. As the researchers had access to key population parameters at the CAO (age, gender, HEI type, school type, region), they were able to reweight the data to ensure that it better represented the target population. Thus, the results reported are estimates of the true population parameters (O'Connell et al., 2006, p. 40). The universities and Colleges of Education have a considerably greater intake of Leaving Certificate graduates with multiple honours.

Table 6.2 Educational backgrounds of new college entrants by college type (%)

No. of Hons	Universities	IoTs	Colleges of Education	Other	Total
0–3	17.5	70.9	8.4	80.5	43.7 (14649)
4–5	33.5	22.3	23.7	16.9	27.5 (9179)
6 or more	49.0	6.8	67.9	2.8	28.7 (9616)
Total %	100.0	100.0	100.0	100.0	100.0
Total N	15,607	15,086	1,316	914	33,444

Source: O'Connell (2006. p. 76).

As we can see, Leaving Certificate students with six or more honours (Grade C or higher on Higher Level papers) make up the greater proportion of university (49 per cent) and College of Education (67.9 per cent) students, relative to the IoTs, where only 6.8 per cent of new entrants obtained six or more honours in their Leaving Certificate.

Regional Variation in College Entry

As has consistently been the case since studies of this kind were first carried out, entry rates to higher education vary significantly by region. They are highest in the western seaboard, for example, Sligo (70.5 per cent), Galway (67.4 per cent), Kerry (67 per cent) and Mayo (66.8 per cent). What is the explanation for this? Possibly it is due to a higher population of small farmers, a group which has traditionally placed a high value on education, perhaps increasingly so in an era when it becomes difficult to make a living on small farms. Very low rates of entry to higher education are found in some Dublin postal districts, particularly those with higher concentrations of lower SES (socio-economic status) households, for example, Ballyfermot (11.7 per cent) and other inner-city areas.

The availability of a college locally would not appear to be an overwhelming determinant. Higher than average entry rates are recorded in some counties with no college (Roscommon, 57.8 per cent; Longford, 60.3 per cent; Leitrim, 64.2 per cent). Nationally, the lowest admission rate is Co. Westmeath (40.8 per cent), despite the presence of Athlone Institute of Technology.

O'Connell et al. (2006) examined the factors impacting on inter-county variability in university and IoT admission rates. They report that rates of entry to university are higher where there is a higher proportion of households engaged in farming and where there is geographic proximity to a university. In the IoT sector, counties with lower per capita income have greater admission rates:

> It appears that the key underlying processes 'explaining' county level variability in admission rates to higher education are different for admission to the university and Institute of Technology sectors. The educational attainments of the population and the prominence of farming, along with proximity to a university, appear to be the key factors distinguishing counties with high and low admission rates to university. For the Institutes of Technology on the other hand, counties with lower levels of economic development (as measured by income per capita) have higher admission rates (O'Connell et al., 2006, p. 114).

Irish College Entry Relative to Other Countries

While the increase in progression to higher education in Ireland has been dramatic in recent years, it is surpassed by many other wealthy nations. For example, in 2004, 44 per cent of the relevant age cohort in Ireland entered tertiary type A education, defined by the OECD (2004, p. 6) as 'largely theoretically-based and designed to provide qualifications for entry to advanced research programmes and professions with high skill requirements', essentially, honours degree programmes. For the same year, almost 90 per cent of the relevant youth cohort in New Zealand, and almost 80 per cent in Sweden and Iceland, progressed to tertiary type A education (OECD, 2006). Notwithstanding the dramatic growth in numbers progressing to higher education in Ireland in recent years, there is still considerable scope to increase the numbers further to match the progression rates in other wealthy countries.

At the highest educational level, the doctorate, Ireland also has some catching up to do. Ireland's number of PhD graduates per 1,000 head of population aged 25 to 29 is 1.8 per cent, compared to the EU average of 2.9 per cent and far below countries like Finland and Sweden – both at 5.8 per cent (OECD, 2004, p. 36).

IS IRISH HIGHER EDUCATION IN DANGER OF 'MISSION DRIFT'?

As a result of this growth and expansion, the clear division between degree-providing universities and sub-degree-providing technical colleges has become blurred. As they attempt to shift up the 'academic ladder', several of the larger Institutes of Technology are offering degree and post-graduate education. This is particularly noticeable in the case of the largest IoT, the Dublin Institute of Technology. For the 2006 September intake, DIT offered 32 Level 6 and 7 programmes (its 'traditional' area of operation) and 47 Level 8 degrees. In addition, it offers 45 taught post-graduate programmes. At the time of writing, both Dublin Institute of Technology and Waterford Institute of Technology (WIT) have active campaigns underway to acquire university status.

Some commentators see this as 'mission drift', with the potential to dilute the benefits of the existing binary system. Two major reports have been commissioned in recent years to advise the Higher Education Authority (HEA) and government on how best to develop the higher education sector: the Skilbeck Report (2001) and the OECD Report (2004).

The Skilbeck Report was published by the Higher Education Authority in 2001, with financial support from a private philanthropic organisation – Atlantic Philanthropy, which is funded by Irish American billionaire Chuck Feeney, who has provided enormous sums of money to Irish universities in recent years. The main thrust of the Skilbeck Report, *The University Challenged*, is that universities must change and adapt to a fast-growing economy and changing society. They should co-operate more closely to become a strong national system, rather than a collection of individual organisations. They should establish systems to monitor the quality of teaching and research; they should broaden student intake and increase the proportion of mature age and post-graduate students 'to better meet access and equity targets' (2001, p. 13). Teaching should be more flexible to facilitate part-time learners and others returning to education. Also, they should co-operate more closely with the wider community, industry and the Institutes of Technology. In summary:

> To gain strength and impact and to maximise their human and financial resources, the universities need to work more closely together, in various partnerships, yet with more entrepreneurial flair. The readiness to address the challenges creatively and effectively, while maintaining the intellectual and moral values of free inquiry and the disinterested pursuit of truth, will be a demonstration of the Irish university's continuing relevance and vitality (ibid., 2001, p. 13).

Skilbeck does not address the binary nature of the higher education system in Ireland directly in his 2001 report. He does this in a subsequent 2003 report where he argues that the binary system is rigid, highly regulated and less capable of strategic innovation (Skilbeck, 2003). That is, the lack of a cohesive, unified, single 'system' of third-level education in Ireland may lead to gaps and duplication. He argues for a more integrated, coherent tertiary system. He argues that the present system gives the universities considerably greater freedom, power, prestige and influence than even the largest and strongest IoTs. He recommends the establishment of two new universities to be established from the existing Waterford Institute of Technology

(WIT) and Dublin Institute of Technology (DIT). Such new universities would provide a spectrum of sub-degree, degree and post-graduate qualifications, as occurs in numerous other jurisdictions, often in the form of 'technological universities'.

A second major report on higher education was undertaken by the OECD (2004) as a result of an invitation by the Department of Education and Science to undertake a review of Irish higher education. The OECD authors echo Skilbeck (2001) and argue that Ireland needs a better-integrated tertiary system. For example, management of the entire 'system' is split between the HEA (for the universities) and the Department of Education and Science (for the IoTs). Unlike Skilbeck, however, the authors of the OECD report argue that this can occur while retaining the divide between the universities and the Institutes of Technology. They argued that DIT should remain as separate and distinct from the university sector:

> The role of DIT is significantly different to other institutes by reason of its age, size, academic range and location in Dublin but we believe that its mission … as a comprehensive higher education institution serving the very broad educational and vocational needs of Dublin must be retained. The success of the institute sector needs to be nurtured and celebrated so that its differentiation from the university sector is not seen as conferring lower status but defining it as an equal partner in a dynamic higher education system which covers a diverse range of functions (OECD, 2004, p. 20).

Indeed, the first of the 52 recommendations in this OECD review of higher education is that 'the differentiation of mission between the university and the institute of technology sectors is preserved and that for the foreseeable future there be no further institutional transfers into the university sector' (OECD, 2004, p. 63). To summarise, the OECD (2004) was clear in its recommendation to government that there should be no new university. However, other international experts disagree (see Skilbeck, 2003), pointing to the model of the technological university common in Europe. In addition to DIT, both Cork IT and Waterford IT have launched campaigns off and on over the years for university status. At the time of writing, WIT has a formal application with the Minister for Education and Science to be assigned university status. This application took a step forward in November 2006 when the government appointed an international higher education expert to assess WIT's application. Other Institutes of Technology will watch with interest.

Why Do Some Institutes of Technology Seek University Status?

As noted in both Skilbeck (2001) and OECD (2004), many of the bigger actors in the IoT sector have long campaigned for university status. In 1998, an application by DIT to the Department of Education and Science for university designation was refused, based on the recommendations of an international review group (the Nally Report). In 2004, the DIT became a membe of the European University Association, suggesting its research and course provision is akin to those of a university, but it remains, in Irish law, an IoT under the control of the Department of Education and Science, with little of the independence enjoyed by the universities.

A primary reason for seeking a change in designation is to acquire greater academic and management independence; for example, the creation of a new degree course in the IoT sector requires approval from the Department of Education and Science. However, this is not the case for universities. This gives an unfair advantage to the university sector, particularly in an era of decreasing student numbers. Similarly, the universities have much greater freedom to divert income from fees for development initiatives. This freedom is not available to management in the IoT sector, thus stifling innovation and development.

There is also the issue of greater international recognition. The term 'university' is internationally recognised as a place of higher education. The same is not true of 'institute of technology'. It is felt that this can hinder efforts to recruit students internationally and to foster links with European and international universities.

CONCLUSION

Education of its population is a strategic goal of Irish governments and is highly valued by the general population. However, Irish funding of education does not match our international counterparts and there are numerous areas where there is considerable scope for improvement, such as school completion, access to third level and numbers of PhD graduates. A vibrancy and dynamism has been created at further and higher education level in the last decade and this must be extended to provide even greater access to more sections of the population, including school-leavers, mature students, work-based students and other 'life long learners' if Ireland is to compete with other countries in creating a knowledge-based economy.

RECOMMENDED READING

Hannan, D., Smyth, E., McCullagh, J., O'Leary, R., & McMahon, D. (1996). *Coeducation and gender equality. Exam performance, stress and personal development.* Dublin: Oaktree Press/ESRI. A comprehensive study on the effects of coeducation on exam performance that highlights the importance of family and social background, and prior academic ability, on exam performance and illustrates that, all other things being equal, single-sex or mixed-sex schooling does not have a significant impact on exam performance.

OECD. (2004). *Review of higher education in Ireland.* Paris: OECD. The most recent comprehensive analysis of the Higher Education sector.

7

Values and Attitudes

INTRODUCTION

At a time of very rapid social change, such as Ireland has experienced in recent years, it is common for adults to express concern about the younger generation and to worry that the values they themselves hold dear, the things they believe in and they regard as being a central part of their culture, are under threat. Even when the pace of social change has not been so dramatic, there has been a long-standing perception that there is a 'generation gap' between older and younger people, involving not just the obvious differences of chronological age but also marked differences of behaviour and lifestyle and – more fundamentally – of basic values and beliefs. Is this the case in Ireland today? Do young people see things, or at least some things, differently from adults? And if so, how might the differences be interpreted and what might their implications or significance be? This chapter will consider some recent evidence regarding the values and attitudes of young people in Ireland, comparing it where possible with findings relating to other age groups in contemporary Ireland, to Irish young people in the past and to young people in other countries, particularly within Europe.

Firstly, it is necessary to define some terms. Values can be defined as the standards that people have about what is good and bad (Macionis and Plummer, 2005, p. 111); in other words, they have a moral dimension (the concept of moral development is introduced in Chapter 2). Values vary not just from one person to another, but from culture to culture. In fact, the word 'moral' comes from the Latin word for 'custom', reflecting the fact that our morals are to a substantial extent 'customary' or cultural. Beliefs are specific statements that people hold to be true. While values are abstract standards relating to what is good and bad, beliefs are more specific expressions of what people hold to be true or false, valid or invalid (ibid); for example, if 'democracy' is a value (a general commitment to, literally, the 'rule of the people'), a belief that the citizen has the responsibility as well as the right to exercise his or her vote might follow. Attitudes and beliefs are very similar. Early uses of the concept of attitude referred to physical posture or body position, and that remains part of the dictionary definition. A social attitude can therefore be defined as the position someone takes (or a whole group takes) regarding a social issue or topic or another social group; it is a 'standpoint' on a matter of social significance.

The remainder of this chapter will consider young people's values, attitudes and beliefs in relation to politics, religion, sexual morality and social issues.

POLITICS

In the broadest sense, 'politics' is about power, and power refers to the capacity of individuals and groups to implement their will, fulfil their goals or further their aspirations and ambitions, with tensions necessarily arising when wills, goals or aspirations are incompatible. In this sense, there is a political dimension to all social life. However, in practice the term is usually employed with a more specific meaning, referring to what might be called 'institutional' or 'constitutional' politics (Hackett, 1997). The designation 'party politics' captures much of the sense of these terms. It is this dimension of politics on which most research effort has focused so it will be the one highlighted here; although it will also be suggested that a significant aspect of contemporary social and generational change may be the fact that people are becoming politically aware and active in new and diverse ways, and that we should not interpret young people's political attitudes and behaviour simplistically.

Attitudes to Politics and Public Institutions

There has been a concern in Ireland for many years that young people have become disaffected from institutional politics. The National Youth Policy Committee (see Chapter 10) was established in 1983 not least because there was a 'real fear that many young people will, in frustration, become alienated from their society' (Department of Labour, 1983, p. 1) and in particular a concern that these alienated young people could be lured by 'the appeal of the non-democratic path' (Government of Ireland, 1985, p. 13). More recently there has been a sense that the *apathy* of young people, rather than their radical activism, might itself be subversive of democracy. One of the considerations which led to the preparation of the EU White Paper *A New Impetus for European Youth* was the 'widening gap between young people and public affairs at national, European and international levels, with the attendant risk of a "citizenship deficit"' (European Commission, 2002, p. 10). Figures 7.1 and 7.2 support the contention that there is such a gap. Drawing on the European Commission's Eurobarometer survey (conducted twice a year throughout the EU), they show the contrasting responses in May/June 2005, by age group, to the statements 'I am interested in what is going on in politics and current affairs' and 'I feel well informed about what is going on in politics and current affairs'. Young European citizens (15- to 24-year-olds) are considerably less likely to respond positively to both statements than older ones (with a difference of 12 per cent and 11 per cent, respectively). The younger they are, the less interested or informed they are likely to be. The data also suggest that young people in the 10 member states that had just recently joined the EU at the time of this Eurobarometer (referred to in the charts as 'NMS' or 'New Member States') were less informed about politics and current affairs (or, strictly speaking, were more likely to *think* they were less informed) than the longer-established EU members, and the difference in their level of interest was even greater. This relatively unenthusiastic response to politics and current affairs among young people was in keeping with the actual voter turnout in the elections for the European Parliament in 2004; only one-third of 18- to 24-year-olds participated in the elections, compared with a turnout of 45.6 per cent for the electorate as a whole (European Commission, 2005).

Figure 7.1 'I am interested in what is going on in politics and currents affairs'

% of 'Agree'

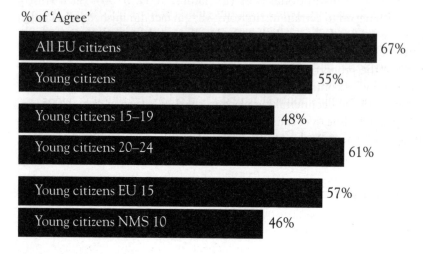

Figure 7.2 'I feel well informed about what is going on in politics and currents affairs'

% of 'Agree'

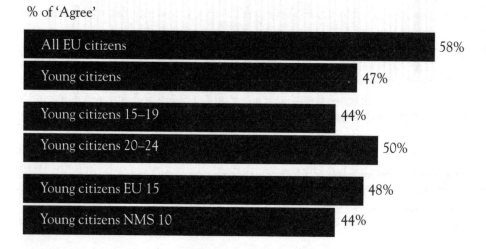

Irish research findings are broadly in line with this pattern. It should firstly be said that Irish confidence in public institutions is very high by European standards. Figure 7.3 shows levels of confidence in public institutions in European countries (not limited to the EU) as measured in the European Values Study (EVS) in 1999–2000. The public institutions in question include the armed forces, the education system, the press, trade unions, the police and the civil service. The diagram shows mean scores calculated on a scale ranging from 1 (no confidence at all) to 4 (a great deal of confidence).

Ireland is second highest in ranking, exceeded only by Finland. This is unusual in international terms because countries with a dominant Roman Catholic tradition tend to score low on institutional trust (Elchardus, 2003, p. 33). Such trust – particularly with regard to certain institutions – has in fact diminished in Ireland in the period since the first European Values Study was carried out in 1981. Confidence in the Catholic Church itself has fallen considerably (as will be seen in the next section); while the proportion expressing confidence in the Dáil (either 'a great deal' or 'quite a lot' of confidence) fell from 52 per cent in 1981 to 31 per cent in 1999, with most of the decline taking place in the 1990s (Fahey et al., 2005, pp. 194–5). Despite a decline over time, however, Irish people's levels of confidence in their national parliament, in the government and in political parties remains ahead of the EU average (European Commission 2006, p. 19).

Figure 7.3 Confidence in public institutions in Europe

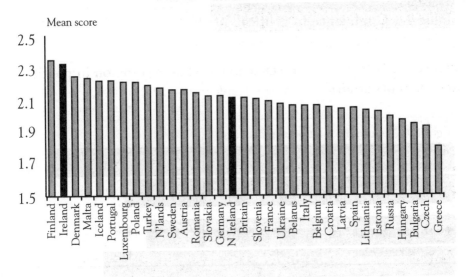

Note: Mean scores are based on a four-point scale ranging fom 1 (none at all) to 4 (a great deal). Institutions included: armed forces, education system, the press, trade unions, the police, the civil service.

Source: European Values Study, 1999–2000; Fahey et al. (2005).

As is the case throughout Europe, there are age-related differences in the Irish findings. The European Values Study 1999–2000 shows differences between younger people and older people with regard both to confidence in political institutions and to orientations towards political action ('younger people' here means those aged 18 to 30 years as the European Values Study does not include people under 18). Table 7.1 presents the data relating to both of these variables cross-tabulated with gender and age. A number of public institutions are specified, as are a number of types of political action. The table shows that men and women differ hardly at all in their degree of confidence in political institutions but do differ significantly with regard to all items of political action, with the exception of voting itself. As Fahey et al. conclude (2005, p. 205), 'gender makes no difference in terms of confidence in politics or of turning out to vote but has significant effects on a range of other forms of political involvement'.

The differences relating to age are more pronounced. The 18- to 30-year-olds tend to have less confidence in public institutions, including political parties and the Dáil, than the older age groups (although the pattern is not straightforward in the case of the civil service and the health care system). They are less likely to be 'very interested' or 'somewhat interested' in politics, although more likely than most of their elders to say they have helped or might help a political party. They are also more likely to have taken part in a demonstration or an occupation of a building. Finally, they are much less likely to follow politics in the media regularly and to say they will vote in the next election.

Table 7.1 Confidence in political institutions and orientation to political action by gender and age, Ireland

	Gender		Age			
	Male	Female	18 to 30 years	31 to 45 years	46 to 60 years	61 years or more
A great deal plus quite a lot of confidence in:						
Political parties	19	19	15	15	21	27
Dáil	32	32	26	30	39	34
Civil service	61	60	58	54	66	64
Gardaí	85	86	81	84	89	89
Health care system	59	57	62	51	59	63
Social welfare system	56	58	50	49	62	69

	Gender		Age			
	Male	Female	18 to 30 years	31 to 45 years	46 to 60 years	61 years or more
Political action:						
Very interested in or somewhat interested in politics	53	39	39	43	53	46
Have helped or might help a political party	54	40	49	44	51	41
Have occupied or might occupy buildings	21	14	21	20	19	7
Have attended or might attend lawful demonstrations	73	57	73	69	68	46
Follow politics in the media every day or several times a week	57	46	33	49	60	58
Would vote in next election	79	81	69	79	84	87

Source: European Values Study, 1999–2000; Fahey et al. (2005).

Voters and Non-Voters

The 'next election' in that particular case was the General Election of 2002. A survey conducted by the Central Statistics Office after that election (as a 'module' within the Quarterly National Household Survey) assessed the extent to which people described themselves as having voted (CSO, 2003b). Not surprisingly, it found that voter abstention was highest among young people (see Figure 7.4 below). Just over 40 per cent of those aged 18 to 19 and 53 per cent of those aged 20 to 24 indicated that they had voted in the election. The figure increased rapidly with age thereafter, reaching a high of almost 90 per cent for 65- to 74-year-olds, and then declining somewhat to 85 per cent for those aged 75 to 79 and 79 per cent for those aged 80 and over. Male and female rates were almost identical at 75.9 per cent and 75.2 per cent, respectively, bearing out the EVS findings cited above. The overall self-reported turnout of 75.5 per cent in the survey compares with an actual voter turnout at the election of 62 per cent. Such an overstatement of participation is usual in surveys like this. It may reflect the likelihood of a lower turnout among non-respondents to the survey; in other words, those actually responding to the survey are also those most likely to vote. There may also be a reluctance to admit to not voting. Despite the discrepancy, the CSO believes the survey findings provide a sound basis for analysing the socio-demographic characteristics (including age) and attitudes of voters and non-voters.

Figure 7.4

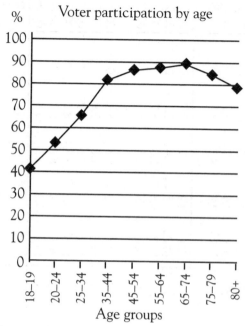

Source: CSO (2003b).

Table 7.2 provides information on the reasons given by the abstainers for not voting, broken down by age but also by other variables (respondents were asked to pick one reason only). Among younger people, the most important reasons are clearly not being registered and not being interested. (We do not know the reasons for not being registered but presumably in many cases that could be attributable to not being interested, although there are undoubtedly other factors involved, such as being away from home, preoccupied with study and so on.) Two out of five 18- and 19-year-old abstainers are not registered, almost double the national rate. Not being registered accounts for more than one quarter of 20- to 24-year-old non-voters and almost as many 25- to 29-year-olds. About a quarter of the abstainers aged 18 to 24 say they have 'no interest' in voting. Interestingly, the younger age groups express very low levels of 'disillusionment' with politics as compared with older people. This is both good news and bad news for politicians! The figures also show low levels of interest among single people and those on home duties, and high levels of non-registration among single people and students, but a relatively low proportion of students attribute their abstention to lack of interest.

Table 7.2 Non-voters in the May 2002 general election classified by reason(s) for not voting

	No interest	Disillusioned	Lack of knowledge/ information	My vote would make no difference	Illness/ disability	Away	Too busy	Not registered	No polling card	Lack of transport	Other	Not stated	% Total
State	20.4	10.6	2.9	3.7	6.0	15.6	8.5	21.8	3.8	1.3	5.6	0.1	100.0
Sex													
Male	19.9	13.2	2.7	3.8	4.1	16.2	9.5	21.0	3.9	0.6	5.1	*	100.0
Female	20.8	8.1	3.1	3.6	7.7	15.0	7.4	22.6	3.6	1.9	6.0	0.2	100.0
Age group													
18–19	24.0	4.6	2.6	4.0	*	9.0	5.8	39.4	6.3	0.7	3.6	*	100.0
20–24	25.8	5.8	4.5	2.6	0.9	17.3	9.6	25.5	4.3	0.3	3.5	*	100.0
25–34	21.1	11.6	2.5	3.3	2.5	16.3	9.9	24.6	3.8	0.4	4.0	*	100.0
35–44	17.8	15.2	2.5	4.0	4.0	14.6	9.8	19.8	3.7	0.8	7.9	*	100.0
45–54	16.7	17.4	2.0	5.2	6.2	18.0	9.7	10.8	2.1	1.0	10.5	0.5	100.0
55–64	13.8	16.0	1.9	4.1	12.4	21.5	6.7	9.5	3.7	1.7	8.7	*	100.0
65+	11.0	9.6	1.9	5.5	37.9	11.8	1.3	3.5	0.9	8.3	8.3	*	100.0
Marital status													
Single	22.9	9.3	3.4	3.4	2.7	14.0	8.0	27.0	4.4	0.7	4.3	0.1	100.0
Married	16.9	12.8	1.8	4.1	7.7	20.6	10.8	14.0	2.5	1.4	7.2	0.2	100.0
Separated	19.0	16.6	2.2	4.1	4.8	11.3	8.3	19.7	4.3	1.0	8.7	*	100.0
Widowed	10.5	8.8	2.9	4.9	35.8	13.2	2.1	3.7	1.9	7.3	8.9	*	100.0
Principal economic status													
At work	20.6	10.9	2.5	3.2	1.9	18.3	11.2	22.6	3.2	0.4	5.1	0.1	100.0
Unemployed	24.5	12.2	4.3	4.8	2.7	10.2	3.6	23.6	7.3	1.0	5.9	*	100.0
Student	14.7	6.1	4.6	3.7	0.1	18.0	6.4	38.4	4.5	0.6	2.9	*	100.0
On home duties	24.3	10.1	2.6	5.1	13.7	9.8	6.2	13.3	3.5	3.3	8.1	*	100.0
Retired	11.1	14.2	1.9	3.8	31.1	13.7	1.8	6.5	1.9	6.0	8.2	*	100.0
Others	22.0	13.9	1.4	2.6	25.9	8.2	2.3	13.1	5.5	1.3	3.8	*	100.0

* sample occurrence too small for estimation

Source: CSO (2003b).

The unemployed respondents score highly both on disinterest and non-registration, and are much more likely to be numbered among the non-voters in the first place (only 59 per cent of the unemployed said they had voted, compared with 76 per cent of those at work). This is in keeping with the findings of the 1999 EVS survey, in which 29 per cent of the unemployed, as compared with 49 per cent of the employed, said they were 'very interested' or 'somewhat interested' in politics (Fahey et al., 2005, p. 207). That study (like most other research) also found significant social class differences in interest in politics and propensity to engage in political action, with people in manual occupations less likely than their non-manual counterparts to take part in almost all types of political activity except voting itself (the proportion expressing an intention to vote in the next election was identical for manual and non-manual workers, 80 per cent in both cases). Education (which is itself of course related to social class) is the biggest influence on levels of political interest and activism. Two-thirds of the EVS survey respondents with third-level education were interested in politics, compared to just 40 per cent of those with 'some secondary education or less' (ibid.). This is consistent with the view of some writers who argue for a 'resource-based' as opposed to 'disaffection-based' model of political action (or inaction) among young people.

> Those who are more educated feel they are able to influence the course of political events, whereas those without these cognitive and social resources feel powerless to affect them. In terms of identity, the political engagement dimension reflects the degree to which engagement in politics and political activity is important or central to one's self-concept. For those high in engagement, a distinctive ideological position will be a salient aspect of their identity, while those who are low in engagement will not strongly define themselves in political terms (Bynner et al., 2003, p. 320).

As well as asking respondents whether they had voted in the previous election, the CSO survey conducted in 2002 also inquired about their 'satisfaction with the workings of democracy in Ireland'. The findings are provided in Table 7.3, broken down by sex and age. Males are more likely to be 'very satisfied' than females; females are more likely to be undecided. As regards age, what is most striking is the very high level of 'don't knows' among the younger age groups. Considerably more than a quarter of 18- and 19-year-olds, and one in five 20- to 24-year-olds, say they don't know whether they are satisfied. These two groups also have the fewest 'very satisfied' respondents. Not surprisingly, there are significant differences between voters and non-voters regarding degree of satisfaction. More than three-quarters (75.6 per cent) of those who said they voted also said they were 'very' or 'fairly' satisfied with the workings of democracy, compared with not much more than half (54.2 per cent) of the non-voters, while the latter were more than three times as likely as the former to say they didn't know whether they were satisfied (22.1 per cent and 7.3 per cent, respectively). The survey found other significant attitudinal and behavioural differences between voters and non-voters, with voters much more likely to say they have definite views on political issues, that they think most politicians are honest and that most of their own families and friends vote too.

Table 7.3 Persons entitled to vote in the May 2002 general election classified by their satisfaction with the workings of democracy in Ireland

	Very satisfied	Fairly satisfied	Not very satisfied	Not at all satisfied	Don't know	Not stated	% Total
State	16.2	54.1	12.6	6.0	10.9	0.3	100.0
Sex							
Male	18.1	54.1	12.5	6.5	8.5	0.2	100.0
Female	14.3	54.1	12.6	5.5	13.2	0.3	100.0
Age group							
18–19	10.7	45.5	9.6	6.1	28.1	*	100.0
20–24	12.5	52.3	10.6	5.0	19.4	0.2	100.0
25–34	13.5	55.6	13.2	5.9	11.5	0.3	100.0
35–44	16.7	57.1	12.5	6.0	7.3	0.3	100.0
45–54	17.8	54.1	13.8	6.9	7.0	0.3	100.0
55–64	18.6	54.3	13.7	6.3	6.9	0.2	100.0
65+	20.1	52.0	11.8	5.4	10.3	0.3	100.0
Marital status							
Single	13.4	52.2	12.4	6.3	15.6	0.1	100.0
Married	18.2	56.6	12.4	5.6	7.0	0.3	100.0
Separated	14.1	49.7	16.7	8.5	10.7	0.4	100.0
Widowed	19.3	51.3	12.1	5.2	11.8	0.4	100.0
Principal economic status							
At work	16.6	56.4	12.2	5.7	8.8	0.3	100.0
Unemployed	10.7	43.4	16.3	11.2	18.2	0.2	100.0
Student	13.1	50.8	12.5	6.0	17.6	*	100.0
On home duties	15.0	52.9	12.7	5.0	14.2	0.2	100.0
Retired	21.6	51.7	12.4	6.3	7.7	0.3	100.0
Others	14.2	48.7	12.6	8.9	15.5	*	100.0
Electorate							
Voters	18.2	57.4	11.9	5.2	7.3	0.2	100.0
Non-voters	10.1	44.1	14.7	8.5	22.1	0.5	100.0

* Sample occurrence too small for estimation
Source: CSO (2003b).

Making Politics More Attractive to Young People

Youth workers and youth organisations have been arguing for some years that the systems of registration and voting (among other things) should be reformed to make it easier and more attractive for young people to become involved in institutional politics. In response to the CSO survey findings, McLoughlin (2003, p. 9) noted: 'The main reason for poor turnout amongst young voters is amenable to remedy, i.e. not being on the register or being on the register in the wrong place.' He recommended a number of practical measures, including the (voluntary) combination of voter registration with other events such as the issue of driving licences or registration with state websites, and other innovative uses of ICTs (information and communication technologies) (ibid). The National Youth Council of Ireland has called on several occasions for a change in the arrangements regarding polling days: 'Mid-week elections restrict the ability of young people to vote. The constant change in election day from poll to poll is also confusing. All future elections should be held at a weekend' (NYCI, 1998, p. 13).

As we saw at the start of this section, the pattern of diminishing involvement by young people in institutional politics is by no means exclusive to Ireland. In an analysis based on the experience in Britain but with relevance throughout Europe and beyond, Kimberlee (2002) suggests that there are at least four different categories of explanation for young people not voting (and not being actively involved in mainstream politics in other ways). The first consists of what he calls 'youth-focused' explanations. These suggest that young people's non-participation is a result of their age and/or aspects of their lifestyle: the fact that they are more mobile, may have a less established pattern of residence, may be removed from strong family and community ties, may have less responsibilities and be more apathetic regarding institutions in general.

Secondly, there are 'politics-focused' explanations which draw attention to barriers created either by state institutions or political parties. These include the factors mentioned above – arrangements for registration, timing of elections and so on – as well as the ethos and organisation of the parties themselves, their lack of interest in the views and experiences of young people (particularly as young people make up a declining proportion of the population as a whole), their intolerance of youthful innovation and dissent, and the fact that they are dominated by older people.

'Alternative-value' explanations suggest that young people are attracted to politically 'unconventional' ideas and movements such as environmental and identity politics and a variety of social issues, and that they choose to express a commitment to these values by other means than voting in elections, not least because election candidates are unlikely to reflect their own interests and commitments. (The EVS survey cited above does indeed show that young people are more likely to take part in certain types of political activism than older people, especially demonstrations and occupations, but it also suggests that they are more likely to help, or be willing to help, a political party.)

Finally, what Kimberlee calls 'generational explanations' highlight the influences of evolving social and political events, and broader cultural developments, on the views and behaviour of each generation. In this view, young people's lack of political engagement is a reflection of and response to broader social changes which have increasingly delayed their acquisition of traditional 'adult statuses' (like secure employment, marriage and independent residence) and made their lives more precarious and 'uncertain':

> [L]ong-standing sources of reference like class, family, community and religion, are less apparent than before, making collective identities less relevant and harder to sustain. These certainties used to be seen as vital to ensure that young people develop a partisan attachment to a political party, particularly for young people from the working class ... (Kimberlee, 2002, p. 95).

Obviously our choice of explanation for the relative lack of engagement of young people with political institutions (whether one of the four options just outlined or another explanation altogether) will shape our opinions regarding what would be an appropriate remedy or response. It is unlikely that any one explanation is sufficient on its own. At any rate, it is important to conclude this section with a caution against interpreting young people's relationship to political culture in an overly simplistic way, or seeing them necessarily as a problematic 'special case'. For one thing, and as shown above, there is evidence that adults, too, have come to have less confidence in at least some public institutions than they had in the past, and this is likely to have an influence on young people's values and behaviour. The concern with an overall decline in social engagement and community activism lay behind the establishment by the Taoiseach in 2006 of a Task Force on Active Citizenship to explore ways of boosting Ireland's 'social capital', an idea most associated with the American writer Robert Putnam (2000). Moreover, a lack of 'engagement' with any social phenomenon need not mean a lack of awareness or interest, and in certain instances a lack of engagement may represent a highly intelligent and sophisticated response; it may reflect 'not just the absence of political interest, knowledge or commitments, but a self-definition as more actively averse to, or disenchanted with, the political sphere ... [Research shows that] significant numbers of young people are more than indifferent about politics – they are highly cynical and actively avoid engaging with politics' (Bynner et al., 2003, p. 327). If this is the case, the challenge is clearly not just, or not primarily, to change young people's (and older people's) values, attitudes and behaviour relating to political institutions, but to reform the institutions themselves so as to make them more likely to command young people's respect and involvement.

RELIGION

It was mentioned earlier that confidence in the Catholic Church has declined considerably in Ireland in recent years. In fact, as Figure 7.5 shows, even among regular church attenders (in this case those who attend at least once a month), the proportion of Catholics expressing a 'great deal' of confidence in the Church has fallen by almost half from 57 per cent in the first European Values Study in 1981 to 29 per cent in 1999–2000 (the equivalent figure for 'irregular attenders' in the most recent EVS being only 5 per cent). Figure 7.5 also makes it clear that the pattern of decline in Northern Ireland has been much less marked. While the clerical sex abuse scandals of recent years have for the most part occurred in Ireland, some commentators have argued that they did not so much cause a radical new loss of confidence in the Catholic Church in the South as 'carry forward a downward momentum that had begun up to two decades earlier' (Fahey et al., 2005, p. 49). Differences in the two parts of the island are likely to reflect at least in part the fact that in Northern Ireland religious differences continue to overlap to a substantial extent with political ones, as well as the influence of divergent social and economic conditions North and South in recent years.

Figure 7.5 Declining confidence in the Church among regular church attenders in Ireland and Northern Ireland, 1981–1999

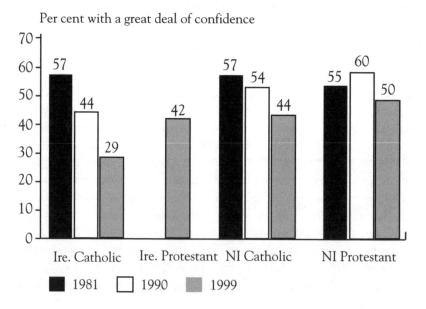

Note: Regular attenders attended religious services at least once a month. Data for Ireland Protestants are available for 1999 only.
Source: European Values Study, 1981, 1990, 1999–2000; Fahey et al. (2005).

Increasing Secularisation

Nonetheless, the findings of the EVS and other relevant research suggest that the process of secularisation has intensified throughout Ireland in the 1990s and in the early years of the twenty-first century, and that its 'pioneers' are more likely to be young, as well as male and better educated (Fahey et al., 2005, p. 52). Secularisation has a number of dimensions. One is a decline in church membership. As Figure 7.6 shows, the number of religiously non-affiliated has grown significantly since the 1970s, with a particularly steep rise in Ireland, between the end of the 1990s (8.6 per cent) and 2003 (17 per cent, the latter figure taken from the European Social Survey). Older people are much less likely to be non-affiliated: in the most recent EVS, only 3.3 per cent of people in Ireland aged 65 and over said they had no religious denomination, compared with 10.8 per cent of those aged 18 to 24, although an even higher proportion of 25- to 34-year-olds (14.4 per cent) were non-affiliated (Breen, 2002, p. 112).

Figure 7.6 The growth of the religiously non-affiliated in Ireland and Northern Ireland, 1968–2003

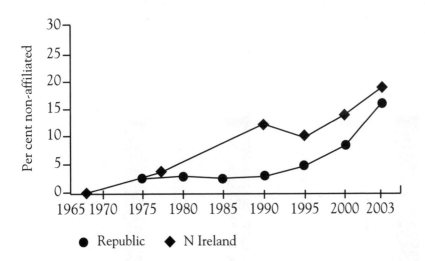

● Republic   ◆ N Ireland

Source: Ireland: Eurobarometer Surveys, 1975, 1980, 1985, 1990, 1995, European Values 1999–2000; Northern Ireland: Loyalty Survey, 1968, Social Attitudes Survey, 1978, Northern Ireland Social Attitudes Survey, 1989 and 1995; European Values Study, 1999–2000; European Social Survey, 2003.
Reproduced from Fahey et al. (2005).

A second dimension of secularisation is a decline in traditional religious practice, most obviously regular church attendance. Table 7.4 shows patterns of religious attendance in 1999–2000. Here the figures show a clear contrast in levels of church attendance in Ireland by age, as well as differences by urban or rural location, occupation and gender. Younger adults, in particular urban manual workers and especially young men, have very low levels of weekly attendance. According to Fahey et al. (2005, p. 44), 'The figures suggest, though obviously do not prove, that, as the present young adults grow older, decline in weekly churchgoing could become precipitous'. The figures also show that differences by age, occupation and gender are much less marked in Northern Ireland. It is also the case that, seen in an international context, both parts of Ireland 'remain in the upper range of church attendance rates in Europe' (ibid, p. 45).

Table 7.4 Weekly church attendance by age, occupation and rural–urban location in Ireland and Northern Ireland

	(Percentages)				
	18 to 30 years	31 to 45 years	46 to 60 years	60+ years	All
Ireland					
Occupation and rural–urban location:					
Non-manual					
Rural	61	69	86	94	76
Urban	24	42	73	91	49
Manual					
Rural	32	63	78	85	63
Urban	13	45	78	82	50
Gender					
Male	20	46	72	86	51
Female	34	66	81	90	66
All	27	56	77	89	59
[N]	[214]	[270]	[189]	[140]	[813]
Northern Ireland					
Occupation:					
Non-manual	39	33	59	62	49
Manual	41	35	55	60	48
Gender:					
Male	39	30	55	52	46
Female	40	36	60	67	50
All	40	33	57	60	48
[N]	[225]	[240]	[311]	[224]	[1,000]

Source: European Values Study, 1999–2000; Fahey et al. (2005).

A third aspect of secularisation can be termed 'privatisation'. This suggests that people can 'believe without belonging'; they can continue to believe in God and value a spiritual dimension in their lives but purely as a private matter (Fahey et al., 2005, p. 34). The EVS data do suggest that even among irregular church attenders, certain key religious beliefs (in God, in life after death and so on) continue to be held by considerable majorities. Even among the non-affiliated, more than two-thirds of people in Ireland (68 per cent) express a belief in God (although the figure in Northern Ireland is significantly lower, at 53 per cent). Overall, belief in God is high across all age groups, and is in fact marginally higher among 18- to 24-year-olds in Ireland (as opposed to Northern Ireland) (94.8 per cent) than 25- to 34-year-olds (92.5 per cent) or 35- to 44- year-olds (93.8 per cent) (Breen, 2002, p. 114).

A national survey of 15- to 24-year-olds conducted for *The Irish Times* newspaper by TNS mrbi in 2003 also found a high level of belief in God among young people (86 per cent overall) despite relatively low levels of church attendance (44 per cent said they attended; frequency of attendance was not given). Belief in God was found to be marginally stronger among young women (88 per cent) than young men (84 per cent), and was highest in Connaught/Ulster (93 per cent) and lowest in Dublin (82 per cent). It was considerably higher in rural areas than urban (93 per cent and 82 per cent, respectively), and declined somewhat with age, falling from 89 per cent among 15- to 17-year-olds to 87 per cent among 18- to 22- year-olds and 81 per cent among 23- to 24-year-olds. It was strongest among young people from farming backgrounds (95 per cent), who were also much more likely to attend church (72 per cent) (Brennock, 2003).

Table 7.5 Gender and age differences among irregular church attenders in Ireland

| | (Per cent who attend church less than monthly) | | | | | | | | | |
| | Men | | | | | Women | | | | |
Age	1981	1990	1999	#1	#2	1981	1990	1999	#1	#2
18–26	16	14	45	-2	+31	11	11	42	+0	+31
27–35	21	16	41	-5	+25	16	12	33	-4	+21
36–44	9	16	41	+7	+25	7	2	22	-5	+20
45–53	6	8	19	+2	+11	4	9	13	+5	+4
54–62	10	7	10	-3	+3	0	1	3	+1	+2
63+	4	7	7	+3	+0	1	4	7	+3	+3
All	13	11	30	-2	+17	8	7	22	-1	+14

Note: #1 and #2 shows the net change for each of the gender-specific age groups from 1981 to 1990 and from1990 to 1999, respectively.
Source: European Values Study, 1981, 1990, 1999–2000; Fahey et al. (2005).

With regard to the persistence of religious belief in a context of declining church attendance and lower levels of confidence in the institutional church, Fahey et al. argue that 'such incipient secularisation as has occurred has indeed been as much a matter of the privatisation of religion as of a complete shift towards irreligion' (ibid, p. 55). As to whether the age-related differences in religious practice reflect fundamental change at a societal level or simply 'life-cycle effects' (for instance, people being less 'religious' in their youth but more committed to traditional belief and practice as they get older), the same authors suggest that at least in Ireland there is evidence of an overall shift in behaviour across the three waves of the EVS survey, and particularly between the second and third. This can be seen in Table 7.5, which shows that the number of irregular church attenders (that is, less than once a month or not at all) increased during the 1990s among both males and females and across all age groups, with the exception of males aged 63 or older. Overall, the proportion of irregular attenders almost trebled, from 8 per cent to 22 per cent in the case of women and from 11 per cent to 30 per cent in the case of men.

Despite this, the overall conclusion drawn by Fahey et al. from the European Values Study and other research is that, both in Ireland and in Northern Ireland, 'the typical end-point of decline in religious adherence is not total rejection and indifference towards religion but a shift from strong and highly institutionalised attachment towards more intermittent and lukewarm adherence and towards various forms of privatised belief and commitment' (Fahey et al., 2005, p. 56). Future research will show whether this trend continues, and will also show whether and how the marked increase in the multicultural nature of Irish society in recent years is reflected in changing patterns of religious belief and practice.

FAMILY AND SEXUAL MORALITY

Issues relating to the family and sexual morality have been a source of consistent contention and debate in Ireland since the 1970s, and have been the subject of several constitutional referenda and high-profile court cases (including cases taken to the European Court of Human Rights). They remain at the heart of social and political debate today: the age of sexual consent, the recognition of same-sex marriage and the rights of cohabiting couples (whatever their sexual orientation) have all been considered by commissions or committees and have been the focus (directly or indirectly) of litigation in very recent times. It is generally found in social research that young people are more liberal, or tolerant, in relation to matters of sexual morality than older people, and this is true in Ireland as elsewhere. However, just as in the case of religious beliefs (which in many cases relate directly to sexual morality), we need to be cautious in interpreting the findings. In particular it is important to distinguish between life-cycle effects (which, as stated above, refer to changes in the attitudes of a single generation of people as they get older) and cohort effects, 'where each succeeding generation is more liberal than the one that preceded it' (Fahey et al., 2005, p. 126).

Figure 7.7 Opposition to divorce, abortion and homosexuality by age group and age cohort in Ireland, 1981–1999

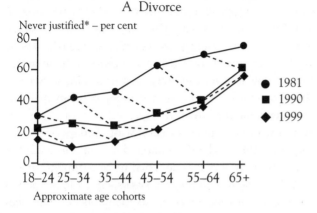

A Divorce

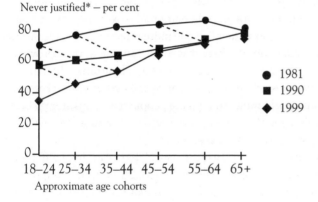

B Abortion

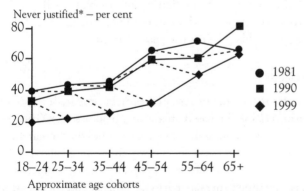

C Homosexuality

* Scores 1 and 2 on 10-point scale, where 1 = never justified, 10 = always justified.
Source: European Values Study, 1981, 1990, 1999–2000; Fahey et al. (2005).

Figure 7.7 makes this distinction with regard to levels of disapproval of divorce, abortion and homosexuality in Ireland in each of the three European Values Studies to date. In the three graphs (one dealing with each issue), the solid lines plot the differences between people in different age groups in each round of the EVS (that is, in 1981, 1990 and 1999–2000). For the most part, these lines slope upwards from left to right, showing that at any one time the old are more conservative (show more disapproval) than the young. The fact that almost without exception the solid line for each round of the EVS falls below that for the previous round is indicative of a *cohort shift* towards liberalism: people in any given age group are less likely to disapprove of these matters than people used to at that age.

The dotted lines allow us to trace the attitudes of specific age groups over time. The EVS is not strictly a 'longitudinal' study: the sample does not consist of the same respondents in each case. Nonetheless, it is designed to be representative in each case of the population as a whole and therefore gives us a good indication of the changes in attitudes within any one age group as its members get older. For example, those who were 35 to 44 in 1990 were much less likely to disapprove of divorce than they had been (as 25- to 34-year-olds) in 1981, and their level of disapproval continued to decline, although only marginally, over the next decade. The graph shows that each age cohort in fact became more tolerant of divorce during the 1980s, although among older cohorts there was some increase in disapproval in the 1990s. Opposition to abortion followed the same general pattern, 'though at a higher level overall and with a less steep age gradient in the earlier years' (Fahey et al., 2005, p. 127). The graph clearly shows that young people have consistently been less likely to disapprove of abortion than older people, and that during the 1990s the gap between the views of young and old became wider.

In the case of homosexuality there is also a clear age-related attitudinal difference in each of the three EVS rounds. There was very little reduction in the disapproval rating of any age group between 1981 and 1990, and in fact those aged 35 to 44 in 1981 became much more disapproving over the ensuing decade. By the turn of the century, however, the level of disapproval had fallen by almost half in all but the oldest age groups. Overall, then, the data would seem to support the argument that the generations are becoming more liberal with the passage of time.

Changing Attitudes to Sex

This is also the conclusion of a recent major research project, the Irish Study of Sexual Health and Relationships (ISSHR), based on a survey of almost 7,500 people aged 18 to 64 years of age as well as a comprehensive review of earlier research. It concludes:

> Irish sexual attitudes have changed substantially over the last three decades. People are now more accepting of behaviours previously seen as wrong. The rate of change has been fastest among younger age groups. There is an increasing gap

between the attitudes of younger and older individuals. Young people now tend to see sex as a matter of individual conscience, or even as a lifestyle choice, whereas older respondents still tend to view sex within a more traditional moral framework (Layte et al., 2006, p. 96).

The authors of the ISSHR study point out that between 1973 and 2005 the proportion of Irish people agreeing that sex before marriage is 'always wrong' fell from 71 per cent to 6 per cent. Figure 7.8 summarises the ISSHR's own findings on attitudes to sex before marriage, broken down by age group and gender. It suggests that men are more accepting of sex before marriage than women and that younger people are much more accepting than older people. The difference between men and women declines with each successive age group.

Figure 7.8 Attitudes to sex before marriage: by gender and age group

Source: Layte et al. (2006).

These findings (and the others which follow) should be qualified by the ISSHR authors' observation that 'the Irish population still holds comparatively conservative attitudes in a West European context' and that 'this is as true of young people as of older' (Layte et al., 2006, p. 119). In fact, this is borne out by Eurobarometer research from the year 2001, although the question regarding pre-marital sex was put somewhat differently (requesting the respondents' assessment of the attitudes of 'people their age' rather than their own view). The Eurobarometer found that close to nine out of ten 18-24 year-olds (88 per cent) across what were then the 15 countries of the EU believed that 'young people their age' looked favourably on sex before marriage, whereas in Ireland the figure was 76 per cent, the lowest of the 15 countries and just one point below the UK (76 per cent) (European Commission, 2001). Nonetheless, seen over time the pattern undoubtedly appears to be one of convergence (Layte et al., 2006, p. 119).

The ISSHR survey also assessed attitudes to 'one-night stands' or casual sex. Overall, 40 per cent of respondents considered one-night stands to be 'always wrong', 14 per cent 'mostly wrong', 30 per cent 'sometimes wrong' and 16 per cent 'never wrong'. Figure 7.9 presents the findings broken down by age group and gender. Once again, younger people display significantly more liberal attitudes than older people, and men are more permissive than women. Only 15 per cent of men under 25 thought one-night stands were always wrong, compared to 56 per cent of men aged 55 to 64. Among women, this view was taken by 29 per cent of the under 25-year-olds, but 84 per cent of the 55- to 64-year-olds.

Figure 7.9 Attitudes to 'one-night stands': by gender and age group

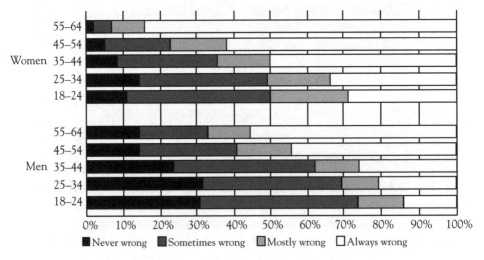

Source: Layte et al. (2006).

The same broad pattern underlies responses to other items in the ISSHR study. In addition to age and gender, a highly significant factor shaping attitudes to sex and sexuality is level of educational attainment and – clearly related to this – social class background.

> The analysis ... showed a dramatic liberalisation of attitudes since the 1970s. Only a small minority now see pre-marital sex as 'always wrong'. The young, better educated and less religious tend to be least likely to say that pre-marital sex is wrong ... This pattern is present across all of the attitude issues, including

those on homosexuality and abortion. It indicates a division on world view between the generations in Ireland and considerable differences between those at different socio-economic levels (Layte et al., 2006, p. 119).

While the ISSHR study notes that the relationship between sexual attitudes and behaviour is complex and that 'increasing liberalism does not directly translate into more risky behaviour or unsafe practices' (ibid), it expresses considerable unease at the low levels of knowledge among young people about certain aspects of sexual and reproductive health.

The group with the lowest level of accurate knowledge about a woman's fertility is young men and women: 75 per cent of men and 56 per cent of women aged 18 to 24 could not correctly name the most fertile part of a woman's cycle. This knowledge deficit also seems to be marked among those with lower educational attainment and/or of lower socio-economic position. It could have serious consequences in terms of the level of crisis pregnancy. In other areas of knowledge, such as the time limit for emergency contraception, and chlamydia and HIV/AIDS, young people appeared to have higher levels of knowledge than older people. However, even among young people, 73 per cent of men and 36 per cent of women under 25 did not know the correct time limit for use of EC [emergency contraception] (Layte et al., 2006, p. 118).

Further information about young people's attitudes to sexuality as well their sexual behaviour is presented in Chapter 4 of this book. There is little doubt about the nature of the trends in recent years. Whether viewed positively or negatively, much more liberal attitudes among the young to sexual matters and much earlier commencement of sexual activity present challenges to all those concerned with the welfare and development of young people. Whatever choices people make, at whatever stage of their lives, it is in their interest to do so armed with as full a knowledge as possible of the implications and an appreciation of the possible risks as well as the rewards. This requires both adequate information and a capacity for critical self-reflection. As Inglis (1998, p. 177) says in the context of a discussion of relationships and sexuality education (RSE):

A frank, open and honest approach to teaching children and young people about relationships and sexuality may also involve critical reflection ... [Young people] need to learn to ask fundamental questions such as: Who is it who speaks about sex? What do they say? What is the motivation behind what they are saying? I have argued that there is no one truth about sex and sexuality. Different truths emerge from different discourses and perspectives. These divisions and contradictions make relationships and sexuality education more necessary now than ever before.

SOCIAL ISSUES

The European Values Study conducted in 1999–2000 (and in two earlier waves, as indicated above) explores values and attitudes towards a range of social issues apart from those directly related to politics, religion and sexual morality. Respondents were asked among other things for their opinions about various 'targets' for the creation of a more just society and about the extent of their concern for different named groups in society. Figure 7.10 (reproduced from Breen, 2002, p. 100) summarises the pattern of responses by age group when people were asked how important it was to address three social targets: eliminating social inequalities, providing basic needs for all and recognising people on the basis of their merits (rather than, for instance, social background or family connections). Respondents could give an answer ranging from one to five, with one meaning 'not at all important' and five meaning 'very important'. This makes it possible to calculate a mean score for different groups.

Figure 7.10 Importance of social targets, by age

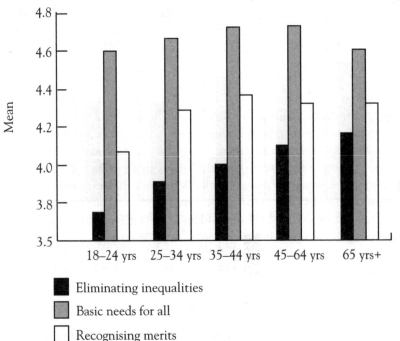

Eliminating inequalities
Basic needs for all
Recognising merits

Source: Breen (2002, p. 100).

In the case of the target of meeting basic needs for all, there is no significant difference by age group: people of all ages agree that this is a very important goal (the mean exceeds 4.5 in all cases). There is a different pattern in the responses regarding the recognition of merit: while the very oldest groups fall slightly below the middle-aged, the scores for all age groups are relatively closely clustered except for the 18- to 24- year-olds, who accord this target somewhat less importance than their elders. The target of eliminating inequalities is regarded as less important among all age groups than the other two targets, and the younger the age group, the less important it gets.

Figure 7.11 presents the results regarding concern for the living conditions of several vulnerable (or potentially vulnerable) groups, again broken down by age (Breen, 2002, p. 101). The scoring in this case was in the opposite direction, so that a lower score indicates higher concern. Overall, the pattern corresponds to the previous findings: younger people in general expressed lower levels of concern than older people. While the increase in concern with age group is only marginal in some instances, in the case of all four groups it is the 18- to 24-year-olds who express least concern.

Figure 7.11 Concern for vulnerable groups, by age

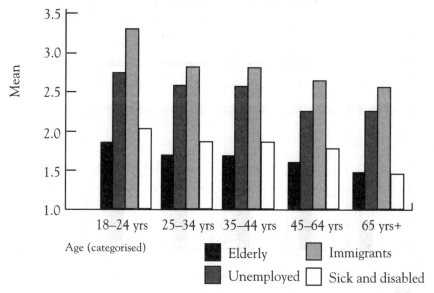

Source: Breen (2002).

These findings can be compared with the results of survey research conducted for the organisation Development Education for Youth (DEFY) in 1995 -and 1999 (McDonell and Wegimont, 2000; Wegimont, 2000; Wegimont and Farrell, 1995). In both cases the focus was on attitudes to development and justice issues, and the more recent survey included a sample of adults for comparative purposes. Figure 7.12 presents summary data from the 1999 survey in response to the question: How much, if at all, do you think about the problems of poorer countries, such as those in Africa, South America and parts of Asia?

Figure 7.12 Incidence of thinking about the problems of poor countries

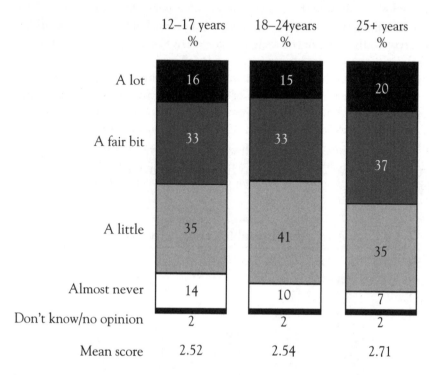

	12–17 years %	18–24 years %	25+ years %
A lot	16	15	20
A fair bit	33	33	37
A little	35	41	35
Almost never	14	10	7
Don't know/no opinion	2	2	2
Mean score	2.52	2.54	2.71

Source: Wegimont (2000).

Figure 7.12 shows that the three groups, 12- to 17-year-olds, 18- to 24-year-olds and those aged 25 and over, are broadly similar in the extent to which they think about poor countries, but with some differences, particularly at both ends of the continuum (with a higher number of the older group saying 'a lot' and a higher number of the youngest group saying 'not at all'). However, the mean scores are not far apart, particularly for the 12- to 17-year-olds and the 18- to 24-year-olds. A comparison with the 1995 results for the full youth sample of 12- to 24-year-olds (not shown here) suggests contrasting trends: an increase of 5 per cent (from 11 per cent to 16 per cent) in those thinking 'a lot' about poor countries but also an increase of 3 per cent (from 9 to 12 per cent) in those thinking about them 'almost never' (McDonnell and Wegimont, 2000, pp. 23–4).

Table 7.6 indicates extent of involvement or willingness to get involved in voluntary organisations or groups set up to help countries in the Third World. It includes aggregate data for 12- to 24-year-olds in 1995 and 1999, with an indication of the increase or decrease in the interim, as well as disaggregated figures for the 12- to 17-year-olds and 18- to 24-year-old groups in 1999. There are also figures for those aged 25 and over in 1999. The findings among young people are generally positive.

The total proportion of young people aged 12 to 24 already involved has increased from 5 per cent to 8 per cent, although the proportion not yet involved but prepared to participate has fallen by the same amount. However, the proportion neither involved nor willing to get involved (the most negative possible response) has fallen by 9 per cent. To the right of the table it can be seen that in 1999, younger people were much more open to the idea of involvement than those aged 25 and over. The proportion of the latter group 'not yet involved but willing' was barely a third (34 per cent), whereas it was almost half of 18- to 24-year-olds (47 per cent) and considerably more than half (56 per cent) of the 12- to 17-year-olds.

Table 7.6 Involvement and willingness to be involved with voluntary organisations set up to help the countries of the Third World (per cent)

	1995	1999	% change	1999	1999	1999
	12–24 yrs average			12–17 yrs	18–24 yrs	25+
Already involved	5	8	+3	8	8	10
Not currently but prepared to be involved	55	52	-3	56	47	34
Involved previously but no longer	–	9	n/a	6	12	12
Not prepared to be involved	39	30	-9	28	32	43

Source: McDonnell and Wegimont (2000); Wegimont (2000).

The target of eliminating social inequality was one of the attitudinal items explored in the European Values Study, as discussed earlier. An Irish study of young people's attitudes towards and experiences of 'equality concerns' in the educational context (Lodge and Lynch, 2003; Lynch and Lodge, 2002) throws additional light on this area. The study involved 12 second-level schools (varied according to type of school and gender mix) located across six different counties. It included a total of 1,557 students as well as their teachers. A variety of methods and media were used: informal discussion, tape recordings, essay writing, focus groups, a questionnaire survey and observations in classrooms, playgrounds and at school events. The study found that the young participants were 'keenly aware of the inequality they experienced because of their youth and lack of power vis-à-vis adults' (Lodge and Lynch, 2003, p. 16). However, there was a striking lack of awareness of other types of inequality or of equality as a broader issue. For example, of all the 1,202 students who wrote essays about 'their most pressing equality concerns', almost half (48 per cent) expressed concern about the way adults exercised power and authority over them, but 'only a tiny proportion named any minority identity as a contributory factor in their (and anyone else's) experience of inequality' (ibid. p. 17). Only 20 young people (1.7 per cent) spontaneously identified race or ethnicity as an equality concern, while only eight (0.7 per cent) mentioned sexual orientation. These figures are less surprising when we consider the responses of their teachers. When asked about important equality issues in Irish education, 12 per cent of teacher respondents spontaneously mentioned gender (itself a very low figure) but less than 1 per cent identified disability, sexual orientation, religious identity, race or ethnicity.

The young people in the study were not only lacking awareness but were often actively hostile and negative towards lesbian and gay people. In the questionnaire survey, a majority (55 per cent) thought that discovering a friend to be gay or lesbian would be grounds for terminating the friendship. Homosexuality evoked sentiments of ignorance, fear and hostility among boys in particular. Again, the role of teachers appears crucial. When the attitudinal data showing a high level of homophobia was presented to teachers in all 12 schools, only in one of those schools did the teachers themselves raise the subject in their discussions with the researchers (ibid, p. 23). Given that other survey research, including the EVS findings presented earlier in this chapter, consistently shows relatively tolerant attitudes towards homosexuality among young people aged 18 to 24, the question arises whether the negative attitudes that appear (according to the research under discussion) to prevail among younger age groups can be attributed to developmental factors, the school environment, the dynamics of the adolescent (especially male) peer group or some combination of these.

Travellers were also found to be subject to very negative attitudes in the research by Lodge and Lynch (2003). Almost all the young people in their survey (91 per cent) thought that 'having Travellers in this school would make life difficult for the teachers and the pupils' and more than half agreed that 'if I made friends with a Traveller, my other friends might not go around with me anymore'. Attitudes towards other ethnic minorities were less negative, although the authors note that their fieldwork took place prior to the 'very significant increase in the number of migrant workers, refugees and asylum seekers entering Ireland' (Lodge and Lynch, 2003, p. 35). Attitudes towards people with disabilities were also more benign, if anything more characterised by ignorance and pity than hostility. Not surprisingly, direct knowledge and experience of people with disabilities was associated with much more positive attitudes (although there were few young people with disabilities in the schools studied). In this as in other areas of inequality, teachers, schools as institutions and the educational system as a whole are implicated in the findings.

[I]t is important to recognise that young people's cultural attitudes and values are played out within an education system which, for a long period of time, has been characterised by segregation and lack of recognition for difference and diversity in its institutional processes and structures. We found that where young people had the opportunity to study and socialise in a more diverse environment, differences (such as disability, or membership of minority ethnic groups) could cease to be seen as deviant or subordinate. Schools themselves have failed to provide an inclusive environment in which young people are afforded the opportunity to learn to respect and recognise difference (Lodge and Lynch, 2003, p. 31).

Despite the evidence earlier in this chapter that young people are more liberal and tolerant in relation to many matters than their elders, the findings presented above in relation to social justice are not so straightforward. In the EVS research, young people show less concern than older people with issues of inequality or the living conditions of vulnerable or excluded groups. In the educational research by Lodge and Lynch, they show scant awareness of inequality issues and active antipathy towards some minority groups, although the researchers did not find much evidence of more positive attitudes among their teachers. In the DEFY research on attitudes to development and justice issues, young people think about poorer parts of the world somewhat less than older people, yet they express a greater willingness to get involved in groups working in the interests of developing countries. It is likely, of course, that, especially for the youngest age groups, levels of actual knowledge and experience colour the findings, and in the case of all age groups there are differences relating to educational attainment and socio-economic status which have not been detailed here (but have been shown to be at play in the case of other types of values and attitudes). In relation to all matters pertaining to the formation of values and attitudes, educators, both formal and non-formal, clearly have key roles and responsibilities.

Table 7.7 Can young people help to bring about improvements in their locality, their country and their world? (per cent)

		1995 12–24 yrs	1999 average	% change	1999 12–17 yrs	1999 18–24 yrs
Local	Yes	74	61	-13	64	59
	No	18	31	+13	27	34
National	Yes	66	52	-14	51	52
	No	26	35	+9	33	37
Global	Yes	66	71	+5	70	71
	No	24	20	-4	19	20

Source: McDonnell and Wegimont (2000).

One final matter is worthy of mention here. People's level of motivation and commitment regarding social issues, whatever their age, is likely to be influenced by the extent to which they think they can actually have an impact on the society around them. Table 7.7 shows the extent to which young people in 1995 and 1999 thought they could 'help to bring about improvements in their locality, their country and their world' according to the DEFY research (McDonnell and Wegimont, 2000,

p. 10). For the overall 12- to 24-year-old group, the proportion thinking they could do so declined by 13 per cent (from 74 per cent to 61 per cent) in relation to the local level and by 14 per cent (from 66 per cent to 52 per cent) in relation to the national level in the period between the two surveys. The percentage thinking they could make an improvement globally increased, but only by 5 per cent overall. The breakdown of the 1999 figures into the 12- to 17-year-olds and 18- to 24-year-olds shows that confidence in being able to make a difference does not increase with age, particularly at local level. This is a worrying trend, and one worthy of close attention by those who hope to promote an active interest among young people in issues relating to social justice at home and abroad.

POSTMATERIALIST VALUES

This chapter has presented data relating to young people's values and attitudes on a range of matters: politics, religion, the family and sexual morality as well as various social issues. It has suggested that there has been a considerable change in recent decades in Irish people's attitudes, for the most part in the direction of a more liberal approach (especially in relation to sex and sexuality) and to a great extent pioneered by the young (as well as by the better educated, who are also more likely to be young). Looked at broadly, it has been suggested by some commentators that advanced industrialised countries (including Ireland) have been experiencing a move in the direction of postmaterialist values as they have developed in economic and social terms. If 'modernising' societies in the twentieth century emphasised economic growth and economic achievement, the postmodern age is seeing an increasing emphasis on freedom of expression, cultural enrichment and environmental protection. This is a view particularly associated with Ronald Inglehart:

> The shift from materialist to postmaterialist values is only one aspect of a much broader shift from modern to postmodern values that is taking place throughout advanced industrial society. Postmodern values are uncommon in most developing societies; they are still moving from traditional to modern values. Both traditional and modern values were shaped by economic scarcity, which prevailed almost everywhere until recently. But during the past few decades, a new set of postmodern values has been transforming the social, political, economic and sexual norms of rich countries around the globe. These new values reflect conditions of economic security. If one grows up with a feeling that survival can be taken for granted, instead of the feeling that survival is uncertain, it influences almost every aspect of one's worldview (Inglehart, 2000, p. 223).

However, the interpretation by Fahey et al. (2005) of the European Values Study data over recent decades raises questions about the applicability of Inglehart's postmodern/postmaterialist thesis in the Irish context (or indeed elsewhere). There have certainly been changes in attitudes towards such matters as gender roles and environmental protection – both of which are aspects of what might be called the 'new politics' (Fahey et al., 2005, pp. 150 ff.) – and as in other areas these changes are more marked among the young and better educated. However, the application of a scale developed by Inglehart himself for measuring postmaterialism, based on a question that asks respondents what they think their country's first and second most important priorities should be over the next 10 years, produces results which are not persuasive (Fahey et al., 2005, pp. 156–7). Respondents have four options:

1. Maintaining order in the nation.
2. Giving people more say in important government decisions.
3. Fighting rising prices.
4. Protecting freedom of speech.

According to Inglehart (1990) those who select (2) and (4) as their top two priorities are postmaterialist and those who select (1) and (3) are materialist, with people selecting other combinations deemed to be mixed. Using these criteria, it is not possible to detect any clear increase over the past few decades in the proportion of Irish people who are postmaterialist. There have been fluctuations but no long-term trend: the proportion of postmaterialists in Ireland 'showed a significant increase in the late 1980s, but by 1997 it had fallen back more or less to the level of the 1970s', and in both parts of Ireland, north and south, the results overall are 'unexceptional among European countries' (Fahey at al., 2005, p. 157).

Figure 7.13 Postmaterialism by age group in the pooled EVS samples for Northern Ireland and Ireland, 1981–1999

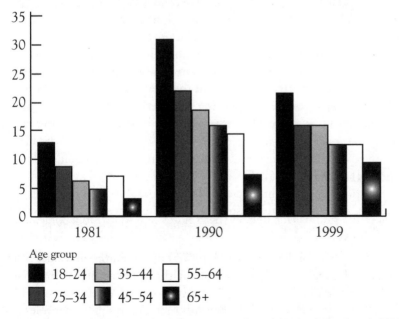

Source: European Values Study, 1981, 1990 and 1999–2000; Fahey et al. (2005).

In Inglehart's view the shift to postmaterialist values should also be marked by a high 'age gradient' on the postmaterialism scale at different successive points in time, with the young scoring more highly than the old in each case. To check whether this is the case, Figure 7.13 shows the results for Ireland as a whole in each of the three rounds of the EVS since 1981, broken down by age group. It does appear to give some support to Inglehart's thesis since the young are indeed consistently more likely to be postmaterialist than the old. However, the suggestion of a broader cultural shift towards postmaterialism in the 'postmodern era' is undermined since the proportion of postmaterialists declined in the 1990s, even among the youngest age groups. In fact, the only people who became more postmaterialist with each wave of the EVS were those aged 65 and over (Fahey et al., 2005, p. 158).

CONCLUSION

Overall, there does appear to be a consistent difference in the values and attitudes of younger people and older people at different points in time, and as the material presented throughout this chapter shows, the difference ranges across a wide variety of issues and topics. Some of the differences may be due to life-cycle effects (the fact that people change as they grow older), others to broader social and cultural transformations which expose each new generation to a different set of circumstances and influences, with the pace of change increasing all the time.

People's attitudes towards their free time provide us with an example of the impact of these two contrasting factors. Young people may see their free time differently, and spend it differently, because by virtue of their age they are less likely to be earning an independent income or to have other people depending on them for their welfare. This is a life-cycle effect. On the other hand, recent social and technological change have transformed the relationship between education and employment, with significant cultural and material effects on the transitions into adulthood of today's young people, more and more of whom are now likely to be in school and work at the same time (as shown in the previous chapter), and this will inevitably have an impact on their 'free time'; for one thing, there is less of it. We examine to the topic of young people's recreation and leisure time activities in the next chapter.

RECOMMENDED READING

A comprehensive analysis of data from the European Values Study 1999–2000, which places the findings for Ireland (both north and south) in a comparative European context and highlights changes since the early 1980s, can be found in Fahey, T., Hayes, B. & Sinnott, R. (2005). *Conflict and consensus: A study of values and attitudes in the Republic of Ireland and Northern Ireland*. Dublin: Institute of Public Administration.

Regarding attitudes towards sex and sexuality (and related matters) an important recent study is Layte, R., McGee, H., Quail, A., Rundle, K., Cousins, G.,

Donnelly, C., Mulcahy, F., & Conroy, R. (2006). *The Irish study of sexual health and relationships*. Dublin: Department of Health and Children and Crisis Pregnancy Agency.

Both the above sources are very valuable in demonstrating differences in values and attitudes between the generations and over time, but they are confined to persons aged 18 and over. The European Commission's regular Eurobarometer surveys include periodic studies specifically focused on 15- to 24-year-olds throughout the EU. These can be found at: http://ec.europa.eu/public_opinion/index_en.htm

8

Recreation and Leisure

INTRODUCTION

This chapter discusses leisure and the functions it serves for young people. Gender, age and socio-economic patterns in young people's leisure are presented and discussed.

In considering the various forms of leisure young people engage in, the categories of general free-time activities, sports, hobbies and community or charity group involvement are used as a framework. The chapter concludes by exploring the constraints and facilitators to young people's leisure.

LEISURE

There are many different conceptions of leisure.

- Leisure as residual time: all free time outside of school or work.
- Leisure as a range of activities a person chooses to engage in during his or her free time, including sports, hobbies, general free-time activities, community group involvement and simply hanging around doing nothing in particular.
- Leisure as functional, a means to achieving desired ends such as identity, a sense of belonging, skills mastery, esteem and enjoyment.
- Leisure as freedom: being autonomous with the capacity to exercise choice, to be and develop oneself.

(Haywood et al., 1995)

Each of these, individually, provides only a partial understanding of leisure. Consequently, conceptions of leisure tend to revolve around all of these dimensions, acknowledging that leisure involves:

- Free-time use.
- Activities a person chooses and has (some) autonomy in.
- Constant change, being dynamic, constantly changing.
- Activities that may serve different purposes for a young person.

Leisure is a key context where 'young people decide for themselves what they will do, how they will do it, as well as who they will do it with' (Green et al., 2005 p. 34).

Doing something enjoyable, having fun, switching off from school or study, pursuing an interest, being with friends and feeling a sense of belonging to something like a club or group are all reasons cited for engaging in leisure. Leisure that young people freely choose is a means through which they actively construct their personal development and identity.

The significance of leisure cannot be overestimated, comprising 40–50 per cent of a young person's life and constituting social worlds in which they are more likely to be producers of their own development, directing their own personal growth and individuation (Caldwell et al., 1992). Leisure is also a forum through which social and cultural forces influence young people, shaping how they perceive and experience the world they live in. The growth in mobile phone, Internet and computer game use by young people are recent examples of cultural changes central to young people's leisure.

The importance of young people's leisure is addressed by policy. The UN Convention on the Rights of the Child 1989 (Article 31) states that 'State Parties shall respect and promote the right of the child to participate fully in cultural and artistic life and shall encourage the provision of appropriate and equal opportunities for cultural, artistic, recreational and leisure activity'. In terms of Irish government policy, Objective D of the National Children's Strategy states that 'children will have access to play, sport, recreation and cultural activities to enrich their experience of childhood' (Department of Health and Children, 2000, p. 57). New Irish policy on recreation and leisure for young people is, at the time of this book going to print, currently in the final stages of its development.

Using leisure as a means of working with young people, helping them to build their self-esteem and resilience, to enhance their social skills and identity is common for a number of Irish professionals, such as social care practitioners, youth workers and physiotherapists. Most young people in care in Ireland have hobbies and leisure interests which they see as enjoyable and important sources of friendship and confidence (Emond, 2002). In addition, interest into the therapeutic role of leisure has proliferated over recent decades. The Barretstown Gang camp in Co. Kildare is an example of where this approach is used in working with children (and their families) affected by cancer.

Categorising Youth Leisure

Four distinct categories or types of youth leisure or 'lifestyles' have been identified (Glendinning et al., 1995):

- **Commercialised leisure:** Shopping, listening to music, going to discos.
- **Conventional (adult-approved) activities:** Hobbies (art, playing a musical instrument) and community groups (Scouts or Guides, youth clubs).
- **Sports or games-oriented activities:** Playing or watching sports, playing computer games.
- **Street-based, peer-oriented activity:** Hanging around outside.

Some of these show a social class association, conventional activities being common among middle-class young people and street-based activity being more prevalent among working-class young people (Karvonen et al., 2001). Commercial and street-based leisure is *sometimes* associated with health risks such as drinking, smoking and drug-taking, whereas structured leisure (organised sports and family leisure) tends to inhibit these health risks, but not necessarily, as some studies report organised sport to be associated with drinking (Piko and Vazsonyi, 2004).

Developmental Functions of Leisure

Leisure has many developmental functions for the young person. Firstly, there is identity formation and 'self-knowledge'. Young people formulate their own 'leisure biographies' by identifying talents and abilities contributing to their sense of self (Zeijl et al., 2003). In describing personal strengths, many mention their involvement in sports or other youth activities.

A second function is the development of initiative, that is, 'the capacity to direct attention and effort over time toward a challenging goal' (Dworkin et al., 2003 p. 24). Learning to set realistic goals, time management and taking responsibility are part of this.

Yet another function is emotional development and resilience, including self-regulation, stress management and relaxation. Hobbies, sports, clubs and cultural pursuits are all free-time activities that enhance resilience by nurturing self-worth and self-efficacy and by providing a positive developmental social context (Gilligan, 2000).

Forming new friendships with, and knowledge of, peers is another developmental function of leisure. When a young person joins a team, club, or activity group, other participants often become friends or simply part of that person's social network (Brown, 1990). Youth activities are a common context for young people to meet and learn about peers who are different from them in ethnicity, race and social class. Yet another function is the development of social skills and competencies, such as communication skills, teamwork and leadership skills (Dubas and Snider, 1993). Learning co-operation and how to work with others is part of the 'hidden curriculum' of youth activities. Through uniting around a shared goal, young people learn to handle each other's emotions, divide responsibilities and give and take feedback, thereby enhancing social skills and confidence.

Finally, the acquisition of 'social capital' and the formation of relationships with adult leaders and others in the community is another function of leisure. Participation in community activities assists young people to forge a strong connection to their local community that may become a source of social and emotional support to them.

Leisure Across the Adolescent Years

Early adolescence, according to Larson and Kleiber (1991), is a critical period during which greater interest is shown in leisure activities. Leisure that facilitates autonomy and self-controlled actions (rather than 'other-directed' by a leader or parents) is especially important for enhancing interest in that leisure activity and minimising the risk of boredom. Some young people need assistance with focusing their attention, but if this assistance is too directed (where leisure activities are too structured or directed by others), boredom is more likely. This is consistent with the theory that intrinsic motivation (enjoying leisure activities for their inherent pleasure) and self-determination (exercising choice in leisure activites to take part in) are antithetical to the experience of boredom, highlighting the significance of autonomy and choice in adolescent leisure (Caldwell et al., 1999).

Leisure involvement alters across the adolescent years. Across adolescence, unstructured socialising progressively replaces specific free-time activities. Young people increasingly move away from formal, organised leisure towards more informal and individualised activities, such as hanging around and chatting over the phone. As emphasised by McHale and colleagues (2004), an increasing interest in the peer social world underpins a shift from involvement in specific leisure activities to general socialising.

For young women, greater intimacy and self-disclosure in close relationships across adolescence appears to be very influential in this shift towards greater socialising over specific leisure activities (ibid).

Relating to this trend, Kelly (1987) proposed that people have 'core' leisure behaviours they engage in throughout their lives and transitional or 'balance' leisure activities that meet specific developmental needs at given stages of their lives. Consequently, 'balance' leisure activities tend to be dropped when needs are fulfilled. An example of this may be where a leisure activity that is joined to acquire more friends is dropped because the young person now feels they have made enough friends.

GENDER AND LEISURE

Gender exerts a very strong influence on leisure involvement for all age groups. In the 1990s, sociological literature on youth leisure highlighted a change: youth leisure no longer paralleled that of adults. In the past, female leisure was devalued, constrained and domestically bound (Green et al., 1990). Much attention was paid to the 'bedroom leisure culture' of teenage girls, who spent more time than males on indoor activities such as reading, talking on the phone, listening to music and activities involving fashion and make-up. However, from the 1990s, gender divisions in youth leisure altered, with young women no longer as constrained by cultural norms, greater value now being attached to leisure for teenage girls. The leisure of teenage males has in turn become domestified as they came to spend more of their leisure time in the home, using new media technologies including playing computer and video games (Drotner, 2000). Gender differences in 'street-based' leisure, such as hanging around on the street (previously more male), have also diminished slightly (Sweeting and West, 2003), but types of preferred leisure still vary between the sexes. In this chapter leisure activities are looked at in terms of general free-time activities, hobbies, community or charity groups and sport. Cultural factors also influence the leisure activities of each gender. In some cultures, girls of a particular age are *not* encouraged, and are even discouraged, from participating in particular types of leisure, reinforcing deep cultural norms (Caldwell et al. 2004). In Ireland, this applies to young people from ethnic minorities whose values may differ regarding appropriate free-time use and leisure for young men and women.

As well as gender and culture, other factors need to be considered in exploring young people's leisure, such as individual differences, location and disability or health needs. Research undertaken by Karvonen and colleagues (2001) illuminated how 'local peculiarities' affect leisure but are often masked if attention is paid only to the broader picture. Influence of the local milieu and social context thus needs to be acknowledged in considering leisure patterns. Cultural choices available to young people are influenced and constrained by both the ideological positions and material conditions of their immediate environment, especially the school (Thurlow, 2002).

Young people with particular needs, such as those with visual and hearing impairments or learning disabilities, may have very different leisure experiences to other young people. Leisure is one context in which people with disabilities have experienced a lack of social acceptance and inclusion (Devine, 2004). This in turn has negatively influenced the leisure lifestyle of people with disabilities (see Chapter 11).

TYPES OF LEISURE

In considering the various forms of leisure young people engage in, the following sub divisions will be used.

Table 8.1 Different types of leisure

General free-time activities: Hanging around, watching TV, playing computer/video games, reading and listening to music are included in this and examined in this chapter. Other common forms of this leisure include looking at shops, going to the cinema, going to discos, talking/texting on the phone.

Sports: Recreational and competitive individual and team sports.

Hobbies: Activities pursued in leisure time excluding the general free-time activities listed earlier.

Community/charity groups: Youth clubs/groups, Scouting and Guide associations, Gaisce and involvement in a charity voluntary work.

General Free-Time Activities

Hanging Around

Well over half of Irish young people report hanging around outside every day or most days (de Róiste and Dinneen, 2005). Over half spend between five and 14 hours per week hanging out with friends (Lalor and Baird, 2006). This reflects how much of Irish young people's leisure time is spent 'not doing' any particular structured activity and is in agreement with international research that hanging out with friends is extremely prevalent, especially for older children and young people (Child Accident Prevention Trust, 2002; Hendry et al., 1993). In the UK, hanging out with friends is the third most popular leisure activity, after TV and listening to music (Child Accident Prevention Trust, 2002). Hours spent talking on the phone may also be seen as just another manifestation of hanging out.

From a peak at 14 years, hanging around outside declines across adolescence, especially for young women. Variance in hanging around is also linked to socio-economic status (SES); young people from higher SES groups hang around outside less frequently than other SES groups (de Róiste and Dinneen, 2005; Sweeting and West, 2000).

Hanging around is clearly a normal feature of youth. As a social context, hanging around fulfils important developmental functions, such as group membership and role negotiation (Van Vliet, in Hendry et al., 1993).

As indicated earlier in Chapter 2, Abbott-Chapman (2000) and others have drawn attention to the need for young people to 'make space', to have moratoriums and individual and collective safe havens in which to reflect and rejuvenate. Features of hanging around such as 'fooling around', 'having a chat' and 'having a laugh' are perceived by young people as among their most fulfilling activities. In some instances, hanging around involves 'going around in a group looking for excitement' or 'annoying the neighbours' (Connor, 2003, p. 163).

Friends are central to a young person's life and by hanging out together young people can spend time enjoying the company of friends, chatting, seeing others and being seen. Young people enjoy simply being in each other's company, free of the constraints of structured activities. Hanging around is valued particularly *because* it is not confined by adult supervision. However, as Katz (1998) noted, internationally young people are faced with lessening choice and fewer opportunities of where they can go without adult interference. Katz (1998), among others, voiced concern over the increasing elimination of public environments for outdoor play or 'hanging out'. One of the most consistent responses young people in Co. Kildare cite as a need is having 'somewhere to go/something to do/a place to hang out' (Lalor and Baird, 2006). The difficulty of being viewed as 'a problem', 'unwelcome' or 'out of place' for simply hanging around outdoors is a common experience for young people (Percy-Smith, 1999).

In sociological literature, the concept of the 'third place' has been proposed (Oldenburg, 1999). This refers to a location that is not work or school and not home, rather it is a public place where young people can easily meet, relax and interact. Such places contribute to social capital and community life. For Irish adults, the pub is a very popular third place; other examples include cafés, public libraries and hairdressing salons. Young people have fewer 'third places' available to them than adults, though 'youth cafés' represent a measure to address this. This has become more pronounced with the greater erosion of public space through increased privatisation via property development (Byrne et al., 2006). In relation to this, the United Nations Committee on the Rights of the Child expressed concern that little political and financial importance was given in Ireland to the creation of recreational facilities for children and young people and recognised that housing demands hindered the development of public space for these age groups. It recommended that 'the State party place more emphasis on the creation of facilities for children to enjoy leisure, recreation and cultural activities' (www.ohchr.org/english/bodies/crc/index.htm).

An alternative perspective considers hanging around to be associated with risk and problematic behaviour. Hanging around outside has long been associated with gangs and delinquency and is of concern given the relationship found in some studies between unstructured and unsupervised activities with school drop-out and deviance (Vazsonyi et al., 2002). Irish research has highlighted problematic relationships of young people in disadvantaged communities with local gardaí and how the high visibility of young people hanging around brings them to the attention of neighbours and the gardaí (Byrne et al., 2006). Research in Scotland with 11- to 16-year-olds found smoking, drinking and drug use were strongly associated with hanging about the street (or going to discos) and that while girls are more likely to smoke, boys are more likely to drink or to take drugs (Sweeting and West, 2000). Participation in structured activities, on the other hand, is argued to reduce health risks, including obesity, drug use and teenage binge drinking, all significant concerns in Ireland today (Department of Health and Children 2004-Strategic Task Force on Alcohol, 2004; Hibbell et al., 2000). For young people at risk for anti-social behaviour, participation in structured activities is contended to reduce the risk of criminal arrest and school drop-out (Mahoney, 2000). But this is not a clear-cut pattern. Some studies have found that participation in unstructured leisure is associated with enhanced self-worth as well as higher educational attainment and aspirations. Other studies show structured sports participation to be linked with higher rates of alcohol and drug use (Eccles and Baber, 1999).

In sum, the value of simply hanging around with peers cannot be ignored and caution should be exercised in seeing it as a risky activity. As noted by Hendry and colleagues (2002), a balance needs to be negotiated between young people's need for space to develop socially and to have leisure meaningful for them with adults' desire for 'socialisation and control' as the power-holders in society. Consideration also needs to be given to the social forces that pressurise young people towards conformity in leisure. 'From nursery school onward leisure is safeguarded and organised *for* young people – instead of *by* them. This continues into adolescence so that many feel the need to create their own leisure challenges away from parents but in adult society' (Hendry et al., 2002 p. 372).

Television Viewing

The majority of Irish young people (70 per cent) watch television every day and just under a quarter watch television most days (de Róiste and Dinneen, 2005). In terms of hours spent watching TV, about 40 per cent of young people watch two to three hours of television per day (Fahey et al., 2005). Lalor and Baird (2006) report that almost a quarter of young people from Co. Kildare watch TV, DVDs or videos for more than 10 hours per week. These findings are not surprising, as watching TV is one of the most frequently reported adolescent leisure activities internationally, differing little between age groups, gender or SES (Bartko and Eccles, 2003). Most Irish families now have two or three TVs and one-third of children have a TV in their bedroom (Foley-Nolan et al., 2005).

TV watching is integral to family life; over one-third of Irish families eat weekday meals while watching TV and patterns of watching are related to parental patterns (Foley-Nolan et al., 2005). Television programmes are also one of the most common topics of general social conversation for young people, reflecting the contribution of TV programmes to social interaction (Leyser and Cole, 2004). When watching TV, young people experience states of detachment, relaxation and 'vegetativeness' rather than those of involvement and enjoyment typical of other activities. Another perspective is that television may be watched primarily to fill in time due to a lack of desirable alternative leisure or because of constraints to alternative leisure, discussed later in this chapter.

Many are concerned about the impact of TV on the health of children and young people. This is understandable as time spent in sedentary activities, such as TV watching, is related to greater body weight, regardless of age or gender (Vandewater et al., 2004). On top of this, such sedentary leisure is associated with snacking between meals. Other research, however, reports no association between TV or video game use and being overweight, implying that the relationship is not clear cut (McMurray et al., 2000).

Overall, it is clear that TV is a source of much young people's leisure, contributing to social interaction, socialisation and relaxation for the young person. Television is a part of family life and of the young person's social world.

Computer Games

The rapid rise in the use of computers in young people's leisure is a major technological development over recent decades. It is estimated that in 2005, 54.9 per cent of all Irish households had a home computer, 35 per cent a games console and 45 per cent of households were connected to the Internet (CSO, 2005a). E-mail, 'blogs' or online diaries, Internet searches and downloading of music are some of the many uses of computers in leisure time. The Internet in particular provides an online gateway for social communication with other young people, from a local or distant location. Computer use, along with other forms of technology, is the fourth most popular hobby for 12- to 18-year-old Irish males (de Róiste and Dinneen, 2005). Computer games represent a very popular form of technology use by young people, especially males. Over a third (37 per cent) of Irish young people play computer games such as 'play stations' every day or most days; as few as 2 per cent report never playing (ibid).

Figure 8.1a Computer games female frequency

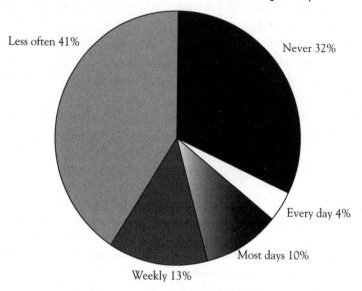

Less often 41%
Never 32%
Every day 4%
Most days 10%
Weekly 13%

Figure 8.1b Computer games male frequency

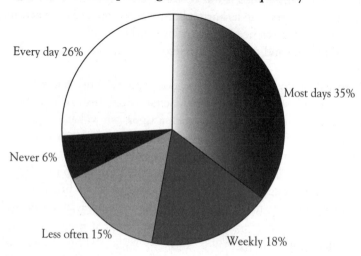

Every day 26%
Most days 35%
Never 6%
Less often 15%
Weekly 18%

Source: de Róiste and Dinneen (2005).

This pattern is in agreement with international trends and tends to continue into adulthood (Griffiths et al., 2004; Sweeting and West, 2000). Research with primary school pupils in Dublin found that almost a quarter spend over two hours per day playing computer games and this increases with age. Six per cent of children in fourth class play between two and three hours a day compared to 13 per cent of pupils in sixth class (INTO, 2005). This suggests that an interest in computer games is inculcated in the childhood years and continued into adolescence.

An overwhelming gender difference is present; adolescent males play computer games significantly more than females. In contrast to 60 per cent of males who play computer games every day or most days, only 13 per cent of young women report this frequency of use (de Róiste and Dinneen, 2005). Young males are more interested in computers, more confident and less anxious about using them (Jackson et al., 2001). This may be because they have interiorised a stereotyped view that men are more able than women in technological areas. They see computers more as a toy, using them for entertainment and diversion, such as downloading software, acquiring information and for play. Adolescent females, on the other hand, perceive the computer more as a tool, using it to communicate via e-mail rather than to play games (Wolfradt and Doll, 2001).

Reading

More than half of Irish young people, especially females, read every day or most days, indicating the popularity of reading as a free-time activity. Consistent with international research, Irish teenage females read significantly more than males (de Róiste and Dinneen, 2005). Based on research with 15-year-old Australian males, Martino (2001) identified three categories of male response to reading:

- Males who rejected reading, claimed it was boring, preferring other activities.
- Males who did not refer to reading as boring but preferred to read only certain kinds of text: action, fantasy, science fiction, horror and humour.
- Males who enjoyed reading and/or saw it as an escape.

For young men there appears to be something 'uncool' about reading. According to Martino (2001, p. 68), adolescent male reading is caught in a 'dualistic gender bind' whereby more masculine and active activities, such as sport, are valued over more passive and feminised activities such as reading. However, many young men do read but not perhaps the books aimed at young people. Young men tend to be more interested in reading comic books and newspapers (possibly focusing on the comics and sports sections) while young women are more interested in reading books of fiction as well as fashion or beauty magazines (Leyser and Cole, 2004; Sweeting and West, 2000).

Children and young people's reading is also associated with parental educational level, which is in turn linked to parental occupation (van Schooten et al., 2003).

Family reading habits also enhance young people's reading. A positive attitude towards reading and the cultural level of the home environment are associated with greater reading by children and young people (ibid). Much research has been undertaken into the impact of reading frequency on educational attainment and linguistic abilities, with a clear association between reading and academic achievement and vocabulary size (ibid). Individual factors such as Attention Deficit Hyperactivity Disorder, intellectual and sensory disabilities and a young person's past reading experience also all influence popularity of reading. In addition, some young people feel 'left out' because of a poor range of reading literature available to them. Research in the UK illuminated the social exclusion young people with visual impairments experience because they are not able to read new and popular books (Murray, 2002).

Listening to Music

The ubiquitous popularity of music for young people is overwhelming. Over four-fifths (80 per cent) of Irish young people listen to music every day or most days (de Róiste and Dinneen, 2005). Morgan's (2000b) finding that 'CDs and music' are major items of expenditure by Irish young people with their earnings from part-time work is in keeping with this. Similarly, Scottish research indicates that over 90 per cent of 11- to 16-year-olds listen to music 'every day' or 'most days' and nearly 95 per cent had a music system in their bedroom (Sweeting and West, 2000).

Listening to (as well as playing) music is one of the most widely reported remedies young people cite for dealing with 'feeling down' (Lalor and Baird, 2006), highlighting its role as a coping mechanism. Young people also use music to assert their individuality, develop relationships, conform to a group and learn about things. A shared taste in music is one of the most common shared features of adolescent friendship groups (Thurlow, 2002). Music listening is related to developmental issues such as individuation, self-awareness, autonomy, identity, love and sexuality. According to the uses and gratifications approach (Arnett et al., 1995), individuals make different media choices dependent upon personal characteristics. Music listeners gravitate to particular kinds of music because of certain personality characteristics, issues and/or needs that are either reflected in the music they choose or that the music satisfies; for example, teenagers with few friends, as compared to those with many friends, prefer music with themes of loneliness and independence.

Shopping

The frequency with which young people shop or simply look at shops in their free time shows a clear gender difference consistent with international research (Leyser and Cole, 2004; Sweeting and West, 2000). Half of Irish young women (50 per cent) compared to just under one-third (32 per cent) of young men shop on a weekly basis. Nearly a quarter of young women (24 per cent) shop every day or most days compared to only 15 per cent of their male counterparts. Little difference occurs between young people of different ages in shopping, although unsurprisingly, locality is influential; young people in urban settings shop more often than their rural counterparts (de Róiste and Dinneen, 2005).

Young women tend to strongly 'peer orientate': to form and maintain friendship groups or cliques on the basis of a shared appreciation of clothes (as well as music and personal qualities). This may be integral to explaining the high female frequency in shopping. Male youth, on the other hand, 'peer orientate' primarily on the basis of a shared interest in sport and/or computers (Thurlow, 2002). Gender socialisation, marketing influences and cultural mores also contribute to the gender difference. It is also worth noting that shopping centres and streets may be popular as areas for young people to hang out and meet each other, which understandably would further enhance the popularity of shopping for young people.

Hobbies

Nearly two-thirds (65 per cent) of Irish young people have one or more hobbies. This diminishes across adolescence due to a wide variety of factors, including a move towards more unstructured leisure and constraints to leisure (discussed later), including more homework and study, part-time work and greater identification with specific leisure interests to the exclusion of others (de Róiste and Dinneen, 2005).

Young women report significantly more hobbies than young men, possibly because of the greater popularity of sport for the latter. These findings are consistent with international trends. Many studies state that females report more hobbies, whereas males report more sports, and across adolescence, unstructured socialising activities increasingly replace hobbies and sports (Eccles and Barber, 1999; Passmore and French, 2001).

Types of Hobbies

Overall, the most popular hobbies reported by Irish young people are 'playing a musical instrument', 'looking after pets' and 'art'. A clear gender difference is also present, with the most popular hobbies for males being 'playing a musical instrument,', 'looking after pets' and 'pool or snooker', while for females they are 'dance', 'playing a musical instrument' and 'art' (de Róiste and Dinneen, 2005).

The popularity of playing a musical instrument (30 per cent) is unexpected and may be artificially high. In their study with American adolescents, for example, Passmore and French (2001) found that 15 per cent played a musical instrument or engaged in other expressive activities such as dancing or painting. Connor (2003), in a study with young people from Waterford, found that as few as 8 per cent 'played music'. 'Pool or snooker' was a popular activity for young Irish males, and 'art' and 'looking after pets' were popular leisure activities for both young Irish males and females.

Looking in particular at pets as a hobby, research with American young people also found this to be a frequent leisure activity (Zarbatany et al., 1990). Pets are sources of pleasure, fun, security, exercise and protection and help impart a sense of responsibility and respect for life (Ottney Cain, 1985), although empirical support for these findings is lacking. Pet ownership and care is a way of nurturing autonomy and self-esteem in young people and can contribute to well-being (Hagerty Davis and McCreary-Juhasz, 1985; Hanafin and Brooks, 2005).

Table 8.2 Top five hobbies of Irish young people

	Males	Females
1	Playing a musical instrument (29%)	Dance (35%)
2	Pets (19%)	Playing a musical instrument (32%)
3	Pool/snooker (17%)	Art (27%)
4	Technology (15%)	Pets (24%)
5	Art (14%)	Cooking (16%)

Source: de Róiste and Dinneen (2005).

It is clear that 'dance' is a very popular hobby for Irish adolescent females. Dance can enhance self-mastery through being in charge of the body, contributing to positive self-perception, body image and esteem (Hanna, 1988). Research with 7- to 8-year-old children found that dance enhances social skills although the extent to which these findings are generalisable to all types of dance and age groups is questionable (von Rossberg-Gempton et al., 1999). Dance may also be a healthy and fun way to keep fit and reduce the risk of obesity.

Sport

Sport has been defined as 'all forms of physical activity which through casual or organised participation aim at expressing or improving physical fitness and mental well-being, forming social relationships or obtaining results in competition at all levels, (Cospóir, 1994, p. 4). In keeping with the European Sports Charter, the Irish Sports Council differentiated between *competitive sports:* 'which include all forms of physical activity, which through organised participation, aim at expressing or improving physical fitness and at obtaining improved results in competition at all levels' and *recreational sports:* 'all forms of physical activity, which through casual or regular participation, aim at expressing or improving physical fitness and mental well-being and at forming social relationships' (Irish Sports Council Act, 1999, pp. 3–4). Another categorisation of sport is into game sports, fitness sports, survival sports and national games (Cospóir, 1994).

The 1997 Department of Education report *Targeting Sporting Change* stated that it 'is vital that sport is introduced and nurtured in our young people. It is vital that our children learn sporting and personal skills, it is vital that our children experience the sense of well-being, the benefits are life-long' (1997, p. v). An increasing association has arisen over recent years between sports and public health policies (Fahey et al., 2004). Liston and Rush (2006) noted the association between sports, social capital and public health.

The Gaelic Athletic Association (GAA) has used the contribution of sport to social capital and identity in advertising. These adverts include the portrayal of fathers and sons who follow the same local club, with the slogans 'It's not DNA, it's GAA' and 'Belong'. Such advertising represents the significance of playing Gaelic sports for identity and a sense of belonging to a shared culture and community.

According to Fahey and colleagues (2004, p. vi), key challenges for sports policy with respect to children and young people are to 'develop better integration between formal PE and extra-curricular sport … [and] its understanding of what a holistic, developmental approach to children's sport would entail'. Many sports organisations now have schools liaison officers who liaise with schools and local clubs in working with young people. Formal physical education and extra-curricular sport should support each other, 'facilitating young people to find and maintain a personal interest in some form of physical activity that occurs within and extends beyond the school environment. Over recent years there has also been a shift away from Sports for All (Council of Europe, 1975) policy towards an implicit emphasis on individualisation, physical exercise and targeted health promotion' (Fahey et al., 2004, p. 55).

Table 8.3 Top five sports of Irish young people

	Male	Female
1	Soccer (70%)	Basketball (38%)
2	Gaelic football (56%)	Gaelic football (36%)
3	Hurling (30%)	Swimming (33%)
4	Basketball (15%)	Soccer (27%)
5	Swimming (14%)	Camogie (19%)

Source: de Róiste and Dinneen (2005).

Others, such as the Physical Education Association of Ireland (PEAI), contend that irrespective of the availability of extra-curricular activities, quality physical education should be available to all school-going children at both primary and secondary levels. According to the PEAI (2006, p. 1), 'Physical Education provides the bedrock on which safe and sustainable physical activity patterns are established. At a time when the Government is showing increased commitment to investment in sport and physical activity, it is essential that children of school-going age be provided with comprehensive Physical Education experiences.'

A large majority (88 per cent) of Irish young people are involved, recreationally and/or competitively, in at least one sport (de Róiste and Dinneen, 2005).

Interestingly, young people take part more frequently in extra-curricular sport in schools, and outside of schools, than they do in physical education (Fahey et al., 2005). International comparisons show similarly high participation levels. In England, participation in sport (excluding walking), outside of physical education classes in school, is 97 per cent amongst 11- to 16-year-olds, while in the Netherlands, 89 per cent of 6- to 18-year-olds play sport (Sport England, 2003; Zeijl et al., 2003).

Table 8.4 Top five hobbies by gender

	Total	n=1475	Male	n=660	Female	n=815
1st	Play music 30.7%	n=454	Play music 28.7%	n=190	Dance 34.9%	n=285
2nd	Pets 21.5%	n=318	Pets 19.2%	n=127	Play music 32.3%	n=264
3rd	Art 21.4%	n=317	Pool/snooker 16.5%	n=109	Art 26.9%	n=220
4th	Dance 20.3%	n=300	Technology 15%	n=99	Pets 23.8%	n=191
5th	Cooking 10.4%	n=148	Cooking 14%	n=97	Art 16%	n=131

Table 8.5 Top five sports of Irish adults

	Male	Female
1	Golf (17%)	Swimming (17%)
2	Soccer (13%)	Aerobics/keep-fit (10%)
3	Swimming (12%)	Cycling (3%)
4	Gaelic football (8%)	Golf (3%)
5	Snooker/billards (6%)	Tennis (3%)

Source: Fahey et al. (2004)

The sports young people engage in differ significantly from adults, as outlined above, with individual sports more prominent in adulthood.

GENDER AND SPORT

A very strong gender difference is present in young people's sport, with young men significantly more likely to play a sport, recreationally or competitively, than young women (91 per cent of males versus 86 per cent of females) (de Róiste and Dinneen,

2005). This gender difference is well documented. According to Fahey and colleagues (2004, p. 83), 'boys and young men spend more time at sport and enjoy it more and are more enthusiastic about its rough and tumble aspects'. According to Hendry and colleagues (1993, p. 66), 'young women are less likely than young men to be competitors and are more likely either to play sport for fun or not at all'. From early childhood, boys are given greater encouragement to engage in sport by parents and teachers, and this increases with age (Balding, 2001; Sport England, 2003). However, rates of young females playing sport have increased over past decades and, as Roberts (1999) notes, have broken out of the recreational 'bedroom culture' and are now as likely as young men to use indoor sports facilities at least.

Table 8.6 Sports participation by Irish teens

Age	Male		Female		Total	
12	95%	(n= 95)	98%	(n= 93)	96%	(n=188)
13	95%	(n=196)	92%	(n=200)	93%	(n=396)
14	93%	(n=215)	90%	(n=257)	92%	(n=472)
15	88%	(n=184)	90%	(n=149)	89%	(n=334)
16	88%	(n=176)	76%	(n=133)	82%	(n=309)
17	88%	(n=123)	72%	(n=109)	80%	(n=232)
18	87%	(n= 33)	68%	(n= 30)	77%	(n=63)
TOTAL	91%	(n=1022)	86%	(n=971)	88%	(n=1994)

Source: de Róiste and Dinneen (2005).

Young women participate in sport weekly on average, whereas males, on average, participate in sport most days. Over two-thirds (70 per cent) of young men who participate in soccer and Gaelic football do so every day or most days, compared to just over a third (38 per cent) of young women. Even in sports that are more popular with young women, the frequency of male participation is higher. In basketball, 45 per cent of males who play basketball participate every day or most days compared to only 26 per cent of females (de Róiste and Dinneen, 2005). These results are in line with other research (Connor, 2003; Hendry et al., 1993).

There is also a decline in sports participation across the adolescent years, from 96 per cent at the age of 12 to 80 per cent at the age of 17 and 77 per cent at 18. The most striking drop-off in sports involvement occurs for female 15- to 16-year-olds (de Róiste and Dinneen, 2005).

This trend is found internationally. In 1998 the number of adolescents partaking in moderate exercise at least four times per week was 63 per cent of 10- to 11-year-olds, decreasing to 40 per cent of 15- to 17-year-olds. In 2002 these figures had decreased to 57 per cent and 35 per cent, respectively. The participation decline was present in both genders but again was more noticeable for girls, dropping from

55 per cent of 10- to 11-year-olds to 25 per cent of 15- to 17-year-olds in the 2002 survey (Kelleher et al., 2003). The public health implications of this decline in adolescent physical activity will be enormous. An individual's risk for all causes of mortality and in particular for premature death and/or morbidity from non-communicable diseases is significantly increased by having a sedentary lifestyle. Given that involvement in sport is for some, although not all, associated with a decreased likelihood of drinking, smoking and illicit drug use, bolstering young people's involvement in sport may also hinder risky health behaviour (Kilbarrack Coast Community Project, 2004). Many argue for targeted physical activity promotion during adolescence and, in particular, in the transition from adolescence to early adulthood. Providing opportunities for adolescents to develop the skills necessary to participate in individual sports seems particularly useful given that individual sports are more likely to be maintained into adulthood (Dinneen and de Róiste, 2006; Fahey et al., 2004).

Table 8.7 Top four community/charity groups of Irish young people (of those who report participating in groups)

	Male	Female
1	Youth clubs/groups (68%)	Youth clubs/groups (53%)
2	Scouts/guides (11%)	Choir/folk group (38%)
3	Voluntary work (9%)	Voluntary work (12%)
4	Choir/folk group (9%)	Scouts/guides (10%)

Source: de Róiste and Dinneen (2005).

A wide breadth of sports undertaken in childhood and adolescence is also important in determining whether a person remains active in sports into adulthood. As noted by Roberts (1999, p. 139), 'The extremely low rates of participation in physically active recreation within the present-day older age groups are not due solely to them having dropped out of sport during their adult lives but are also due to the poverty of their childhood sports socialisation and the limited opportunities that were available for them to continue playing after leaving school.'

Type of Sports

More Irish young people participate in team than individual sports with a ratio of almost exactly 2:1 (Connor, 2003; de Róiste and Dinneen, 2005). This is in complete contrast to the sporting patterns of Irish adults (Fahey et al, 2004).

Not surprisingly, gender has a major bearing on type of sport cited, though Gaelic sports feature prominently for both young Irish males and females. The Gaelic Athletic Association (GAA) in 2004 had 8,891 and 5,431 registered underage teams for Gaelic football and hurling, respectively. Taking even a conservative average of 18 players per team, this equates to 257,796 individuals involved in Gaelic games.

Even allowing for the fact that many young people play on more than one team, these numbers are impressive (GAA, 2005).

The top three most popular sports for young Irish males are soccer, Gaelic football and hurling, while for their female counterparts they are basketball, Gaelic football and swimming (de Róiste and Dinneen, 2005). Similar findings were reported for young males in Connor's (2003) study. However, while basketball (34 per cent) and swimming (23 per cent) are the top two sports for young females, Gaelic football did not even feature in the top 10 female sports of that study. This may be explained by the fact that Connor's (2003) study included predominantly urban respondents from a narrow geographical area or it may reflect an increase in the popularity of Gaelic football amongst females in the seven-year gap between the studies.

Soccer is the most common male sport and this is not surprising given its media prominence. Following a particular premiership team may be linked to identity and a sense of belonging to peers who follow the same team. Soccer and other sports are also popular topics of conversation for young men.

The most common female sport is basketball. Basketball has popularity as a school sport, both in PE and extra-curricular sport, that is in contrast with its rather limited presence outside of the school environment (Fahey et al., 2005). The schools division of Basketball Ireland report that approximately 40,000 children and young people play basketball (Basketball Ireland, 2005).

Interestingly, young women are significantly more likely to participate in individual sports than males, which again is consistent with international research. In addition, the predominance of individual and non-competitive sports in adult participation in Ireland can be further used as an argument for encouraging young people to participate in more individual and recreational physical activities (Dinneen and de Róiste, 2006; Fahey et al, 2004).

Research by McPhail and colleagues (2003, p. 67) emphasised young people's 'dissatisfaction with the overrepresentation of a small number of sports in schools' and at the same time their interest to experience a wider choice of activities. What is important for facilitating lifelong participation in sports and physical activities is the need to provide young people with a repertoire or portfolio of sports and physical activities (Green et al., 2005). It is to be expected that some of these will endure while others will be dropped, replaced or supplemented.

COMMUNITY OR CHARITY GROUPS

Nearly one-third (32.2 per cent) of Irish young people participate in one or more community or charity groups (de Róiste and Dinneen, 2005). This is similar to the findings of Connor (2003), who reported that only 35 per cent of young people were involved in a group. In contrast, membership of sports clubs tends to be higher, particularly for males (McGee et al., 2005; Zeijl et al., 2003). While sampling and methodological differences may compromise comparisons with other research studies, research suggests greater participation by Irish young people in youth clubs and other groups, such as Scouts and Guides, compared to other countries (de Róiste and Dinneen, 2005). In the UK, 17 per cent of young people report being in a youth club and 7 per cent in Scouts or Guides (Child Accident Prevention Trust, 2002). In the Netherlands, 11 per cent of young people are members of a youth club, 11 per cent of a drama or singing club and 6 per cent members of a hobby club (Zeijl et al., 2003).

Young women participate more in groups than young men, which is in agreement with international research. In America, Eccles and Barber (1999) found that young women participate more in church and volunteer activities while young men participate more in Scout clubs. Gender socialisation into caring may contribute to this. Females are over-represented in the caring professions and in training courses in the social care, social work and nursing sectors. In contrast, males of all ages are more likely to be members of sporting clubs and associations (McGee et al., 2005). Relating to this is Buhrmester's (1996) contention that females are more likely to participate in activities that support communal awards (such as interpersonal connection) whereas males are more likely to engage in activities where agency awards (such as personal achievement, recognition and power) are sought, for example through sports and competitive games.

The most popular groups are youth clubs or groups, choirs or folk groups and voluntary work. A slight gender difference is apparent: for young men the most popular groups are youth clubs or groups, Scouts and voluntary work; for young women the most popular groups are youth clubs or groups, choirs or folk groups and voluntary work. Youth clubs or groups and Scouts or Guides are amongst the most popular groups mentioned, similar to Connor's (2003) research. Other comparisons (such as choirs) are difficult to make due to methodological differences between the studies. Youth clubs and groups play a significant role in young people's lives, particularly in the younger adolescent years (12 to 15 years). Young people particularly value the social aspects of clubs and groups (Hennessy and Donnelly, 2005). National youth organisations such as Youth Work Ireland and Foróige incorporate an extensive number of clubs in both urban and rural locations throughout Ireland. In addition, a number of schools in disadvantaged areas have an after-school youth club; however, young people have voiced the need for different and separate services and facilities for different age groups (12 to 14 and 15 to 17) (Byrne et al., 2006).

The popularity of voluntary and charity work may reflect the impact of the transition year school programme. This can introduce young people to voluntary work, as can fundraising. Another example is Gaisce (The President's Award). This is a formal means of encouraging young people to undertake community and voluntary work.

The Irish White Paper on Voluntary Activity (2000) and the National Youth Work Development Plan (2003–2007) (discussed in Chapter 10) identify the value of volunteering and the community or voluntary sector.

Volunteering has many potential benefits, both for young people and those they are helping. Voluntary work can empower young people, encouraging a greater sense of responsibility and understanding and help them to see that they can make a difference. It can expand a young person's social worlds, possibly leading them to mix with people they otherwise would not meet and to enhance their social capital.

Research has shown that a variety of factors influence participation in clubs and groups, such as pre-adolescent participation, SES, family values, self-efficacy and peer attachment (McGee et al., 2005). Participation in clubs and groups widens an individual's 'social capital', socio-emotional development and social skills (Kahn and Antonucci, 1980). Participation in voluntary activities can also be personally expressive, enabling a young person to communicate their identity and sense of who they are and stimulate assessment of values, talents, interests, culture and social belonging (Barber et al., 2001). According to McGee and colleagues (2005, p. 2), membership of community or charity groups may

> facilitate social development by increasing friendships within groups; linking like-minded peers; strengthening the relationship between individual and family; exposure to other world views and enabling young people to develop skills such as acting cooperatively and taking different perspectives ... membership might also be seen as a dynamic process linking the adolescent to larger social forces within the community.

Research exploring the impact of participation in such extra-curricular groups on self-esteem and other indices cannot disentangle whether participation enhances self-esteem or vice versa (Hart and Fegly, 1995).

As with sports and hobbies, participation diminishes across the adolescent years, from 45 per cent participation at the age of 12 to 34 per cent at the age of 17 to 34 per cent at 18 years. This decline has been found by other Irish studies and is common internationally (Connor, 2003; Hendry et al., 1993; McGee et al., 2005; Zeijl et al., 2003). In the UK, the Child Accident Prevention Trust (2002) reported that adolescents are more likely to be members of youth clubs or groups in their early years at secondary school, with a pattern of increased drop-out then evident across the rest of adolescence.

With respect to youth clubs and groups, this decline is in keeping with current trends. Ógra Chorcaí, for example, reported that for 2004 in the 10- to 14-year-old age group they had 1,710 males and 2,189 females attending their 87 youth groups across Cork city and county, while for the 15- to 19-year-old age group the corresponding numbers were 862 and 930. The principle objective of Ógra Chorcaí is to 'engage young people in development and educational opportunities in order that they may more fully participate in their community and society'. Ógra Chorcaí works with and for young people in three ways: through adult volunteers and leaders, through community-based special intervention projects and through training for prospective youth workers (Ógra Chorcaí, 2005). Similar organisations operate throughout the country.

The Irish Girl Guides also report a decline across age. Currently there are 131 Guide Units for 10- to 15-year-olds and 13 Ranger Units for 15- to 21-year-olds. In

2004, 1,578 girls attended these. Over two-thirds (67.3 per cent, n=1,062) were aged 12 to 13, a fifth (21 per cent, n=343) were aged 14 to 15 and 10.9 per cent (n=173) were aged 16 to 18 (Irish Girl Guides, 2005).

According to Hendry and colleagues (1993), close links between such clubs and the school's organisational structure, the location of the club in the school building or strict rules or discipline may contribute to drop-out. With age, adolescents move from structured to more unstructured, casual leisure and thus may reject the disciplined and structured nature of such clubs in favour of hanging around and involvement in informal groups (Coleman and Hendry, 1990).

With respect to policy, the National Youth Development Plan (2003–2007, p. 11) identifies as a challenge for youth work 'attracting and sustaining the interest and involvement of young people, especially older young people'.

Another example of youth groups are those run by Foróige, which has over 45 active youth groups across Ireland. Foróige clubs are purposively structured youth development groups made up of young people from the local community. These are usually groups of less than 30 young people, aged 12 to 18 years, and voluntary adult leaders, in a ratio of approximately 10 to 1. They enable young people to experience democracy by electing their own club committee and managing and operating the club in co-operation with their adult leaders. Foróige clubs plan and carry out activities designed to meet the interests and needs of members, and to assist in this regard, Foróige has developed eight education programmes: Leadership, Culture, Youth Co-operative Education, Family and Lifeskills, Science, Health, Agriculture or Horticulture and Citizenship.

In 2004, 14,110 young people were members of Foróige groups; 54.1 per cent of these were female and 48.2 per cent were male. The majority of their members – over two-thirds (70 per cent) – are rural dwellers. In contrast to other youth clubs and associations, figures from Foróige do not show a steep decline in participation rates over the adolescent years: 51.5 per cent of their members were aged 12 to 14 years and 48.2 per cent were aged 15 to 18 years, the national average being 14.6 years (Foróige, 2005).

CONSTRAINTS AND FACILITATORS TO YOUNG PEOPLE'S LEISURE

Young people live in environments with features that simultaneously both hinder and facilitate leisure participation. These factors are a particular source of interest with respect to structured or formal leisure, such as organised hobbies, sports or community or charity groups, as opposed to informal leisure such as watching TV, hanging around or playing recreational sport with friends.

Constraints are defined as 'factors that are assumed by researchers and perceived or experienced by individuals to limit the formation of leisure preferences and to inhibit or prohibit participation and enjoyment in leisure' (Jackson, 1997, p. 461). Facilitators are defined as 'condition(s) that exists, whether internal to the individual, in relation to another individual, or to some societal structure, that enables participation. The facilitator is the condition itself, not the process through which that condition energises or motivates behaviour leading to (i.e. facilitating) or limiting (i.e. constraining) participation' (Raymore, 2002, p. 4).

Constraints and facilitators are seen by some, but not all, theorists as two sides of a coin; the absence of one meaning the presence of the other. For example, if body image is not a barrier to leisure, it can be seen to be a facilitator. Others contend, however, that this is not the case and rather see facilitators and constraints as operating independently of each other.

It is worth asking at this point what you feel are the factors that constrain your structured (organised) or formal leisure participation. In general, people typically report 'structural constraints', such as a lack of facilities or transport. These are very obvious and visible leisure barriers. However, as illustrated below, other types of constraint (and facilitators) act even before a person gets to the point where structural constraints or facilitators may be experienced.

In order to examine constraints and facilitators to leisure, the model developed by Crawford, Jackson and Godbey (1991) will be used. They proposed three types of constraints on leisure: intrapersonal, interpersonal and structural, representing a hierarchy of constraints beginning with those that affect preferences and leading to those that affect participation (or non-participation) (see Figures 8.7 and 8.8). Each level of the hierarchy (from intrapersonal to structural) requires successful negotiation before a person can progress closer to their desired leisure activity. Consequently, intrapersonal constraints or facilitators are experienced before interpersonal ones. Structural constraints and facilitators are the last type encountered.

Table 8.8 Examples of constraints

Intrapersonal constraints
- A perceived lack of skill.
- A dislike of competition.
- Poor body image.

Intrapersonal facilitators
- Self-confidence.
- An enjoyment of competition.
- Positive body image.

Interpersonal constraints
- A lack of family support.
- Not knowing anyone in a desired leisure activity.
- Bullying.

Interpersonal facilitators
- Family support.
- Having friends who share the same leisure interests.
- Peer support.

Structural constraints
- A lack of leisure facilities in the locality.
- Transportation difficulties to/from leisure activities.
- A lack of money to partake in the leisure activity.

Structural facilitators
- Leisure facilities that are nearby and easily accessible.
- Having money to participate in leisure interests.
- A positive cultural ethos towards leisure.

Figure 8.2 Crawford, Jackson and Godbey's (1991) model of leisure constraints and facilitatiors

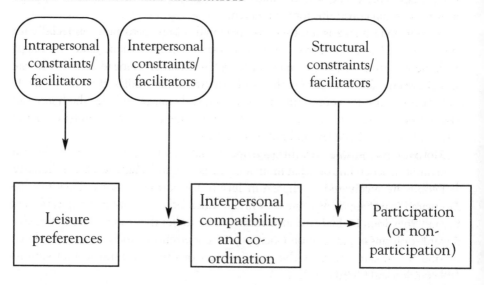

Caution should be exercised regarding a simplistic assumption that a particular constraint cited by a person will result in non-participation, as some people 'negotiate through constraints' and succeed in initiating or continuing leisure participation. Equally, while a facilitator may be present, that in no way guarantees participation.

Intrapersonal Constraints and Facilitators

Intrapersonal facilitators are individual characteristics, traits and beliefs that enable or support the formation of leisure preferences and encourage participation in leisure.

Intrapersonal constraints refer to where such characteristics, traits and beliefs act as barriers to leisure participation.

One of the most prominent intrapersonal constraints is a perceived lack of skill. This is a key barrier to participation in Gaelic football and soccer, where skill is perceived as important to membership of a club (de Róiste and Dinneen, 2005).

Competition is another intrapersonal constraint that also can be a facilitator depending on the individual's personality profile. Many studies recommend minimising the importance of winning in order to maximise enjoyment and finding a balance between intense competition and an enjoyable amount of competition (National Heart Alliance, 2001). Recent research suggests that competition is not a strong barrier for most Irish young people. Over three-quarters of Irish young people enjoy competition, implying that competition is more likely to be a facilitator rather than a constraint in leisure. This is more especially true for young men, as a significant gender difference was evident; young men are twice as likely to report enjoying competition (de Róiste and Dinneen, 2005).

Another intrapersonal constraint is where a young person does not enjoy joining new clubs and groups. Over half of Irish young people enjoy joining new clubs and groups, especially young women (ibid). This suggests that this is more likely to be an intrapersonal constraint for young men.

A poor body image is another intrapersonal leisure constraint, especially for females (Hendry et al., 1988). Over three-quarters of Irish young males are happy with the way they look compared to only just over half of young females (de Róiste and Dinneen, 2005), suggesting that, as in international studies, this is more likely to be a constraint for young women. However, body image and ideal body size can also act as strong motivators for girls and young women to exercise, in particular in late adolescence (Ingledew and Sullivan, 2002).

Motivation is another key intrapersonal variable, serving as a leisure constraint or facilitator, depending on what motivates the person to undertake a leisure activity.

People are motivated to engage in leisure for various reasons. They may be motivated to participate because they find it inherently interesting or enjoyable and because they want to do it (intrinsic motivation) and/or they want to attain tangible rewards or forms of recognition (such as prizes or attention and praise from others) or due to pressure from or the expectations of others (extrinsic motivation) (Alexandris and Grouis, 2002).

High levels of both intrinsic and extrinsic motivation are intrapersonal facilitators of leisure. However, intrinsic motivation is a stronger predictor of a person maintaining their leisure involvement than extrinsic motivation. Intrinsic motivation incorporates:

- **Motivation to know:** Performing an activity for the satisfaction derived from learning, exploring or trying to understand new concepts or skills.
- **Motivation to accomplish things:** Engaging in an activity for the satisfaction experienced in attempting to reach personal objectives.

- **Motivation toward experiencing stimulation:** Engaging in activities to experience stimulating sensations such as sensory pleasure, fun and excitement (Alexandris and Grouis, 2002).

A lack of leisure motivation, or 'amotivation', is an intrapersonal leisure constraint. Amotivation is where a person cannot be bothered to make an effort to engage in leisure. This may often be because of negative experiences with leisure or social groups or institutions in previous years. It may also be because they see no point in undertaking any leisure, perceiving themselves as passive, rather than active, agents in their life, including their leisure. According to Alexandris and Grouis (2002, p. 8), 'amotivated individuals are neither intrinsically nor extrinsically motivated. They do not perceive contingencies between their actions and the outcomes of these actions and their behaviour is out of their control.'

Amotivation is proposed as one of the most powerful predictors of a lack of leisure participation and of drop-out in hobbies, sports and other organised activities (Alexandris and Grouis, 2002). It may arise due to a lack of community resources, negative past experiences with leisure, a lack of cognitive ability and a poor sense of self-efficacy. As a dimension, it is negatively associated with optimal leisure experience as well as positively associated with substance abuse, though in the latter it is unclear if amotivation causes the substance abuse or vice versa (Caldwell et al., 2004).

The vast majority of Irish young people show high levels of intrinsic motivation in their leisure. They report that what they do is done out of personal choice rather than as a result of parental or familial pressure. Most report that they enjoy what they do, that they want to have fun and that what they choose to do is important to them (de Róiste and Dinneen, 2005). A small minority (just under 6 per cent) of Irish young people can be described as low in leisure motivation, or 'amotivated'. These young people participate significantly less than others in hobbies, sports and community or charity groups (ibid). Research on these motivation dimensions, though, is quite new and caution needs to be exercised about their validity, reliability and usefulness.

Having a strong desire to try out some type of leisure, feeling confident in oneself and one's abilities, enjoying joining new clubs and meeting new people are other types of intrapersonal facilitators which are all highly prevalent in Irish young people with respect to their leisure (ibid).

Interpersonal Constraints and Facilitators

Interpersonal facilitators or constraints are the result of interpersonal interaction. Having friends to engage in a leisure activity with is an example of an interpersonal leisure facilitator, while the absence of this is an interpersonal leisure constraint. Familial or peer support for leisure participation are other interpersonal facilitators, while their absence are constraints.

Not knowing anyone else involved in an activity is one of the foremost barriers to young people's leisure in Ireland today. Nearly one-third of Irish young people report this interpersonal barrier to participation (ibid). It is most likely in dance and swimming and least likely to be an issue in soccer and Gaelic football.

A lack of parental permission and support are other examples of interpersonal constraints. Most Irish young people (over three-quarters) do not report being constrained in their leisure by their parents not giving permission and over half (61 per cent) report that their family encourages them in their leisure pursuits, indicating the high prevalence of family support and encouragement for young people's leisure (de Róiste and Dinneen, 2005).

Family encouragement is a clear facilitator to Irish young people's leisure. Over three-quarters (86 per cent) of young people indicate that their parents allow them to do what activities they would like and nearly two-thirds indicate their families encourage them to join new clubs and groups (de Róiste and Dinneen, 2005). Parents facilitate by being leisure educators and models and by providing leisure opportunities and encouragement. Research has highlighted the importance of the family and interestingly, the father in particular, for involvement in leisure (Lewko and Greendorfer, 1998). When tensions between adolescent autonomy and adult control are played out in the leisure context, the family may be experienced as a leisure constraint. Adults may choose a young person's leisure for them, feeling they know what's best rather than the young person herself or himself. Parents of young people with disabilities are often over-protective, limiting the leisure their son or daughter engages in for reasons of perceived safety. The young person again may experience this as a leisure constraint.

Given the salience of friendship groups in adolescence (O'Donovan, 2002 in Green et al., 2005), friends are a critical support for young people in their leisure. Leisure is a context where young people can come together with their friends doing something enjoyable together, being 'part of the same thing'. For a young person, a form of leisure is valued if it is valued by their friends as well (Green et al., 2005). It is thus understandable that young people are more likely to be involved in leisure that their friends are engaged in and drop out of leisure that their friends have dropped out of.

Being either mixed or single-sex, leisure may be an interpersonal facilitator or constraint for young people. Overall, more than two-thirds of Irish young people, especially young women, prefer leisure activities with both sexes together, while young teenage males prefer more single-sex activities (ibid).

Structural Constraints and Facilitators

Structural facilitators and constraints are physical or material barriers such as finance, time, transport and weather.

The primary leisure barrier for Irish young people's leisure today is a structural barrier: inadequate provision of leisure facilities or activities in their locality. This can refer to a lack of dance classes, lack of a local swimming pool or a lack in the choice of sports available. Over half (59 per cent) of young people believe that there is very little leisure provision in their area, while under a third (32 per cent – the remainder of the sample) were undecided on the issue (ibid). Location is most likely to be a barrier for swimming and least likely to be an issue for those who would like to join Gaelic football. This reflects the ubiquitous coverage of the GAA and the poor provision in terms of swimming pools, particularly public swimming pools.

A gender difference is present, with young women reporting less leisure provision in their area than young men (64 per cent vs. 55 per cent). Not surprisingly, there is also an urban-rural divide in this. Less than half (45.5 per cent) of city dwellers compared to over two-thirds (68.1 per cent) of those who live in the countryside experience this structural barrier. Young people from lower socio-economic groups also report this barrier significantly more than those of the higher groups (de Róiste and Dinneen, 2005).

Transport difficulties in terms of getting to and from leisure activities is another one of the most prominent structural leisure constraints experienced by young people. Over a quarter of Irish young people identify transport difficulties as a barrier. As with location, transport is more likely to be a barrier for joining swimming but least likely to be a barrier for joining Gaelic football, which is easier to get to than swimming pools (de Róiste and Dinneen, 2005). However, factors such as two-car households, the recent economic upturn and improved rural transport networks may have reduced transport difficulties for some young people. There is a smaller than expected urban-rural divide in this, as although it would be expected that those in rural (compared to urban) areas would have greater transport difficulties, this is only slightly the case. The widespread prevalence of GAA sports may contribute to this. Older adolescents are significantly more likely to report transport difficulties, probably reflecting the broadening horizons of the late adolescents' recreational sphere. Seventeen- and 18-year-olds are likely to want to travel further from home for leisure and also are likely to want to be out later at night (ibid).

Not having sufficient money to undertake a particular leisure activity is another structural constraint. Membership fees, equipment and travel costs can all be too expensive for a young person in their leisure participation. However, in contemporary Ireland this seems to be a leisure constraint for only a minority (15 per cent) of young people. As anticipated, young people from lower SES groups are more likely to experience it as a barrier. Allied to this, young people from lower socio-economic groups are more likely to report that there is little for them to do in their area (ibid).

Older adolescents are also more likely to identify money as a constraint (ibid), reflecting the trend towards more commercial recreation across adolescence (Hendry et al., 1993). A lack of money is a difficult barrier to mediate on an individual level because young people do not generally have control of household finances and, where money is scarce, leisure pursuits are unlikely to be prioritised. At a community level, particularly in areas of high disadvantage, leisure activities for young people should be free or heavily subsidised and matched to their leisure interests (de Róiste and Dinneen, 2005).

Time is a common structural constraint in both youth and adult leisure, for example, where a young person feels they don't have enough time for leisure activities because of study and homework, part-time work or other factors. For Irish young people, time is more likely to be a leisure constraint for older age groups. Only one quarter of 12-year-olds experience a time constraint, compared to 62 per cent of 17-year-olds and 71 per cent of 18-year-olds. A gender difference is also present, with time being more likely to be a constraint for young women than young men. A key reason for this may be the greater time adolescent females spend on studying and homework (de Róiste and Dinneen, 2005).

Perception of safety is a factor that can be seen to be both structural and intrapersonal in nature, as it depends on a person's judgment of their environment. 'Feeling safe' is a much documented leisure facilitator, while its opposite, 'not feeling safe', is a known constraint. Young people who may not feel safe in different types of leisure with a consequential negative impact on their leisure involvement include young people from ethnic minorities, young people who are gay, lesbian or transsexual, young people with disabilities and young women. Irish research has found that the vast majority of the general population of young people feel safe going to and from activities in the evening, although 15 per cent (primarily young females aged 14 to 15 in Dublin) report not feeling safe (ibid).

In terms of facilitators, a social ethos that values leisure and a good economy whereby funding is available to support the provision of a leisure infrastructure, including facilities and transport, also supports leisure involvement. Policy development with respect to leisure is central to this and the Department of Health and Children's emerging policy on recreation and leisure for young people will hopefully enhance leisure provision for this age group in the future.

Overall, it is clear that the most common constraints Irish young people experience with respect to leisure are:

- Inadequate provision of leisure facilities or activities in the locality.
- Not knowing anyone else involved in the leisure activity.
- Transport difficulties in terms of getting to and from activities.
- A perceived lack of skill integral to the activity.

Some of the most common facilitators include:

- Family support and encouragement.
- Friends engaging in the same leisure activity.
- Enjoyment of competition.
- Finance.

Caution needs to be exercised in considering these; such constraints and facilitators reflect young people's experiences in 2005. Social and cultural changes as well as local contextual factors play an integral role as to how leisure is perceived and experienced by young people.

Leisure is only one component of a lifestyle embedded in the wider social structures of family, community and culture. Socio-economic status and membership of a minority ethnic group in the UK are associated with a lower level of participation in hobbies and sports (Seefeld et al., 2002).

A large number, particularly males, of Irish early school leavers speak of being barred from cinemas, pool halls, shops and other locations. This suggests marginalisation and a sub-group of youth who are disenfranchised. These young people, who are no longer attending school and are from economically disadvantaged and ethnic minority backgrounds, thus appear to encounter further obstacles in their leisure time. While these young people do not report high levels of participation in structured sports or hobbies, activities such as pool or snooker and the cinema were popular for them. However, many report that they or their friends had been barred from pool or snooker clubs or the cinema. As a consequence they report spending more time 'hanging around outside' and less time engaged in what they would like to do in their free time (de Róiste and Dinneen, 2005; see also Devlin, 2006, pp 29–32). While hanging around can be positive in itself, some research also suggests that it may lead to being more 'at risk' for crime, substance abuse and increasing social exclusion. Further research is warranted in this to better understand the complex relationships between all of these variables.

Drop-out

Dropping out of activities is a natural part of adolescence; research has shown that young people are likely to drop particular activities as particular development needs are met (Kelly, 1987). Three-quarters of young people have typically dropped out of one or more leisure activities. Dance (predominantly Irish dance), basketball, drama and music are the activities most commonly dropped out of by young women. A high number of young men drop out of soccer, martial arts and swimming (de Róiste and Dinneen, 2005).

Young Irish women are significantly more likely than their male counterparts to drop out of a leisure activity (ibid). There are predictable gender differences in the leisure activities that young people drop out of. Females are more likely to have dropped out of dance (predominantly Irish dance), drama, basketball and music than males. However, apart from music, they are more likely than young men to have joined these activities in the first place. Gender-neutral activities in terms of drop-out include Scouts or Guides, Gaelic football and hurling or camogie. Young men are more likely than young women to have dropped out of soccer, martial arts and swimming. Apart from swimming, these are also activities young men are more likely to join in the first place.

Looking at reasons cited for drop-out, the most common reason given by Irish young people is 'loss of interest' in the activity (ibid). This is not surprising, as adolescence is a time of transition during which the individual may be exposed to a broad spectrum of activities and will enter adulthood having ceased involvement in all but a few of these. This concurs with studies showing that young people 'outgrow' activities as they mature. By the age of 16, young people's leisure becomes more focused around a smaller number of retained pastimes. These are then more likely to be carried forward into adulthood (Roberts, 1999). As a response for drop-out, 'loss of interest' may mask more deep-seated constraints on participation. Further research is clearly needed into this to unravel what constitutes such loss of interest.

Table 8.9 Top five reasons for drop-out

1.	Loss of interest in the activity	55%
2.	Times of the activity not suitable	34%
3.	Not liking the activity leader(s)	27%
4.	Skill level not good enough	21%
5.	Friends dropped-out	16%

Source: de Róiste and Dinneen (2005).

Time is a reason for dropout for over one-third of Irish young people. This applies particularly to swimming more than other leisure activity. Reasons for this may be the huge time commitment, including early morning sessions, competitive swimmers give to their sport.

Over a quarter of young people cite not liking the leader as a reason for drop-out. This is consistent with the findings of Hultsman (1993) and others, that while parents are more salient in a young adolescent's decision whether or not to join a leisure activity, cessation of an activity is more influenced by *other* adults. An interesting trend is the difference between the response for youth clubs or groups and Scouts or Guides. Over one-third (39 per cent) of young people who dropped out of Scouts or Guides cite not liking the leader as the reason, in contrast to only 17 per cent of those who dropped out of youth clubs or groups. This may be because of stronger structural constraints (rules, leader-led activities) in the former.

Not having a good enough skill level is cited as a reason for drop-out by over one-fifth of young people. Not surprisingly, this reason for drop-out is highest in sport where skill level is closely associated with both success and enjoyment. Nearly one-third (32 per cent) of those who dropped out for this reason did so out of Gaelic football. Additionally, over a quarter (27 per cent) of those who dropped out of soccer cited skill level as a reason for drop-out (ibid). Dropping out because friends have also dropped out is the fifth most likely reason for young people to drop out of an activity. This reason is more commonly cited with regard to clubs and groups than with sports or music. A problem with transport was the next most popular reason for dropping out of an activity, especially swimming.

CONCLUSION

Leisure has a prominent place in the lives of young people today. Most young people engage in a range of activities (sports, hobbies and groups) as well as enjoying hanging out with their friends and doing less directed activities, such as watching TV and listening to music. A high proportion (88 per cent), especially males, play sport recreationally or competitively, though this declines significantly across the adolescent years. Nearly two-thirds of Irish young people, especially females, have one or more hobbies and nearly one-third participate in one or more community or charity groups.

Gender differences are prevalent throughout young people's leisure and may be due to gender socialisation, cultural values and sex-typing of activities, among other factors. However, gender differences in sport and hobby participation over past decades are diminishing, suggesting, as Roberts (1999) notes, a move towards more leisure forms becoming 'genderless' in participation terms.

Across the adolescent years there is a marked decline in leisure participation, especially in hobbies and groups. While experimentation with different activities is a feature of adolescence, the level of drop-out is a concern, particularly with respect to those who, by late adolescence, are not committed to any hobby or group.

Using Crawford, Jackson and Godbey's (1991) model, intrapersonal, interpersonal and structural constraints to young people's leisure were discussed. Inadequate provision of leisure facilities or activities in the locality and transport difficulties stand out as barriers to young people's leisure.

In order to provide optimally for leisure in this age group, young people, in any particular social context, need to have a say in the content and format of such leisure provision. In this way young people's needs and preferences in leisure can be addressed and their growing autonomy respected.

RECOMMENDED READING

Coleman, J.C., & Hendry, L. (1999). *The nature of adolescence*. London: Routledge.

Connor, S. (2003). *Youth sport in Ireland: The sporting, leisure and lifestyle patterns of Irish adolescents*. Dublin: The Liffey Press.

de Róiste, A. and Dinneen, J. (2005). *Young people's views about opportunities, barriers and supports in recreation and leisure*. Dublin: National Children's Office.

9

Juvenile Justice

INTRODUCTION

The focus of this chapter is young people's experiences of the justice system. The structures of the justice system for young people shall be described, commencing with a focus on the Children Act 2001, the primary piece of legislation governing young people and criminal behaviour. The characteristics of young offenders as detailed in various research reports shall be described. We shall examine the available data on the nature and incidence of juvenile crime (primarily from statistics in the Garda Síochána Annual Reports). The workings of the Garda Juvenile Diversion Programme and the Garda Youth Diversion Projects are described. Next, this chapter looks at the workings of the Special Residential Services Board and the newly established Irish Youth Justice Service. The operation of the Children Court is described, as are the various detention facilities for young people (the Children Detention Centre and Children Detention Schools). Finally, this chapter concludes with a description of the implications for youth justice arising from the Criminal Justice Act 2006.

THE CHILDREN ACT 2001

The Children Act 2001 is the primary piece of legislation governing juvenile justice in Ireland. It is a complex piece of legislation, which affects the working of three government departments: the Department of Justice, Equality and Law Reform, the Department of Education and Science, and the Department of Health and Children. Overall responsibility for implementation of the Act lies with the Minister for Children.

The Children Act 2001 replaces the outdated Children Act 1908. As Cotter (2005) notes, 'The Act ... shifts the emphasis away from the idea of punishment and detention and proposes a comprehensive range of community sanctions' (p. 288).

Age of Criminal Responsibility

The age at which a child is considered capable of committing a criminal offence is covered both in the Children Act 2001 and the Criminal Justice Act 2006. Historically, Ireland has had one of the lowest ages of criminal responsibility in

Europe. The 1908 Children Act allowed for children as young as seven to be prosecuted. Part 5 of the Children Act 2001 provided for the raising of the age of criminal responsibility from seven to 12 years. Section 52 states 'It shall be conclusively presumed that no child under the age of 12 years is capable of committing an offence'.

This part of the Children Act 2001, however, was not implemented and was replaced by s.129 of the Criminal Justice Act 2006, in which the age of criminal responsibility was raised to 12, but for serious crimes such as rape, murder and manslaughter only to 10 years. This commenced in October 2006.

This reversal of a provision (that did not come into force) to raise the age of criminal responsibility to 12 years for a number of serious crimes has the effect of keeping Ireland's age of criminal responsibility one of the lowest in Europe because of the extremely remote possibility of a 10- or 11-year-old being tried for rape, murder or manslaughter.

Kilkelly (2006, pp. 52–3) details a presentation by Minister Michael McDowell to the Joint Committee on Equality, Justice, Defence and Women's Rights in September 2005, where he stated:

> It could seriously scandalise public perceptions of criminal justice if 11- or 12-year-old rapists went unpunished, were told their offences were bad behaviour and society did nothing about it, particularly now that 11-year-old children are getting pregnant … we could have a serious collapse of social confidence in our criminal justice system, especially now that children mature younger and are engaged in sexual behaviour, if all sexual activity up to the age of 12 years was, in every circumstance, regarded as being incapable of being criminal.

These are unconvincing arguments on a number of points:

- The Minister presents no evidence that there has been a single incidence of an 11- or 12-year-old committing rape.
- The reference to 11-year-olds becoming pregnant is doubly misleading. There have only been a very small number of 11-year-olds who have become pregnant. Also, the Minister seems implicitly to make a connection between 11-year-old rapists and pregnant 11-year-olds. This is spurious, as in the majority of (the small number of) cases of young adolescents becoming pregnant, the father is invariably an older teenager, brother, father or relative of the girl.
- There is no evidence that children under 12 are engaging in sexual intercourse earlier or more frequently than they did in the past. As we saw in Chapter 4, numerous studies have indicated that first sexual intercourse typically occurs in the late teens and early twenties. The most recent (and comprehensive) survey of Irish sexual behaviour (Layte et al., 2006) found that the median age is 18 for men and 19 for women.

Kilkelly (2006) concludes that 'the intention of the Minister for Justice to legislate for an age of criminal responsibility of 10 is contrary both to the prevailing approach in other jurisdictions and to Ireland's international obligations. It is also contrary to the ethos of the Children's Act 2001 itself' (p. 55).

This aspect of Ireland's juvenile justice system has long been a source of considerable controversy and numerous children's rights organisations have argued for the age of criminal responsibility to be raised so as to bring Irish law into line with European norms.

GARDA DIVERSION PROGRAMME AND FAMILY CONFERENCES

The Children Act 2001 puts the Garda Diversion Programme on a statutory footing (discussed in greater detail later in this chapter). The purpose of the Programme is to deal with relatively minor offences without exposing the young person to the criminal justice system and to 'divert' him or her from further offending, which may lead to a criminal lifestyle. If a young person accepts responsibility for a crime and agrees to be cautioned, he or she can be admitted to the Programme. Should the child be prosecuted, this is done through the District Court, sitting as the Children Court (Kilkelly, 2006).

Recognising the role of families in supporting young people in conflict with the law (and the frequent need for family support amongst young offenders), the Children Act 2001 allows for a number of different family conferences:

- Family welfare conferences run by the Health Services Executive (health board)
- Family conferences run by the gardaí under the Diversion Programme
- Family conferences ordered by the Children Court and run by the Probation and Welfare Service (Kilkelly, 2006).

The Garda Conferences have been evaluated by the Garda Research Unit (O'Dwyer, 2006). He examined 147 restorative events: 134 restorative cautions and 13 garda conferences. Overall, participants reported high levels of satisfaction with the process – 93 to 94 per cent were satisfied or very satisfied.

In most cases (73 per cent) victims, or their representatives, were in attendance, but in 23 per cent of cases they declined the invitation to attend and their views were represented by the gardaí. O'Dwyer (2006) describes restorative justice as 'resource-intensive' and the cases evaluated took an average of 11.8 hours each to process (with a range of one to 51 hours).

O'Dwyer (2006) sees a key strength of the restorative process as its 'humanising effect', that is:

the offender sees the victim as a real person, perhaps not unlike himself or herself, affected by the incident in ways that are sometimes unpredictable. One child, for example, was struck and upset by the fact that the victim of his burglary was pregnant.

Overall, O'Dwyer concludes that the number of restorative events needs to be increased significantly to have an impact and 'at the moment, restorative justice remains a marginal activity in the Irish juvenile justice system. Garda restorative events currently represent a tiny percentage of potential cases processed under the Juvenile Diversion Programme.'

Garda figures show a recent increase in the numbers of restorative cautions and conferences, from 118 in 2003, to 177 in 2004, to 262 in 2005 (Garda Síochána Annual Report, 2003, 2004, 2005). These are significant increases, but from a very low base, especially when we consider that approximately 17,500 young people are referred to the Garda Juvenile Diversion Programme each year (as we shall examine in greater detail later).

Delays in the Commencement of the Children Act 2001

Despite widespread praise for the community-based and welfare-oriented provisions in the Children Act, there has been considerable delay in commencing (as the process is referred to in law) many of them; for example, Sections 115–132 and 137–141, which deal with community sanctions such as supervision orders and family support orders, and Section 77, which allows the court to refer a child to a Health Board to convene a family welfare conference (Anderson and Graham, 2006). Numerous agencies have called for the necessary resources to be put in place for the additional child care, social work and probation service resources required for the full implementation of the Act.

Table 9.1 Commencement of the Children Act 2001

1 May 2002	Part 4	Garda Diversion Programme
	Part 6	Treatment of Children in garda custody
	Part 7	Children Court
	Part 9	Community sanctions (partially)
6 Nov 2003	Part 11	Special Residential Services Board
24 July 2004	Part 8	Probation-led family conferencing
30 Sept 2004	Part 2	Family welfare conferences
	Part 3	Special care orders

Source: Adapted from Kilkelly (2006, pp. 41–2).

The following is a selection of Parts that still have not been commenced (as of November 2006):

Part 2   Convening of Family Welfare Conferences (HSE)
Part 6   Parental supervision orders, community sanctions
Part 7   Operation and inspection of Children Detention Schools
Part 10   Children detention schools
Part 12   Protection of children (dealing with, amongst other things, cruelty to children, begging, allowing a child to be in a brothel and causing or encouraging sexual offence upon a child).

A summary of progress on the commencement of the Children Act 2001 can be found on the website of the National Children's Office (www.nco.ie/work_of_the_national_childrens_office/children_act_2001/).

Why has there been a delay in fully implementing such a widely welcomed Act? There are probably two main reasons. Firstly, many of the community-based provisions require additional resources in terms of extra social workers, probation officers and social care staff. Secondly, juvenile offenders have few 'champions' – they are unlikely to win any politician many votes and are widely disliked (to put it mildly) by the public at large.

Kilkelly describes the implementation of the Children Act 2001 as 'piecemeal', 'regrettable' and a cause for 'serious concern'. She suggests:

> it will take some time – at least a decade – before its [Children Act 2001] full impact is felt both by those working with and for young people in this area and, of course, the young people themselves. Moreover, the decision to introduce a wide range of amendments to the legislation in 2006, before it is all fully operational, confirms suspicions as to the level of political commitment to the area. There is also a general criticism to be made here about the extent to which this inaction on the part of the Executive represents an ignoring of the will of the Oireachtas, which so enthusiastically supported the legislation when it was going through the Dáil and the Seanad (Kilkelly, 2006, pp. 43–4).

Characteristics of Young Offenders

The characteristics of young offenders in Ireland have been described in numerous studies. Overwhelmingly, they are the children of the poor; they are early school leavers; they have experienced broken homes and many have lived in residential child care. Barnes and O'Gorman (1995) describe 100 admissions to St Michael's Assessment Centre, Finglas (now known as Finglas Child and Adolescent Centre) between 1989 and 1991. Young people are sent here on conviction for assessment (psychological, psychiatric, social and physical) and the assessment report aids the judges of the Juvenile Court (now called Children Court) in sentencing. Barnes and

O'Gorman studied 100 boys younger than 16, all from the Dublin area. They found that only 54 per cent of the sample lived with both natural parents. Only 24 per cent of the heads of household were in full-time or part-time employment. Alcohol abuse was described as a major problem in 31 of the families studied.

Perhaps most shocking, the psychiatrist who examined the boys' family backgrounds 'considered that only three families could offer a caring and stable environment for their sons' (Barnes and O'Gorman, 1995, p. 54). In general, these boys had IQ scores significantly below the norm – 94 per cent had IQ scores below the mean (100) and 21 were classified as 'mentally handicapped' (with an IQ below 70, today termed 'intellectually disabled'). In terms of personality, the sample in general were described as 'immature emotionally, peer-dependent for self-esteem, lacking in initiative with few goals in life, unreliable, and impulsive with low frustration tolerance' (p. 55).

A study by the Centre for Social and Educational Research, DIT (2001) described the participants of Garda Special Projects. The study examined 130 participants with a view to developing a profile of the risk factors that expose young people to offending behaviour. The researchers looked at community, family and personal factors. They found that the participants typically came from areas characterised by high youth populations, a general lack of youth facilities and high levels of anti-social behaviour and intimidation. Furthermore, 'unemployment rates, rates of dependency on social welfare, levels of early school leaving, numbers of one- parent families and households with more than four children were above the national average' (p. 7).

The characteristics of female offenders have been described by Mark Smyth (2006), who studied the backgrounds of 59 girls at Oberstown Girls' School. They were mostly admitted for offences such as assault, criminal damage, larceny and breach of the peace. One-third were already in the care of the State prior to their admission to Oberstown. Like their male counterparts, a significant number (31 per cent) had IQ scores in the mild intellectual disability range or lower. Perhaps not surprisingly, given how many of them had been previously taken into care, 36 per cent of them were victims of physical or sexual abuse.

Nature and Incidence of Juvenile Crime

The numbers of young people who come to the attention of the gardaí and the justice system are small relative to the numbers of young people in the general population. For instance, the total number of young people cautioned in 2005 was highest in Dublin (at 16.43 per 1,000 of the population) and lowest in the Northern region (9.56 per 1,000); that is, between 1 and 1.6 per cent of the relevant population (Garda Síochána, 2005).

Elsewhere in this book we consider how young people are portrayed in the media but, as an aside here, we can note that no newspaper is likely to run with a headline such as '99 per cent of young people do not come to the notice of the Garda Síochána'!

Figure 9.1 shows that the number of young people referred to the National Juvenile Office (NJO) of the Garda Síochána has remained fairly constant in recent years.

Figure 9.1 Total and individual referrals to Garda National Juvenile Office, 2002–2005

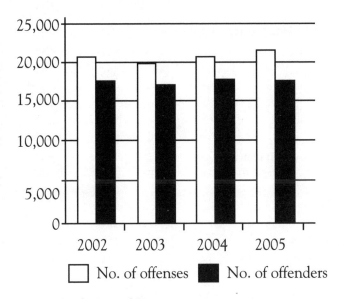

Source: Garda Annual Reports.

As we can see, the NJO received 20,585 referrals (relating to 17,634 individual children) in 2004 and 21,497 referrals (relating to 17,567 individuals) in 2005. Similar levels are reported for 2002 and 2003. For the most part, juveniles are involved in relatively minor offences, with few instances of serious, or 'headline', crimes. The 2005 Garda Annual Report details the 21,497 offences involving juveniles.

Table 9.2 Juvenile offences in 2005

Offence	No.	%
Alcohol related offences	4,217	19.62
Theft	3,922	18.24
Criminal damage	2,099	9.76
Public order	1,861	8.66
Other traffic offences	1,652	7.68
Drugs (possession)	1,356	6.31
Trespass/found on enclosed premises	1,126	5.24
Assault (non-headline)	1,125	5.23
Vehicle offences (unauthorised taking, carriage, interference)	951	4.42
Burglary	832	3.87
Serious assault	325	1.51
Miscellaneous	299	1.39
Possession of offensive weapons, etc.	291	1.35
Handling stolen property	286	1.33
Robbery (incl. demanding money with menaces)	191	0.89
Drugs (sale/supply)	177	0.82
Fraud-related offences	143	0.67
Begging	122	0.57
Firearms-related offences	112	0.52
Sexual offences	109	0.51
Arson	90	0.42
Public mischief (incl. hoax telephone calls)	63	0.29
Casual trading offences	55	0.26
Possession of articles with intent	38	0.18
Railway acts (trespass line, stone throwing, non-payment of fare)	23	0.11
Aggravated burglary	14	0.07
Assault garda/peace officer	7	0.03
False imprisonment	4	0.02
Offences against animals	4	0.02
Street and house-to-house collections	3	0.01
Total	21,497	100

Source: Adapted from An Garda Síochána Annual Report 2005.

Serious crimes such as murder, rape, sexual assault and assault causing serious bodily harm were committed by juveniles in 2005 (the categories detailed in Table 9.2 are broken down to reveal this in the 2005 Garda Annual Report). However, the vast majority of offences are connected with theft, alcohol offences and traffic or motor offences. The breakdown of the above figures detailed in the 2005 An Garda Síochána Annual Report show that 4,164 offences (19.4 per cent of the total) were 'intoxication in a public place' or 'purchase/possession/consumption of alcohol'.

McCullagh (2006) describes the difficulties in determining just how many young people are involved in criminal behaviour. He notes that while all juvenile offending (committed by persons younger than 18 years) is reported to the National Juvenile Office of An Garda Síochána, their reports do not distinguish between headline and non-headline offences. Official crime figures issued annually by the gardaí do distinguish between headline and non-headline offences, but they do not break age categories down into 'younger than 18' or 'older than 18'; instead they use the categories of 'under 14 years', '14–16 years', '17–20 years' and '21 years and over'. He concludes that this makes it 'impossible to be definitive about the level and seriousness of the criminal behaviour of those aged less than 18 years (2006, p. 162).

Walsh (2005), too, highlights the difficulties in deciphering the incidence of juvenile crime. In his foreword, Walsh describes Ireland's criminal justice statistics as 'a bit of a mess' (p. ix). An example of this is that the Garda Commissioner's Annual Reports do not present data on the annual total of cases in which juveniles were convicted. Also, there is no data on the arrest and detention of juveniles (Walsh, 2005, p. ix).

The Garda Commissioner's Annual Report does not use age 18 as a breakpoint, so for the purposes of identifying trends in juvenile offending, Walsh (2005) examines indictable offences for under 21-year-olds. The figures show a significant downward trend from the mid-1980s. From a high of 5,636 in 1983, they drop slowly through the 1990s, to a low of 999 in 1999. In 2002, the last year for which figures were available for Walsh's study, 1,856 indictable offences were recorded for 'under 21s'. Walsh (2005) attributes the decline from 1991 to the extension of the juvenile diversion programme to the whole country in that year. This inconsistency in reported age bands could be fairly simply rectified by more detailed age bands being reported in annual crime statistics.

What is not so easily overcome is the disparity that exists in all jurisdictions between official crime figures and the reality of what happens 'on the ground'. For a whole host of reasons, not all crimes are brought to the attention of the police, and this unquantified (real) level of crime is known as the 'dark figure'. Victim surveys and self-report delinquency surveys attempt to access this dark figure. At the time of writing, an International Self-Report Delinquency Study is underway in 25 countries, including Ireland, where the research is being undertaken by the Department of Social Sciences and Centre for Social and Educational Research at Dublin Institute of Technology (DIT), the Institute of Criminology at University College Dublin and the Institute for Criminology and Criminal Justice at Queen's

University, Belfast. The results will provide an important alternative source of information about juvenile offending in Ireland, including age of onset, frequency and seriousness of offending as well as data on cross-national variation (www.cser.ie).

In 2001 the National Crime Council published a review of crime figures in Ireland from 1950 to 1998. Again, the fractured nature of the statistics available is noted. For instance, specific figures for juvenile offences were only kept between 1950–1957 and 1991–1998. Nevertheless, the findings indicate that juvenile recorded crime peaked in 1961 with 3,333 offences being recorded. There was a fall in the mid-1970s, from 3,108 in 1975 to 1,650 the following year. Then, since 1992

> there has been a decline in recorded crimes in all offence categories for juveniles except damage to property ... The mid-1990s registered an increase in the number of juveniles being referred to and accepted into the Juvenile Liaison Officer Scheme ... It is possible that the irregular yearly figures for juveniles reflect recording practices and/or prosecution decisions rather than 'real' increases or decreases in the number of offences being committed by juveniles. Further investigation and research would be required to fully appreciate the irregular pattern of juvenile recorded crime (National Crime Council, 2001, p. 72).

GARDA JUVENILE DIVERSION PROGRAMME AND GARDA YOUTH DIVERSION PROJECTS

The Garda Juvenile Diversion Programme was established in 1963 to try to divert offending juveniles away from court and criminal activity by means of cautions and restorative conferences. Since then, 178,485 children (aged seven to 17 years, inclusive) have engaged with the Programme (Garda Síochána, 2005). The Children Act 2001 places the Garda Juvenile Diversion Programme on a statutory footing.

The Garda Juvenile Diversion Programme is administered by the Director of the Garda National Juvenile Office in Harcourt Square, Dublin – the Programmes are implemented nationwide by Gardaí known as Juvenile Liaison Officers, usually selected for their experience of, or interest in, working with young people. Young people are referred to the Garda Juvenile Diversion Programme for the types of offences detailed in Table 9.2. For instance, the primary reasons in 2004 were alcohol related (20 per cent), theft (18 per cent), criminal damage (10 per cent), public order offences (8 per cent) and traffic offences (7 per cent). A similar pattern has existed for the last five years (Garda Síochána, 2004). The philosophy is to 'divert' the young person away from criminality and the formal justice system by offering guidance and support to them and their families, administered by the Garda Juvenile Liaison Officer.

Once a juvenile offender is referred to the Juvenile Diversion Programme, what happens to him or her? The process is explained each year in the Garda Annual Report:

Every child who is admitted to the Garda Juvenile Programme is given a caution. The caution can be either formal or informal. An informal caution is used where the act committed by the child is of a less serious nature than one requiring a formal caution. The caution is administered by the local JLO and it is normally given at the offender's home and in the presence of parents or guardians. Where the offence is of a more serious nature, a formal caution is administered and the child is placed under Garda supervision for a period of 12 months. This caution may be given by the local Superintendent or a JLO trained in mediation (An Garda Síochána Annual Report, 2004, p. 53).

Once cautioned, the JLO monitors and supervises the child, usually for one year. The level of supervision is variable from one young person to another, depending on the seriousness of their offence and the level of family support and control. In certain circumstances the Director of the Garda National Juvenile Office can direct that the victim be invited to attend the formal caution as outlined under the restorative justice provisions set out in Sections 26 and 29 of the Children Act 2001. Section 26 provides for a restorative caution. Section 29 provides for a restorative conference. In both cases the Act allows for the victim of the offence to be invited to attend at the formal caution of the offending child. The victim, or in some cases the victim's representative, is given an opportunity to outline to the offending child the effect that the behaviour had on his or her life. The offending child is given the opportunity to take responsibility for his or her actions and is then encouraged to agree to take some action that might assist in restoring matters to where they were prior to the offence. This may be in the form of an apology, some type of community work or payment of compensation. An action plan is then agreed with the child with a view to preventing any further offending (Garda Síochána Annual Report 2004, p. 54).

The Garda Youth Diversion Programme provisions for restorative conferences (described earlier in this chapter) are an example of *restorative justice*, whereby efforts are made to confront offenders with the impact of their crimes on victims and to give victims a sense of 'right' or 'justice' being 'restored' to them, of damage being repaired. Restorative justice emerged from 'the apparent failure of the traditional adversarial justice system to impact on offending, and the dissatisfaction of victims with their experience and treatment in the process' (McCullagh, 2006, p. 165).

For more serious offences, a young person may be deemed 'unsuitable' for the Diversion Programme and the case is referred to the Director of Public Prosecutions, or to the local Superintendent, to be considered for a prosecution. In 2005, 3,998 young people out of the 17,567 individuals referred to the Diversion Programme were deemed 'unsuitable' (Garda Síochána Annual Report 2005). McCullagh cautions that a two-tier system of juvenile justice is emerging. Offenders who are easy to work with, involved in less serious offences and less likely to re-offend are diverted to various community-based programmes. More serious offenders, typically with more disturbed, chaotic backgrounds, are more likely to receive custodial sentences.

McCullagh suggests (2006) that the proliferation of community-based projects may be offering services to young people who do not really need them: 'our attention and resources may be directed at what are termed "soft" offenders: those whose initial offences are relatively minor and whose prospects of re-offending are slight.'

Garda Youth Diversion Projects

In addition to the Garda Juvenile Diversion Programme, there are now over 70 Garda Youth Diversion Projects (formerly known as Garda Special Projects) nationwide.

These projects, primarily staffed by professional youth workers or community workers, have a specific crime-prevention focus and their main goal is 'to divert young people from becoming involved (or further involved) in anti-social and/or criminal behaviour by providing suitable activities to facilitate personal development and promote civic responsibility' (CSER, 2003, p. 7).

The first two were established in 1991 in Ronanstown, West Dublin, following clashes between young people and the gardaí (Kilkelly, 2006, p. 91) and they are now to be found nationwide. The purpose of youth crime prevention work is detailed in a 2003 publication, *Garda Youth Diversion Project Guidelines*:

> To engage young people who have offended in a process of learning and development that will enable them to examine their own offending and to make positive lifestyle choices that will protect them from involvement in criminal, harmful or socially unacceptable behaviours. To implement this, the work involves linking young people with non-offending peer groups and the forming of stable and trusting relationships with adults in the community. The intended impact of this process is that those who are engaged in this process develop into responsible and valued citizens and the intended outcome is that young people engaged do not offend and do not progress into the criminal justice system (Centre for Social and Educational Research, 2003, pp. 4–5).

One of the risks is that Garda Youth Diversion Projects will become little more than neighbourhood youth clubs. The Guidelines for Garda Youth Diversion Projects (Centre for Social and Educational Research, 2003) specify that the primary target group is young people who have entered the Garda Juvenile Diversion Programme and are considered at risk of remaining within the justice system. A secondary target group are young people who 'have come to the attention of the Gardaí, the community or local agencies as a result of their behaviour and are considered at risk of entering the justice system at a future date' (Centre for Social and Educational Research, 2003, p. 34).

The Guidelines for the operation of Garda Youth Diversion Projects identify the following criteria for admission:

- Poor school attendance or early school leaving
- Offending behaviour or offending peer group
- Known to the JLO or local gardaí
- Alcohol or drug use
- Family involvement in crime
- Difficult relationship with parents or authority figures.

(Centre for Social and Educational Research, 2003).

THE SPECIAL RESIDENTIAL SERVICES BOARD AND THE IRISH YOUTH JUSTICE SERVICE

The Special Residential Services Board was established by the Children Act 2001 and its function is to advise the Minister for Health and Children on policies and procedures relating to the detention of children. It was designed to bring cohesion to a system which, as we have seen, was previously the responsibility of three different government departments, with little co-ordination between them. In addition to research and policy work, an important day-to-day function is to allocate accommodation for children subject to detention orders or special care orders. All requests for residential accommodation in the five Children Detention Schools are co-ordinated by Court Officers of the SRSB (the Criminal Justice Act 2006 removes this function to the Department of Justice, Equality and Law Reform).

The main activities of the Special Residential Services Board are detailed on its website (www.srsb.ie). These include:

- Operating a monthly information system to monitor bed utilisation in all units
- Commissioning research on topics central to the detention of young people (for example, admission criteria, the impact of placements on young people and their families)
- Review of education and care programmes in children detention schools.

In July 2005, the Department of Justice, Equality and Law Reform published *Report on the Youth Justice Review*. The review team was charged with making recommendations to improve youth justice services. A primary recommendation was the establishment of a Youth Justice Service. This Service would be charged with co-ordinating the various services across the care and justice spectrum, including:

- Youth justice policy development and crime prevention
- Responsibility for detention of offending children under 18 years of age
- Implementation of the provisions of the Children Act 2001 relating to community sanctions, restorative justice conferencing and diversion projects.

(Department of Justice, Equality and Law Reform, 2005, pp. 6–7).

Accordingly, the creation of a new Irish Youth Justice Service (IYJS) was announced in December 2005. For the first time, it will bring all youth justice services together under a single body. This service will be responsible for the detention of all persons under 18 years of age. It will provide a unified approach to all youth justice policies and practices. Specifically, it is tasked with:

> Development of a specific youth justice policy from a single unified perspective; responsibility for services for young offenders including detention, community sanctions, restorative justice conferencing and diversion projects (Department of Justice, Equality and Law Reform, 2005, p. 42).

One immediate implication of the transferring of responsibility for all children under 18 in detention to the IYJS will be the cessation of incarcerating 16- and 17-year-olds in St Patrick's Institution. Instead, all offending children under 18 years of age will be detained in an education-focused detention school. This will bring Ireland closer to international norms, whereby the focus for children in detention shall be education and rehabilitation, as opposed to punishment. However, as we write, 16- and 17-year-old boys are detained in the wholly inadequate St Patrick's Institution and there is not, as yet, a concrete timetable for the transfer of such boys to Children Detention Schools. Current indicators are that this will be commenced in 2010, which is a long way off.

The IYJS's first national director was appointed in April 2006 (Michelle Shannon) and the Service becomes operational in 2007. The budget estimates in November 2006 earmarked €16 million for its operation. At the time of writing, it is too early to evaluate the working of this new structure in the Irish juvenile justice scene.

THE CHILDREN COURT

All offenders under 18 years who are to be prosecuted initially come before the Children Court (previously known as the Juvenile Court), which operate in Dublin, Cork, Limerick and Waterford. The most comprehensive description of the working of the Children Court to date is to be found in a report by Kilkelly (2005). This report details the findings of observations of 944 cases in the Courts in Dublin, Cork, Limerick and Waterford in 2003 and 2004. These research findings are particularly valuable as the proceedings in the Children Court are heard *in camera* (privately, not in public).

Of the 944 cases in Kilkelly's study, 93 per cent of the defendants were male and only 7 per cent were female. All except five were 12 years of age or older. Indeed, the majority (67 per cent) were aged 16 to 17 years. In spite of a requirement in the Children Act 2001 that children in court be accompanied by a parent or guardian, Kilkelly (2005) found that parents were absent in 30 per cent of cases, the most common reason given being ill-health or other family or work commitments. Mostly, mothers (often with a female relative) accompanied the child. Indeed, in 67 per cent of cases there was no father in attendance.

The most common offences recorded were road traffic offences (theft, dangerous driving, drink driving), public order offences (drunken behaviour, urinating in public) and theft (shoplifting, theft of alcohol, DVDs or CDs, mobile phones). As Kilkelly notes:

> alcohol is a significantly influential factor in the lives and offending of young people who face charges in the Children Court. Drunkenness and alcohol misuse appeared to be common occurrences. For example, the public order offences were observed to be almost exclusively alcohol related as were the charges of assault; many of the charges of theft also involved alcohol as the principal item being stolen (p. 23).

Of the 944 cases studied, 151 involved final disposal of charges or the determination of a sentence. These included:

Probation bond	33%
Custody	23%
Probation Act	17%
Fine	13%
Suspended sentence	6%
Community Service order	6%

A probation bond requires monthly supervisory meetings with a Probation Officer. There is a difference between a probation bond and the 'application of the Probation Act' – the latter results in no recorded conviction. It is in effect a rap on the knuckles, with some conditions attached.

While the researchers did observe some young people acting in a cocky, unconcerned manner, Kilkelly says that far more representative is 'the young person who appeared concerned and genuinely vulnerable, frightened and uncertain about the circumstances and what was about to happen' (p. 30).

Kilkelly's (2005) primary focus was to research whether the Children Court conformed to children's rights standards such as the UN Convention on the Rights of the Child. She concluded that a range of practices were extant but that, in general, the young people in the Children Court participated only in a marginal way, and were quite isolated from proceedings. They were rarely addressed unless under examination. They often struggled to hear and follow proceedings and, according to Kilkelly, in numerous cases 'proceedings were concluded without the young person and his or her guardian realising that the case was over. Young people frequently left the courtroom shaking their heads, confused as to what had just happened; in many cases, their only prompt that the case was over was that the next case had been called and another defendant entered the court' (2005, p. 30).

In what seems to be an extraordinary situation, she noted that the judge had no communication whatsoever in 55 per cent of cases: 'the judge neither greeted the young person on his or her arrival in court, made eye contact or any form of non-verbal communication with him or her at any stage of the process, nor informed him or her of the outcome and that he or she was free to leave' (p. 63). However, Kilkelly also records that 'some' judges showed courtesy to young people and that one particular judge:

> welcomed every young person and his or her guardian to his or her court by name, involved them directly in the proceedings throughout the process and explained the outcome – including any bail conditions or conditions attaching to the probation bond – in age appropriate language. At the conclusion of the proceedings, he or she always took a few moments to make sure the young person understood the process and what was to happen next, before wishing them well and/or warning them as to the consequences of future offending or non-compliance with bail conditions (p. 66).

Obviously, it is a matter of some concern that this level of effective communication with children was confined to a single judge. Clearly, more attention needs to be given by judges to ensuring that the proceedings in the Children Court are explained to defendants and their parents, so that the hearing is meaningful. Particularly for young people, exposure to the justice system should be primarily about prevention and rehabilitation. This can only occur if defendants (many of low IQ and low educational attainment) can understand the process.

Kilkelly suggests that the Children Court judge must not only determine a criminal charge, but must also act as 'counsellor, manager and administrator of youth justice' making his or her role the most influential, but also the most challenging, in the youth justice system. She notes that Children Court judges appear to receive no training for the role and recommends that such judges be required to 'undertake training on the principles of youth justice, and related fields of psychology, sociology and criminology before taking up such an appointment. Training on effective models of communicating with young people should also be included' (p. 50).

Further insight to the workings of the Children Court is provided by McPhillips (2005). Fifty young people appearing before the Dublin Children Court in 2004 were studied. The sample had a total of 551 charges against them, illustrating how one incident may lead to a range of charges against a young person. The most common charges were for theft and robbery (27 per cent), public order offences (23 per cent), traffic offences (18 per cent) and criminal damage (10 per cent).

Thirty-six of the sample group were convicted and half of these (18) were sentenced to detention – 50 per cent (nine) to St Patrick's Institution as they were over 16 years of age and 50 per cent (nine) to schools of detention because they were under 16 years of age. The latter sentences were primarily (in seven out of the nine cases) for a period of two years, which strikes us a very protracted period for a young adolescent.

The backgrounds of the sample were characterised by a range of difficulties, with problems including:

> absence of at least one parent for significant periods of the young person's childhood (26 out of the 38 for whom family background information was available); breakdown of relationship between parents (14); young person living without either parent (12); criminal record of family members (14); housing problems (11); large family size (17); parents with serious substance misuse problems (8); and in a small number of cases, self-harm (7), physical (2) or sexual abuse (2) indicators. Many young people (18) were strongly influenced by an anti-social peer group (McPhillips, 2005, p. 8).

To summarise, young people appearing before the Children Court are coming from fractured and disadvantaged backgrounds. They have low IQ and educational attainment, are not very engaged in the proceedings against them and can be sentenced to considerable periods of time in detention.

Placing Children in Custody

The placing of children in custody is perhaps the most controversial area of the juvenile justice system. Although the UN Convention on the Rights of the Child and the Children Act 2001 require that children and young people be detained only as a measure of last resort, Irish judges show a worrying predilection for incarcerating young people, often for considerably long sentences. About one-quarter of the Irish prison population is under 21 years of age, compared to proportions as low as 5 per cent in other European countries (O'Mahony, 2000 cited in Anderson and Graham, 2006). Also, the conditions in which young people over 16 are detained (in St Patrick's Institution) are appalling by any standards.

Upon receiving a custodial sentence, youths may be sent to one of six institutions. They may be sent to the State's only Children Detention Centre (St Patrick's Institution, in the Mountjoy Prison complex), or to one of five children detention schools:

- St Joseph's, Clonmel (formerly an Industrial School)
- Finglas Child and Adolescent Centre (formerly an Industrial School)
- Oberstown Boys' School (formerly a Reformatory School)
- Oberstown Girls' School (formerly a Reformatory School)
- Trinity House School (formerly a Reformatory School).

Of the five children detention schools, only Trinity House School offers high security and complete control of movement.

We shall examine the conditions in each of these six institutions below.

Children Detention Centre

St Patrick's Institution is a large Victorian-style prison for the detention of young people aged 16 to 21. Located on the site of Mountjoy Prison, North Circular Road, Dublin, it is a large facility, with accommodation for 220 people. Children aged 16 to 17 are detained with offenders aged between 18 and 21 with 'greater emphasis placed on rehabilitation and education ... than in adult prisons' (Department of Justice, Equality and Law Reform, 2005). However, despite this stated emphasis, the detention of juveniles with adults is a clear breach of the UN Convention on the Rights of the Child (Article 37) and other international law.

The conditions in which young people are detained in St Patrick's Institution have been severely criticised for many years. Fr Peter McVerry, a long-standing campaigner for young homeless people in Dublin, wrote in October 2006 that 'St Patrick's Institution is a disaster, an obscenity and it reveals the moral bankruptcy of the policies of the Minister for Justice' (2006, p. 3). He notes that in the impoverished 1980s, St Patrick's had 10 workshops, but that it had none from 2003 until September 2006 (when four were reopened) and that, as a consequence, inmates spend 19 hours each day alone in their cells. He adds:

> St. Patrick's Institution is nothing but a 'warehouse' for young people, many of whom were broken by their childhood experiences. In this harsh and punitive system, they are further broken down. Detention in St. Patrick's is a demoralising, destructive and dehumanising experience, with no redeeming features; it is characterised by idleness and boredom for young people who are full of energy, at a critical time in their development. One young person summed the experience of being in St. Patrick's very succinctly when he told me: 'This place brings out the worst in you' (McVerry, 2006, p. 4).

In his introduction to the *Fourth annual Report of the Inspector of Prisons and Places of Detention for the Year 2004–2005* (Department of Justice, Equality and Law Reform, 2006a), Dermot Kinlen described St Patrick's as a 'training ground for criminality'. He was particularly critical of the fact that young men aged 17 to 21 were effectively locked up for 17 to 18 hours each day. In the remaining time they 'have access to dreary yards, inadequate schooling and no workshops at all' (p. 5). He concludes, 'the present situation is a continuing disaster'.

Approximately one-third of the inmates in St Patrick's are under 18 years, legally children. However, the State does not treat *these* children in the same way it treats other children in the care of the State; the staff minding them are prison officers, not social care workers. These children do not have care plans or designated social workers. Their place of detention is not subject to inspection by the Social Services Inspectorate, as most other child residential facilities are, and the Ombudsman for Children has no jurisdiction in St Patrick's Institution. In short, it appears the State is making little effort to care for or rehabilitate these children, unlike their counterparts in secure residential units (many of whom have similar family backgrounds and offence profiles). Thus, it seems a rather arbitrary 'abandonment' by the State of a particular group of children, totally at odds with normal residential care standards and our commitments to international standards such as the UN Convention on the Rights of the Child.

Given the philosophy of prevention and early intervention enshrined in the National Children's Strategy and the Children Act 2001, it is easy to understand the frustration and palpable anger of expert commentators such as Peter McVerry and Dermot Kinlen on the conditions experienced by people under age 18 in St Patrick's Institution.

The Minister for Justice, Equality and Law Reform, Michael McDowell, told the Dáil in October 2006 that St Patrick's was unsuitable and that the government plans to rebuild a replacement (currently planned for Thornton Hall, the new 'super prison' in north Co. Dublin). It is planned to cease the detention of 16- to 17-year-olds in St Patrick's Institution, so that all children are detained only in an education-focused secure care environment, as opposed to a prison environment. This will occur when Part 9 of the Children Act 2001 is fully commenced.

Children Detention Schools (Formerly Industrial and Reformatory Schools)

Juvenile offenders may also be placed in one of five Residential Schools for Young Offenders, managed by the Department of Education and Science (following reforms in the Criminal Justice Act 2006 from early 2007 responsibility for all Children Detention Centres will be transferred to the Department of Justice, Equality and Law Reform):

- St Joseph's, Clonmel
- Finglas Child and Adolescent Centre
- Oberstown Boys' School
- Oberstown Girls' School
- Trinity House School.

Oberstown Boys' School, Oberstown Girls' School and Trinity House School share a large site in a rural setting in Lusk, north Co. Dublin. The National Assessment and Remand Unit is located at Finglas Child and Adolescent Centre. A judge may send a young person to the unit for a three-week psychological, psychiatric, social or physical assessment to assist placement and/or sentencing.

In line with the policy that detention should only be as a matter of last resort, average yearly attendance in these five institutions has fallen from approximately 125 in 2000 to approximately 83 in 2004 (Department of Justice, Equality and Law Reform, 2005). Referrals to Trinity House School and Oberstown Boys' School are made from the courts; the other units also take referrals from the HSE (Health Service Executive).

Are the conditions in the five children detention schools any better than those found in St Patrick's Institution? Kilkelly (2006) provides a useful summary of the care and inspection reports of the children detention schools. As in any inspection, room for improvement was noted in each school, but the tone of Kilkelly's summary is one of a good quality of care and education being provided to young people. For example, she notes the mutual respect between staff and boys and positive atmosphere in St Joseph's (p. 203) and the high levels of qualifications and retention rates of staff (p. 205). Similarly, in Oberstown Girls' School, the care inspection report showed good relations between staff and young people (Department of Education and Science, 2004, cited in Kilkelly, 2006).

The review of Finglas Child and Adolescent Centre (comprising St Lawrence's School and the National Remand and Assessment Centre) was more challenging for management and staff. A report carried out in 2002 found high levels of challenging behaviour from boys and no commonly agreed approach to working with them. The inspectors also note high numbers of inexperienced and unqualified staff, and high staff turnover. Kilkelly lists a series of causes for concern raised by the Inspection team:

the lack of a comprehensive care plan for every young person ...; inconsistent quality of record-keeping and inadequate access by young people to their file; a lack of consensus among and leadership from management regarding key aspects of care including use of the safety room; sanctions and the lack of a care and children's rights culture; the lack of a separate complaints procedure for recording and processing the complaints made by young people (Department of Education and Science, 2002b cited in Kilkelly, 2006, pp. 211–12).

The conclusion was that the Centre was in 'acute crisis' and was 'unsafe for young people and staff'. A further review in 2004 by Michael Donnellan (now Director of the Probation Service) recommended that the Centre could not continue to operate in its present state and that it needed a root and branch review of its procedures and systems. In October 2005, a new Director was appointed and an inspection in February 2006 found a dramatic improvement in service provision.

The experience in Finglas shows the importance of an inspection system. It is a cause for concern, therefore, that changes made to the Children Act 2001 by the Criminal Justice Act 2006, s.152, allow for children detention schools to be inspected only annually, instead of biannually.

Kilkelly (2006) summarises the present situation of youth detention in Ireland as follows:

Two distinct regimes currently exist: Children Detention Schools for those under 16 years and St Patrick's Institution from those over that age. While it is clear that the schools are challenged by a varying population and a lack of common approach, in the main they are positive environments where qualified staff not only are committed [to] maximising the positive potential of the young person's experience in detention, but also enjoy the support and resources to implement that commitment ... St Patrick's Institution is staffed principally by prison officers, rather than care workers, and this, together with the penal nature of the institution and the relentless cost-cutting imposed by the Department of Justice, Equality and Law Reform, continues to reinforce the punitive nature of the environment and its failure to protect and promote the rights of young people detained there (Kilkelly, 2006, pp. 240–241).

THE CRIMINAL JUSTICE ACT 2006

The Criminal Justice Act was passed on 29 June 2006. It contains a number of provisions for juvenile justice. We have discussed earlier in this chapter the implication for the age of responsibility. Specifically, the Criminal Justice Act 2006 sets the age of criminal responsibility at 10 years for certain serious crimes, as opposed to 12 years, as envisioned in the Children Act 2001.

Equally controversial is the introduction of Good Behaviour Contracts and Anti-Social Behaviour Orders (ASBOs), modelled on the UK. The Act extends the operation of the Garda Diversion Programme to include behaviour which is not necessarily criminal, but is anti-social, 'behaviour which has caused or was likely to cause to one or more persons harassment; significant or persistent alarm, distress, fear or intimidation, or significant or persistent impairment of their use or enjoyment of their property' (Kilkelly, 2006, p. 96). These orders shall apply to young people between 12 and 18 years. Where a garda brings a child's anti-social behaviour to the attention of a superintendent, he or she may convene a meeting with the child, his or her parents, the reporting garda and the JLO if the child is in the Garda Diversion Programme (Kilkelly, 2006). If the child acknowledges his or her anti-social behaviour and undertakes to change it, a Good Behaviour Contract is drawn up. If the anti-social behaviour continues, the superintendent may reconvene the meeting and apply for an ASBO to the Children Court, which may last for up to two years. Breach of an ASBO is a criminal offence.

This development has not been welcomed by children's rights groups. A large coalition of NGOs campaigned, ultimately unsuccessfully, against the introduction of ASBOs. The Coalition against Anti-Social Behaviour Orders consisted of over 50 NGOs, academics and legal practitioners, including the Irish Penal Reform Trust, the Children's Rights Alliance, the National Youth Council of Ireland and the ISPCC (Hamilton and Seymour, 2006). Opponents of ASBOs argued that these provisions have the potential to criminalise a young person for behaviour that is not, in fact, criminal, for example, loud and boisterous 'horse play' in a housing estate. On the other hand, proponents of these new provisions argue that a misbehaving adolescent is given two opportunities (GBC and ASBO) to mend his or her ways before coming into contact with the criminal justice system. The present schedule is that the legislation governing ASBOs will commence in March 2007.

CONCLUSION

We are in a period of considerable change in the area of youth justice in Ireland. The Children Act 2001 contains many innovative, community-based responses to 'troubled and troublesome' young people. This Act is being commenced very slowly. Indeed, some sections had not even been commenced before they were modified and inserted to the Criminal Justice Act 2006. Promising developments have occurred, such as the creation of the Irish Youth Justice Service, which has the potential, for the first time, to have a smooth and integrated system, managed and co-ordinated by one body with consistent systems, policies and procedures. At the same time, retrograde steps have been taken such as only increasing the age of criminal responsibility to 10 years for some serious crimes, instead of the 12 years provided for in the Children Act 2001. Also, in spite of a commitment to end the inhumane detention of some adolescent boys in St Patrick's Institution, there is no timeframe for this to occur.

The management of youth justice in Ireland was highlighted as a concern by the UN Committee on the Rights of the Child on the two occasions Ireland came before the Committee, 1998 and 2006. Let us hope that there shall be dramatic improvements in our performance next time around.

RECOMMENDED READING

There have been two significant additions to the literature on juvenile justice in Ireland recently:

Kilkelly, U. (2006). *Youth justice in Ireland: Tough lives, rough justice.* Dublin: Irish Academic Press.

Walsh, D. (2005). *Juvenile justice.* Dublin: Thomson and Roundhall.

For an accessible overview of the criminal justice system as a whole:

Cotter, A. (2005). The criminal justice system. In S. Quin, P. Kennedy, A. Matthews, & G. Kiely (Eds.), *Contemporary Irish social policy.* Dublin: UCD Press.

10

Services and Policy for Young People

INTRODUCTION

This chapter gives an overview of some of the major types of service and policy which are designed specifically with young people in mind (apart from those which are dealt with elsewhere in the book, such as education). It will pay particular attention to youth work, in relation to which there have been significant developments (including new framework legislation) in recent years, and to the National Children's Strategy. It will also look at child care services and the issue of child protection. First, it is necessary to revisit some definitional questions touched on at the start of the book.

We have already suggested that concepts like 'child', 'adolescent' and 'youth' are not essential classifications referring to fixed and unchanging stages of the life cycle or categories of social group, but rather are *cultural constructs*. That is to say that their meaning can vary from one society to another and even from one culture to another within a given society. They can also vary significantly over time: ideas about when childhood ends and when adulthood begins, and about the length and nature of the period in between, have changed a lot in Ireland even in the last 50 years or so, as a period of extended formal education at second level (and, increasingly, beyond) has come to be seen as the norm. In fact there is now considerable cultural ambivalence or uncertainty about definitions of childhood, youth and adulthood, which is reflected in services and policy for children and young people, and even in the legal definitions on which such services and policy are frequently based. As Berger and Berger (1976, p. 236, 239) have put it, 'law always reflects the society in which it has its being and … in this particular area the ambiguities of the law reflect the ambiguities of the society's conception of youth … [In modern society] it is unclear when youth begins and when it ends. And it is far from clear what it means while it is apparently going on.'

Let us take a few examples of these ambiguities. A 'child' is defined in law for most purposes as a person under the age of 18. This is the definition in the Child Care Act 1991 and also in the Children Act 2001, which deals for the most part with matters relating to young people and the law, including the age of criminal responsibility. Society's perception of the age at which a person might be deemed responsible for a crime is one important indicator of prevailing attitudes regarding the process of maturation towards adulthood. As discussed in Chapter 9, the Children Act 2001 provided that the age of criminal responsibility would be increased to 12 from the lower age of seven at which it was set in the Children Act of 1908 (and further, that there would be a 'rebuttable presumption' that a child up to the age of 14 would be incapable of committing an offence because he or she did not have the capacity to know that the act was wrong). However, this change was not implemented (or 'commenced', as the process is referred to in law) and in the amendments to the Children Act 2001 included within the Criminal Justice Act 2006, the age of criminal responsibility, while set at 12 for most offences, is increased only to 10 years for murder, manslaughter, rape and aggravated sexual assault and the 'rebuttable presumption' is abolished. The dilution of the earlier provision in the Children Act 2001 has been strongly criticised by children's and young people's organisations (for example, Children's Rights Alliance, 2006). Here the important point is that this example illustrates the ambiguity, the ambivalent and even contested nature of society's attitudes towards the transition from childhood to adulthood.

Earlier justice legislation actually differentiated between a 'child', referring to someone under 15, and a 'young person', someone who had reached 15 but not 17 years of age (Children Act 1908, s.131, as amended by the Children Act 1941, s.21). A 'young person' is currently defined differently under two separate pieces of legislation. The definition in the Protection of Young Person's (Employment) Act 1996 is 'a person who has reached 16 years of age … but is less than 18 years of age', while in the Youth Work Act 2001, discussed below, a young person means 'a person who has not attained the age of 25 years'.

These examples amply bear out the truth of Berger and Berger's remarks just quoted, and if we also take into consideration the fact that different ages of entitlement apply when it comes to being able to leave school, to vote, to have consensual sex (at the time of writing, also different for males and females), to hold a driving licence (different ages for different types of licence) and to stand for election to public office (different ages for different offices), it is clear that societal attitudes towards children and young people, and specifically towards their transition into adulthood, are far from straightforward. This is not necessarily a bad thing (although from the point of view of young people themselves it might seem confusing and frustrating). While there are undoubtedly aspects of the law and of other institutional provision for young people that are incoherent and inconsistent and in need of rationalisation or reform, it is perhaps also true that the complexity described above is a reflection of the fact that growing up in Ireland today is itself a highly complex process, much more so than in earlier times here or in more traditional societies today. There are multiple dimensions of the transition into adulthood to be provided for – in fact, as is increasingly recognised, *multiple transitions* (see Chapters 2 and 12) – so the framework of legislative provision for young people, and the policies and services flowing from that, will also necessarily be multifaceted.

The remainder of this chapter will outline some of the major types of service and policy relating to young people and summarise where relevant the legislation that applies. As already noted, some key services and policies, for example in the areas of formal education and educational welfare, employment and youth justice, are dealt with not in this chapter but in the other appropriate chapters of the book.

YOUTH WORK SERVICES

The Nature of Youth Work

Youth work, as defined by most contemporary practitioners and providers and as recently enshrined in Irish law (in the Youth Work Act 2001), is essentially a type of non-formal education. In other words, it consists of educational and developmental activities and programmes different from but complementary to the formal schooling system. It is sometimes referred to as 'out-of-school education' but that term is not always strictly accurate since youth work can actually take place in school premises. In addition to being educational it is recreational; it takes place in young people's free time and they participate of their own volition. As well as being non-formal, the learning which takes place in youth work is frequently informal; in other words, it happens spontaneously in naturally occurring settings and situations.

> Non-formal education refers to learning and development that takes place outside of the formal educational field, but which is structured and based on learning objectives. This is differentiated from informal learning, which is not structured and takes place in daily life activities within peer/family groups etc. Youth work interventions typically result in both non-formal and informal learning (Youth Service Liaison Forum, 2005, p. 13).

Historically, youth work has been developed and delivered predominantly by adult volunteers, and the emphasis on the value of volunteers and volunteering remains central to contemporary thinking and practice (see, for example, Department of Education and Science, 2003a, p. 14). It is estimated that there are some 40,000 adult volunteers in youth work in Ireland (NYCI, 2006a). However, in recent years youth work (and especially the practice of youth work in certain types of setting) has increasingly come to be seen also as a professional job for which substantial education and training is required. Youth work's primary focus is on the years of transition from childhood to adulthood rather than on younger childhood (see the section on the Youth Work Act below). Research suggests that roughly a fifth to a quarter of teenagers participate in youth work services, through membership or regular attendance at youth groups or projects, with the pattern varying somewhat by gender and age (see Cunningham 2001; de Róiste and Dinneen 2005, Chapter 5; and Chapter 8 of this book). This is apart from young people taking part in sports clubs or special interest groups (for example, GAA clubs, music or drama groups). These interests can of course also be accommodated within youth work. Youth work's methods and activities vary widely, and include recreational and sporting activities, indoor and outdoor pursuits, artistic and cultural programmes, spiritual development, health promotion, issue-based activities (for example, social justice, the environment) and intercultural and international programmes and exchanges. Youth work programmes are also often designed with the needs or circumstances of particular groups of young people in mind (for example, young people with disabilities, young Travellers, young gay men and women, young rural people).

Research suggests that participation in youth work programmes can have very beneficial outcomes for young people in terms of their own personal development, leading to enhanced confidence and self-esteem (see Canavan, 1998), the development of networks of friendship and support, discovery of aptitudes and interests that would otherwise remain latent, acquisition of new skills and knowledge, and so on (Youth Council for Northern Ireland, 1998). Youth work can also have an impact in other ways and at other levels: it enables and encourages young people and adults to work together, 'building community spirit and playing an active role in the development of their communities' as well as combating disadvantage and enhancing the democratic life of society as a whole (National Youth Council of Ireland, 2006b).

Origins and Development of Youth Work

Youth work as we now know it has its origins in the voluntary efforts of concerned adults in the late nineteenth and early twentieth centuries to take working-class young people 'off the streets' of rapidly growing urban areas and to engage them in 'character-building' pursuits. Their motivation was a mixture of genuine philanthropy and 'moral panic' about the masses among the more privileged sectors of society. In this respect and in many others, there are close parallels between youth work in Ireland and Britain (understandably, since until the early 1920s the whole island was part of the United Kingdom) and some of the earliest youth groups established in Ireland were part of British uniformed organisations such as the Boy Scouts and Girl Guides and the Boys' and Girls' Brigades. Of course, reflecting the political tensions of the time, there were also nationalist alternatives such as Na Fianna Éireann and Inghinidhe na hÉireann, established in 1909 and 1900, respectively, and, somewhat later, Catholic versions of the scouting and guiding movements emerged (1927 and 1928). In 2004, after several years of negotiation, the two separate scouting organisations formally joined together as Scouting Ireland.

The development of youth clubs in Ireland can be dated at least to 1911 when 'a well-known probation officer, Miss Gargan' founded the Dublin Boys' Club, later to become the Belvedere Newsboys' Club (Belvedere Newsboys' Club, 1948). An emphasis on the particular danger posed both to society and themselves by idle young males (there was also, separately, early youth work provision for girls), a concern with inculcating Christian values, and a difference in class background between the young people and the youth leaders or 'helpers' was common to much early youth work.

A club is what happens when a group of young men actuated by Christian charity, and more or less of middle class, and a group of boys of the slums form individual and collective friendships. A club is not a building or anything else on the material plane. It is like a bridge across the great gulf of class, environment, age, that exists between the two groups (Belvedere Newsboys' Club, 1948, p. 8).

The first significant statutory initiative in youth work came in the early 1940s and was at least partly due to pressure from the Archbishop of Dublin, Dr John Charles McQuaid, who was keen to see a response to the problem of youth unemployment. In 1942 the Department of Education wrote to the City of Dublin Vocational Education Committee (CDVEC) on behalf of the Minister for Education, requesting it to make provision for the 'very many young unemployed people of 15 to 20 years of age in the county borough [city] on whom no organised social or educational influence is brought to bear'. This situation represented a 'grave danger', and action was needed to prevent 'further deterioration of character and an increase in undisciplined conduct – all too common in recent years' (Department of Education correspondence, quoted in Devlin, 1989, p. 18). The Department requested the establishment of a youth welfare sub-committee of the CDVEC under section 21(2) of the Vocational Education Act of 1930 (the section providing for 'continuation education'). As a result, Comhairle le Leas Óige (now known as the City of Dublin Youth Service Board) came into existence, and in its early years primarily fulfilled its functions through running a number of 'brughanna' (centres for young people offering recreation and practical training) as well as financially supporting youth clubs around the city of Dublin and training youth leaders. While several other VECs have in the intervening years used their powers under the 1930 legislation to support youth work services or establish youth work committees, these have been entirely discretionary, and Dublin city has remained the only area with securely established statutory youth work provision. This situation is now changing with the implementation of the Youth Work Act 2001 and the establishment by all the VECs of Youth Work Committees (see below).

In the meantime, it has largely been the voluntary organisations which have driven the development of youth work in Ireland. The two largest national organisations are Foróige, founded in 1952 as Macra na Tuaithe, and Youth Work Ireland, until recently known as the National Youth Federation, founded in 1961. Foróige has a national network of youth clubs ('Foróige clubs') and also runs local and regional youth services in partnership with VECs. Youth Work Ireland is a federal organisation with a membership of 22 local and regional youth services (Donegal Youth Service, Waterford Regional Youth Service, Kerry Diocesan Youth Service, and so on) and also hosts at its head office the Irish Youthwork Centre (a library, resource and study centre) and other training and programming services. Macra na Feirme (founded 1944) is an organisation for young farmers and young people in rural areas. Other large regional organisations include Catholic Youth Care (founded 1944), which operates within the Dublin archdiocese and runs local youth work services in partnership with VECs and Ógra Chorcaí in Cork (founded 1966).

There are also a wide variety of organisations with special interests or concerns or working with young people with particular identities or circumstances, such as (in the former category) the National Association of Youth Drama, Feachtas, an Irish language youth organisation and ECO (environmentally focused); or (in the latter category) the youth service of Pavee Point Travellers' Centre, the Irish Wheelchair Association Youth Group for young people with disabilities and BeLonG To for LGBT (lesbian, gay, transgender and bisexual) young people.

All of these organisations, along with the uniformed ones mentioned earlier and the youth organisations of the political parties (for example, Labour Youth, Ógra Fianna Fáil, Young Fine Gael), come together under the umbrella of the National Youth Council of Ireland (NYCI). NYCI, which in 2006 had 40 full member organisations and eight affiliates, was formed in 1967 by a group of just 15 organisations that had been called together the year before by the Minister for Education, Donough O'Malley, to discuss their co-operation with each other and their relationship with his department. Two years after the establishment of NYCI, Bobby Molloy was appointed Parliamentary Secretary to the Minister for Education (a position equivalent to what is now called Minister of State), with responsibility for a new section within the Department dealing with youth and sport. In April 1970 the first youth service grants were distributed to the voluntary organisations: a total of £33,000 to 12 bodies. Since then the system has remained largely unchanged (although the section is now known as Youth Affairs and sport is dealt with by a different government department). The individual youth organisations receive annual funding from the Department of Education under two main headings: the Youth Service Grant Scheme and the Special Projects for Youth, the latter mainly to employ full-time youth work staff to work with disadvantaged young people. The Youth Affairs Section also funds a network of youth information centres and supports a number of other initiatives (for example, Gaisce, the President's Award; the national youth arts and health programmes; North-South and international youth exchanges). In 2006 the total Youth Affairs budget was approximately €47 million. The vast majority of the money disbursed by the Youth Affairs Section comes from the proceeds of the National Lottery.

While having a clear institutional, and now also legislative, link with the education system and education policy, youth work is also very much influenced by (and may in turn help to influence) policy developments and initiatives in other areas. The *National Drugs Strategy 2001–2008* (Department of Tourism, Sport and Recreation, 2001) provides a good example of this. The Strategy built on earlier Task Force Reports of 1996 and 1997 which resulted in the establishment of a Cabinet Drugs Committee chaired by An Taoiseach and the setting up of a National Drugs Strategy Team and Local Drugs Task Forces in the areas worst affected by drugs. Regional Task Forces were set up under the Strategy in each of the regional Health Board areas. Also closely related to the Strategy is the Young People's Facilities and Services Fund (YPFSF), which was first introduced in 1998 and was aimed at young people most at risk of drug use in the designated Task Force areas and other major urban areas. It was designed to support a variety of capital and non-capital projects including youth, sports and recreational facilities and has had a dramatic impact on youth work services, at least in some parts of the country. In the city of Dublin, where the bulk of the funds have been targeted, the YPFSF led to a fivefold increase in project funding and in youth project staff in the first five years of its existence. Up to 2007, expenditure under the YPFSF amounted to approximately €135 million (Dáil Debates 24/10/06).

A further area of concern, and source of funding, for youth organisations today is the interface of youth work and youth justice through the Garda Youth Diversion Projects (formerly known as Garda Special Projects) funded by the Department of Justice, Equality and Law Reform. From the original two projects in 1991, the total grew to approximately 75 by late 2006 and the Minister for Justice announced his intention to increase the number to 100 by the end of 2007. Funding for these projects in 2006 was €6.6 million (Department of Justice, Equality and Law Reform, 2006b). For youth organisations availing of such funding, a tension is likely to arise between their youth work ethos (with an emphasis on voluntary participation) and the essentially crime-prevention purpose of these projects and their frequent use of referral systems for the young people participating.

Complexity of Practice and Provision

For many decades the dominant model of youth work provision was the club or unit run entirely by voluntary effort and open, more or less, to 'all comers'. This began to change in the 1970s and 1980s. It was Comhairle le Leas Óige in Dublin which first employed a number of community-based youth workers to work directly and intensively with disadvantaged young people. As the social problems associated with disadvantaged urban areas (including drugs problems) became more severe in the early 1980s, the demand for such intervention rapidly increased, and by the end of the 1980s, when National Lottery funding was made available to the youth work sector, the number of full-time paid youth workers had increased enormously. Professional training in youth work (or 'youth and community work') had begun to develop in Britain in the late 1960s, and some of the first professional youth workers in Ireland in the 1970s had undertaken one or other of the British programmes. Professional training began to be offered at NUI Maynooth in 1981, initially in community work but subsequently in integrated programmes dealing with 'community and youth work'. Official recognition of the importance of such training for those undertaking the increasingly complex job of youth work came in 1990, when the Department of Education offered financial support for the provision of in-service professional training at Maynooth.

The increasing complexity of youth work, and indeed of young people's lives, had for many years been leading the youth organisations to call on the government to develop a more co-ordinated approach to the full range of services for young people, i.e. to develop a coherent youth policy. In September 1983, at a time of widespread concern about the threat to social order from disaffected young people in disadvantaged neighbourhoods (echoing the 'grave danger' of the early 1940s), the Taoiseach, Garret FitzGerald, appointed the National Youth Policy Committee, chaired by High Court Judge (and former prominent Fine Gael TD) Declan Costello. Almost exactly a year later the Committee presented its *Final Report* (National Youth Policy Committee, 1984), which included an in-depth study of the state of young people and youth services in Ireland and set out detailed proposals for the development of a comprehensive national youth service built on a system of local youth committees. The proposals were for the most part adopted by the government in 1985 (which was UN International Youth Year) in the White Paper *In Partnership With Youth: The National Youth Policy*. However, no significant progress had been made in implementing the policy by the time of a general election in 1987 and the incoming government allowed it to lapse. Nonetheless, the Costello Report remains of very considerable historical significance in youth policy terms, not least because the framework it proposed for the delivery and co-ordination of youth services very closely corresponds to that which was eventually enshrined in the Youth Work Act of 2001.

In the absence of such a framework from the late 1980s until the early 2000s, youth organisations continued to develop their own programmes and services, often (as indicated above) through agreements and/or contractual relationships with VECs and other statutory services and making use of a proliferation of funding opportunities. This has meant that a single local youth service or project might have staff funded from a variety of different sources: Special Project for Youth funding from the Department of Education; funding from a Local Drugs Task Force for a youth drugs worker; a Garda Special Project worker funded by the Department of Justice, and so on. This has undoubtedly resulted in a very significant increase in the range of much-needed services for disadvantaged young people, and is far preferable to youth workers (or other professionals) working in isolation in single-worker projects (of which there are unfortunately still a significant number around the country). Moreover, in many instances the organisations or projects in question have very good systems in place for managing the complexities of multi-member teams funded by multiple sources.

There is also, however, inevitably a danger of duplication or inefficient use of resources in such a situation, all the more so since at regional and national level there has been an almost complete absence of co-ordination of these various initiatives targeted at disadvantaged young people. There are also inconsistencies between the various schemes, relating to funding timescales and to the amounts and proportions of funding devoted to programming as opposed to salaries; and also relating to the salary scales themselves and conditions of employment for staff. (The idea behind the Funding Review conducted as part of the *National Youth Work Development Plan*, outlined below, was to begin to address some of these anomalies). Finally, there is a danger of the practice with young people itself suffering from the tensions inherent in trying to meet the expectations and criteria of different funders, with their different and not necessarily compatible agendas and priorities.

In the early to mid-1990s a process of review of the education system as a whole was undertaken and spanned the terms of two (opposing) governments and several Ministers for Education. It included the publication of the Green Paper *Education for a Changing World* (Government of Ireland, 1992) and the White Paper *Charting our Education Future* (Government of Ireland, 1995a). There was an extensive national consultation exercise involving the major education 'partners' (National Education Convention Secretariat, 1994) and, in parallel, the Department of Education instigated a consultative process with youth organisations and the VECs about a framework for the development of youth work, which led to agreement on most, but not all, of the major structural issues (Consultative Group on the Development of Youth Work, 1993). Both the Green Paper and the White Paper had sections on youth work, the latter expressing a commitment to the introduction of youth work legislation. This came to pass in the Youth Work Act 1997.

As a statute, the legislation was somewhat anomalous since it was framed as 'an Act to extend the powers of education boards in relation to youth work' and yet the much larger and more contentious Education Bill 1997 – which provided for the establishment of those boards in the first place and would have ultimately resulted in the abolition of the VECs – had not in fact been passed when there was a further change of government in 1997. The incoming government deemed the Youth Work Act 'inoperable' and stated its intention to introduce its own amended youth work legislation. It may be that it would not have seen the need for legislation in this area at all, but its options were somewhat limited by the fact that in the very final days in office of the previous Minister for Education and Minister of State for Youth Affairs, one very important element of the Youth Work Act 1997 had already been implemented: the appointment of the National Youth Work Advisory Committee (NYWAC).

This had at least two direct consequences. Firstly, as just indicated, it made it difficult for the new government simply to ignore the Act or leave it to gather dust, and secondly, in securing ministerial approval after a relatively short time to prepare proposals for a National Youth Work Development Plan, NYWAC established itself as having a significant contribution to make in the longer term.

THE YOUTH WORK ACT 2001

The revised (and current) legislation, the Youth Work Act 2001, was introduced after further consultation with the relevant voluntary and statutory organisations. The crucial difference from the earlier legislation was that, far from undermining the VECs, it made them responsible for the co-ordination of youth work within their areas of operation. However, apart from the appointment of a (slightly reconstituted) NYWAC, its main provisions remained inactive for several years, partly for reasons of cost and partly because agreement needed to be reached between the parties involved (the Department, the VECs, the voluntary organisations) about the precise shape some elements of the legislation would take in practice. NYWAC, on which all of these parties and others are represented, took a leading role (in keeping with its own statutory functions) in preparing detailed guidelines for the implementation of key components of the Act. In 2006, funding was finally provided by the Department of Education and Science to enable the VECs (or at least those which did not already have specialist youth work staff in place, which was the majority) to recruit Youth Officers and thereby to begin to fulfil their functions under the legislation.

The Youth Work Act (s.3) 2001 defines youth work as follows:

A planned programme of education designed for the purpose of aiding and enhancing the personal and social development of young persons through their voluntary involvement ... which is –
(a) complementary to their formal, academic and vocational training; and
(b) provided primarily by voluntary organisations

Two elements of this definition echo the formulation in the 1997 legislation, and both are very much in keeping with the position taken in Irish youth work policy documents for decades. These are, firstly, the voluntary participation of young people and, secondly, the fundamentally educational nature of the work. The third element – the idea that youth work is 'primarily provided by voluntary organisations' – was added to the amending legislation after lobbying by the voluntary organisations themselves. The Act refers throughout to 'youth work programmes and services', 'programmes' here referring to direct provision for young people and 'services' to any provision which directly or indirectly assists or supports such work.

As already mentioned at the start of this chapter, the Act defines a young person as 'a person who has not attained the age of 25 years', but specifies that 'particular regard will be had' to the youth work requirements of young people between the ages of 10 and 20 (inclusive) and of young people who are socially or economically disadvantaged. The age band specified is broadly in line with the distinction normally drawn within the 'social professions' between youth work provision and children's services (the latter for the younger age groups), although some would argue that this distinction is artificial and hinders the ability of youth work organisations to engage in valuable developmental and preventative work with younger children.

The Youth Work Act also makes explicit mention of the issue of access and participation by both young women and young men, the information needs of young people and the youth work requirements of young Irish speakers.

Under the Act, the Minister for Education has statutory responsibility for ensuring the development and co-ordination of policies relating to youth work programmes and services. The Minister must also ensure the co-ordination of youth work with other services for young people, educational and otherwise. Other ministerial functions relate to financial support, research, monitoring and assessment (dealt with separately below).

As stated already, the Vocational Education Committees (VECs), originally charged with responsibility for vocational and 'continuation' education under the

Vocational Education Act of 1930, and operating for the most part at county and city level, were given responsibility under the Youth Work Act for ensuring the provision of youth work programmes and services in their areas of operation. This involves:

- Providing assistance, including financial assistance, to voluntary youth work organisations
- Preparing and implementing three-yearly Youth Work Development Plans within their areas (while ensuring co-ordination with other local services for young people)
- Drafting annual youth work budgets and reporting on youth work services to the Minister for Education.

Very importantly, both from their own point of view and that of the voluntary youth organisations, VECs have been given the responsibility to 'monitor and assess youth work programmes and services' and evaluate the expenditure incurred. To support VECs in carrying out their functions and in keeping with the principle of statutory-voluntary partnership, the Act provides that each VEC will establish a Youth Work Committee and a Voluntary Youth Council. As explained earlier, it was only in 2006 that the VECs secured funding for staff to enable them to begin to fulfil their functions under the Act, and therefore at the time of writing the structures are only just beginning to be put in place.

The role of the Youth Work Committee is to advise and make recommendations to the VEC on the performance of its youth work functions. It has a membership of 16 to 20 members comprising, in equal proportion:

(a) Persons nominated by the relevant local statutory agencies (for example, local authorities, health services, FÁS, the gardaí)
(b) Nominees of the Voluntary Youth Council for the area.

In effect, and allowing for differences of detail, this means that every VEC has a committee such as has existed in the City of Dublin VEC since 1942.

The Voluntary Youth Council role is to advise the VEC on matters related to the Youth Work Development Plan and to act as a forum for voluntary youth work organisations in the VEC area, including, as just stated, the nomination of members to the Youth Work Committee. The Voluntary Youth Council has 10 to 20 members, of whom, 'as far as practicable', at least one-fifth should be under 25 years old, and at least three-quarters should be volunteers. The Act also refers to the 'desirability' of having representation from youth work services for young Travellers on the Voluntary Youth Council (the Youth Work Act of 1997 had made such representation mandatory). The members are elected in accordance with directions issued by the VEC, following Ministerial guidelines. The National Youth Work Advisory Committee (NYWAC) prepared such guidelines for the Minister's consideration, as well as other documentation such as standing orders for the Voluntary Youth Councils and criteria for the 'designation' (registration) of local youth groups to enable them to become entitled to take part in the elections and to avail of VEC services and support.

NYWAC first came into existence, as indicated earlier, under the Youth Work Act of 1997. Its slightly expanded membership under the 2001 legislation numbers 31 to 33 and apart from one to three ministerial nominees is made up of:

- Nominees of the various government ministers and statutory organisations with an involvement in the provision of services for young people, including four nominees of the Irish Vocational Education Association (the VEC representative body)
- Nominees of the 'prescribed national representative organisation' for the voluntary sector. The National Youth Council of Ireland was explicitly named in the Act as having that status for the first three years, and at the expiry of that period the status was renewed. The Act provides that the voluntary sector representatives will equal in number the total of all other members, excluding the chairperson.

The role of NYWAC is to advise the Minister in relation to the provision of youth work programmes and services, the development and implementation of youth work policies, the co-ordination of youth work with other services for young people, the equitable treatment of young men and women in youth work, and the implementation of the detailed provisions of the Youth Work Act at national and VEC level.

For a short period in the early 1990s the Youth Affairs Section of the Department of Education employed a professional Youth Work Assessor, whose work resulted, among other things, in the publication of a review of youth work practice in community-based projects (Treacy, 1992) and fed into the youth work consultative process mentioned above. When the incumbent left the post to take up another position, it was left unfilled. The Youth Work Act 1997 provided for the formal assessment of youth work programmes and services; the 2001 Act went further by establishing the statutory position of Assessor of Youth Work, somewhat analogous to the formal educational inspectorate. The Assessor has two principal functions: the assessment and monitoring of youth work programmes and services, and the review of various aspects of the Minister's and VECs' functions. An Assessor was appointed to the Youth Affairs Section in 2006, but not strictly to the statutory post as provided for in the legislation. The new Assessor made quality standards in youth work practice a priority on taking up office.

At the time of writing, a number of issues remain to be clarified regarding the implementation of the provisions of the Youth Work Act. The Act provides that VECs will provide assistance, 'including financial assistance', to voluntary organisations. It is not clear how this will impact on existing arrangements whereby voluntary youth work organisations receive funding from the Youth Affairs Section of the Department of Education and Science (under two major schemes as noted above, the Youth Service Grant Scheme and the Special Projects for Youth scheme), in some cases for disbursement to regional or local affiliates.

Under the terms of the Act, and as already noted, the primary providers of youth work services will remain the voluntary youth work organisations. Where a VEC considers there to be a need for a youth work programme or service to be provided, it must publicly advertise for tenders from organisations in its area for the delivery of such a programme or service. Only when no suitable tender is received may the VEC directly provide such a programme or service itself, and even then it must re-advertise for tenders after three years.

What is less clear in the Act is the precise nature of the relationship to be entered into between the VEC and organisations that are successful in their application to provide a programme or service, and whether such relationships are to be contractually time-limited or open ended. These matters are obviously of considerable importance to existing voluntary organisations which have up to now been receiving ongoing financial assistance from VECs to provide local services, and there has been a concern that the procedures stipulated in the Act might introduce a climate of unnecessary and unconstructive competition between (in many cases relatively small) voluntary youth organisations. For these and other reasons, NYWAC recommended to the Minister for Education that the relevant section of the Youth Work Act should not be commenced.

A further potentially very significant provision of the Youth Work Act is that which requires the VEC to 'ensure co-ordination within its vocational education area of youth work programmes and youth work services with education programmes and other programmes that provide services for young people'. This has the potential of remedying the current unsatisfactory situation whereby there is no systematic co-ordination between the various types of provision for young people, which have increased and diversified enormously in recent years (with funding from a wide range of statutory sources, each largely without reference to the others).

Given that the Youth Work Committees of the VECs will bring together representatives of these statutory agencies (along with voluntary sector representatives), there will be the possibility for a planned, coherent and co-ordinated approach to cross-sectoral youth work provision, but this will require commitment, compromise and concessions on all sides. Otherwise, a 'minimalist' interpretation of the Act will prevail, whereby the VEC simply ensures that none of the youth work programmes or services in its own development plan duplicates any of the other youth provisions locally, but these various other provisions continue as before without any overall co-ordination. From the point of view of those individuals and organisations who have been calling for comprehensive youth work legislation for many years, this would be an opportunity missed.

NATIONAL YOUTH WORK DEVELOPMENT PLAN

It has already been indicated that the National Youth Work Advisory Committee (NYWAC) has been in existence since 1997. In 1999, NYWAC considered and approved a proposal from the National Youth Council of Ireland (which nominates almost half of its members) that it prepare for the Minister of State for Youth Affairs a set of proposals for a National Youth Work Development Plan, intended to complement the amending youth work legislation then in preparation. The Minister endorsed the idea in principle and the preparation of the Development Plan was financially supported by the Department of Education and Science.

After a lengthy process of research and consultation with young people, youth workers and relevant statutory and voluntary interests, the proposals were presented to the Minister late in 2001 as the basis for a plan covering the years 2002 to 2006. Government approval, however, was not formally granted for 18 months and the document was published in August 2003 as the *National Youth Work Development Plan 2003–2007*. Further difficulty in securing financial resources meant that in effect its implementation did not begin until 2005. The most recent national social partnership agreement, *Towards 2016*, states: 'Following a review of the Youth Work Development Plan, to be undertaken in 2008, consideration will be given to the need for a further plan' (Department of the Taoiseach, 2006, p. 44).

The 'vision of youth work' presented in the Development Plan, taking the definition in the legislation as its starting point, stressed the fundamentally educational nature of youth work, the importance of the voluntary participation of young people and the special role of the voluntary organisations. It emphasised the rights of young people as citizens (rather than simply participants in activities or recipients of a service) and aimed to uphold 'in spirit as well as in letter the provisions of the Equal Status Act, whereby no adult or young person may experience discrimination on the basis of gender, marital status, family status, sexual orientation, religion, age, disability, race, nationality or ethnicity, including membership of the Traveller community (Department of Education and Science, 2003a, p. 15).

The Development Plan set out four broad goals, with related 'actions' in each case (46 actions in total):

- **Goal 1:** *To facilitate young people and adults to participate more fully in, and to gain optimum benefit from, youth work programmes and services.*
  The actions relating to this goal included additional support for geographical areas under-resourced in youth work terms (primarily rural areas), the phasing in of specific criteria regarding the active participation of young people as part of the funding requirements for youth work programmes, the development of 'peer-managed' projects and programmes and the preparation of charters of rights for young people and adult volunteers involved in youth work.
- **Goal 2:** *To enhance the contribution of youth work to social inclusion, social cohesion and citizenship in a rapidly changing national and global context.*
  Youth organisations and Vocational Education Committees (in the preparation of their own area development plans, as provided for under the Youth Work Act

2001) are encouraged to use the categories specified in the Equal Status Act (outlined above), and other relevant categories (for example, 'rurality'), in a positive way 'as a template for the active promotion of equality within their areas of operation, and for the monitoring and evaluation of youth work programmes and services' (p. 22). Other actions relate to racism, multiculturalism and intercultural education, international exchanges and the enhancement of 'North-South' (all-Ireland) and 'East-West' (Britain-Ireland) links.

- **Goal 3:** *To put in place an expanded and enhanced infrastructure for development, support and co-ordination at national and local level.*

Under this goal, a Development Unit for youth work was identified as 'a priority action and one on which the implementation of much of the rest of the Plan depends' (Department of Education, 2003a, p. 24). The Unit's functions would include developing guidelines for all aspects of good practice, managing and co-ordinating research, piloting innovation and overseeing and monitoring the Development Plan itself. NYWAC's own proposals to the Minister, included in the Development Plan as published, set out four options for the manner in which the Unit might be constituted (as part of the existing Youth Affairs section of the Department of Education and Science; as a company limited by guarantee; as a statutory body under new legislation; or as a body corporate set up by 'establishment order' under Section 54 of the Education Act 1998). The decision announced in late 2005 was to establish the Development Unit in an existing institution associated with youth work education and training, namely NUI Maynooth.

Also under the third goal, an important action in the Development Plan was the establishment of a funding review of the youth work sector to examine all aspects of the allocation of finances, including funding lines, criteria, categories of activity supported, arrangements within funded organisations regarding salary scales and conditions of employment, and so on. Independent consultants were appointed by the Department of Education and Science in 2005 to carry out such a review, the results of which were not available at the time of writing.

- **Goal 4:** *To put in place mechanisms for enhancing professionalism and ensuring quality standards in youth work.*

The key action set out under this goal was the establishment of a 'Youth Work Validation Body, with the purpose of developing a comprehensive framework for accreditation and certification in youth work' (p. 27). Such a body had first been recommended in 1984 in the Final Report of the National Youth Policy Committee (Costello Report). In the Development Plan, the desirability was expressed of setting up the body on an all-Ireland basis, particularly since the Youth Council for Northern Ireland (a statutory body established under the Youth Service [Northern Ireland] Order 1989) was already in the process of taking over the 'licence' for endorsing professional youth work training in the North (a function previously exercised by the National Youth Agency in England). Discussions began at an early stage between NYWAC, the Youth Council for Northern Ireland, and the Departments of Education in both jurisdictions, and in January 2006 the North South Education and Training Standards Committee for youth work (NSETS) was launched in Armagh by the Minister for Education for Northern Ireland, Angela Smith, MP, and the Minister of State for Youth Affairs in the South, Síle de Valera, TD.

The NSETS is broadly representative of all the relevant youth work interests throughout the island: the government departments, national policy and advisory bodies, youth work organisations and employers, youth work practitioners and (in the North) their trade union, and the higher education institutions that provide programmes of education and training in youth work. The role of the committee is to assess all aspects of the quality of such training and professionally endorse (or not) the programmes submitted to it on behalf of the sector as a whole. Negotiations with the relevant equivalent bodies in Britain have ensured mutual recognition of endorsed programmes on an 'East-West' basis, thereby enhancing the professional mobility of graduates. It was envisaged in the National Youth Work Development Plan that ultimately the endorsement process would extend beyond the third-level professional programmes to include all levels and types of training for youth work, and it is likely that in the longer term this will happen.

NATIONAL CHILDREN'S STRATEGY

As we saw in Chapter 1, the publication of *Our Children – Their Lives: The National Children's Strategy*, targeted at all young people up to the age of 18 years of age, came in November 2000 after several years of stringent criticism, both nationally and internationally, of the inadequate and uncoordinated state of Irish child care services. Despite the passing of the Child Care Act 1991 and more recent initiatives such as the publication of *Children First: National Guidelines for the Protection and Welfare of Children* (Department of Health and Children, 1999), the last comprehensive examination of issues affecting children had been undertaken by the Task Force on Child Care Services (1980). The government itself acknowledged the scale of the problem when in 1998 it made a presentation to the United Nations Committee that monitors adherence to the UN Convention on the Rights of the Child (which Ireland ratified in 1992). The Committee was forthright in its criticisms of Irish provision for children 'on a whole range of fronts' (Gilligan, 1999, p. 234). These included:

- The lack of a 'comprehensive, national policy'
- The inadequate emphasis on measures of a preventive nature
- The lack of co-ordination among organisations and bodies providing for children
- The lack of a mechanism such as an ombudsman for children
- Problems of access to education and health services experienced by certain minority groups
- Inadequate procedures for hearing the voice of children

- Inadequate measures to ensure the rights of children with disabilities
- The exclusion of certain children from the school system
- The low age of criminal responsibility

> (Committee on the Rights of the Child, 1998; summarised in Gilligan, 1999, p. 234).

The last point above, and related matters pertaining to juvenile justice, were addressed in the Children Act 2001, which provided for the raising of the age of criminal responsibility from seven to 12, although as mentioned at the outset of this chapter, that provision of the Act was never actually implemented and was subsequently amended by the Criminal Justice Act 2006 (see Chapter 9). The National Children's Strategy dealt with the broader issues of children's care and well-being. It was designed to run until 2010.

The Strategy adopted a 'whole-child' perspective and set out a vision of an Ireland where 'children are respected as young citizens with a valued contribution to make and a voice of their own; where all children are cherished and supported by family and the wider society; where they enjoy a fulfilling childhood and realise their potential' (p. 4). Six operational principles were intended to underpin all the Strategy's provisions. Actions taken under the Strategy should be (p. 10):

- **Child-centred:** 'The best interests of the child shall be a primary consideration and children's wishes and feelings should be given due regard.'
- **Family-oriented:** 'The family generally affords the best environment for raising children ...'
- **Equitable:** 'All children should have equality of opportunity in relation to access [and] participation in ... services. A key priority ... is to target investment at those most at risk.'
- **Inclusive:** 'The diversity of children's experiences, cultures and lifestyles must be recognised and given expression.'
- **Action-oriented:** 'Service delivery needs to be clearly focused on achieving specified results to agreed standards ...'
- **Integrated:** 'Measures should be taken in partnership, within and between relevant players ... services for children should be delivered in a co-ordinated, coherent and effective manner.'

Clearly, at least some of the above principles overlap with elements of the Youth Work Act 2001, which also provides for targeting in the case of socio-economic disadvantage, for raising standards through monitoring and assessment and for enhanced co-ordination in service delivery.

The 'substantive' content of the Strategy was built around three broad goals, each of these reflected in a series of practical measures.

Goal 1

'Children will have a voice in matters which affect them and their views will be given due weight in accordance with their age and maturity.'

This first goal is closely based on Article 12 of the UN Convention on the Rights of the Child:

'State Parties shall assure to the child who is capable of forming his or her own views the right to express those views in all matters affecting the child, the views of the child being given due weight in accordance with the age and maturity of the child'.

The following measures were provided for under the first goal.

Office of Ombudsman for Children

This office, in addition to having the function of investigating complaints from children against public bodies such as schools and hospitals (in accordance with the traditional role of Ombudsman), has the additional broader functions of promoting the welfare and rights of children, consulting with children on issues of importance to them and advising government on such issues. The legislation providing for the establishment of the Office of Ombudsman for Children was enacted in April 2002 and the first Ombudsman was appointed in 2004.

Dáil na nÓg

Dáil na nÓg, the National Children's Parliament, is intended 'to provide a national forum where children can raise and debate issues of concern to them on a periodic basis' (p. 32). The first Dáil na nÓg was convened in September 2001 and it has been an annual event ever since, involving hundreds of children. Recruitment or selection of the children is primarily through schools and City or County Development Boards (see below).

National and Local Fora

According to the Strategy, 'children's views will be represented on existing national and local fora in relation to relevant services such as education and health' (p. 33). The County and City Development Boards (CDBs) were identified as providing 'an ideal opportunity for children's views to be captured' at local level. These Boards were placed on a statutory footing by the Local Government Act 2001. They bring together the local authority, state agencies (including VECs), local development bodies and the 'social partners' (including the community and voluntary sector), and they are charged with drawing up comprehensive strategies for economic, social and cultural development (with which the VEC youth work development plans, mentioned in the previous section of this chapter, must be compatible). Many of the CDBs have established a local youth council (Comhairle na nÓg) to select participants to the national 'parliament' and to act as a forum for consultation with children and young people. However, an independent review conducted for the Office of the Minister for Children in 2005 found that the operation and activities of the Comhairle varied considerably throughout the country and that structures were not functioning effectively in all areas. In 2006 the Minister for Children announced the establishment of a Comhairle na nÓg Planning Group to 'ensure the establishment and development of effective Comhairle na nÓg by every City and County Development Board in the country' (Office of the Minister for Children, 2006).

Other Measures

Additional measures under the first goal of the National Children's Strategy relate to:

- Introduction of 'family conferencing' in judicial proceedings involving children (subsequently provided for in section 78 of the Children Act 2001)
- A review of the Guardian *ad Litem* service (which remains incomplete and inconsistent; see Children's Rights Alliance, 2006, pp. 22–3)
- Ratification of the European Convention on the Exercise of Children's Rights, intended to promote the rights of children in family law proceedings (not yet ratified)
- Consideration by the All-Party Oireachtas Committee on the Constitution of the Constitution Review Group's recommendations (1996) relating to children's rights.

The Constitution Review Group had recommended that the Constitution be amended to include the 'welfare principle' (whereby 'the best interests of the child' are paramount in all actions involving children), and also to provide an 'express guarantee' of other children's rights deriving from the UN Convention. The Group's recommendation was endorsed by the Commission on the Family in its final report (1998). In January 2006, the All-Party Oireachtas Committee on the Constitution proposed the following text (2006, p. 124):

All children, irrespective of birth, gender, race or religion, are equal before the law. In all cases, where the welfare of the child so requires, regard shall be had to the best interests of the child.

This proposed wording has been described by the Children's Rights Alliance (2006, p. 8) as 'inadequate ... and a radical departure from the commitment made by the state when it ratified the Convention [on the Rights of the Child] in 1992'. The

Alliance argues that the first sentence merely reinforces the existing constitutional requirement of equality for all citizens contained in Article 40.1 and thereby does not improve the situation of children, and that 'regard' being had to the child's interests is much weaker than such interests being 'paramount'. Most importantly, the proposed amendment requires that an individual child's welfare be under consideration before the 'best interests' provision would apply, and therefore it does not 'provide for the range of children's rights generally' (Children's Rights Alliance, 2006, p. 8).

Goal 2

'Children's lives will be better understood.'

This goal in the Strategy aimed to build up a more 'coherent understanding of children's development and needs', develop an 'evidence-based approach' to decision-making at all levels, improve the commissioning, production and dissemination of research and information and also improve the evaluation and monitoring of services (p. 39).

The measures included:

- The establishment of a National Longitudinal Study of Children, examining their progress and well-being at critical periods from birth to adulthood (the commencement of the study was announced in 2006, to be undertaken by the Economic and Social Research Institute and the Children's Research Centre at Trinity College Dublin).
- A Children's Research Programme, with fellowships and research grants (in operation).
- Development of a set of 'child well-being indicators' building on the work already done in Ireland by the Economic and Social Research Institute and the Combat Poverty Agency and internationally by UNICEF, WHO and others (see the resulting work in Hanafin and Brooks, 2005, to be used as the basis for a report on the 'state of the nation's children', to be published every two years).
- Establishment of a National Children's Research Dissemination Unit.
- Introduction of a system of 'child impact statements' by all departments seeking a government decision on new policies and initiatives.

Goal 3

'Children will receive quality supports and services.'

The approach taken in this part of the Strategy was more complex than in the previous two. It included a set of 14 objectives (but stressed that 'it is essential that they are understood as interrelated and reinforcing of each other': p. 46). These were in turn grouped into three categories, designed to reflect three headings, or 'statements'.

- **Group 1:** *All children have a basic range of needs.* The needs referred to here include basic educational and health needs as well as opportunities to develop positive relationships 'through sport, play, leisure and cultural activities'. The Strategy noted that a major gap in such services is in relation to play and leisure facilities. This ultimately led to the publication by the Office of the Minister for Children in 2005 of a consultation document on the development of a recreation policy for young people of secondary school age, and the commissioning of a major national survey of young people's recreation and leisure (de Róiste and Dinneen, 2005; see also Chapter 8 of this book).
- **Group 2:** *Some children have additional needs.* The government here expressed a commitment to a 'policy of social inclusion and equity' and to a set of objectives concerned with such problems and issues as child poverty, homelessness, disabilities, behavioural problems and the recognition of cultural diversity so that all children, including Travellers and other marginalised groups, could achieve their full potential.
- **Group 3:** *All children need the support of family and community.* The Strategy noted the provisions of the Irish Constitution relating to the family and reiterates the commitment to protect the family through political, social, economic and other measures. It also stressed the importance of community involvement in providing support for children and referred to the White Paper *Supporting Voluntary Activity*, which was published in 2000 and set out a framework of support for the community and voluntary sector across government departments and agencies. The Family Support Agency was established in 2004.

According to organisations working for and with children and young people, it is in relation to the third goal of the National Children's Strategy ('children will receive quality supports and services') that progress has been slowest and most sporadic to date (Children's Rights Alliance, 2006).

Management at National Level

A number of mechanisms were put in place to implement and manage the National Children's Strategy at national level (in addition to those already mentioned, such as the Ombudsman's Office and the National Research Dissemination Unit). These have all been established in the intervening years. They include:

- A *Cabinet Sub-Committee* to oversee the Strategy, chaired by the Taoiseach, and a Minister of State with special responsibility for children within the Department of Health. This Department was renamed the Department of Health and Children after the 2002 general election, and more recently the Office of the Minister for Children has been established with links not only to Health but to the Departments of Education and Justice (see below).
- A *National Children's Advisory Council*, with a membership 'reflecting the partnership of interests required' and with the functions of advising the Minister

on all relevant matters, of undertaking research and contributing to the monitoring and evaluation of the Strategy itself. The National Children's Advisory Council was launched in May 2001, with representation from the statutory and voluntary sectors, research and training interests, children themselves and independent nominees.

• A *National Children's Office*, established as an independent body in 2001 under the terms of the Public Service Management Act 1997, headed up by a board comprising the Assistant Secretaries from the main departments involved in the implementation of the Strategy and with a professional staff with the functions of: preparing an annual work programme for implementing the Strategy; ensuring that 'priority cross-cutting' issues and actions are co-ordinated and integrated; monitoring the strategy and promoting capacity building through training initiatives.

In 2005 the National Children's Office was incorporated within the newly established *Office of the Minister for Children*. This is a unit within the Department of Health and Children, headed up by a Minister of State and bringing together (as well as all the NCO functions) the Equal Opportunities Childcare Programme (formerly in the Department of Justice, Equality and Law Reform), the Early Years Education functions of the Department of Education and Science, and the new Youth Justice Service of the Department of Justice, Equality and Law Reform. The latter two – the early years and youth justice initiatives – will formally remain the responsibility of the Ministers for Education and Justice, respectively, but they will be located within the 'strategic environment' of the Office of the Minister for Children (Dáil Debates, 28/3/06).

It remains to be seen how effectively this system ('co-location' of services, but continued dispersal of authority and responsibility) will work in practice. Ministers of State (or 'junior ministers', as they are often called in the media) are not members of Cabinet, but under the new arrangements the Minister of State for Children is invited to attend Cabinet meetings. However, the Minister of State does not have a vote and therefore the extent of influence 'over children's issues which are the primary responsibility of other departments remains unclear' (Children's Rights Alliance, 2006, p. 10).

To conclude, the National Children's Strategy was widely welcomed by individuals and organisations involved in providing services for children and young people – a reflection, perhaps, of the fact that an unusually extensive consultation process had been undertaken as part of its preparation. It was certainly an ambitious and comprehensive document, and if implemented in full over the 10 years of its time span will go a long way towards redressing the problems and shortcomings of previous arrangements for meeting children's health-related, educational, social, cultural and developmental needs. The lack of urgency in relation to certain key initiatives, particularly under the third goal, has been criticised.

Childhood does not stand still while yet another strategy is developed or expert working group convened. In the eight years since the last UN Committee examination, a generation of children have lived out their childhood: during this time we have made only limited progress towards creating a society where all children are truly respected, listened to and enabled to develop to their full potential (Children's Rights Alliance, 2006, p. iv).

Hayes (2002) has argued that even after the launch of the Strategy, the basis for policy on child-related matters in Ireland has remained welfare-based rather than rights-based and sees children as the passive recipients of protection. She calls for the strengthening of the Ombudsman for Children legislation to include the responsibility to protect as well as promote children's rights, and argues that the exemption regarding children in detention and children of refugees and asylum-seekers should be removed (a point echoed by the Childrens Rights Alliance, 2002 and 2006). Not surprisingly, the lack of progress in relation to children's rights is also the key criticism made in the most recent report of the Committee on the Rights of the Child, issued in late 2006. The Committee welcomed a range of new legislation and policy initiatives since its first report in 1998, including the Equal Status Acts 2000 to 2004, the Education (Welfare) Act 2000, the Children Act 2001 and of course the National Children's Strategy itself. It particularly welcomed structural initiatives such as the appointment of the Ombudsman for Children and the establishment of the Office of the Minister for Children.

However, the Committee expressed regret that some of its original recommendations had not been acted on, 'in particular those related [to] the status of the child as a rights-holder and the adoption of a child rights-based approach in policies and practices' (Committee on the Rights of the Child, 2006, p. 2). It also expressed concern about the slow pace of enactment of specific provisions, in particular of the Children Acts 1997 and 2001 (stating in the case of the latter that it was 'very disappointed' at developments relating to the age of criminal responsibility); and it expressed regret that the UN Convention on the Rights of the Child has not been incorporated into domestic law 'as recommended by the Committee in its previous [i.e. 1998] concluding observations' (Committee on the Rights of the Child, 2006, p. 3). Towards the end of 2006, after the publication of the UN Committee's report and also in the wake of a number of high-profile legal judgments with significant implications for children, the government announced its intention to hold a constitutional referendum on the rights of the child.

CHILD CARE SERVICES

Children's 'natural and imprescriptable rights' are already mentioned in the Constitution but they are not explicitly defined. The reference occurs in Article 42.5 of Bunreacht na hÉireann, which provides the constitutional basis for Irish child care services.

[I]n exceptional cases, where the parents for physical or moral reasons fail in their duty towards their children, the State as guardian of the common good, by appropriate means shall endeavour to supply the place of the parents, but always with due regard for the natural and imprescriptible rights of the child.

The history of child care services in Ireland actually goes back much further than the Constitution (passed in 1937). Its origins lie in the industrial and reformatory school system of the nineteenth century (Robins, 1980). The Reformatory Schools (Youthful Offenders) Act 1858 certified a number of voluntary (generally religious-run) institutions as suitable for the reception and reformative treatment of 12- to 16-year-olds committed through the courts. The industrial school system, also run for the most part by religious orders, began some 10 years later and catered for younger children and those who committed only minor offences or none at all. Separate laws (of 1862 and 1897) provided for foster care ('boarding out') for children under five years of age. The Children Act of 1908, referred to at the start of this chapter, consolidated the earlier legislation and dealt with children in need of care and protection as well as providing for juvenile offenders. In 1924 responsibility for the industrial and reformatory schools was transferred from the Minister for Justice to the Minister for Education.

The system that developed in the nineteenth century 'was not appreciably altered until the 1970s' (Kelleher et al., 2000, p. 40). In 1970 a report on the industrial and reformatory schools was published, usually referred to as the Kennedy Report after its chairperson, District Justice Eileen Kennedy. Key recommendations of the Kennedy Report were for an emphasis on prevention and for the de-institutionalisation of the care system. Fostering should be the preferred form of care, and where residential care was required, it should be in the form of smaller units.

The whole aim of the child care system should be geared towards the prevention of family breakdown and the problems consequent on it. The committal or admission of children to residential care should be considered only when there is no satisfactory alternative (Department of Education, 1970, p. 6).

The Kennedy Report also emphasised the need for a child-centred approach which would take into consideration the emotional and psychological needs of the child, and in keeping with this recommended that care staff should be professionally trained. Much of the philosophy of the report was shared by the *Report of the Task Force on Child Care Services* (1980), and both documents called for composite updated child-care legislation and for responsibility to be unified in one government department, the Department of Health. In fact, the Task Force had its origins in 1974 following a government decision to allocate the main responsibility for child care to the Minister for Health and its own terms of reference included drawing up a new child care bill but it did not do so (Curry, 2003).

The Child Care Act was eventually enacted in 1991. It raised the legal definition of a 'child' to 18 years and placed a statutory duty on Health Boards (now the Health Services Executive) to 'promote the welfare of children who are not receiving adequate care and protection', as well as to provide a range of child care and family support services. In performing these functions, the health authorities must regard the welfare of the child as the first and paramount consideration, have regard to the rights and duties of parents, give due consideration to the wishes of the child and also have regard to the principle that it is generally in the best interests of the child to be brought up in her or his own family. The Act 'strengthens the legal duties of health boards to support young people in their care and empowers them to prepare young people to leave care' (Kelleher et al., 2000, p. 160).

Under the terms of the Child Care Act, children and young people can be taken into care under care orders of the District Court. A supervision order (section 19) authorises the Health Board to have a child visited at home 'in order to satisfy itself as to the welfare of the child and to give to his parents or to a person acting *in loco parentis* any necessary advice as to the welfare of the child'. An emergency care order (section 13) authorises the placement of a child in the care of the Health Board for a period of up to eight days where there is 'an immediate and serious risk to the health or welfare' of the child. In the event of a member of the Garda Síochána believing that such a risk exists, he or she may enter a house without warrant and remove a child to safety, accompanied by other persons if necessary (for example, a social worker). The child must then be delivered to the Health Board as soon as possible so that an emergency care order can be sought (section 12). A care order (section 18) commits the child to the care of the Health Board until the age of 18, or for any shorter period determined by the District Court, if the court is satisfied that the child has been or is being assaulted, ill-treated, neglected or sexually abused, or if the child's health, development or welfare has been, is being or is likely to be avoidably impaired or neglected.

The health authorities fulfil their functions under the Child Care Act, and carry out the different types of order outlined above, through the employment of social workers and different types of child care worker. Community child care workers, as the name suggests, 'do most of their work in the community, be it in the client's home, a satellite health centre or other agreed venue' (McKenna-McElwee and Brown, 2005, p. 303). They are normally assigned their work through the social work team leader and work closely with other relevant professionals involved in a given case. Where it is deemed impossible to maintain the child in its own family, he or she may be placed in foster care or in a residential centre staffed by residential care workers. These centres now tend to be 'based on group homes rather than the traditional large institutions' (Curry, 1993, p. 155). In 2001 there were 126 residential children's homes across the 10 Health Board areas. Almost two-thirds of these were in the former Eastern Health Board area (Counties Dublin, Wicklow and Kildare). However, it is difficult to ascertain the exact number of residential centres at any one time 'given the short-term nature of some of the units' (Byrne and

McHugh, 2005, p. 314). All the centres are funded by the Department of Health and Children, with almost half run by voluntary organisations or groups. Many provide care for just one child, while others can cater for up to 24 children (ibid). 'Special care' and 'high support' services are designed to deal with young people who regularly abscond from non-secure centres or whose behaviour is particularly challenging or difficult. Several court cases in recent years have highlighted the lack of adequate facilities and support for such young people.

Recent figures presented in the Dáil by the Minister of State for Children indicated that over 5,000 children and young people were in the care of the Health Services Executive (Dáil Debates, 23/11/06). Of these, almost 4,250 (84 per cent) were in foster care, an increase of 4 per cent on the previous figures. The Minister was introducing the Child Care (Amendment) Bill which provides that a foster parent or a relative with a child in their care for five years might apply for increased autonomy from the health authorities in relation to the child's care (for further information on children and young people in care, see Chapter 11).

Since the passing of the Child Care Act 1991, the Department of Health and Children has introduced a number of sets of regulations governing the provision and delivery of different types of care, and in 1999 the Social Services Inspectorate (SSI) was established. In its early years the work of the SSI focused on children in care. It assisted in the development of national standards for residential centres, foster care services and special care units. The SSI conducts inspections of children's residential centres and foster care services. The Health and Social Care Professionals Act 2005 provided for a statutory system of registration for a range of professions – including social workers and social care workers – through a Health and Social Care Professionals Council and Registration Boards for each of the professions in question (12 in all).

CHILD PROTECTION

The publication in 1999 by the Department of Health and Children of *Children First: National Guidelines for the Protection and Welfare of Children* was a 'clear acknowledgement that the profile of child abuse as a social problem had risen considerably in Ireland and was urgently in need of a structured, centralised, socio-legal response' (Martin, 2000, p. 64). The guidelines were intended to assist people in identifying and reporting child abuse and to improve professional practice in both statutory and voluntary agencies and organisations providing services for children and families. It was expected that the national guidelines would be complemented by local guidelines specific to the needs of regional Health Boards and to different disciplines and organisational settings. The main objective of the guidelines is to facilitate professionals in identifying child abuse (categorised into four different types: neglect, emotional abuse, physical abuse and sexual abuse) and reporting it, primarily to the Health Board or the Garda Síochána. Standard reporting procedures are stipulated in detail, and this is 'possibly the most important provision in the guidelines overall'.

The implication for professionals and the public at large is that anyone who suspects that a child is being abused, or is at risk of abuse, should make a report to the Health Board or the police. The core maxim is that everyone now has a duty to protect children and reports should be made to the statutory authorities without delay. Furthermore, the guidelines provide principled, practical, clear and powerful criteria for various organisations on the reporting mechanism to be adopted, requiring each to appoint a designated person to act as a liaison with outside agencies' (Martin, 2000, p. 67).

In keeping with the intention that *Children First* might be used as a national framework within which different disciplines or sectors might develop their own more focused guidelines, the Irish Sports Council published its *Code of Ethics: Good Practice for Children's Sport* (2000) and the National Youth Work Advisory Committee prepared the *Code of Good Practice: Child Protection for the Youth Work Sector* (Department of Education and Science, 2002c). The Department of Health and Children itself published *Our Duty to Care: The Principles of Good Practice for the Protection of Children and Young People* (2002a), which was particularly aimed at community and voluntary sector organisations.

More recently, the Arts Council has published guidelines for the protection and welfare of children and young people in the arts sector (2006), which include a template for a child protection policy statement, a code of behaviour for staff and recommended procedures regarding recruitment and selection, management and supervision, reporting, allegations and complaints and handling accidents. This last point is a reminder that the welfare and protection of children and young people extends beyond a concern with child abuse.

A further outcome of increased awareness and concern with child abuse and child protection in recent years was the establishment in 2002 of the Garda Central Vetting Unit (GCVU) to deal with criminal record vetting, initially in the health and social services sectors. In 2006 the Minister of State for Children announced a phased expansion of vetting to *all* those who have substantial, unsupervised access to children and vulnerable adults, irrespective of whether they work in a full-time or part-time capacity or whether they are volunteers or students on placement. Vetting was extended to:

- All prospective full-time and part-time employees of the Health Service Executive (HSE) and certain agencies funded by the HSE (previously only full-time employees were vetted)
- New teachers in the primary and post-primary education sectors, as well as non-teaching staff such as caretakers
- New employees and volunteers working in the youth work sector and in selected sports organisations.

It was also announced that vetting would subsequently be further extended to such sectors as private hospitals, residential child care centres, agencies working with the homeless, local community initiatives, arts organisations, and private tuition centres and organisations.

It was explained in Chapter 4 that, arising from a Supreme Court decision in 2006 that a provision of the Criminal Law Act 1935 was unconstitutional, new legislation regarding the age of consent was introduced in the form of the Criminal Law (Sexual Offences) Act 2006. In the wake of the Supreme Court judgment and following a public outcry concerning the sexual vulnerability of young people, in particular young women, the government appointed two Child Protection Rapporteurs (both lawyers) whose job is to review and 'audit' legal developments for the protection of children and assess what impact, if any, litigation in national and international courts will have on child protection. The Child Protection Rapporteurs are independent and accountable to the Oireachtas, to which they report annually.

CONCLUSION

This chapter began with a reminder that perceptions and definitions of age-associated categories are culturally constructed, and particularly that in contemporary Irish society there is considerable cultural ambivalence about the boundaries between childhood, youth and adulthood, an ambivalence reflected both in the law and in social policies and services for children and young people. It was suggested that while this ambivalence, and the apparent inconsistencies to which it can give rise, may appear irrational and frustrating to young people themselves, it can also be seen as a reflection of the fact that growing up in today's Ireland is in fact a very complex and multifaceted process and that simple definitions of life stages may not be possible. However, the diverse aspects of children's and young people's policy and services are undoubtedly in need of much greater coherence and co-ordination than is there at present. The major recent policy and legislative developments outlined in this chapter are partly designed to provide this, as well as to meet the needs of the young more effectively and to facilitate their more active involvement and participation in all aspects of the society in which they live. It is, of course, still too soon to gauge the success of these initiatives.

RECOMMENDED READING

The journal *Youth Studies Ireland* and the magazine *Youth Work Scene*, both published by the Irish Youth Work Centre (www.iywc.ie), provide up-to-date information and perspectives on youth work and other youth services in Ireland.

The Children's Rights Alliance (www.childrensrights.ie) and the National Youth Council of Ireland (www.youth.ie) have a range of reports and publications dealing with the issues raised in this chapter.

11

Marginalised and Excluded Young People

INTRODUCTION

While this is a textbook about young people in contemporary Ireland, the authors have attempted to remember throughout (and to remind you, the reader) that young people do not form an undifferentiated group, any more than the people designated by such terms as 'children', 'adults' or 'older people' do. Several decades ago, sociologists at the Centre for Contemporary Cultural Studies (CCCS) at the University of Birmingham, in a very influential challenge to widely accepted conceptions of the nature of youth culture, proclaimed: 'Youth as a single, homogeneous group does not exist' (Hall et al., 1976, p. 19; see also Chapters 2 and 12 of this book).

Certainly, age is a vitally important feature of social stratification in societies such as ours, and it is an organising principle for the operation of major social institutions, most obviously the education system in which attendance is compulsory until a certain age (which has increased over the years) and people for the most part go through the various 'levels' of learning in the company of others of a very similar age to themselves. Spending a lot of time together inevitably enhances the sense of a shared identity and culture among young people, and this is reinforced by the way in which the media target the youth market, and in many of their own practices express a 'bias' towards youth and youthfulness (O'Boyle, 2006). In addition, of course, all young people are engaged in the gradual physical and psychological processes of growth into adulthood. However, just as important as the ways in which young people are similar by virtue of their age are the ways in which they differ by virtue of other aspects of their lives, circumstances and identities. A failure to recognise that there is more to being young than the age-related aspects runs the risk of stereotyping young people, whether negatively ('they're all psychologically unstable, at the mercy of their hormones and mood swings'; 'they seem to care about nothing but drink, drugs and sex') or positively ('they're full of energy and idealism'; 'they're having the time of their lives, without a care in the world'). In either case, such stereotyping is a simplification of a complex social reality (Devlin, 2006, p. 11). It is particularly damaging because it ignores the issues and concerns confronting young people who are socially marginalised and excluded and for whom 'youth culture' may seem to hold limited relevance or attractiveness, may be difficult to access or participate in, or may itself be experienced as actively marginalising and excluding. The remainder of this chapter deals with the situation of a number of groups:

- Young people with disabilities
- Young Travellers
- Young separated asylum seekers
- Young people in care and leaving care
- Young homeless people
- Rural young people.

The situation of young LGBT people (lesbian, gay, bisexual or transgender) is dealt with in Chapter 4, while gender-related inequalities and the experiences of young people who suffer socio-economic exclusion, affecting (for instance) their participation in education or their interaction with the justice system, are addressed in other chapters.

YOUNG PEOPLE WITH DISABILITIES

Disability is itself a complex and contested concept, and there are different ways of understanding the experience of people with disabilities, their relationships with others and their position in society. It is common to distinguish between different models of disability (Whyte, 2006, Chapter 3). The medical model focuses on the health status of the individual and sees other aspects of his or her personal and social experiences as flowing from this, whether it is a physical, sensory, intellectual or mental health condition or a combination of some or all of these. Alternatively, the social model places the emphasis on the exclusion (and, according to some analysts, oppression) of people with disabilities by 'disabling' social structures and systems, and argues that it is these which need to be challenged and changed so that people with 'disabilities' can get on with their lives like everyone else. Whyte (2006) suggests that an adequate theory of disability should include 'all the dimensions of disabled people's experiences – bodily, psychological, cultural, social, political – rather than claiming that disability is either medical or social'.

The definition adopted by the National Disability Authority (NDA) takes account both of individual 'impairment' and of the crucial role of externally imposed constraints: disability is 'the disadvantage or restriction of activity caused by contemporary social and cultural organisations which take little account of people who have impairments and thus exclude them from mainstream social and cultural activities' (NDA, 2002, p. 76). Disability can take a wide range of forms. Section 2(1) of the Disability Act 2005 defines it to include 'enduring physical, sensory, mental health or intellectual impairment'. This definition, and others like it in related legislation, has been criticised by some commentators as relying on a 'seriously flawed functional deficiencies model' of disability (Kenny et al., 2003, p. 139).

Gathering Information on Young People with Disabilites

Despite the recommendations of the Commission on the Status of People with Disabilities (1997) and the actions proposed in the National Children's Strategy (2000), there is still a lack of comprehensive information about the number and circumstances of children and young people (or indeed older people) with disabilities in Ireland. The NDA is providing support to the Central Statistics Office in the development of a National Disability Survey (NDS) which will create comprehensive baseline data regarding disability in Ireland for the first time. Meanwhile, existing large nationally representative household samples – the Living in Ireland Survey and the Quarterly National Household Survey (QNHS) – do provide some valuable information on disability. In addition, the 2002 Census of Population included for the first time some specially designed questions on disability.

Both the above-mentioned sample surveys include data about people aged 15 and over (stopping at age 64 in the case of the QNHS). In the Living in Ireland Survey conducted by the Economic and Social Research Institute (ESRI) in 2001, it was found that 10.2 per cent of 15- to 24-year-old respondents reported having a 'chronic physical or mental health problem, illness or disability' (the figures here are taken from Gannon and Nolan, 2005, Chapter 2). This compared with 21.6 per cent for the sample as a whole. Looked at differently, of all those reporting a chronic illness or disability, 7.9 per cent were aged 15 to 24. Of course, these relatively low figures for younger people might be expected given that the definition being used includes chronic illness. Respondents were also asked whether their chronic illness or disability 'hampered' them, with the possible answers being 'severely', 'to some extent' or 'not hampered'. Here it was found that the youngest group, the 15- to 24-year-olds, were most likely to say they were not hampered: 40.6 per cent of them said so, as compared with 24.9 per cent of the total. Significantly, however, they were also among the groups with the highest rates of people saying they were severely hampered (23.9 per cent, compared with an overall average of 21 per cent). It must be remembered that these figures represent the respondents' subjective assessments of their own condition and circumstances and are likely to be affected by their views of what would be the standard or the 'norm' for people of their own age.

Using a number of existing sources to arrive at 'reasonably reliable estimates', the Commission on the Status of People with Disabilities (1997, p. 288) concluded that there were at least 30,000 children in Ireland with some form of disability. These included approximately 8,000 pupils with disabilities enrolled in special schools and some 3,800 attending special classes in primary schools. An additional 8,000 pupils with specific disabilities were in ordinary classes in primary schools, 2,300 in special classes in post-primary schools and finally about 100 pupils with disabilities enrolled in five designated post-primary schools (ibid, p. 171). More recent Department of Education and Science statistics show that in 2002/03 there were 16,191 pupils with assessed special educational needs at primary level (9,384 in national schools and 6,807 in special schools), which represents 3.6 per cent of the total primary population, while at second level there were 5,322 students with special educational needs in vocational schools, 3,443 in community and comprehensive schools and 1,208 in secondary schools (National Disability Authority, 2005a, pp. 7–9). This amounts to less than 3 per cent of the overall second-level student population. Department of Education and Science figures for third-level applications in the same year (2002/03) suggest that there were about 1,100 students with disabilities attending third level, approximately 1 per cent of the total at this level (National Disability Authority, 2004, p. 6).

Experiences of School

These figures alone tell one important part of the story of young people with disabilities: as they grow up, their participation in the education system diminishes markedly in comparison with their non-disabled peers. Experiences of education are important in shaping the identities and opportunities of all young people, but even more so, perhaps, those of young people with disabilities: 'The definition and categorisation of people as disabled is an institutional and social practice and for most young people so categorised the main institution involved has been the school' (Blackburn, 1990, p. 152). Young people with disabilities have traditionally been provided with a segregated education, either in separate schools from non-disabled young people or in separate classes in the same schools (as the figures above show).

While some young people have positive experiences of special schools and value the opportunity to 'develop alongside similarly disabled children and the freedom from day-to-day barriers' (French and Swain, 1997, p. 200), many dislike the isolation from other young people of their own age and from their own neighbourhoods (they frequently attend special schools as boarders) and believe that integrated education is better for all young people: 'I didn't have the opportunity to mix with my able-bodied peers and therefore failed to realise the negative reactions that form a part of everyday life … Attitudes towards disability would improve if children were allowed to gain direct experience of each other from an early age' (Noble, 2003, pp. 65–6).

A further common experience of young people with disabilities is that little is expected of them and it is assumed that they have limited interest in academic study and low aspirations for the future. The education sector is 'full of stereotyping' in this regard, according to one young disabled participant in a recent Irish study. Others spoke of being largely ignored by teachers and left 'just sitting around' in school, or complained of not having the same range of subject options as other young people. The following is an excerpt from a focus group discussion involving young people with a range of physical disabilities (Devlin, 2006, p. 37):

Bronagh: Why do most disabled schools not teach Irish?
Conor: Yeah, Irish and religion. The two most hated subjects!
Bronagh: They may be horrible but why are we not given a choice?

Barry: It would give you more options. You might be great at Irish.

Others: Yeah! [general agreement]

Bronagh: It's our native language. We have a right to learn it, like every other Irish citizen.

If special or segregated education for young people with disabilities can be criticised for not making the full range of subject options available, mainstream secondary schools (as opposed to other schools at second level) can also be faulted for insisting on a 'classical liberal' curriculum and not offering the technological and practical subjects such as wood technology, home economics and metalwork, or music at Junior Certificate level. Referring to Gardner's (1985) theory of multiple intelligences, a recent Irish study has pointed out that subjects such as those just mentioned frequently appeal to students whose interests and intelligences are in the bodily kinaesthetic, musical or visual-spatial spheres, rather than in the linguistic or mathematically based disciplines (although of course the different types of intelligence are not mutually exclusive). A failure to offer such subjects, or to provide the Leaving Certificate Applied or 'other curriculum options that appeal to students with abilities outside the traditional academic spheres', means that secondary schools are often responsible for a 'de facto exclusion' of young people with disabilities, a matter which needs to be addressed both by the schools themselves and by policy makers at national, regional and local level (Lodge and Lynch 2004, pp. 82–3).

The problem lies not only with curriculum options but also, and more fundamentally, with enrolment policies. In fact, late in 2006 the Minister for Education and Science ordered an audit of school enrolment policies amid increasing concern that some schools were excluding special needs students (as well as foreign national children). Figures published in a national newspaper a year earlier had indicated that special needs provision in Dublin schools was largely concentrated in disadvantaged areas (*The Irish Times*, 1 November 2005).

Where steps *have* been taken in recent years towards integrating young people with physical or sensory disabilities in mainstream schools (of whatever kind), insufficient attention has sometimes been paid to the complexity of this task and the range of factors to be taken into account to ensure that the experience is a positive and educationally beneficial one for all the young people involved. These factors include the need for adequate infrastructure, the provision of sufficient resources and appropriate training and an acknowledgement of the impact of societal attitudes on school experiences for the young people in question (Kenny et al., 2003, p. 139). One study of the experiences of young people who have transferred from special to mainstream schools (O'Donnell, 2003) highlights many positive outcomes relating to the participants' involvement in community activities, enhanced self-concept and expanded sense of opportunities for the future. However, it also documents the persistence of disadvantage and unequal treatment regarding both the formal curriculum and extra-curricular activities: 'Exclusion from involvement in physical education and class outings supports the literature that inclusive education means more than integration. The fundamental principles of equality and inclusion were not being practised with regard to these pupils' (O'Donnell, 2003, p. 250).

Level of Educational Qualifications

The negative experience of young people with disabilities in the education system relative to their peers without disabilities is reflected in the statistics regarding educational outcomes. In the 2001 Living in Ireland Survey referred to above, the proportion of all those over 15 with a chronic illness or disability who had no formal educational qualification was almost exactly 50 per cent, compared with just over 20 per cent of the rest of the population. Among the non-disabled population, the proportion with a third-level qualification was 22 per cent, more than double the figure for those with a disability or chronic illness (10 per cent). The Quarterly National Household Survey conducted in the second quarter of 2002 (with a sample of approximately 100,000 15- to 64-year-olds) included a special additional 'module' on disability. Its key identifying question ('Do you have any long-standing health problem or disability?') differed somewhat from the one used in the Living in Ireland Survey, leading inevitably to some differences in the findings, but the overall pattern regarding educational attainment is along similar lines: 'ill/disabled' respondents in the QNHS were much more likely to have no qualification than the rest of the respondents (41.9 per cent as compared with 19.7 per cent) and much less likely to have a third-level qualification (22.1 per cent as compared with 34.3 per cent).

Employment

Not surprisingly, differences in qualification levels are reflected in employment opportunities and experiences of young people (and older people) with disabilities. Using the same datasets referred to above, Gannon and Nolan (2004) reported that the labour market status of those reporting a long-standing illness or disability differed systematically from the rest of the samples. About 40 per cent of those reporting a long-standing or chronic illness or disability were in employment, and most of the remainder were inactive (outside the labour force) rather than unemployed. This compared with an employment rate of close to 70 per cent for those not reporting such a condition. Labour force participation appears to be clearly related to the extent of physical restriction associated with the illness or disability.

> [I]n the QNHS the employment rate for men who said they were severely restricted in the kind of work they could do was only 18 per cent, and for women in that situation it was only 15 per cent. In the Living in Ireland Survey, the employment rate for those who said they were severely hampered in their daily activities by a chronic illness or disability was only 24 per cent, compared with 64 per cent for those who were not hampered (Gannon and Nolan, 2004, p. 40).

These statistics are in keeping with other qualitative and quantitative Irish findings. Many participants at a national series of seminars for young people with disabilities a few years ago had never been employed on a full-time or even part-time basis (Browne, 2003). The obstacles they described were partly physical and practical, relating to the availability and accessibility of transport, design of buildings externally and internally and of public space in general. 'Getting a job is one thing, getting to and from work and overcoming problems which may arise in the workplace is another' (Browne, 2003, p. 11).

At least as significant are the obstacles posed by the attitudes of employers and other employees, just as the research shows that the attitudes of teachers and others students are often decisive in shaping the experiences of young people with disabilities in schools (Kenny et al., 2000). Not having a job, or (as a young person) a reasonable prospect of a job, is a profound material and psychological disadvantage in a society in which much of the 'sense of self' of adults is bound up with their occupational or professional identity, and in which many (if not most) leisure pursuits, which also enhance that sense of self and contribute to personal and social development, cost money. This is why it is increasingly common for young people to engage in part-time employment (see Chapter 6). A recent national study (de Róiste and Dinneen, 2005) found that among young people with special needs and sensory impairments, virtually none worked part-time, compared to more than one-third of the main sample.

Leisure Activities

The focus of the study just mentioned was on young people's leisure time activities, and it included a consideration of the particular barriers facing young people with disabilities. These included structural barriers like cost, lack of tailored programming and provision (for example, subtitling in cinemas), access and transport difficulties, inadequate changing facilities or the lack of appropriately adapted equipment in sports contexts, or the lack of provision for wheelchairs beside standard seating in cinemas and concert venues. One research participant made an important distinction: 'Most cinemas are wheelchair accessible but not necessarily wheelchair-friendly. For example, some don't have spaces for people to sit beside the wheelchairs which is needed as some of the lads need help to eat popcorn or to tap you on the shoulder to let you know if they want something' (de Róiste and Dinneen, 2005, p. 139).

As already mentioned, many young people with a sensory impairment, physical disability or special needs often attend boarding school or travel a long distance to school. This means that friendship groups can be widely dispersed, making it difficult to meet up informally to hang out, go to the cinema or play recreational sport. There are also interpersonal barriers, such as over-protectiveness on the part of parents, communication difficulties and negative attitudes of peers, similar to those encountered in school and the workplace. It is not surprising, therefore, that individual sports such as cycling, athletics, martial arts and aerobics tend to be more popular, particularly among young people with sensory disabilities.

Sexual Identity

Given the barriers mentioned above, and given that for most young people leisure activities are valued not just for their intrinsic enjoyment but for the opportunity to establish and develop relationships, it follows that young people with disabilities face particular difficulties when it comes to the exploration and expression of their sexual identities. Again, the challenge in this area is sometimes a fundamental attitudinal one:

> People with disabilities are denied their sexuality primarily by the stigma which surrounds and pervades disability. In a society in which the cult of the 'body beautiful' reigns one becomes less sexually acceptable the further one is from the stereotypes of beauty. For many people with disabilities this is a further burden on top of low economic and social status (Commission on the Status of People with Disabilities, 1997, p. 231).

As with the other areas described above, the challenges associated with sexual identity and expression can be experienced differently by young people with different types of disability, or by young men and women, or by those whose sexual orientation is gay, lesbian or bisexual, in which case they may have to deal with a 'double prejudice' (National Disability Authority, 2005b, p. 13). In any case, many of the difficulties encountered may arise from an unconscious need on the part of the rest of society to suppress the sexuality of people with disabilities. 'It is this need which must be tackled if those with disabilities are to enjoy equality in sexual matters' (Commission on the Status of People with Disabilities, 1997, p. 232).

Steps Towards Equality for Young People with Disabilities?

In concluding this section, it is important to acknowledge that significant steps have been taken towards achieving equality for people with disabilities in Ireland in recent years, although a lot remains to be done. The Employment Equality Acts 1998 and 2004 and the Equal Status Acts 2000 to 2004 both include disability as one of the nine grounds on the basis of which discrimination is prohibited. They also both include one significant 'positive duty' (Crowley, 2006, p. 71), namely a requirement on employers and service providers to make reasonable accommodation for people with disabilities. This means that service providers, including schools and other educational establishments, must do all that is reasonable to accommodate the needs of a person with a disability by providing special treatment or facilities in circumstances where without these it would be impossible or unduly difficult for the person to avail of the services, and as long as such provision would not incur more than what is referred to as a 'nominal cost'.

In the case of schools, the provisions of the Equal Status Acts 'rest on a presumption of mainstreaming for students with disabilities' (Lodge and Lynch, 2004, p. 78). A school is exempt from the requirement to provide service to a student with a disability only to the extent that doing so would have a seriously detrimental effect on the provision of service to other students, or make such provision impossible. The 'presumption' of mainstreaming was taken further with the Education for Persons with Special Educational Needs Act 2004, which provides that every child who has special educational needs must be educated in an inclusive environment with children who do not have such needs, unless this would not be in the child's own best interests or would impair the effective provision of education to others. However, the provisions of the Act are 'subject to available resources' and in practical terms will take several years to implement (National Disability Authority, 2005a, pp. 4–5).

A significant recent development, which it is hoped will have a very positive impact not just in Ireland but globally, was the agreement by the United Nations in August 2006 of a new treaty on the rights of people with disabilities. It does not invent new rights but seeks to ensure that existing human rights are fully and equally enjoyed by all. The treaty was warmly welcomed by disability organisations in Ireland. Despite the existence of equality legislation, it is clear from the information presented above that this country still has a long way to go in ensuring equality for people with disabilities, whether young or not so young.

YOUNG TRAVELLERS

A distinctive feature of the Traveller community is its age structure. In fact, almost two-thirds of Travellers are under 25 years of age. Travellers are a minority ethnic group indigenous to Ireland. They have many cultural similarities to the Gypsy communities in Britain and to the Roma communities of other parts of Europe, including a history and tradition of nomadism and of extended families living in close proximity. Travellers have their own language, known as *Shelta*, or by Travellers themselves as *Gammon* or *Cant*. While some Travellers live in houses, nomadism and the freedom to travel are vital aspects of Traveller culture and identity. As has been observed elsewhere (McCann et al., 1994, p. 96), just as settled people remain settled when they travel, Travellers remain Travellers even when they are not travelling! Other important aspects of Traveller culture are music and storytelling. The latter fulfils very significant social as well as recreational functions, in relation, for instance, to the dissemination of important information about health matters or work: 'Word of mouth is a strong and influential method of communication among the Traveller community in Ireland' (Jackson, 2005, p. 256).

Traditionally, Travellers gained employment through horse-trading, market-trading and tinsmithing, but today there are relatively few opportunities for work in these areas and many Travellers work in recycling. As regards 'mainstream' employment, and reflecting the growth of the Travellers' movement and of community development initiatives involving Travellers, most options nowadays probably exist in the community and voluntary sector. 'However, many of these jobs are over dependent on funding from active labour market [support] programmes and as a consequence are often low paid, with limited opportunities for sustainable employment' (Pavee Point, 2005, p. 37). Travellers are eight times more likely to be unemployed than settled people (Irwin, 2006).

Travellers and Ethnicity

The Irish government has so far resisted acknowledging that Travellers are a distinctive ethnic group, despite being urged to do so by the UN Committee on the Elimination of Racial Discrimination. For instance, the main equality legislation (the Employment Equality Acts 1998 and 2004 and the Equal Status Acts 2000 to 2004), in stipulating nine grounds on the basis of which discrimination is prohibited, identifies membership of the Traveller community as a separate ground from the race ground (which covers 'race', skin colour, nationality and ethnic origin). And yet the definition of the Traveller community used in the legislation highlights characteristics normally associated with ethnicity: 'people who are commonly called Travellers, who are identified both by Travellers and others as people with a shared history, culture and traditions, identified historically as a nomadic way of life on the island of Ireland'. A recent report by the Equality Authority (2006) points out that such an 'ethnic definition' of Travellers in the legislation was specifically understood by the Oireachtas as removing any doubts as to whether Travellers were entitled to the protections for ethnic groups provided for in the UN Convention, making the refusal of explicit recognition all the more surprising. The report reviews all the key academic literature on the issue and concludes that Travellers unquestionably meet the criteria for ethnicity. These include biological self-perpetuation; shared fundamental cultural values (including nomadism); obligations based on kinship, self-employment and distinctive beliefs relating to cleanliness and pollution; distinctive language and communication; and a name for themselves, just as settled people have a name for Travellers, and know to whom it applies.

The fact that Travellers have been regarded as a 'special case' rather than an ethnic minority has been reflected in their categorisation within the Census and in the practice of data gathering, meaning that statistics have been very unreliable in the past. Prior to 1996, Census records of the Travelling community were based on the enumerators' own determinations, meaning that only those Travellers in halting sites and on the roadside were counted and the overall Traveller population was underestimated by almost 100 per cent (Fanning, 2002, p. 161). This changed in 2002. According to that year's Census, there were about 24,000 Travellers in Ireland, although Traveller organisations argue that this is still an underestimate and that the true figure is likely to be closer to 30,000 (Pavee Point, 2005, p. 17).

Age Structure

According to the most recent Census figures, Travellers account for 0.6 per cent of the national population. As noted at the outset, the age structure of the Traveller community is very different from that of the settled population. Figure 11.1

demonstrates this diagrammatically. The pyramid representing the overall population is relatively narrow at the bottom, narrows further before bulging somewhat in the late teens and early twenties, and then tapers gradually up through the older age groups. The shape reflects the fact that the 'total fertility rate' in Ireland declined steadily from the 1970s to the early 1990s and has recovered slightly since then, while life expectancy for the population as a whole has continued to improve. The Traveller pyramid looks strikingly different, reflecting both higher birth rates and higher mortality rates. Only 3.3 per cent of Travellers are over 65, less than one-third of the proportion in that age group for the population as a whole (11.1 per cent). About 42 per cent of Travellers are aged under 15 years, double the rate for the general population (21 per cent); while 63 per cent of Travellers are under 25 (compared with less than 38 per cent). The average age of Travellers is 18; the national average is 32.

Figure 11.1 Population pyramid for the percentage of Irish Travellers and of the total population of the State at each age group

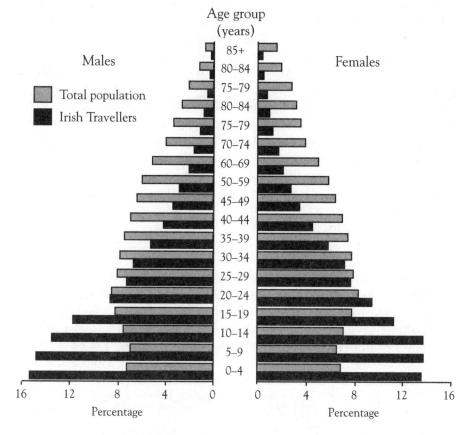

Source: Census of Population (2002).

These figures clearly have important implications for social policy. On the one hand, health policy and provision faces a massive challenge to enable Travellers to live longer and healthier lives. On the other, and especially relevant in the present context, all the various dimensions of youth policy (relating to education, training, youth and community work, social care services, play and leisure provision, and so on) have a particular relevance, indeed urgency, in the case of the Traveller community.

Obstacles and Inequalities

Young Travellers are confronted in their daily lives with a multitude of obstacles and disadvantages. At the most obvious material level, their accommodation and living conditions are often inferior to those of their settled peers because inadequate public provision continues to be made for suitable accommodation such as halting sites and group homes. Given such material inequality, it is not surprising that young Travellers are much more likely than young settled people to be in State care (see the section on care later in this chapter). Many Travellers continue to live on the side of the road without access to the most basic facilities. According to the 2002 Census, 56 per cent of Travellers were in permanent accommodation and 37 per cent in temporary accommodation (with the remainder not stated). Despite the publication of the *Report of the Task Force on the Travelling Community* (Government of Ireland, 1995b), the accommodation circumstances of Travellers had deteriorated by the end of the 1990s. The Monitoring Committee on the Task Force Report regarded it as 'particularly unsatisfactory' that one in every four Travellers was living without access to water, toilets and refuse collection and the number of Travellers living on the roadside had actually increased (Pavee Point, 2005, p. 26). Poor accommodation compounds existing health inequalities and, if anything, makes it more unlikely that Travellers of all ages will pay sufficient attention to their health: it is understandable that 'health programmes will have a low priority … as long as more immediate requirements such as food, shelter and warmth are unmet' (Jackson, 2005, p. 258).

Participation in Education

Research has clearly shown that (leaving aside cultural considerations, which will be returned to below) material inequalities have an impact on participation in and attitudes towards education (Drudy and Lynch, 1993, p. 162). Young Travellers are severely disadvantaged in terms of educational participation and outcomes, a pattern that continues to have profound implications for the Traveller community as a whole. Figures from the 2002 Census show that of those Travellers who answered the question as to what age they ceased full-time education, 66 per cent said they left school before the age of 15, as opposed to 15 per cent of the general population.

This is not to say that there has not been progress in relation to Traveller education in recent years. There has, in fact, been a pronounced improvement in the levels of Traveller enrolment, even at post-primary level. Drawing on figures provided by the National Education Officer for Travellers, Forkan (2006) shows that the number of young Travellers enrolled in post-primary schools increased from 100 in 1992 to 1,729 in 2003, an increase of 1,600 per cent over 12 years. However, there are persistent problems in the form of poor attendance at primary level (in one local case study, almost 30 per cent of the children missed more than 100 days from school in a year, with a further 22 per cent missing between 50 and 100 days) and very poor retention at second level. Of the cohort of 478 Traveller entrants to second level nationally in 1999, only 63 (13 per cent) remained until sixth year, and 33 per cent dropped out after first year (ibid).

A number of factors appear to be contributing to the problem. The study from which the statistics just cited are drawn also gathered qualitative data which suggests that the relationship between Traveller culture and formal education is complex. It is certainly not a question of young Travellers or their parents simply 'not liking' education or not seeing it as relevant. On the contrary, parents had a very positive attitude towards school and were very keen to see their children do well. They also had the perception that their children enjoyed school, a view generally borne out in discussions with young people themselves. However, it is still the case that family occasions like weddings, funerals and baptisms generally take precedence for Travellers over attendance at school.

The majority of Traveller boys still opt out of school after confirmation, attracted by the working life and its association with adulthood (Forkan, 2006, pp. 86–9). For girls, there is an expectation that they will get married young, at 16 or 17 or not long after, and if there is a choice between marriage and school, as one young woman said, 'Travellers will pick marriage' (ibid, p. 86). However, this too is changing, and the young women in the same study also had hopes of gaining access to courses in the future that would enhance their job prospects, even if married, and said that they would encourage their own children to stay on in post-primary education.

The organisation and culture of educational institutions themselves represent a further very significant factor in shaping the experiences and opportunities of young Travellers. There have been many positive recent developments, such as material and financial supports for pupils, the work of visiting teachers and home-school liaison officers, the complementary and supportive work of youth and community projects which offer pre-school, after-school and homework clubs as well as valuable opportunities for non-formal learning. However, Traveller young people continue to experience a pervasive lack of understanding or tolerance of their culture in mainstream schools. They also regard themselves as being treated differently – for instance, removed from integrated classes in Maths or English or kept back at primary level for longer than their settled peers – 'just because they are Travellers'. Their participation in extra-curricular activities is also an area in relation to which it appears schools should be more proactive (Forkan, 2006, p. 90). Of course, the climate of mainstream schools will to a large extent reflect the attitudes and practices which prevail in society more broadly, and this is a further crucial factor (perhaps the decisive one) which much be taken into account. As Kenny (1997, p. 90) suggests, what appear to be the 'innate cultural practices' of a particular group are often actually the outcomes of 'structural exclusion and inequalities', and must be addressed at that level.

Leisure Activities

Not surprisingly, young Travellers' experiences in their leisure time also differ considerably from those of their settled peers, and again this can be explained by a variety of factors. One recent study found that as girls in the Traveller community move towards their teens, they may be discouraged from participating in sports and hobbies and instead encouraged and expected to participate in helping out at home. Mixed sports are more likely to be discouraged. For boys and young men, looking after animals is a popular pastime, and in keeping with traditional Traveller lifestyles, many have a particular interest in horses; it is often a 'family thing' with their fathers or grandfathers being 'horse men', although one young man in the study also spoke about his grandmother's keen interest in horses (de Róiste and Dinneen, 2005, pp. 141–2). Part-time work is common for young male Travellers (as it has increasingly become for young settled people). It is done mostly over the weekend with fathers, uncles and cousins and might include gardening, tarring and selling. Again, there is a gender difference here, with young women more likely to be engaged in unpaid cooking, cleaning and baby-sitting duties (ibid).

Travellers of all ages regularly encounter prejudice and discrimination in their dealings with leisure facilities and public amenities. There have been numerous cases under the Equal Status legislation highlighting the unequal treatment (usually a refusal of service) of Travellers in pubs, restaurants and hotels. In the study by de Róiste and Dinneen (2005, p. 137–8), young Traveller men spoke of being discriminated against in some sports clubs. A 'quota system' might be in place, meaning that once two or three Travellers were in membership, no more would be admitted. This could be dealt with by 'passing' (concealing some aspect of one's identity): 'Sometimes you'd hide your identity until you'd get in and then after a while you'd let them know you were a Traveller'. While perhaps effective (in a sense), this strategy was considered wrong by the young men, and the necessity to do it was seen as an infringement of their rights. For both young men and women, being turned away at pubs and clubs is another common experience. As one young Traveller woman explained in a recent study of stereotyping and inequality (Devlin, 2006, p. 31):

When we want to go out at the weekend, there's nowhere to go because we're not allowed into pubs and nightclubs. They say you have to show your ID, so you're not let in that week, so you go the following week and they say 'No, you're not a regular'. But how can you become a regular when you're not allowed in?

The following exchange from the same study shows how anti-Traveller prejudice can be compounded by negative views of young people in general. Some young Traveller men had been recently refused entry to a cinema (Devlin, 2006, pp. 31–2):

John:	She wanted us out [the woman at the door].
Patrick:	But we wouldn't get out.
Researcher:	And can I ask you if she wouldn't let you in because you were young men or because you were young Travellers?
John:	Young Travellers.
Patrick:	Both. We were Travellers.
John:	Young Travellers. Young Travellers.

This passage is a practical illustration from young people's own perspective of the point made at the outset of this chapter. Understanding young people's experiences means taking into account the ways in which they are similar by virtue of their age *and* the ways in which they are different by virtue of other aspects of their identities.

YOUNG SEPARATED ASYLUM SEEKERS AND AGED-OUT MINORS

The history and traditions of the Traveller community provide one example of how Ireland is, and has long been, home to more than one culture. However, the multicultural character of this society has increased markedly in recent years. As the *National Youth Work Development Plan* puts it (Department of Education and Science, 2003a, p. 2):

Ireland has never been entirely monocultural: it has long been home, to one degree or another, to people of different cultures, different religious, political and ethnic backgrounds, including the Travelling community. For generations it has had the linguistic diversity of two languages, Irish and English. The multicultural nature of Irish society has, however, in recent years become much more pronounced, as people have increasingly come here from other parts of the world, whether because they have been actively encouraged to come here to work, or because they are seeking asylum.

Immigration to Ireland

Immigration has been a striking feature of Irish demographics in recent years. Although there has been a natural increase (the difference between births and deaths, which in 2006 was twice the level recorded in the mid-1990s but still lower than it was in the 1970s), immigration is the primary reason for the increase in the population from 3.9 million in 2002 to 4.2 million as recorded in the 2006 Census, the highest total since 1861 and the highest rise (proportionately) in the European

Union. The level of inward migration is such that 10 per cent of the population – 400,000 people – are foreign nationals. Many of these are migrant workers from the more recently acceded EU member states. In the two years 2004 to 2006, almost 230,000 people from these countries received PPS (Personal Public Service) numbers in Ireland, with more than half of these being received by Polish people. There is also a long-established Chinese community in Ireland, which currently numbers approximately 60,000. Many people have also come to live in Ireland in recent years from Africa, in particular Nigeria (close to 30,000). And of course there are significant numbers of people from other English-speaking countries, especially the UK (25,000) and the US (6,000).

The experience of the immigrants in these different groups can vary significantly, and the experience can also vary within each group, depending on when they came, the reason for coming here and the way in which the person's (or family's) arrival has been dealt with. It can also vary, of course, by age. Arriving in Ireland as a migrant worker can present many challenges, linguistically and culturally, and whatever their reason for being in Ireland, people from different national and ethnic backgrounds are vulnerable to racist abuse (European Monitoring Centre on Racism and Xenophobia, 2006).

Seeking Asylum

Immigrants are likely to be more vulnerable in every sense if they have come here seeking asylum. This is particularly true if they are young and alone, or accompanied by people other than those who would normally care for them. An asylum seeker is any individual who has applied for refugee status under the criteria of the United Nations Geneva Convention Relating to the Status of Refugees (1951). Section 2 of the Irish Refugee Act of 1996 incorporates the Convention's definition of a refugee (in Article 1) into national law:

> A person who is outside his/her country of nationality or habitual residence; has a well-founded fear of persecution because of his/her race, religion, nationality, membership of a particular social group or political opinion; and is unable or unwilling to avail himself/herself of the protection of that country, or to return there, for fear of persecution.

The process of granting refugee status can take up to two years. Once such status is granted, the holder has the same rights and privileges as Irish citizens. While the application is being considered, the applicant has the temporary status of asylum seeker. Asylum seekers cannot leave the State without the permission of the Minister for Justice, Equality and Law Reform and cannot seek or take up employment. Those who entered Ireland before 26 July 1999 and have waited for at least a year for a determination on their case may be given a 'right to work' by the Department of Justice, Equality and Law Reform. Those who arrived after April 2000 are provided for by 'direct provision' and are regionally resettled in full-board accommodation (Keogh and Whyte, 2003, p. 4). A person who does not meet the requirements of the definition of refugee under the UN Convention may be granted humanitarian 'leave to remain' at the discretion of the Minister under section 3 of the Immigration Act 2003. People with such leave to remain have almost all the same social and economic rights as refugees, including access to full-time education (ibid).

A particularly vulnerable group of asylum seekers are separated children, people under the age of 18 who arrive in Ireland alone or in the company of people other than their carers. While a detailed age breakdown of asylum seekers is not available, one estimate has placed the proportion which is under 18 at 27 per cent (see McRea, 2003, p. 1). The reasons for leaving their country of origin may include war or political upheaval, parental detention or death, poverty, discrimination or persecution, trafficking, exploitation or abuse. Their journey to Ireland may frequently have exposed them to further danger or ill treatment (Veale et al., 2003). The United Nations Convention on the Rights of the Child requires in Article 22(1) that signatory states take measures to ensure that such children receive 'appropriate protection and humanitarian assistance' in the enjoyment of the rights set out in the Convention and other relevant international instruments. In Ireland, the provisions of the Child Care Act of 1991 (discussed in Chapter 10) oblige the health authorities to identify children within their geographical area who are not receiving adequate care and attention and to take them into their care. This does, of course, include children who are separated asylum seekers, but since the Act does not make specific provision for such children, they are treated as homeless Irish children for welfare purposes, meaning that their care is often 'inappropriate and disordered' (McCann James, 2005, p. 324), a point returned to below.

It is very difficult to accurately establish the number of separated children seeking asylum in Ireland. This is because data are gathered by a number of different agencies and not all use the same systems or procedures. Phillips (2006, p. 3) highlights the following difficulties:

- Not all Health Service Executive (HSE) areas enter the children in the asylum process and not all children are entered.
- Some HSE areas do not differentiate between separated children seeking asylum and other children in their care.
- Some children are smuggled into the country and come to the attention of the authorities at a late stage or not at all.
- National, age or status-referenced figures on the total number of children in the system are not readily available.

One estimate suggests that in 1999 there were 32 separated children seeking asylum in Ireland and that by 2003 the total (over the four years) referred to the North Eastern Area Health Board had come to approximately 2,717 (McCann James, 2005, p. 322, citing unpublished Health Board figures). Of these, nearly half were reunited with family members already in Ireland and the remainder made applications for asylum or had them made on their behalf. Reunification is not by any means a straightforward process (Phillips, 2006, p. 4). There have been concerns about the lack of checks for young asylum seekers reunited with adults claiming to be family members and there is little if any follow-up care or monitoring (O'Brien, 2006a). At any one time there are approximately 200 young asylum seekers in State care in Ireland (ibid).

HSE statistics show that the majority of separated children have originated in Nigeria (accounting for the largest proportion by far, at 44 per cent), with lower figures for other African countries including Sierra Leone, Congo, Ghana, Cameroon and Zimbabwe (Phillips, 2006, p. 4). Close to 100 have also come from Romania (McRea, 2003, p. iv). According to studies to date, all separated children seeking asylum are living in Dublin. As regards age, one study suggests that about half were 17 to 18, more than a third 18 to 21, a further 10 per cent 16 years old and the remainder under 16 (Phillips, 2006, p. 4). Just as the process of leaving care for Irish young people is a fraught and troubled process (discussed later in this chapter), so too there can be additional difficulties for separated young asylum seekers who cease to be children in legal terms and whose status therefore changes. Such young people are usually referred to as 'aged-out minors'.

Once they have come to the attention of the health authorities, officials can seek refugee status on behalf of separated children and pay the costs incurred. The young people are then placed in emergency accommodation and supported through supplementary welfare allowance and exceptional needs payments, depending on their age and circumstances. They are entitled to educational and other services (Keogh and Whyte, 2003, p. 5). Aged-out minors are accommodated separately in centres operated under contract with the Reception and Integration Agency (RIA), which is under the aegis of the Department of Justice, Equality and Law Reform.

Separated children face enormous challenges. They are unquestionably among the most vulnerable groups in Ireland. Simply dealing with the trauma (in most cases) that prompted them to leave their country of origin is a continuing burden. Like other immigrants, they regularly have to deal with racist incidents and being relatively young and inexperienced, and in a foreign context (in every sense), they may be ill-equipped to do so. McRea (2003) has identified a number of other challenges:

- They are forced to deal with the refugee determination process and with adapting to a new country without the support of family or other social networks.
- They lack the usual support or assistance with everyday tasks like managing money or getting up for school.
- They face restricted educational and leisure opportunities.
- Most live in communal accommodation with few recreation facilities.
- They are susceptible to feelings of boredom, cultural dislocation and loneliness.

These points are borne out in a recent questionnaire survey (complemented by focus group discussions) of 47 separated children and aged-out minors staying in HSE centres and RIA hostels in Dublin (Phillips, 2006). More than half of the young people (53.5 per cent) had experienced racist abuse. The vast majority had known nothing about Ireland or about the asylum process when they came here (89 per cent in both cases). They found the application process difficult and the wait for an outcome troubling and unsettling.

They were generally unhappy with the overcrowding and lack of privacy in their accommodation (some spoke of their personal mail being opened) and criticised the food for its lack of quality, freshness and variety (there were accounts of big improvements in the food immediately prior to inspection visits, which are meant to be unannounced, with a return to the usual standards afterwards). The young people were generally not consulted or asked to contribute to decisions about food, visiting hours, reporting requirements or other matters affecting them, and gave examples of rules that were inconsistent and/or unexplained. They had little or no recreational facilities in their hostels or centres. There was a lack of support for their own mother culture. In a telling sign of their extreme vulnerability, a fear was expressed at all the focus groups of making complaints about standards of accommodation or about poor treatment by hostel or centre staff, in case it would jeopardise the young people's asylum applications.

Difficulties in Education

Many of the concerns and difficulties of the young people in the study related to education. It was difficult even to gain access to a place in school if their arrival was after September. The school would have little incentive to accommodate them because late entrants are not counted for school capitation grants or for teacher allocation grants the following year. Of course, the school might also be full. In any event, as Phillips says (2006, p. 28), 'there seems to be an over-concentration of [separated children seeking asylum] in certain inner city schools, some of which may be excellent in terms of cultural supports, but the distance factor is a real issue'. Distance is an issue because most of the children reside in south County Dublin. Travelling a long way every day is difficult and tiring in itself (as many Irish students and commuters know all too well), but there are additional implications for young people without the usual supports of family and friendship groups. Cost is one obvious concern. Some students who travel long distances and who have a 'favourably disposed Community Welfare Officer' (ibid, p. 30) receive money for a bus pass. Others do not, adding to the difficulty of gaining access not just to educational but also recreational and cultural facilities. Going to school locally would cost less and give the young people more time and opportunities to get involved with local social activities and young people.

In school, English language support is of insufficient quality and duration (and the research suggests that the young people may overestimate their own proficiency).

Unqualified teachers often provide such support, and there is no formal curriculum relating to English as an additional language (EAL). No supports are available to enable them to retain their mother tongue, a very serious omission in a situation where only a minority will be successful in their application for asylum. Just nine per cent of all applications up to March 2003 resulted in refugee status, with 65 per cent refused, 11 per cent withdrawn and 15 per cent under consideration (Veale et al., 2003). Compounding these obstacles, it is very difficult for the young people to study or do 'homework' in hostels where separate study facilities are rare or non-existent and the norm for sleeping arrangements is 'at least two and sometimes four to a room' (Phillips, 2006, p. 16). Finally, although the vast majority (98 per cent) are interested in further or higher education, they face considerable policy, institutional and financial barriers, such as having to pay 'non-EU' college fees, which are far beyond their means in the overwhelming majority of cases.

Accommodation and Care Facilities

Given their circumstances, the nature of the care received by separated children seeking asylum is of key importance, yet as suggested above, there are very serious weaknesses and disparities in the current system. In effect, the Irish care system is a two-tier one with separated children being placed in privately run hostels operated by staff who for the most part are not professionally qualified. There are poor ratios of staff to residents, the hostels do not meet the standards required for other children and are not subject to inspection by the Social Services Inspectorate. In 2006 the media reported that a residential centre accommodating 24 young people was continuing to be funded by the HSE a year after it had failed to meet the standards for registration. The same journalist reported that 250 separated children had disappeared from care over the previous five years, noting that if the same thing happened to Irish young people, 'there would be cries of protest and anger', but instead there was 'barely a whimper of public debate' (O'Brien, 2006a). The Ombudsman for Children has said that the inferior care provided to separated children seeking asylum is unacceptable and 'places the State in breach of its obligation to prevent discrimination under the UN Convention on the Rights of the Child and the European Convention on Human Rights' (Ombudsman for Children, 2006.)

The young people surveyed in the recent study had limited levels of contact and support from social work and social care staff: almost half of them saw a professional social or project worker only once a month or less frequently, and even then the contact was likely to be only for 15–30 minutes (Phillips, 2006, p. 18). While some hostels are of course well managed and run, there are many accounts of staff, who in most cases are not qualified social care workers, abusing their position or behaving in a manner that is far from 'caring'. The research report recommends that all hostel staff should be care workers, and that in addition there should be a system of trained adult mentors for all separated children. The care setting itself is in most cases inappropriate:

No children should be placed in hostels. Foster care or supported lodgings (i.e. family placement) should be the first preference. Other semi-independent arrangements in small units with resident trained house parents may be appropriate for some older children or aged-out minors. There should be a constant presence of HSE staff in existing hostels. Ideally, these should be round the clock care staff ... [R]epresentative systems should be established to allow residents to make some input into day-to-day food, visitor access, and study arrangements (Phillips, 2006, pp. 43–4).

The transition to aged-out minor status requires additional psycho-social support. Those aged 18 to 21 and under the justice system may at present have no form of adult support or guidance at all. Again, this is a reflection of a two-tier system since Irish young people in that age group leaving care are often provided with such a service (although not always, which is itself a problem, as will be seen later in this chapter).

Adapting to Cultural Differences

While this section has highlighted the position of separated children and young people because of their particular vulnerability, they are part of a larger pattern of increasing migration and a marked increase in the multicultural nature of Irish society. As the *National Youth Work Development Plan* acknowledges (Department of Education and Science, 2003a, p. 3), this means that there is an enhanced need for 'intercultural attitudes and awareness among young people and those who work with them'. Such an awareness should take account of the fact that the concept of youth itself is culturally constructed, a topic discussed earlier in this book. As one respondent in a study of youth work responses to separated children put it: 'Calling something youth work may not appeal to a 17-year-old Cameroonian girl who is perceived as an adult and is given adult responsibilities in her country of origin' (McRea, 2003, p. 28). The challenge extends beyond youth work to social work, care work and of course the education system. There is a need both for targeted initiatives recognising and responding to the needs and circumstances of particular groups – for instance, Lesovitch (2005) reports on the context and challenges relating to Roma educational needs in Ireland – and for broader strategies of training and awareness-raising to equip young people and adults to run institutions and organisations interculturally, using cultural diversity as a resource. A recent study of the experiences of immigrant students in second-level schools (including but not limited to separated children) highlights some of the features of their 'extraordinary lives' (Keogh and Whyte, 2003, p. 17).

All of the immigrant students had experienced great change in their lives through moving to Ireland. Coming to a new country means leaving friends and family behind. One girl who had only been here for two months talked about how much she missed her friends. Another had not seen her mother for two years. In addition, starting life in a new country means trying to adapt to a new culture and becoming familiar with social practices. For some students, simple things like sex roles and the way people socialise are totally different. Family roles and relationships have to alter and adapt, and this may be a difficult process. Some students found that they are now part of a religious or ethnic minority and have had to deal with hostility and prejudice. In many ways, people who are starting a new life in a new country have to reinvent themselves.

In welcoming these migrant young people and living and learning with them, there are also, of course challenges and opportunities for Irish young people and those of us who work with young people or work to further their interest, to do some reinventing of our own.

YOUNG PEOPLE IN CARE AND LEAVING CARE

The issue of child care has arisen several times already in this chapter. The structure of the Irish child care system was outlined in Chapter 10, which summarised the main provisions of the Child Care Act 1991 and indicated that at the end of 2004 there were 5,060 children in care in Ireland. These were fairly evenly divided in gender terms (2,451 girls and 2,609 boys). There are many reasons why children and young people find themselves in need of State care. However, in the vast majority of cases, these reasons relate in one way or another to social class. As Gilligan (1991, p. 19) has suggested:

> Socio-economic factors play a major part in shaping the destinies of Irish children. Social class has an overwhelming, if largely unacknowledged, influence on their chances in life. There is an inexorable association between lower social class and inferior outcome on a whole series of measures, such as infant mortality, general health, educational attainment or employment prospects ... Children from lower social classes are more at risk of becoming involved in drug abuse, delinquency or of being subjected to abuse. They are more likely to live in physical environments that are barren and impoverished.

Child Poverty

Poverty appears to be the underlying cause behind most children being admitted into care. There may be a perception that physical or sexual abuse in the home is a dominant factor but about half of admissions into care are due to neglect, difficulties with housing or finance, or parents' inability to cope. Families in such circumstances 'have often fallen through society's cracks and find themselves unable to access support because of educational disadvantage, addiction problems or social exclusion' (O'Brien, 2006b). Kelleher et al. (2000, p. 2) note that middle- or upper-class families are better placed to finance the supports needed in a situation of family crisis or breakdown, whereas 'lower-income families, lacking such supports, are more likely to come to the attention of the Gardaí and social work services'.

If poverty and deprivation are the main factors behind children needing State care, then clearly a question arises about the adequacy of the support available to families in such circumstances. O'Brien (2006b) highlights figures from an unpublished Department of Health report which show that the west of Ireland has the highest level of investment in family support services, while the east has the lowest level, and concludes: 'It is hardly a coincidence that the west has the lowest rates of children in care (31 per 10,000) while the east has the highest (57 per 10,000) … [T]hese regional variations indicate that children's chances of ending up in State care depend on where they live.' A greater preventative emphasis on family support, parenting skills, youth advocacy programmes and access to therapeutic services would, according to O'Brien, play a major role in reducing the need for State care. Given the decisive underlying role the State plays in so many cases, eradicating poverty would be the most effective strategy of all, and yet child poverty remains a persistent problem even in a society awash with money (see Chapter 12).

Being in Care

The proportion of young people in care who are being fostered has increased markedly in recent decades. In 1982 it was 52 per cent (Gilligan, 1991, p. 188). In 2004 it was 84 per cent, up 4 per cent on the previous year's figure (Irish Association of Young People in Care, 2006). Almost one-third of the young people being fostered are with relatives, and the number in relative foster care increased by 112 per cent between 1998 and 2004 (ibid). Children in foster care for the most part lead fairly 'regular' lives, especially if the fostering arrangement has continued for some time. A study by Daly and Gilligan (2005) found that 98 per cent of 13- to 14-year-olds in long-term foster care regularly attended school, 90 per cent had regular friends and 90 per cent a hobby they engaged in at home. With a view to 'normalising' the fostering arrangement from the point of view of both adults and children, the Child Care (Amendment) Bill 2006 provided that relatives and other foster parents who had taken care of a child for a continuous period of five years would no longer need to seek HSE permission in regard to certain decisions pertaining to the young person's welfare, such as medical and dental treatment or going on school trips.

Of the 5,060 children in care in 2004, 365 (7 per cent) were in residential care and 452 (9 per cent) in 'high support' or 'special' care (Irish Association of Young People in Care, 2006). Obviously being in care in a residential centre is very different from being fostered in a family home. In the previous section we saw that separated children seeking asylum appear for the most part to have negative experiences of residential care. We might expect the experience for Irish young people to be very different. For one thing, the centres they live in are subject to inspection by the Social Services Inspectorate, which has clear implications for standards and facilities. In most cases they also do not have to deal with the linguistic and cultural obstacles facing the separated children, although young Irish Travellers certainly face difficulties in this regard, and they are more likely than young settled people to end up in care (in the study by Kelleher et al. (2000), young Travellers made up 9 per cent of the Health Board population and 12 per cent of the special school population despite accounting for only 0.4 per cent of the national population according to the Census figures at the time). In any case, wherever they are from, it is likely that young people in care will have a profound sense of displacement. However considerate and personable their social workers and care workers, there will almost inevitably be some sense of institutionalisation in residential centres, particularly those catering for relatively large numbers of young people. Care workers operate in an environment which is frequently highly stressful, where they are in a position of responsibility for very vulnerable people and where they have to be conscious that 'even their most innocent remarks or normal displays of affection' may be open to misinterpretation (Kelleher et al., 2000, p. 31). In such a climate, there is a sense that 'the remedies being put in place to redress abuses of the past are leading to practices that lack spontaneity and are clinically devoid of feeling' (ibid).

The Views of Young People About Being in Care

The Irish Association of Young People in Care (IAYPIC) used focus-group research to seek the views of young people in care themselves as part of the consultation process surrounding its establishment. Issues identified included the need for separate provision for different age groups; the age of care staff; school arrangements; being uprooted from family; and – a familiar topic – the lack of opportunities for the young people to participate in decision-making which affected them. In fact, the authors remarked: 'Many times when we told young people why we wanted to talk to them, they asked what would be the point in talking about what they thought, as it wouldn't change anything anyway' (Costello and Carty, 2003, p. 14). The following excerpts give a sense of the young people's views in their own words (ages are given if available):

> There should be more places for young people to live in. They should be divided into places for 7- to 12-year-olds; 12- to 15-year-olds and 15- to 18-year-olds. 18-year-olds shouldn't be in with 7-year-olds. It's not fair – the older person gets treated like the 7-year-old, so that there is hassle about bedtimes etc., but the older person isn't treated like an adult and that leads to problems in the long run. Older young people feel mistrusted and feel that they are being treated like children (Linda, 18).

> The staff are too young. In my unit some of the staff are 19. They are the same age as me and come into the unit telling me what to do when I've been living there all my life. It's my home and they forget that. The staff shouldn't be the same age as the children and young people they are working with (Jennifer, 19).

Staff don't treat you badly – it's just like a normal house. You get treated well. You don't get hit. You get attention. They let you have a say about your food. If you're feeling down they'll come over to ask you what's wrong. I like having a keyworker, that person knows your business and they wash your clothes and everything (Mary, 12).

In moving to the residential home I was already losing out on many choices including changing schools, moving away from friends and family. I think that the staff of my house were very aware of this and tried as much as possible to accommodate me, even by giving me the choice of what local school I attended. Going to school was not something that was forced upon me but it was something that was encouraged and emphasised, and I chose to continue with my education with which I was given great help (Tammy).

I had a review but I didn't want to be there when everyone was talking about me. I didn't like the review form – I found it really hard to be able to write down positive things about myself. Some questions were stupid. In my report they said that I couldn't settle down … I'm a twin, I didn't understand why I was in care and why he wasn't. (Jason, 19).

Do you see here, I'd change this whole place, I'd paint the walls peach or something, I'd get different curtains, I'd make the room a little bit darker, and I'd have a lampshade or something like that. (Tony)

After Leaving Care

Some of the young people quoted above are in their late teens. A major issue in Irish child care services in recent years has been the lack of 'after care' for young people in care who reach the age of 18 and are no longer legally children. The Child Care Act 1991 (section 45) empowers the health authorities to provide after care support up to the age of 21 to young people who have been in their care, by visiting them where they live, arranging for the completion of their education (in which case the age limit of 21 may be extended), placing them in work, arranging for hostel or other forms of accommodation and co-operating with housing authorities. This provision of the legislation represented a 'significant extension' of the powers of the health authorities in relation to after care (Kelleher et al., 2000, p. 162). However, it is a discretionary power rather than a statutory responsibility (a point returned to below).

Ideally, young people in State care should be given the opportunity not just to get away from the impoverished, dysfunctional or abusive circumstances in which they had found themselves. but to experience an affirming, nurturing and supportive environment which would enable them to grow up with a 'positive self-worth and identity' (Kelleher et al., 2000, p. 1). While never a substitute for a loving and stable family, it would assist them to explore options and begin to plan and prepare for the future, and then support them further as they set out to build that future. As Gilligan (1991, p. 208) has put it: 'Care is not just about maintenance and shelter. It is about the transmission of skills and values which will sustain young people when they are no longer in care.' However, the research evidence to date regarding the effectiveness of the care system in practice is 'at best ambivalent' (ibid, p. 190). A detailed Irish study of young people leaving care makes it clear that the care system can in fact compound the young person's disadvantage.

> Being in care can cause further disruption and instability in children's lives. They can feel stigmatised for being in care and not living in a 'normal' family environment. Young people in long-term health board care may lack a basic knowledge of their family background. Separation from parents and siblings for young people in care can cause enormous hurt, grief, shame and anger. Multiple admissions to care, multiple placements while in care, and inappropriate placements can undermine their already fragile sense of their own identity. When placements break down, the young person is often made to feel that it is his or her own fault, and this can result in an increased sense of insecurity and anxiety (Kelleher et al., 2000, pp. 2–3).

Kelleher et al. studied 165 young people leaving different types of care setting: one-third leaving health board care, just under two-thirds leaving 'special schools' and a small number leaving probation hostels run by the Probation and Welfare Service of the Department of Justice. They found that 'the majority of young people leaving State care fail to make successful transitions from care' (Kelleher et al., 2000, p. 3). Their study set out to track the young people six months, and again two years, after leaving care, and they succeeded in doing so with a large majority of the sample (although they were not able to conduct the second tracking exercise with the young people leaving the probation hostels, who were a small minority of the total). Two years after leaving care, the lives of many of the young people were characterised by 'despair, hopelessness and chronic social instability'. Care staff and social workers estimated that 59 per cent of the Health Board population, and 76 per cent of the special school population, were in need of additional services such as supported accommodation, addiction treatment, counselling and intensive probation supervision (ibid, p. 14). Table 11.1 presents figures for some of the main difficulties facing the two groups: problems with addiction, 'unresolved problems surrounding childhood sexual abuse', suspicion (on the part of care staff and social workers) of involvement in prostitution, being (or having been) in a place of detention, and – the highest figures of all – experiencing homelessness. This latter issue will be returned to in the following section.

Table 11.1 Difficulties two years after leaving care

Difficulties	Health Board (%)	Special Schools (%)
Accommodation difficulties	27	30
Addiction	30	43
(Unresolved) childhood sexual abuse	23	12
Prostitution	14	3
Detention	25	65
Homelessness	68	33

Source: Kelleher et al. (2000).

Planning for After Care

The authors of the study just cited highlighted the lack of any written policy on aftercare on the part of the Department of Health and Children and the fact that such provision was at the discretion of social work managers in community care areas. They also noted that many foster families frequently provide aftercare for young care leavers in their own time and from their own resources. In keeping with their findings, one of the key recommendations arising out of the research was that there should be a Ministerial Order under the Child Care Act 1991 to ensure adequate aftercare for young people leaving the care of the health authorities and a similar order or, if necessary, new legislation relating to special schools. Since the study was published, some progress has been made in that national *Guidelines on Leaving Care and Aftercare Support* have been prepared and have been disseminated to all the area health authorities by the Social Services Inspectorate – a body which was not in place at the time the research was carried out and whose establishment was called for in the report. The guidelines document recognises that the ultimate challenge is to ensure that young people leave care in better circumstances than they arrived, and urges providers of care to put strategies in place to plan for the young person's departure from care *as soon as he or she is admitted*. The guidelines also recommend helping young people to develop and maintain social networks appropriate to their age, state that health authorities will maintain links so as to continue to promote the young person's welfare at least until the age of 21, and highlight the value of 'specialist leaving care schemes' which actively engage young people in decisions affecting them, 'often in ways that contrast starkly with their experiences whilst in care' (SSI, 2004). The guidelines are an elaboration of the relevant section of the *National Standards for Children's Residential Centres* (Department of Health and Children, 2001b). They also complement the 'Aftercare Protocol' outlined in the *Youth Homelessness Strategy* (Department of Health and Children, 2001a, pp. 27–8), which states that aftercare is 'an integral part of the care process, not an optional extra', and says that an aftercare support plan will be drawn up as part of the overall care plan for young people.

These developments are, of course, to be welcomed and are an improvement on the situation which pertained before. However, they still do not impose a statutory responsibility on the health authorities for the welfare of young people leaving care. This contrasts with the situation in England and Northern Ireland, where, respectively, the Children Act 1989 and the Children (NI) Order 1993 place a duty on local authorities to advise and befriend young people under 21 years. They also have a duty to accommodate any child in need who is 16 or more and whose welfare is otherwise likely to be seriously prejudiced (Kelleher et al., 2000, p. 52).

YOUNG HOMELESS PEOPLE

As the figures in the previous section indicate, there is a strong relationship between leaving care and homelessness. This is not because leaving care 'causes' homelessness, but because the factors associated with needing State care overlap substantially with the factors that predispose people to a risk of homelessness, and because the care system has not been sufficiently effective in countering the effects of these factors. While youth homelessness and adult homelessness have much in common, they are also different, particularly when we are talking about younger children. This is acknowledged in the *Youth Homelessness Strategy*:

> The key difference is that the vast majority of children under the age of 18 have a place of residence from which to operate; this may be their home, or an alternative form of accommodation supplied by a health board or a voluntary agency. In essence, when a young person becomes homeless, it is because they can no longer operate from this base. The term 'out of home' ... is sometimes used when referring to children who are homeless, as this takes cognisance of the fact that there is a place of residence available which has become, for whatever reason, a place where the young person feels that she or he can no longer live (Department of Health and Children, 2001a, p. 11).

Homelessness is a broad concept, encompassing a range of circumstances or experiences from sleeping rough to living in highly insecure or unsatisfactory conditions (Gilligan, 1991, p. 50). In addition, and related to this last point, when giving consideration to the issue of youth homelessness, it is now generally agreed that we need to take into account a 'continuum of housing situations', ranging from young people at risk of homelessness to those who are temporarily without shelter to those individuals who are persistently homeless (Mayock and Vekic, 2006, p. 4).

Youth homelessness in Ireland, as elsewhere, is primarily an urban phenomenon and Dublin city has consistently had the highest numbers of homeless young people. In the late 1980s, a study by the Streetwise National Coalition found that there were 405 homeless young people in Dublin and 225 in other cities, including Cork, Limerick, Waterford and Galway (ibid). Throughout the 1990s a variety of studies by statutory and voluntary agencies confirmed the existence of a serious problem of children and young people out of home, or at risk of homelessness.

In March 2005 the Homeless Agency carried out an assessment of the number of homeless persons in Dublin, which included people sleeping rough and in emergency accommodation as well as those on local authority lists. It found that there was a total homeless population of 2,015 individuals, comprising 1,552 adults and 463 child dependents (under 18). Of the adults, 62 were aged 18 to 20 and a further 203 aged 21 to 25. The figures showed a significant reduction from the previous survey in 2002, but since the earlier figures had not been validated in the way the more recent ones were, it is difficult to be confident about the extent of the drop in numbers (Homeless Agency, 2005). Of course, a numerical reduction does not make the experience of homelessness any less damaging or demeaning for those who remain affected.

In any case, national figures compiled by the Health Services Executive and the Department of Health suggest that the problem of homelessness, at least among young people, has not diminished and may even be getting worse. According to their estimate, there were 492 homeless children in Ireland in 2004, up from 476 in 2003. Most of these were in their mid- to late teens (although there were 22 under the age of 12) and the largest proportion – 210 – were in greater Dublin (O'Brien, 2006c). These figures relate to homeless children on their own and do not include children in homeless families (for a discussion of the particular difficulties facing children in families living in emergency accommodation, see Halpenny et al., 2002).

Pathways into Homelessness

A recent qualitative study of homeless young people in Dublin (Mayock and Vekic, 2006) uses the research method of 'life history interviewing' to explore the participants' 'pathways into homelessness' and their 'homeless careers' to date (this is the first stage of a planned longitudinal cohort study; in other words, the intention is to do follow-up research with the same people in the future). The sample consisted of 40 young people (23 male and 17 female) whose ages ranged from 12 to 22, with the vast majority between 15 and 21. They included five young people who had not been born in Ireland (two from Nigeria and one each from Romania, Bosnia and South Africa). Of the 35 Irish young people, 29 had grown up in suburban Dublin and the remainder in the inner city.

Almost half of the young people in the study had become homeless for the first time at the age of 14 or younger. Almost all had resided in poor neighbourhoods and the majority had experienced multiple forms of adversity in childhood: economic hardship, family conflict and poor relationships with parents (or step-parents), family illness, inadequate or inconsistent care, neglect and/or abuse (physical abuse featuring more often than sexual). For most, schooling had been severely disrupted and several of the young people reported literacy and/or numeracy problems (with a smaller number having attended a special school for children with learning difficulties). On the basis of the life histories, the researchers identify three broad pathways to homelessness. These are not mutually exclusive and in fact there is considerable overlap between them.

The first pathway, and one that is in keeping with the findings of the quantitative research by Kelleher et al. (2000) summarised above, is a *care history*. Sixteen of the young people (40 per cent) reported a history of State care, whether in foster care (of varying durations), residential care or a mixture of both. For a large number of these young people, the care experience was 'dominated by a pattern of rule-breaking, accompanied in some cases by deliberate attempts to orchestrate their removal from one or more settings' (Mayock and Vekic, 2006, p. 14). Resentment about having been separated from parent(s) and/or sibling(s) was a prominent factor.

The second pathway is *household instability and family conflict*, including parental alcohol and drug abuse and in some cases physical violence. The authors note that while the home-based difficulties experienced by the young people were almost always long-standing, leaving home was often triggered by a specific crisis or 'trigger'. The final pathway is *negative peer associations and problem behaviour*. Nine of the study's young people reported a pattern of behaviour leading to persistent disagreement with their parents, whether it was drinking, drug-taking, staying out late, trouble at school, socialising with 'troublemakers' or breaking the rules at home. The researchers stress that it is difficult to disentangle this behaviour on the part of the young people from other home-based problems and difficulties, and in fact they suggest that family conflict is a unifying theme across *all* the pathways into homelessness.

First Experiences of Homelessness

The young people in the study by Mayock and Vekic had a variety of experiences on becoming homeless, some sleeping rough for a while locally or in the city centre, perhaps returning home intermittently, before making contact with the HSE's Out-of-Hours Service (OHS). However, most made immediate contact with the OHS – initially through presenting as homeless at a garda station – and were placed in an emergency or short-term care setting. A small number (mainly young women) were immediately placed in emergency accommodation by a social worker without first making contact with the gardaí. There was also a lot of variation in the type and number of accommodations used, including one or more hostels (as the young people call the residential care centres), but also squats, friends' homes, short-term renting or staying with a family member. Generally positive comments were made about the residential centres, with the young people expressing their appreciation of the food and shelter and the care and commitment of staff however, there was a pervasive sense of powerlessness on the part of the residents (Mayock and Vekic, 2006, p. 21).

> There is one thing about staying in the hostels, you're in them. The bad thing about being in them, you're in them full stop and it's not your choice full stop whether you're in them or not. At 16 or 17, you can't get a flat really. I mean, so that the only, that's the bad thing about them really. It's the actual situation or else you're walking around the streets all night. (Young man, 17).

The researchers discuss the tensions that arise in hostel living due to the prevalence of rules, the residents' perception that they are subject to constant surveillance, the lack of private space and the uncertainty and instability associated with a high client turnover, which also means that it is difficult to form meaningful and lasting friendships. They also highlight the impact of the city centre homeless 'scene' on those young people who use the OHS repeatedly and move around various hostels, as opposed to those who remain in one hostel for a considerable period and have a relatively stable and structured routine, with the possibility of regular attendance at school or a training programme.

Acculturation

On the street, young people are particularly vulnerable to alcohol and drug use, criminal activity, intimidation and violence. These young people go through a *process of acculturation*, learning the street competencies they need to survive 'by becoming embedded in social networks of homeless youth' (Mayock and Vekic, 2006, p. 23). The authors suggest that the social networks and activities of the homeless scene may actually serve to 'further marginalise and isolate' homeless young people, making it more difficult for them to find stable and secure accommodation (ibid, p. 24). Their vulnerability is made all the worse by health problems, often associated with drug and alcohol use and increasing in severity as they get older, as well as by the risk of physical and sexual victimisation. Successful care or welfare intervention is difficult at this stage. The research suggests that much more intensive efforts should be made earlier, when the young person's reluctance to make an enduring break from home provides a 'window of opportunity' that is too often not taken.

This view is confirmed by another recent qualitative study of slightly older (18- to 30-year-old) homeless men in Dublin. Its authors suggest that there is perhaps an element of complacency in relation to homeless young people, since nowadays they appear to be so much the exception, and suggest further that whatever responses have been made to date have not been made early enough, a theme which has featured before in this chapter:

> The temptation may be to ignore the (relatively small) group identified as vulnerable in this report, when most chldren and young people are doing well. A solution would require a concerted and comprehensive approach. Perhaps the failure of some past initiatives is related to the fragmentation of education, family support, employment and health initiatives, and the fact that these interventions may not have been introduced early enough in the child's life (Cleary et al., 2004, p. 130).

RURAL YOUNG PEOPLE

In the classification used in the Census of Population, an urban area refers to any town (including suburbs and environs) with a population of 1,500 or more persons;

if the population is under 1,500, the area is classified as rural. Less than one-third of the population lived in urban areas in 1926. The 1971 Census was the first one in which the urban population exceeded the rural one. By 2002, approximately 60 per cent of the population was urban, up 2 per cent from the 1996 Census (CSO, 2002, p. 14). The national figures reflect the dominance of the greater Dublin area: outside Dublin, considerably more than half of the population lives in rural areas, and in the BMW (Border, Midland and West) region, the figure is approximately two-thirds (Heanue, 2002, p. 11). Overall, the process of urbanisation has accelerated over the past few decades, and many rural areas have not only remained static but have experienced a decline in population. This can have very damaging social and economic effects on communities, leading to 'an unfavourable age structure, higher than average dependency levels, an inability of the rural area to gain an adequate share of new investment and extreme forms of marginalisation' (Government of Ireland, 1999, p. 3).

Cultural Impact of Urbanisation

Such processes can also have a very detrimental impact in cultural terms. In the early years of Irish independence, public life (politics, business, culture) was dominated by an elite originating from and orientated towards rural society, a fact reflected in Eamon de Valera's often quoted vision of a 'countryside bright with cosy homesteads, whose fields and villages would be joyous with the sounds of industry'. This meant not just that rural life and living were highly valued in themselves, but also that rural areas were (relatively) well provided for in terms of public services (schools, shops, post offices, health services, and so on). This is no longer the case. As Tovey and Share (2003, p. 345) have remarked:

> In the early decades of independence, the culture of rural Ireland was elevated to a position of prestige and symbolic importance ... Politicians, church leaders, writers, artists and film-makers agreed that the real Ireland was rural Ireland, while urban life and culture were often regarded with suspicion as 'foreign' to Irish ways. But since the 1960s it has been urban culture that has increasingly established itself as the expression of the real (modern) Ireland, while the rural has been labelled backward and traditional. Urbanisation is more than a shift in regional population balance and the concentration of population around Dublin. It is a state of mind.

The material and cultural dominance of the urban places rural young people at an obvious disadvantage. 'Youth culture' is itself essentially urban, both conceptually and in practice; it is above all else about the collective use by young people of public, urban space (both outdoor and indoor). Youth culture, like all urban culture, also has a relationship with rural life, but it is primarily a 'visiting' relationship, as when music festivals or 'raves' descend upon remote rural areas, or when young urban adults visit the country for a break. Technological change is of course transforming perceptions and experiences of the urban-rural divide (as well as other social distinctions and boundaries) and making it possible for people of all ages to become part of online communities and consumers (and possibly creators) of cyber culture. In principle, a new recording by a favourite band can be downloaded as easily in a remote rural location as in a suburban estate (if the family can afford the hardware and software and if the requisite bandwidth has been made available, which may not be the case) and opinions of the new release can be shared quickly and fairly cheaply by text or e-mail. But getting together and just 'hanging around' (young people's favourite pastime, as Chapter 8 shows) is still likely to be a challenge.

Issues and Problems in Rural Areas

It is the nature of rural areas that social problems tend to be less spatially concentrated and therefore less conspicuously visible than in urban settings. This has the unfortunate effect that they can go unnoticed altogether and therefore do not get addressed, or are insufficiently addressed, in terms of social policy and provision. Programmes targeted at social disadvantage in Ireland have for the most part been aimed at urban areas, although recent years have seen some attempt being made to redress the balance. The issues and problems affecting rural areas have been summarised by O'Dwyer (2001, p. 37) as:

> ... poor transport and infrastructure, centralisation of educational, social and other public services, out-migration creating high dependency, decline of traditional farming and diminishing industries, long-term unemployed rates remaining high, poor physical and mental health associated with poverty and isolation.

Youth work and other youth services have had a notable bias towards young people in urban areas, reflecting the fact that historically (see Chapter 10) such provision was substantially prompted by a concern to 'get young people off the streets' and stop them being a nuisance or even a perceived menace to society. This has meant that an infrastructure for rural youth services was very slow to develop, although in recent years there have been a number of significant attempts on the part of youth and community organisations to acknowledge the particular circumstances of rural young people, assess their needs, opinions and aspirations, and develop strategies for a coherent response (see, for example, County Wexford Rural Youth Forum, 2000; Fitzgerald, 1997; O'Dwyer, 2001; McMullan et al., 2006).

While the term 'rural' encompasses a wide variety of types of setting – Phillips and Skinner (1994) suggest a fourfold distinction between remote rural areas, villages, market towns and coastal areas and hinterland – and while we should be cautious about generalising too much regarding the experiences of young people (and older people) living in what may be very different environments, it is possible to identify a number of ways in which rural young people face difficulties and challenges relative to their urban peers.

Lack of Transport

The first and most obvious difficulty is the practical, physical one of access and transport, which is consistently highlighted as an issue in research reports such as those just mentioned. None of the youth groups in a County Wexford study provided transport for their members, meaning that 'those who did not have access to transport did not have the means to access the youth activities and services' (County Wexford Rural Youth Forum, 2000, p. 30), and this seems typical of the situation around the country. In some cases, parents can and will provide transport, and it is important to remember that within the rural population families vary widely as regards their socio-economic position and the material and other resources available to them.

Even when such support from parents is available, it means that young people have to rely on their parents in a way in which they would rather not, particularly as they get older. As one youth work volunteer in Kerry put it: 'Rural young people are much more dependent on parents and for longer than urban young people' (O'Dwyer, 2001, p. 48). This is an issue not just in relation to youth work services, but to after-hour extra-curricular activities in schools (McMullan et al., 2006, p. 141).

Difficulties in Providing Support for Rural Young People

Practical difficulties with transport are bound up with much more serious socio-psychological matters, such as a sense of isolation and a lack of ready access to sources of information and support on a whole range of issues affecting young people. The apparent informality of much youth work practice conceals a very serious purpose and opportunities regularly arise 'spontaneously' (although in truth probably by design, if the youth worker is a good one) to become aware of young people's needs and concerns and to offer advice or just a listening ear or supportive presence. Such informality is easier to provide for in an urban setting:

> It is possible and practicable, in urban areas, to run 'drop-in' facilities which are very much in keeping with the voluntary principle of youth work and which recognise the preference of many young people for relatively casual involvement in youth services. On the basis of this apparently casual involvement, good youth workers are able to build positive and supportive relationships with young people, and to make a significant contribution to their personal and social development (Devlin, 'Introduction', in O'Dwyer, 2001, p. 13).

Such support for young people is all the more important in areas suffering other forms of disadvantage; at least some rural areas have considerably lower than average levels of educational attainment, for example, and this in turn is frequently linked to higher than average levels of unemployment or low-paid employment among parents (see McMullan et al., 2006, pp. 30, 100). Both young men and young women in rural areas may experience stereotypical gender expectations and have a sense of being 'trapped by conventions' (Geraghty et al., 1997, p. 41). Young people in particular groups – young people with disabilities, young lesbians or gay men, young members of ethnic minority communities – may have an increased sense of isolation or loneliness compared with their urban counterparts. Mental health problems and specifically suicide have also emerged as problems of which those working with young people in rural areas are particularly conscious (for example, O'Dwyer, 2001, p. 48).

Improving Provision for Rural Young People

Arising out of the research cited above and other similar action research programmes, a number of ideas have been developed for improving the circumstances of, and services for, rural young people, and some of these are already being implemented. They include very practical proposals for making more use of existing but under-utilised transport facilities (such as school buses) to facilitate access to youth work activities, as well as the introduction of additional community-based rural transport initiatives.

In Britain, independent transport programmes have been piloted, providing vehicle access (through loan or hire) and supporting young people to gain more autonomy over their leisure time, educational and cultural pursuits. Mobile cinemas have made recently released films available to people outside towns and cities. Other mobile services could be made available with relatively little difficulty if policy makers and providers were willing. In a recent research programme in Northern Ireland, health matters emerged as an important consideration: one young woman expressed the concern that that 'everyone knows your business' in a rural area, and a youth worker recommended that that there might be a mobile 'health bus' for young people (McMullan et al., 2006, p. 117).

It has been recommended that funding of services for young people should reflect the additional obstacles and challenges facing rural-based groups and organisations and that greater co-ordination is required on the part of all agencies at local level which have an interest in young people, whether schools, youth groups, community development projects and resource centres, gardaí, social work and health authorities (O'Dwyer, 2001).

In relation to this last point about the need for co-ordination and co-operation, it will be remembered from the previous chapter that the Youth Work Act 2001 places a statutory obligation on the Vocational Education Committees (VECs) not just to ensure the provision of youth work services within their areas of operation but also to ensure the co-ordination of such services with other services for young people. The Development Plans prepared by the VECs are to be based on an assessment of the needs of young people in their areas and on gaps in existing responses to such needs, and particular regard is to be had to those young people experiencing socio-economic disadvantage. This new framework for the delivery of youth work throughout the country has the potential to make a significant difference to rural young people. Time will show if it does. As a starting point, those charged with making decisions about the allocation of resources and the delivery of services (all services with relevance for young people) should acknowledge the significance of the spatial dimension in shaping young people's experiences and opportunities. As Phillips and Skinner (1994, p. 97) have commented:

> Over the past decade, the majority of youth organisations have acknowledged that race, gender, sexual orientation, class and disability are fundamental to the lives of the young people they work with. Most have, therefore, ensured that both their policies and their practice are informed and influenced by those realities. It is now time to add rurality to the list of factors that have a far-reaching effect on the lives of the young people concerned. *Rurality affects life chances.*

CONCLUSION

This chapter has dealt with the situation of young people whose lives may be somewhat different to those called to mind when we hear terms such as 'contemporary youth culture' or see reference in the media to 'young people today'. In one way or another, and to a greater or lesser degree, they face additional challenges which mean they may find it more difficult than others to live the lifestyle commonly associated with their age group in today's society. While for the sake of clarity we have looked at each group separately, these are not mutually exclusive categories and it should be remembered that just as personal identity can have many dimensions, individual young people can also face multiple forms of prejudice or discrimination, through, for instance, being a young asylum seeker who has a disability, or a young gay or lesbian Traveller. It is vital that we do not lose sight of the experiences, needs and aspirations of young people such as those discussed in this chapter. This is important both so that we can gain a fuller understanding of the situation and circumstances of all young people in contemporary Ireland – rather than just the numerical majority – and also so that we can work more effectively towards combating social exclusion and marginalisation among people of all ages.

RECOMMENDED READING

Some of the issues discussed in this chapter are explored at greater length in:

Kenny, M., McNeela, E., & Shevlin, M. (2003). Living and learning: The school experience of some young people with disabilities In M. Shevlin & R. Rose (Eds.), *Encouraging voices: Respecting the rights of young people who have been marginalised* (pp. 138–58). Dublin: National Disability Authority.

Lodge, A., & Lynch, K. (2004). *Diversity at school.* Dublin: Equality Authority/Institute of Public Administration.

Kelleher, P., Kelleher, C., & Corbett, M. (2000). *Left out on their own: Young people leaving care in Ireland.* Dublin: Oak Tree Press/Focus Ireland.

12

Emerging Trends and Issues

INTRODUCTION

This book has attempted to give a comprehensive account of the situation and circumstances of young people in contemporary Ireland. It has outlined a variety of theoretical perspectives which can be drawn on to understand and interpret adolescence and youth in today's society, and explored some of the ways in which these very terms can be subject to contrasting or even contradictory interpretations. It has provided detailed empirical information about a wide range of aspects of young people's lives: their location in (increasingly) diverse types of families and households; their friendships and peer relationships and their sexual identity and development; their health and well-being and the factors which may be helping or hindering these; their experience of and participation in the education system and the workplace, often both at the same time; their attitudes and values and the points of convergence or divergence with older people's; their leisure time and recreational activities; and their position in law and their interaction with the legal system.

In addition to education, employment and the law, the authors have also discussed a range of other institutional frameworks with a significant bearing on young people's lives, in the form of services and policies in fields such as youth work, child care and other children's services (a child, in law, referring to anyone up to 18 years old). We have attempted throughout to remain aware of the fact that 'youth' is not a homogeneous category, that young people's lives are shaped and influenced by many factors other than biological age, including structural inequalities and cultural differences, and have specifically considered the position of a number of groups which in one way or another experience marginalisation and exclusion. These include young LGBT (lesbian, gay, bisexual and transgender) people (in Chapters 4 and 11): young people with disabilities, young Travellers, separated children seeking asylum, young people in care, young homeless people and young people in rural areas. In all chapters of the book, the reader will also have seen examples of how young people's experiences and opportunities reflect the persistence of inequalities related to gender and to social class.

Throughout the text there has been an element, whether implicit or explicit, of looking forward, of wondering how the lives of young people in Ireland and the social context in which those lives are lived will change as the twenty-first century unfolds.

None of the book's authors claims privileged insight into the future, but the remainder of this chapter will present, very briefly and tentatively, some suggestions (and summaries from other sources) of what appear to be some key emerging trends and issues.

DEMOGRAPHY

The demographic situation of younger age groups – that is, their presence in the population not just in terms of absolute numbers but as a proportion of the total – relative to older people has a significant bearing on their lives and circumstances. It influences the extent to which they are seen as a social and/or political 'priority', and the policies and services developed for them as well, of course, as the way in which they are perceived by the media, by business and marketing interests and by society as a whole. When the National Youth Policy Committee was appointed by the Taoiseach, Garret FitzGerald, in 1983 (see Chapter 10), nearly half of the Irish population (48 per cent) was aged under 25. Two decades later in the 2002 Census, the 'youth population' had dropped by one-fifth, to 38 per cent, and that downward trend is very likely to continue (see Figure 12.1).

Figure 12.1 Population pyramids for 2001 and 2036 based on different assumptions about migration (M) and fertility (F)

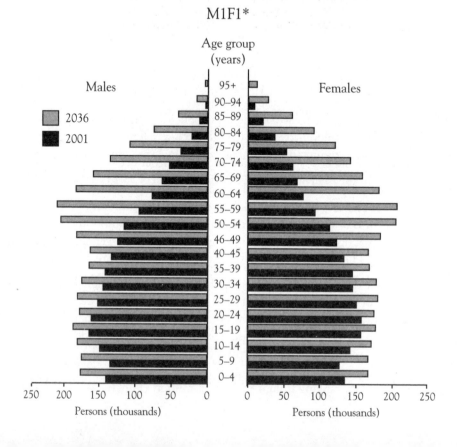

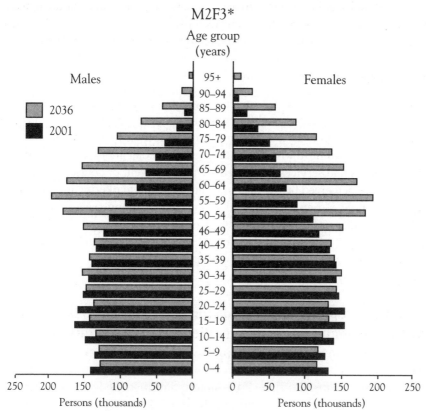

M2F3*

Age group (years)

Males

2036

2001

Females

95+
90–94
85–89
80–84
75–79
70–74
65–69
60–64
55–59
50–54
46–49
40–45
35–39
30–34
25–29
20–24
15–19
10–14
5–9
0–4

250 200 150 100 50   0   0   50 100 150 200 250
Persons (thousands)   Persons (thousands)

*Note: These combinations of assumptions represent the two extremes of the Central Statistics Office's six projections. M1F1 assumes strong though declining net inward migration and the maintenance of a fertility rate of two children per woman; M2F3 assumes moderate and declining net inward migration and a fall in fertility to 1.7 per woman. In either case there will be a major expansion of persons aged 50 and over. The absolute number of under 25s will increase under M1F1 but decrease under M2F3. In proportional terms they will fall in either case, from a level of 38% to 31% under M1F1 and 26% under M2F3.
Source: CSO, 2004.

Ireland is sharing in the overall European pattern of ageing as a society, but it still has a relatively youthful population when compared with other European countries. Projecting future demographic trends is highly complex. It is not simply a matter of taking account of likely trends in fertility and mortality (births and deaths), but also of projected inward and outward migration. Recent projections from the Central Statistics Office for population increase over the next three decades include six different scenarios, with different combinations of assumptions relating to each of the factors mentioned above. These give six different projected totals for the population in 2036, ranging from 4.98 to 5.82 million (Punch, 2006). Whatever the precise figures, demographers are agreed that the proportion of the population made up by the elderly will increase significantly. One estimate is that the number of people aged over 65 will more than treble from the current level of 464,000 to 1.5 million in 50 years' time. This will mean a significantly increased dependency ratio (the ratio between the economically active and their younger and older dependents). 'At present there are more than four workers contributing to the support of every pensioner. This will fall to 2.7 in 2026 and less than 1.5 workers per pensioner in fifty years' time' (O'Brien, 2006d). There are clear implications here for public services and public policy, but partly for that reason there is also the potential for enormous tension and strain on inter-generational relations.

Because it still has a relatively youthful population as compared with the rest of western Europe, Ireland is better placed to prepare for the challenges ahead than many other countries. It is getting a 'demographic lift' at present because the total fertility rate (which refers to the average number of lifetime births per female), after having declined since the 1960s, has recovered to be the highest in the EU, at 1.95 (CSO, 2006). It may decline again, but in the medium term this will not mean fewer births because any overall decline will be counterbalanced by a projected increase in the number of women in the 20- to 39-age group, the prime childbearing years (Punch, 2006). An analysis of population trends by NCB Stockbrokers (2006) estimates that of EU countries, Ireland will have the highest proportion of under-15s in the population by 2010. This will have an obvious knock-on effect on the proportion of young people in the Irish population for some years thereafter. Most population projections also share an assumption of increased net immigration to Ireland in coming years (and decades), which will likely add to the younger age groups and compensate somewhat (but only somewhat) for the ageing process in society as a whole and the likely costs in public services.

In any event, whether young people make up a relatively large or relatively small proportion of the population, the need for adequate youth policies and services will continue. Even if they are diminishing in numerical terms, much more effort will need to be put into all aspects of the care, education and socialisation of the younger generation in a situation where they, as they grow older, will have to exercise an ever-increasing civic responsibility. This is a point made in the National Youth Work Development Plan (Department of Education and Science, 2003a, p. 2):

[An ageing population] does not in any respect lessen the importance of effective and adequately-resourced youth work provision. Quite the contrary: the need for social cohesion, stability and equity in the future, when the dependency ratio will be greater than at present (i.e. the numbers of 'economically active' will be proportionally much lower) makes the social, civic and political education of young people, in formal and informal settings, much *more* important, not less.

CULTURAL DIVERSITY

It has already been mentioned that demographic patterns in Ireland in coming years are widely expected to include continued net inward migration. As recently as the late 1980s, Ireland was experiencing net outward migration of more than 40,000 a year, but the strong economic growth of the intervening period led to an average net immigration figure of 36,000 (58,000 immigrants less 22,000 emigrants) in the five years 2001 to 2006 (Punch, 2006; see also Chapter 11 of this book). According to the expert group advising the Central Statistics Office on its population projections, it is 'unlikely that net immigration [will] be reversed to any sustained degree in the coming decade or two' (ibid). Not all the people immigrating will be completely new to Ireland and many will be coming from countries or cultures which have much in common with Ireland (including, for example, the English language). Many may not intend to stay here very long. Nonetheless, there is no doubt that the multicultural character of Irish society, already much more pronounced than it was just a few years ago, is set to increase further, and this will be particularly the case among the younger age groups since, as already indicated, immigrants tend to include large numbers of young people.

The National Youth Work Development Plan highlights the implications of this for young people themselves as well as for youth workers and other professionals (and so the point made here about youth work applies equally to the formal education system, social care system and so on):

> One way or another, young people in Ireland are growing into adulthood in a much more culturally diverse environment. Ensuring that this diversity is seen as a positive thing from which all can gain enrichment, and by the same token countering racism and intolerance in all their forms, are among the key tasks for those working with young people in Ireland today ... An adequate youth work response requires more than the provision of separate programmes for young people from diverse cultural backgrounds (although these have a role to play); it requires that all young people, and all youth workers, are facilitated in developing the skills appropriate for a more diverse cultural environment (Department of Education and Science, 2003a, pp. 3–4).

GENDER AND FAMILIES

Just as Ireland has experienced an increase in cultural diversity, it has also seen an increase in the diversity of family forms, and this too is a pattern which looks set to continue, with young people not just affected by it but to a large extent pioneering it (see Chapters 3 and 7; and for recent global perspectives on young people and families, see Leccardi and Ruspini, 2006). In the 10 years to 2006, the number of women living as lone parents almost doubled, from 60,000 to 115,000, and the number of men living as lone parents also increased from 8,400 to 10,600 over the same period (CSO, 2006). Census figures also show that in the six years from 1996 to 2002, the proportion of co-habiting couples rose from 3.9 per cent to 8.4 per cent. Some 1,300 couples in 2002 described themselves as same-sex cohabiting. The rights of cohabiting couples, whether of the same or the opposite sex, have been the subject of a great deal of social and political attention and debate in recent times, and have been the subject of reports by the Law Reform Commission (2006) and the Working Group on Domestic Partnerships (2006). On a related issue, the question of the recognition in Ireland of the Canadian marriage of a lesbian couple was the subject of an unfavourable High Court judgment in 2006 which, at the time of writing, was being appealed to the Supreme Court. Whatever the ultimate outcome in terms of same-sex marriage (which is available in a number of countries already), provision of much greater equality for people who live together as partners, whatever their sex or sexual orientation, now seems assured, reinforcing and validating the pattern whereby young people (and older people) have come to expect to have a greater range of options available to them when it comes to establishing families and households.

Figure 12.2 Ages of brides and grooms, 1996 and 2002

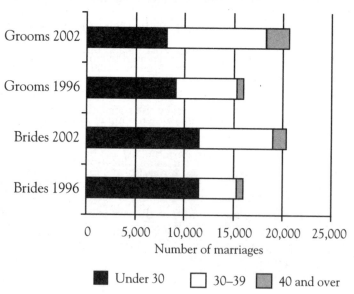

Source: CSO (2005 b).

This is not to say that people do not want to get married at all. In fact, the marriage rate has increased since the mid-1990s, reflecting (as marriage rates have often been seen to do) trends in economic prosperity. However, people now choose to marry later, very often cohabiting for a considerable period of time first. Legal reform to provide equality in financial and revenue terms for cohabiting couples is likely to lead to an increase in this trend. Figure 12.2 illustrates the striking increase in the age of marriage over the period 1996–2002. The proportion of brides under 30 years of age fell from 83.8 per cent in 1996 to 55.8 per cent to 2002, while for grooms the decline was from 72 per cent to 40.7 per cent. The average age of marriage in 2002 was 32.5 for men and 30.4 for women.

The various chapters of this book have shown that while there has been considerable progress in eliminating gender inequalities in Irish society, there is a lot still to be done. While more women are entering the workforce, for instance, there are still significant discrepancies in wages and in the proportions of men and women at senior levels, even in occupations dominated by women (CSO, 2006). Women account for only 14 per cent of TDs in the Dáil and for less than 20 per cent of local authority members. However, while certain forms of inequality appear to be deeply entrenched, the long-term trend in the direction of equal opportunities for young women appears irreversible.

In educational terms, girls have been at an advantage over boys for some time, and this process is continuing and even deepening. There is a marked increase in the number of women entering third-level education, while the number of men is beginning to level off. In 2006, almost 82 per cent of 18-year-old females were students, compared to 62 per cent of males (CSO, 2006). In 1981 the corresponding figures were 35 per cent and 27 per cent (National Youth Policy Committee, 1984). This clearly demonstrates that in the intervening quarter century, while participation in third-level education has greatly increased overall, young women have considerably stretched their lead over young men.

The general expansion of third-level participation is part of the process that took place over the twentieth century in Ireland whereby the social class structure as a whole – and specifically the transmission of inheritance within families – moved from being based on passing on a (usually indivisible) property to one male child towards being based on providing more or less the same educational opportunities for all one's children (Fahey, 1995). While this in itself has obvious implications for gender relations, the fact that young women are availing of such opportunities in much larger proportions than young men (and that the gap is increasing) would appear to raise concerns for the relative positions of young men and women in the future. As the young men who are less likely to go on to third level are those who are already socio-economically disadvantaged, in many cases not even having completed second level (Williamson, 1997), and since, as Bynner (2005) points out, the consequences for young people of not being qualified are getting worse over time, it is clear that overall strategies of gender equality now and in the future should take account of the needs of this group of young men as well as continuing to address the numerous ways in which young women continue to experience inequalities.

SOCIO-ECONOMIC INEQUALITIES

Gender is just one of the areas in which inequality remains evident in Irish society. Despite the economic success of the Celtic Tiger years, about one in five Irish children are in households with below 60 per cent of median income, which is a widely used measure for indicating 'relative poverty' (or being 'at risk of poverty' in current EU usage). This places Ireland among 'a group of countries with a relatively high income-poverty rate for children, together with Spain, Greece, Portugal and the UK' (Nolan et al., 2006, p. 151). Over the years 1994 to 2001, while only 4 per cent of children were below the relative poverty threshold in all eight years, one in four spent at least three years below it. Children experienced substantially more poverty than working-age adults without children, although still less than older people. As regards 'consistent poverty', which refers both to being below the 60 per cent threshold *and* to experiencing basic deprivation on a number of key indicators (being able to afford a warm overcoat or second pair of shoes; being able to heat the house adequately in winter and so on), the overall figure for children fell from 22 per cent in 1994 to 6.6 per cent in 2001, a very significant improvement. However, about 29 per cent of children experienced consistent poverty at some point over the years in question, and about 15 per cent of children spent three or more years in consistent poverty (ibid, p. 153). In a context of economic prosperity at national level that is unprecedented and not long ago would have seemed unimaginable, these figures are remarkable. The challenge for social and economic policy in the future is considerable, 'both to reduce the extent of societal inequalities in childhood socio-economic circumstances, and to weaken the linkages between those circumstances and the opportunities that people face as they progress through the education system and into the labour market' (ibid, p. 163).

The persistence of child poverty is part of a broader phenomenon whereby the gap between the poor and the wealthy has actually increased rather than diminished during Ireland's recent years of economic success. This increased polarisation has been accompanied by a range of other social problems, all of which have a direct impact on young people, particularly those who are socially disadvantaged:

After more than a decade of vigorous economic growth and prosperity, Ireland has been left with some severe problems. So, while much of the transformation has been positive, it has been accompanied by a widening gap between rich and poor; rising crime rates; increased environmental pollution; a large infrastructure deficit; a housing market that excludes many; a huge growth in long-distance commuting; health and welfare systems creaking under pressure; a weakening rural economy with a decline in agricultural incomes; the continued marginalisation of Travellers; and in Northern Ireland sectarianism is still rife. All of these issues are themselves ... uneven and unequal in their manifestations and consequences across Ireland (Kitchen and Bartley, 2007b, pp. 303–04).

The last point that there is a significant spatial dimension to social inequalities is borne out by an analysis of affluence and deprivation throughout Ireland over the period 1991–2002, using a number of indicators (Haase, 2007). It identifies the most deprived areas in the country in 2002 (in urban terms, parts of Dublin and of other cities and towns; in rural terms, most of Donegal and Mayo, large parts of West and

East Galway and significant parts of other counties), but just as importantly concludes that there has been very limited change in the *relative* position of different areas over time:

> This is the key finding of the study. It proves what is intuitively broadly understood, particularly by those who are actively involved in the area-based initiatives: things have hugely improved in the disadvantaged areas with regard to unemployment, educational achievement etc., but at the same time nothing has changed relative to more affluent areas which equally have improved their situation and thus maintained the differentials ... [W]ith very few exceptions, the poorest areas of the 1990s are still the poorest areas in 2002 (Haase, 2007, pp. 275, 278).

This means that area-based initiatives targeted at disadvantaged young people, families and communities will not only need to be continued, but to be intensified in future years and to be reinforced by broader redistributive measures if greater social equality (as opposed to simply lifting those 'at the bottom' out of dire poverty) is to be achieved. Otherwise the effects of social inequalities will continue to be starkly visible in spatial terms, and young people in disadvantaged areas and neighbourhoods, urban and rural, will continue to experience diminished opportunities and persistent social problems:

> Examples of these include the thinning out of certain age cohorts in remote rural locations due to emigration; school-level and neighbourhood effects on educational achievements; the lack of jobs and services ...; drug and crime-related problems in areas of high unemployment, and many more (Haase, 2007, p. 276).

ENHANCED RESOURCES, GREATER RISKS?

Most young people in contemporary Ireland do not experience poverty or other material disadvantages based on their social class background or the area in which they live. In fact, the most commonly accepted view among social scientists is that there has been a dramatic structural movement upwards in Ireland's social class system, meaning that '200,000 people have moved from the poorest social classes to the middle classes, with the poorest class contracting by 29 per cent' (Kitchen and Bartley, 2007a, p. 14) (for a Marxist view which argues that most of Ireland's new 'middle class' is actually its contemporary proletariat, see Allen, 2000). Ireland has quickly become a consumer society, fully integrated within a globalised economy and increasingly globalised forms of cultural expression, particularly among the young.

> Brand name shops from countries across the world increasingly dominate the shopping landscape, and people wearing designer label clothes are a common sight. There has been a massive growth in the restaurant trade, Irish people are

taking more foreign-based and domestic tourist trips than ever before and are spending more on them … [B]etween 1991 and 2002 the proportion of households with at least one car increased from 59.5 per cent to 78.3 per cent. Households with two or more cars increased from 87,174 to 478,660, and the overall number of cars in the state increased from 445,226 to 1,601,619 … This growth far outstrips population growth and has occurred in a country where car prices are the highest in Europe (Kitchen and Bartley, 2007a, p. 15).

Earlier chapters of this book have shown how various aspects of young people's lives have been influenced by this new economic and cultural environment. Shopping malls and centres, for example, have become enormously popular not just as, places to shop, but as places to 'hang out'. In order to help pay for these pastimes, young people are increasingly involved in part-time employment while they are in third-level or even second-level education. Young people today have much more disposable income than they used to, which opens up possibilities both positive and negative. Not just for financial reasons, but also because socially and culturally they have been exposed to more diverse influences than their parents, they see themselves as having a greatly increased range of choices about their lives and lifestyles. There is a inherent 'riskiness' in such an enhanced range of choices (see the discussion of theories of risk in Chapter 5), and we have already seen that, even without buying into a stereotypical 'moral panic' about the younger generation, there is every reason to ensure that adequate supports are put in place for young people's health and well-being, mental and physical (including not just education on alcohol, drugs or sex, but advice and active support on matters relating to diet and nutrition, exercise and mental health and illness). Such supports as are there at present simply have not kept pace with the speed of change in the lives and circumstances of young people in Ireland, for whom the 'choices' on offer may sometimes be overwhelming:

> Too many choices, or 'choices' presented earlier than appropriate, may in fact be experienced as pressures, or may be exercised to harmful effect, whether for the individual him/herself or for others, and often with consequences for the wider community or for society as a whole. There are increasingly complex health issues facing young people today. The link between these and socio-economic and other factors needs to be examined. Issues like drug misuse, suicide and mental health problems are a major concern (Department of Education and Science, 2003a, p. 4).

Another recent analysis of 'youth in a changing Ireland' (Sweeney and Dunne, 2003) has highlighted the precarious nature of young people's position as, on the one hand, enthusiastic consumers with a focus on sustaining a hedonistic lifestyle (relative, at least, to their parents' generation), and on the other, pupils and students (whether enthusiastic or not) within an educational and economic system that expects a great deal of them (again, relative to their parents' experience) and that threatens dire consequences if they are unsuccessful. Caught between the present and the future in this way, young people can be regarded as living their lives 'where two sets of forces meet':

> One has to do with their new status as consumers. Physiological and psychological factors appropriate to their age and the considerable spending power they exercise directly or control indirectly are interacting to make the creation of youth lifestyles an absorbing pursuit, both for young people themselves and an array of commercial interests skilled in the use of media and marketing techniques to reach them ... Another set of forces has to do with societal expectations of their education ... For some young people, the clash between the two sets of forces is like the grinding of opposing tectonic plates. On the one hand, there seems to be little that cannot be experienced and lived now, if only there is enough money to help implement their plans. On the other, the spectre of a failed adult life looms ever larger unless they sacrifice more of their youthful freedoms now in order to knuckle down and secure the right education (Sweeney and Dunne, 2003, p. 12).

TECHNOLOGY, GLOBALISATION AND THE KNOWLEDGE SOCIETY

The increased emphasis in recent years on the education of young people, in greater numbers than before and for longer periods of time, is part of the continuing development of a post-industrial knowledge society in which the basis of the economy is continuing to shift away from industrial activities and manufacturing towards occupations which involve the production and dissemination of information and ideas, often using new technologies. Furthermore, the pace of technological innovation is such that the perception of knowledge itself as something which is acquired, with experience, over a lifetime and passed on from the older to the younger generation is being undermined. As the National Youth Work Development Plan put it, 'in the post-industrial world of information technology [children and young people] often have readier access to certain types of knowledge than many adults, without necessarily having had the opportunity to develop the capacity for critical and responsible use of that knowledge' (Department of Education and Science, 2003a, p. 3).

Such developments have implications for age relations and systems of authority, and along with other changes discussed in this book (diminishing trust in key social institutions, a more individualistic culture, people living busier and more preoccupied lives) may be affecting the willingness or confidence of many adults to take up positions of leadership or authority in relation to young people, particularly on a voluntary basis. On the other hand, the increasing need for education and training (or re-training) throughout people's working lives has made 'lifelong learning' an important social policy goal. It means that people of different age groups are more likely to be engaging in education together, that the education system and other social institutions may become less rigidly 'age calibrated', as Wallace and Kovatcheva (1998) have described it (see Chapter 2), and this could help to counter the trend towards generational 'drift'.

It is important to remember that developments such as these are impacting on different parts of the world in very different ways, and that even within societies at an advanced stage of post-industrialisation (and postmodernisation), routine and manual economic activities still have to be performed. A social class structure remains clearly visible, therefore, often substantially overlapping with other forms of social stratification (for example, more immigrant young people doing relatively menial jobs that most Irish young people are no longer interested in).

Finally, it can be anticipated that the trend towards a more globalised adolescence and youth, with young people in increasingly disparate parts of the world sharing the same interests, pastimes and lifestyles, will continue to be met with countervailing trends towards locally, regionally and nationally specific cultural forms. The subtitle of Helve and Holm's recent edited collection of international youth research (2005), *Local Expressions and Global Connections*, bears this out. The huge popularity at home and abroad of Irish music and dance and the flourishing state of Gaelic sports are obvious examples. In an Ireland where linguistic diversity is becoming much more pronounced, perhaps the time and context might be right for a resurgence of interest in the Irish language among young people.

EMERGING ADULTHOOD OR EXTENDED YOUTH?

This book began with questions of definition, so it is perhaps appropriate that we conclude in a similar way. Is a new term necessary to describe the profound changes that have taken place in young people's lives in recent years? American psychologist Jeffrey Arnett thinks that it is. Because young people now experience much more protracted transitions into adulthood (as seen in the discussion of transitional perspectives in Chapter 2), staying much longer in education and having a relatively unstable and insecure experience of the early years of employment, Arnett (2000, 2007) has introduced the concept of 'emerging adulthood' to refer to the period after adolescence, roughly the years 18 to 25, which he says are characterised (more than other years) by five features:

- **Identity explorations:** 'This means that it is an age when people explore various possibilities in love and work as they move toward making enduring choices.'
- **Instability:** 'A good illustration of this is in how often they move from one residence to another.'
- **Self-focus:** 'As emerging adults, they are in between the reliance on their parents that adolescents have and the long-term commitments in love and work that most adults have, and during these years they focus on themselves as they develop the knowledge, skills and self-understanding they will need for adult life.'

- **Feeling in-between:** 'When asked, "Do you feel that you have reached adulthood?", the majority of emerging adults respond neither yes nor no but with the ambiguous "in some ways yes, in some ways no".'
- **Possibilities:** '[M]any different futures remain possible … It tends to be an age of high hopes and great expectations, in part because few of their dreams have been tested in the fires of real life.'

(Arnett, 2007, pp. 13–14)

Arnett recognises that cultures vary widely in the ages at which young people are expected to enter full adulthood and that therefore 'emerging adulthood does not exist in all cultures' (ibid, p. 15). He also acknowledges the significance of sociological factors – for example, forms of social stratification such as ethnicity – in shaping the experiences of young people in the United States, although his approach is primarily rooted in developmental psychology. His description of the 18- to 25-year-old age group probably does broadly apply to young people of that age in Ireland today, with the caveat that a young person is of a certain gender or social class (for example) is likely to be at least as significant in shaping his/her experiences and opportunities as the fact that he/she is aged between 18 and 25. It is perhaps debatable, however, whether it is necessary to introduce a new term to describe the situation of contemporary 18 to 25-year-olds, particularly given that European sociologists have been drawing attention to the processes and dynamics associated with 'extended youth' for some time. Furthermore, as Bynner (2005, p. 280) suggests: 'The homogenising features of developmental stages also tend to play down the old structural determinacies and polarising aspects of young people's experience that, if anything … are getting stronger in late modern conditions'.

CONCLUSION

This brings us back to some of the ideas introduced in Chapter 2 and elsewhere in this book. Adolescence and youth are being *extended* at both ends, because on the one hand young people are maturing physically earlier than they did in the past and are being 'fast-tracked' into the transition(s) to adulthood by technological and cultural factors and commercial pressures, and on the other the acquisition of the full social status of adulthood is in many cases being delayed 'as young people stay in the education system longer, or for financial reasons find it difficult to develop a sense of (or an objective state of) full autonomy or independence' (Department of Education and Science, 2003a, p. 3).

Transitions, both in the public arena of education and employment and in the personal sphere of relationships and families, are also becoming more complex and contingent, less predictable and unilinear. The idea of completing education or training early in life and embarking thereafter on one stable lifelong career is becoming a thing of the past. Young people in general have more 'choices', but frequently do not have the support to exercise choice in a critically informed and reflective way. The choices, too, continue to be unevenly and unequally divided across the younger generation, with what Bynner (2005, p. 280) calls 'the old structural determinacies' continuing to make their presence felt.

Much has changed for the better, however. There is an increased emphasis on equality and on a rights-based approach to policies for children and young people. Economic prosperity, if sensibly and responsibly managed, creates possibilities for social and cultural enrichment and enhanced opportunities for personal expression for people of all ages. Furthermore, despite the persistence of structural obstacles and problems such as those mentioned in this chapter and earlier, young people continue to exercise individual and collective agency and make their presence felt as a positive force in society. Young people in contemporary Ireland, while certainly constrained by significant structural and cultural forces, are also themselves actively creating and recreating those forces, shaping not just their own lives but the Ireland of the future.

RECOMMENDED READING

For a succinct and recent Irish study of young people's changing experiences and circumstances, see:

Sweeney, J., & Dunne, J. (2003). *Youth in a changing Ireland: A study for Foróige, the national youth development organiation*. Dublin: Foróige.

Comparative international perspectives can be found in:

du Bois-Reymond, M. and Chisholm, L. (eds.), *The Modernization of Youth Transitions in Europe* (San Francisco: Jossey-Bass, 2006)

Helve, H. & Holm, G. (Eds.). (2005). *Contemporary youth research: Local expressions and global connections*. Aldershot: Ashgate.

Leccardi, C. and Ruspini, E. (Eds.). (2005). *A new youth?: Young people, generations and family life*. Aldershot: Ashgate.

References

Abbott–Chapman, J. (2000). Time-out; spaced-out. *Youth Studies Australia, 19*(1), 34–56.

Alexandris, K., & Grouis, G. (2002). Perceived constraints on recreational sport participation: investigating their relationship with intrinsic motivation, extrinsic motivation and amotivation. *Journal of Leisure Research, 34*(3), 233–53.

All-Party Oireachtas Committee on the Constitution. (2006). *Tenth Progress Report: The Family*. Dublin: Stationery Office.

Allen, S. (1968). Some theoretical considerations in the study of youth. *Sociological Review, 16*(3), 319–31.

Allen, K. (2000). *The Celtic Tiger: The myth of social partnership*. Manchester: Manchester University Press.

Allen, O., Page, R.M., Moore, L., & Hewitt, C. (1994). Gender differences in selected psychosocial characteristics of adolescent smokers and nonsmokers. *Health Values, 18*, 34–9.

American Psychological Association. (2002). *Developing adolescents: A reference for professionals*. Washington, DC: American Psychological Association.

Anderson, N. (2004). Brands, identity and young people – ongoing research. *The Psychologist, 17*, 208.

Anderson, S., & Graham, G. (2006). The custodial remand system for juveniles in Ireland: The empirical evidence. *Administration, 54*(1), 50–71.

Arensman, E., Sullivan, C., Corcoran, P., Farrow, R., Keeley, H.S., & Perry, I.J. (2004). Psychosocial factors associated with deliberate self-harm in adolescents. *Psychiatrica Danubinia, 18*(1), 48–9.

Arnett, J.J. (1996). Sensation seeking, aggressiveness and adolescent reckless behaviour. *Personality and Individual Differences, 20*, 693–702.

Arnett, J.J. (1999). Adolescent storm and stress reconsidered. *American Psychologist, 54*, 317–26.

Arnett, J.J. (2000). Emerging adulthood: A theory of development from the late teens through the twenties. *American Psychologist, 55*, 469–80.

Arnett, J.J. (2007). *Adolescence and emerging adulthood: A cultural approach*. (3rd ed.). New Jersey: Pearson/Prentice Hall.

Arnett, J.J., & Balle-Jensen, L. (1993). Cultural bases of risk behaviour. *Child Development, 64*, 1842–55.

Arnett, J.J., Larson, R., & Offer, D. (1995). Beyond effects: Adolescents as active media users. *Journal of Youth and Adolescence, 24*(5), 511–18.

Arts Council. (2006). *Guidelines for the protection and welfare of children and young people in the arts sector*. Dublin: Arts Council.

ASH Ireland. (2001). http://www.ash.ie

Ash, M. (1980). The misnamed female sex organ. In M. Kirkpatrick (Ed.), *Women's sexual development*. New York: Plenum.

AWARE. (1998). *Suicide in Ireland: A global perspective and a national strategy.* Dublin: Aware. www.aware.ie [accessed June 2006].

Back, L. (1997). *New ethnicities and urban youth culture.* London: University College London Press.

Baer, J.S. (2002). Student factors: Understanding individual variation in college drinking. *Journal of Studies on Alcohol,* Suppl. 14, 40–53.

Balding, J. (2001). *Young people in 2000.* Exeter: Schools Health Education Unit.

Barber, B.L., Eccles, J.S. & Stone, M.R. (2001). Whatever happened to the Jock, the Brain, and the Princess? Young adult pathways linked to adolescent activity involvement and social identity. *Journal of Adolescent Research,* 16, 5, 429-55.

Barnes, J., & O'Gorman, N. (1995). A descriptive study of juvenile delinquents. *Irish Journal of Psychological Medicine, 12*(2), 53–6.

Bartko, W.T., & Eccles, J.S. (2003). Adolescent participation in structured and unstructured activities: A person–oriented analysis. *Journal of Youth and Adolescence, 32*(4), 233–42.

Bartley, B. & Kitchen, R. (Eds.). (2007). *Understanding contemporary Ireland.* London: Pluto Press.

Basketball Ireland. (2005). Personal correspondence.

Baumeister, R.F. (2001). *Social psychology and human sexuality.* Sussex: Psychology Press.

Beck, U. (1992). *Risk society.* London: Sage.

Bell, D. (1990). *Acts of union: Youth culture and sectarianism in Northern Ireland.* London: Macmillan.

Bell, R. (1988). *Changing bodies, changing lives: A book for teens on sex and relationships.* New York: Random House.

Bell, A.P., Weinberg, M.S., & Hammersmith, S.K. (1981). *Sexual preference: Its development in men and women.* Bloomington: Indiana University Press.

Belvedere Newsboy's Club. (1948). *A Club for Boys.* Dublin: Belvedere Newsboy's Club.

Benson, C. (1994). A psychological perspective on art and national identity. *Irish Journal of Psychology, 15*(2–3), 316–30.

Berger, P., & Berger, B. (1976). *Sociology: A biographical approach.* (2nd ed.). Harmondsworth: Penguin.

Berndt, T.J. (2002). Friendship quality and social development. *Current Directions in Psychological Sciences, 11,* 7–10.

Berzonsky, M.D. (1999). Identity styles and hypothesis-testing strategies. *Journal of Social Psychology, 139,* 784–9.

Berzonsky, M.D. (2002). Identity processing styles, self construction, and personal epistemic assumptions: A social cognitive perspective. Paper presented at the workshop 'Social cognition in adolescence: its developmental significance', Groningen, The Netherlands, June 28–30, 2002.

Blackburn, D. (1990). Young people, youth work and disability. In T. Jeffs & M. Smith (Eds.), *Young people, inequality and youth work* (pp. 152–78). Basingstoke & London: Macmillan.

Blackman, S. (2005). Youth subcultural theory: A critical engagement with the concept, its origins and politics, from the Chicago school to postmodernism. *Journal of Youth Studies, 8*(1), 1–20.

Blos, P. (1962). *On adolescence*. New York: Free Press.

Blos, P. (1972). The function of the ego ideal in late adolescence. In R.S. Eissler, A. Freud, H. Hartmann, & J. Kris (Eds.), *Psychoanalytic study of the child* (Vol. 22). New York: International Universities Press.

Bolger, S., O'Connor, P., Malone, K., & Fitzpatrick, C. (2004). Adolescents with suicidal behaviour: Attendance at A&E and six month follow–up. *Irish Journal of Psychological Medicine, 21*(3), 78–84.

Booth, A. (1999). Causes and consequences of divorce: Reflections on recent research. In S. McRoe (Ed.), *Changing Britain: Families and households in the 1990s* (pp. 29–48). Oxford: OUP.

Bostik, K., & Paulson, B. (2005). I'm sick of being me: Developmental themes in a suicidal adolescent. *Adolescence, 40*(160), 693–709.

Bowlby, J. (1988). *A secure base*. New York: Basic Books.

Bradford–Brown, R. (1990). Peer groups and peer cultures. In S. Feldman & G.R. Elliott (Eds.), *At the threshold: The developing adolescent* (pp. 176–96). Cambridge, MA: Harvard University Press.

Bradshaw, J., & Miller, J. (1991). *Lone parents in the UK*. London: HMSO.

Bradshaw, J., Stimson, C., Skinner, C., & Williams, J. (1999). *Absent fathers?* London: Routledge.

Brage, D., Meredith W., & Woodward, J. (1993). Correlates of loneliness among midwestern adolescents. *Adolescence, 28*(111), 685–93.

Breen, M. (2002). Different from their elders and betters: Age cohort differences in the Irish data of the European Values Study 1999. In E. Cassidy (Ed.), *Measuring Ireland: Discerning values and beliefs* (pp. 94–120). Dublin: Veritas.

Brennock, M. (2003, 20 September). Religious belief stronger among females. *The Irish Times*.

Bridge, J.A., Goldstein, T.R., & Brent, D.A. (2006). Adolescent suicide and suicidal behaviour. *Journal of Child Psychology and Psychiatry, 47*(3–4), 372–94.

Brinkley, A., Fitzgerald, M., & Greene, S. (1999). *Substance use in early adolescence: A study of the rates and patterns of substance use among pupils in Dublin*. Dublin: Eastern Health Board and the European Commission.

Bronfenbrenner, U. (1979). *The ecology of human development*. Cambridge, MA: Harvard University Press.

Brooks, R. (2002). Transitional friends? Young people's strategies to manage and maintain their friendships during a period of repositioning. *Journal of Youth Studies, 5*(4), 449–67.

Brooks–Gunn, J., & Ruble, D.N. (1983). The experience of menarche from a developmental perspective. In J. Brooks–Gunn & A.C. Petersen (Eds.), *Girls at puberty: Biological, psychological and social perspectives* (pp. 155–78). New York: Plenum.

Brooks–Gunn, J., & Reiter, E.O. (1990). The role of pubertal processes. In S.S. Feldman, & G.R. Elliott (Eds.), *At the threshold: The developing adolescent* (pp. 16–53). Cambridge, MA: Harvard University Press.

Brooks–Gunn, J., Samelson, M., Warren, M.P., & Fox, R. (1986). Physical similarity of and disclosure of menarchal status to friends: Effects of age and pubertal status. *Journal of Early Adolescence, 6*(1), 3–14.

Brown, B., Clasen, D., & Eicher, S. (1986). Perceptions of peer pressure, peer conformity dispositions and self-reported behaviour among adolescents. *Developmental Psychology*, 22, 521–30.

Brown, B.B. (1990). Peer groups and peer cultures. In S.S. Feldman & G.R. Elliot (Eds.), *At the threshold: The developing adolescent* (pp. 171–96). Cambridge, MA: Harvard Press.

Brown, B.B., Lohr, M.J., & Trujillo, C.M. (1990). Multiple crowds and multiple life–styles: Adolescents' perceptions of peer group characteristics. In R.E. Muuss (Ed.), *Adolescent behaviour and society: A book of readings* (pp. 30–36). New York: Random House.

Browne, J. (2003). *Youth – beyond disability: Seminar reports*. Dublin: People with Disabilities in Ireland.

Buchholz, E.S. (1997). *The call of solitude: Alonetime in a world of attachment*. New York: Simon and Shuster.

Buckley, H. (1998). Filtering out fathers: The gendered nature of social work in child protection. *Irish Social Worker*, 16(3), 7–11.

Buhrmester, D. (1996). Need fulfilment, interpersonal competence and the developmental contexts of early adolescent friendship. In W.M. Bukowski, A.F. Newcomb, & W.W. Hartup (Eds.), *The company they keep: Friendship in childhood and adolescence*. New York: Cambridge University Press.

Burtney, E. (2000). *Teenage sexuality in Scotland*. Edinburgh: Health Education Board.

Burtney, E., & Duffy, M. (2004). *Young people and sexual health – individual, social and policy contexts*. UK: Palgrave.

Bynner, J. (2005). Rethinking the youth phase of the life-course: The case for emerging adulthood. *Journal of Youth Studies*, 8(4), 367–84.

Bynner, J.M., Romney, D.M., & Emler, N.P. (2003). Dimensions of political and related facets of identity in late adolescence. *Journal of Youth Studies*, 6(3), 319–35.

Byrne, M., Barry, M., & Sheridan, A. (2005). The development and evaluation of a mental health promotion programme for post-primary schools in Ireland. In B.B. Jensen & S. Cliffs (Eds.), *The health promoting school: International advances in theory, evaluation and practice*. Copenhagen: Danish University of Education Press.

Byrne, J., & McHugh, J. (2005). Residential Childcare. In P. Share & N. McElwee (Eds.), *Applied social care: An introduction for Irish Students*. Dublin: Gill & Macmillan.

Byrne, T., Nixon, E., Mayock, P., & Whyte, J. (2006). *Free time and leisure needs of young people living in disadvantaged communities*. Dublin: Children's Research Centre/Combat Poverty Agency.

Caldwell, L.L., Baldwin, C.K., Walls, T., & Smith, E. (2004). Preliminary effects of a leisure education program to promote healthy use of free time among middle school adolescents. *Journal of Leisure Research*, 36(3), 310–36.

Caldwell, L.L., Darling, N., Payne, L.L., & Dowdy, B. (1999). 'Why are you bored?' An examination of psychological and social control causes of boredom among adolescents. *Journal of Leisure Research*, 31, 103–121.

Caldwell, L.L., Smith, E.A., & Weissinger, E. (1992). Development of a leisure experience battery for adolescence; Parsimony, stability and validity. *Journal of Leisure Research*, 24, 361376.

Canavan, J. (1998). *The North Mayo Schools Project*. Dublin: Foróige.

Carolan, F. & Redmond, S. (2003). *Shout: The needs of young people in Northern Ireland who are lesbian, gay, bisexual and/or transgender.* Belfast: Youthnet.

Carr, A. (2002). *Prevention: What works with children and adolescents? A critical review of psychological prevention programmes for children, adolescents and their families.* Hove: Brunner–Routledge.

Cassidy, C., & Trew, K. (2004). Identity change in Northern Ireland: A longitudinal study of students' transition to university. *Journal of Social Issues, 60*(3), 523–41.

Central Statistics Office. (2002). *Census 2002: Principal demographic results.* Dublin: Stationery Office.

Central Statistics Office. (2003a). *Census 2002 – Volume 3, Household composition and family units.* Dublin: Stationery Office.

Central Statistics Office. (2003b). *Quarterly national household survey, third quarter 2002: Voter participation and abstention.* Cork and Dublin: Central Statistics Office.

Central Statistics Office. (2004). *Population and labour force projections 2006–2036.* Dublin: Stationery Office.

Central Statistics Office. (2005a). *Use of ICT by households.* www.cso.ie [accessed June 2006].

Central Statistics Office. (2005b). *Marriages 2002.* Cork and Dublin: Central Statistics Office.

Central Statistics Office. (2006). *Women and men in Ireland 2006.* Cork and Dublin: Central Statistics Office.

Centre for Social and Educational Research (CSER). (2001). *Study of participants in Garda Special Projects.* Dublin: Centre for Social and Educational Research, DIT.

Centre for Social and Educational Research (CSER). (2003). *Garda youth diversion project guidelines.* Dublin: Centre for Social and Educational Research, DIT.

Child Accident Prevention Trust. (2002). *Taking chances: The lifestyles and leisure risk of young people.* London: CAPT.

Children's Rights Alliance. (2002). *Submission to the National Crime Council.* Dublin: Children's Rights Alliance.

Children's Rights Alliance. (2006). *From rhetoric to rights. Second shadow report to the United Nations Committee on the Rights of the Child.* Dublin: CRA.

Chisholm, L. (1995). Conclusion: Europe, Europeanization and young people – A triad of confusing images. In A. Cavalli & O. Galland (Eds.), *Youth in Europe.* London: Pinter.

Claes, M.E. (1992). Friendship and personal adjustment during adolescence. *Journal of Adolescence, 15,* 39–55.

Clancy, P. (1982). *Participation in higher education: A national survey.* Dublin: Higher Education Authority.

Clancy, P. (2005). Education policy. In S. Quin, P. Kennedy, A. Matthews, & G. Kiely (Eds.), *Contemporary Irish social policy.* Dublin: UCD Press.

Clasen, D.R., & Brown, B.B. (1985). The multidimensionality of peer pressure in adolescence. *Journal of Youth and Adolescence, 14*(6), 451–68.

Cleary, A., Corbett, M., Galvin, M., & Wall, J. (2004). *Young men on the margins.* Dublin: Katherine Howard Foundation.

Cohen, S. (1973). *Folk devils and moral panics: The creation of the Mods and Rockers.* St Albans: Paladin.

Coleman, J.C. (1980). Friendship and the peer group in adolescence. In J. Adelson (Ed.), *Handbook of adolescent psychology* (pp. 408–31). New York: Wiley.

Coleman, J.C., & Hendry, L. (1999). *The nature of adolescence*. London: Routledge.

Coleman, J.S. (1961). *The adolescent society*. New York: Free Press.

Collins, J., Noble, G., Poynting, S., & Tabar, P. (2000). *Kebabs, kids, cops and crime: Youth, ethnicity and crime*. London: Pluto Press.

Commission on the Family (1998). *Strengthening families for life: Final report of the Commission on the Family to the Minister for Social, Community and Family Affairs*. Dublin: Stationery Office.

Commission on the Status of People with Disabilities (1997). *A strategy for equality*. Dublin: Stationery Office.

Conger, J. (1997). *Adolescence and youth: psychological development in a changing world* (5th ed.). New York: Longman.

Connor, S. (2003). *Youth sport in Ireland: The sporting, leisure and lifestyle patterns of Irish adolescents*. Dublin: The Liffey Press.

Constitution Review Group. (1996). *Report of the Constitution Review Group*. Dublin: Stationery Office.

Consultative Group on the Development of Youth Work. (1993). *Report to the Minister of State at the Department of Education*. Dublin: Department of Education.

Cooley, C.H. (1902). *Human nature and the social order*. New York: Charles Scribner & Sons.

Cooper, M.L., Shapiro, C.M., & Powers, A.M. (1998). Motivations for sex and risky sexual behaviour among adolescents and young adults: A functional perspective. *Journal of Personality and Social Psychology, 75*, 1528–58.

Corcoran, M. (2005). Portrait of the 'absent' father: The impact of non–residency on developing and maintaining a fathering role. *Irish Journal of Sociology, 14*(2), 134–54.

Cospóir. (1994). *The economic impact of sport in Ireland*. Dublin: Department of Education.

Costello, J., & Carty, C. (2003). *Teenagers here 2B heard*. Dublin: Irish Association of Young People in Care.

Cotter, A. (2005). The criminal justice system. In S. Quin, P. Kennedy, A. Matthews, & G. Kiely (Eds.), *Contemporary Irish social policy*. Dublin: UCD Press.

Council of Europe. (1975). European Sports Charter. Sport for all. European Sports Ministers' Conference, Brussels. Sport for All.

County Wexford Rural Youth Forum. (2000). *Rural youth work in County Wexford*. Wexford: Ferns Diocesan Youth Service.

Cousins, M. (2006). *Family research in Ireland: A review of the studies published under the first phase of the Families Research Programme*. Dublin: Family Support Agency.

Craft, M. (1974). Talent, family values and education in Ireland. In J. Eggleston (Ed.), *Contemporary research in the sociology of education*. London: Methuen.

Crawford, D., Jackson, E., & Godbey, G. (1991). A hierarchical model of leisure constraints. *Leisure Sciences, 13*, 309–320.

Crosby, R.A., DiClemente, R.J., Wingood, G.M., Cobb, B.K., Harrington, K., Davis, S.L., Hook, E., & Oh, M.K. (2002). Condom use and correlates of African American adolescent females' infrequent communication with sex partners about preventing sexually transmitted diseases and pregnancy. *Health Education and Behaviour, 29*(2), 219–31.

Crowley, N. (2006). *An ambition for equality*. Dublin: Irish Academic Press.

Cunningham, M. (2001). Young people's perspectives. Unpublished research conducted by the Children's Research Centre at Trinity College Dublin for the National Youth Work Development Plan.

Currie, C., Roberts, C., Morgan, A., Smith, B., Settertobulte, W., Samdal, O., & Rasmussen, V. (2003). *Young people's health in context. HBSC study*. Copenhagen: WHO.

Curry, J. (2003). *Irish social services* (4th ed.). Dublin: Institute of Public Administration.

Dahlgren A., & Whitehead, M. (1991). *Policies and strategies to promote social equity in health*. Stockholm: Institute of Futures Studies.

Daly, F., & Gilligan, R. (2005). *Lives in foster care*. Dublin: Children's Research Centre, Trinity College.

Dehne, K.L., & Riedner, G. (2001). Adolescence – a dynamic concept. *Reproductive Health Matters*, 9(17), 11–15.

Dempster, M., Newell, G., & Marley, J. (2005). Explaining binge drinking among adolescent males using the theory of planned behaviour. *Irish Journal of Psychology*, 26(1–2), 17–24.

Department of Education. (1965). *Investment in education*. Dublin: Department of Education.

Department of Education. (1970). *Reformatory and industrial schools systems report* ('Kennedy report'). Dublin: Stationery Office.

Department of Education. (1997). *Targeting sporting change*. Dublin: Department of Education.

Department of Education and Science. (2002a). *Report of the steering group to the PLC review established by the Department of Education and Science*. Dublin: Department of Education and Science. www.tui.ie/Policy%20Documents/PLC%20Review.html [accessed August 2006].

Department of Education and Science. (2002b). *Care inspection report: Finglas Child and Adolescent Centre*. Dublin: Department of Education and Science.

Department of Education and Science. (2002c). *Code of good practice: Child protection for the youth work sector*. Dublin: Department of Education and Science.

Department of Education and Science. (2003a). *National youth work development plan, 2003–2007*. Dublin: Stationery Office.

Department of Education and Science. (2003b). *Summary of all initiatives funded by the Department to help alleviate educational disadvantage*. Dublin: Stationery Office.

Department of Education and Science. (2004). *Care inspection report: Oberstown's Girls' School*. Dublin: Department of Education and Science.

Department of Education and Science. (2005). *DEIS – Delivering equality of opportunity in schools: An action plan for educational inclusion. Summary*. Dublin: Department of Education and Science.

Department of Health and Children. (1999). *Children first: National guidelines for the protection and welfare of children*. Dublin: Stationery Office.

Department of Health and Children. (2000). *National children's strategy – Our children, their lives*. Dublin: Stationery Office.

Department of Health and Children. (2001a). *Youth homelessness strategy*. Dublin: Stationery Office.

Department of Health and Children. (2001b). *National standards for children's residential centres.* Dublin: Department of Health and Children.

Department of Health and Children. (2002a). *Our duty to care: The principles of good practice for the protection of children and young people.* Dublin: Department of Health and Children.

Department of Health and Children. (2002b). *Interim report of the strategic task force on alcohol.* Dublin: Health Promotion Unit.

Department of Health and Children. (2004). *Strategic task force on alcohol. Second report. September.* Dublin: Health Promotion Unit.

Department of Health and Children. (2006). *A vision for change: Report of the expert group on mental health policy.* Dublin: Stationery Office.

Department of Health and Children. (no date). *Working for children and families: Exploring good practice.* Dublin: Department of Health and Children.

Department of Justice, Equality and Law Reform, (2005). *Report on the Youth Justice Review.* Dublin: Department of Justice, Equality and Law Reform.

Department of Justice, Equality and Law Reform. (2006a). *Fourth annual report of the Inspector of prisons and places of detention for the year 2004–2005.* Dublin: Department of Justice, Equality and Law Reform.

Department of Justice, Equality and Law Reform. (2006b). Address by Minister McDowell at the launch of ten new garda youth diversion projects, Castlebar, Co. Mayo (press release), 10 July.

Department of Labour. (1983). *Shaping the future: Towards a national youth policy – a discussion paper.* Dublin: Stationery Office.

Department of Social and Family Affairs. (1997). *National anti–poverty strategy.* Dublin: Department of Social and Family Affairs.

Department of the Taoiseach. (2006). *Towards 2016: Ten–year framework social partnership agreement 2006–2015.* Dublin: Stationery Office.

Department of Tourism, Sport and Recreation. (2001). *Building on experience: National Drugs Strategy 2001–2008.* Dublin: Stationery Office.

de Róiste, Á. (2000). Peer and parent-related loneliness in Irish adolescents. *Irish Journal of Psychology, 21*(3–4), 237–46.

de Róiste, Á., & Dinneen, J. (2005). *Young people's views about opportunities, barriers and supports in recreation and leisure.* Dublin: National Children's Office.

Deutsch, M., & Gerard, H.B. (1955). A study of normative and informational social influences upon social judgement. *Journal of Abnormal and Social Psychology, 51*, 629–36.

Devlin, M. (1989). Official youth work discourse: Aims, orientations and ideology in Irish youth work policy. Unpublished M.Soc.Sc. thesis, University College Dublin.

Devlin, M. (2000). Representations of youth in Ireland. National University of Ireland, Maynooth: Unpublished PhD thesis.

Devlin, M. (2003). A bit of the 'other': Media representations of young people's sexuality. *Irish Journal of Sociology, 12*(2), 86–106.

Devlin, M. (2006). *Inequality and the stereotyping of young people.* Dublin: The Equality Authority.

Devine, M.A. (2004). Being a 'doer' instead of a 'viewer': The role of inclusive leisure contexts in determining social acceptance for people with disabilities. *Journal of Leisure Research, 36*(2), 137–60.

Dolan, P. (2005). Helping young people at risk through social support: NYP youth study summary report – commissioned by Foróige/HSE Western Region.

Donnelly, M. (1995). Depression among adolescents in Northern Ireland. *Adolescence, 30*(118), 339–51.

Douglas, J. (1964). *The home and the school.* London: McGibbon and Kee.

Dring, C., & Hope, A. (2001). *The impact of alcohol advertising on teenagers in Ireland.* Dublin: Health Promotion Unit.

Drotner, K. (2000). Difference and diversity: Trends in young Danes' media uses. *Media, Culture and Society, 22,* 149–66.

Drudy, S., & Lynch, K. (1993). *Schools and society in Ireland.* Dublin: Gill & Macmillan.

du Bois-Reymond, M. & Chisholm, L. (Eds.). *The modernization of youth transitions in Europe.* San Francisco: Jossey–Bass.

Dubas, J.S., & Snider, B.A. (1993). The role of community-based youth groups in enhancing learning and achievement through non-formal education. In R. Lerner (Ed.), *Early adolescence: Perspectives on research, policy, and intervention* (pp. 150–74). Hillsdale, NJ: Erlbaum.

Duggan, A. (2000). *Athlone Institute of Technology Lifestyle Survey.* Athlone: Midland Health Board.

Dunn, J., Cheng, H., O'Connor, T., & Bridges, L. (2004). Children's perspectives on their relationships with non-resident parents. *Journal of Child Psychology and Psychiatry, 45*(3), 553–66.

Dunne, M., & Seery, D. (1997). *What on earth are they doing?* Cork: AIDS Alliance.

Dunphy, D. (1963). The social structure of urban adolescent peer groups. *Sociometry, 26,* 230–76.

Dunphy, D. (1990). Peer group socialisation. In R. Muss (Ed.), *Adolescent behaviour and society: A book of readings.* New York: McGraw–Hill.

Dusek, J. (1991). *Adolescent development and behaviour* (2nd ed.). Englewood Cliffs, NJ: Prentice Hall.

Dworkin, J.B., Larson, R., & Hansen, D. (2003). Adolescents' accounts of growth experiences in youth activities. *Journal of Youth and Adolescence, 32*(1), 17–27.

Ebata, A.T. & Moos, R.H. (1991). Coping and adjustment in distressed and healthy adolescents. *Journal of Applied Developmental Psychology, 12,* 33-54.

Eccles, J.S., & Barber, B.L. (1999). Student council, volunteering, basketball, or marching band: What kind of extracurricular matters? *Journal of Adolescent Research, 14,* 10–43.

Educational Research Centre. (2004). *Education for life: The achievements of 15–year–olds in Ireland in the second cycle of PISA.* Dublin: Educational Research Centre.

Egan, O., & Nugent, J.K. (1983). Adolescent conceptions of the homeland: A cross–cultural study. *Journal of Youth and Adolescence, 12,* 185–281.

Eisenstadt, S.N. (1956). *From generation to generation.* Glencoe: Free Press.

Eisenstadt, S.N (1963). Archetypal patterns of youth. In E.H. Erikson (Ed.), *Youth: Change and challenge.* New York: Basic Books.

Elchardus, M. (2003). Explaining the loss of trust: The case of Flanders. *e–Dare: Newsletter on Human Rights Education and Education for Democracy*. http://www.dare–network.org/newsletter [accessed November 2006].

Elkind, D. (1970). *Children and adolescents: Interpretive essays on Jean Piaget*. New York: Oxford University Press.

Elkind, D. (1981). *Children and adolescents*. Oxford: Oxford University Press.

Emler, N., & Reicher, S. (1995). *Adolescence and delinquency: The collective management of reputation*. Oxford: Blackwell.

Emond, R. (2002). *Learning from their lessons: A study of young people in residential care and their experiences of education*. Dublin: Children's Research Centre, TCD.

Equality Authority. (2006). *Traveller ethnicity*. Dublin: Equality Authority.

Erikson, E.H. (1959). *Identity and the life-cycle: Psychological issues*. New York: International Universities Press.

Erikson, E.H. (1968). *Identity: Youth and crisis*. London: Faber & Faber.

Espito, C., Johnson, B., Wolfsdorf, B., & Spirito, A. (2003). Cognitive factors: Hopelessness, coping and problem solving. In A. Spirito & J. Overholser (Eds.), *Evaluating and treating adolescent suicide attempters: From research to practice* (pp. 89–112). New York: Academic Press.

European Commission. (2001). *Eurobarometer 55:1. Young Europeans in 2001*. Brussels: European Commission.

European Commission. (2002). *A new impetus for European youth: White Paper*. Brussels: European Commission.

European Commission. (2005). *'Youth takes the floor': Young Europeans' concerns and expectations as to the development of the European Union. Background note for the Directorate General on Education and Culture based on Eurobarometer 63*. Brussels: European Commission.

European Commission. (2006). *Eurobarometer 65: Public opinion in the European Union. National report: Ireland*. Brussels: European Commission.

European Monitoring Centre on Racism and Xenophobia. (2006). *Annual report 2006*. Luxembourg: Office for Official Publications of the European Communities.

European Monitoring Centre for Drugs and Drug Addiction. (2003). *Annual report on the state of the drugs problem in the European Union and Norway*. Lisbon: European Monitoring Centre for Drugs and Drug Addiction.

Eurostat. (2006). The family in the EU25 seen through figures. *Eurostat news release*, 59/2006.

Evans, E., Hawton, K., & Rodham, K. (2005). Suicidal phenomena and abuse in adolescents: A review of epidemiological studies. *Child Abuse and Neglect, 29*, 45–8.

Fagan, G.H. (1995). *Culture, politics and Irish school dropouts: Constructing political identities*. Westport, CT: Bergin & Garvey.

Fahey, T. (1995). Family and household. In P. Clancy, S. Drudy, K. Lynch, & L. O'Dowd (Eds.), *Irish society: Sociological perspectives* (pp. 205–234). Dublin: Sociological Association of Ireland/Institute of Public Administration.

Fahey, T. (Ed.) (1999). *Social housing in Ireland: A study of success, failure and lessons learned*. Dublin: Oak Tree Press.

Fahey, T., & Russell, H. (2001). *Family formation in Ireland: Trends, data needs and implications*. Dublin: ESRI Policy Research Series No. 43.

Fahey, T., Delaney, L., & Gannon, B. (2005). *School children and sport in Ireland*. Dublin: ESRI.

Fahey, T., Layte, R., & Gannon, B. (2004). *Sports participation and health among adults in Ireland*. Dublin: ESRI.

Fahey, T., Hayes, B. & Sinnott, R. (2005). *Conflict and consensus: A study of values and attitudes in the Republic of Ireland and Northern Ireland*. Dublin: Institute of Public Administration.

Falkner, N.H., Neumark–Sztainer, D., Story, M., Jeffery, R.W., & Resnick, M.D. (2001). Social, educational and psychological correlates of weight status in adolescents. *Obesity Research, 9*, 32–42.

Fanning, B. (2002). *Racism and social change in the Republic of Ireland*. Manchester: Manchester University Press.

Faulker, A.H., & Cranston, K. (1998). Correlates of same-sex behaviour in a random sample of Massachusetts high school students. *American Journal of Public Health, 88*, 262–6.

Favazzo, A.R. (1998). The coming-of-age of self-mutilation. *Journal of Nervous and Mental Disease, 186*, 259–68.

Fergusson, D.M., & Horwood, L.J. (1997). Early onset cannabis use and psychosocial adjustment in young adults. *Addiction, 92*(3), 279–96.

Ferguson, H., & Hogan, F. (2004). *Strengthening families through fathers: Developing policy and practice in relation to vulnerable fathers and their families*. Waterford: Centre for Social and Family Research, WIT.

Festinger, L.A. (1954). A theory of social comparison processes. *Human Relations, 7*, 117–40.

Fitzgerald, M. (1997). *Rural youth needs in north Offaly and north west Kildare: A youth work response*. Naas/Edenderry: Kildare Youth Service/OAK Partnership.

Fitzpatrick, C., Lynch, F., Mills, C., & Daly, I. (2003). *Challenging times: Psychiatric disorders and suicidal behaviours in Irish adolescents*. Dublin: Department of Child and Family Psychiatry, Mater Misericordiae Hospital.

Flanagan, E., Bedford, D., O'Farrell, A., & Howell, F. (2003). *Smoking, alcohol and drug use among young people*. North Eastern Health Board.

Foley–Nolan, C., Kavanagh, P., Kelly, J., Millar, N., Murray, D., O'Sullivan, M.B., & Ryan, F. (2005). *Our Children...their future...why weight?* Cork: Health Service Executive – Southern Area.

Forde, W. (1995). *Growing up in Ireland: The development of Irish youth services*. Wexford: Cara Publications.

Forkan, C. (2006). Traveller children in education: Progress and problems. *Youth Studies Ireland, 1*(1), 77–92.

Foróige. (1999). *Foróige challenge 2000: Meeting youth needs in the new millennium*. Dublin: Foróige.

Foróige. (2005). Personal communication.

Fortune, S.A., & Hawton, K. (2005). Suicide and deliberate self-harm in children and adolescents. *Current Paediatrics, 15*, 575–80.

Fox, V. (1977). Is adolescence a phenomenon of modern times? *Journal of Psychohistory, 2*, 271–90.

French, J., & Raven, B. (1959). The bases of social power. In D.C. Cartwright (Ed.), *Studies in social power* (pp. 150–67). Ann Arbor: University of Michigan Press.

French, S., & Swain, J. (1997). Young disabled people. In J. Roche & S. Tucker (Eds.), *Youth in society* (pp. 199–206). London: Sage/Open University Press.

Freud, A. (1958). Adolescence. In R.S. Eissler, A. Freud, H. Hartmann, & J. Kris (Eds.), *Psychoanalytic study of the child* (Vol. 13). New York: International Universities Press.

Friedli, L. (1999). From the margins to the mainstream: The public health potential of mental health promotion. *International Journal for Mental Health Promotion, 1*(2), 30–36.

Friel, S., Nic Gabhainn, S., & Kelleher, C. (1999). *The national health and lifestyle surveys.* Dublin: Health Promotion Unit, Department of Health and Children and Centre for Health Promotion Studies, NUI, Galway.

Frith, S. (1984). *The sociology of youth.* Ormskirk: Causeway Press.

Frost, L. (2003). Doing bodies differently? Gender, youth, appearance and damage. *Journal of Youth Studies, 6*(1), 53–70.

Fuligni, A.J., & Eccles, J.S. (1993). Perceived parent-child relationships and early adolescents' orientation towards peers. *Developmental Psychology, 29*(4), 622–32.

Fullerton, D. (2004). *Promoting positive adolescent sexual health and preventing teenage pregnancy – A review of recent effectiveness* research (Report No. 2). Dublin: Crisis Pregnancy Agency.

Furby, L., & Beyth–Marom, R. (1992). Risk-taking in adolescence: A decision-making perspective. *Developmental Review, 12*, 1–44.

Furlong, A., & Cartmel, F. (1997). *Young people and social change: Individualization and risk in late modernity.* Buckingham: Open University Press.

Gaelic Athletic Association. (2005). Personal correspondence.

Gaetz, S. (1997). *Looking out for the lads: Community action and the provision of youth services in an urban Irish parish.* Newfoundland: Institute of Social and Economic Research.

Galland, O. (1995). What is Youth? In A. Cavalli & O. Galland (Eds.), *Youth in Europe.* London: Pinter.

Gannon, B., & Nolan, B. (2004). *Disability and labour market participation.* Dublin: Equality Authority/National Disability Authority.

Gannon, B., & Nolan, B. (2005). *Disability and social inclusion in Ireland.* Dublin: Equality Authority/National Disability Authority.

Garda Síochána. (2002). *Annual report.* Dublin: Garda Síochána.

Garda Síochána. (2003). *Annual report.* Dublin: Garda Síochána.

Garda Síochána. (2004). *Annual report.* Dublin: Garda Síochána.

Garda Síochána. (2005). *Annual report.* Dublin: Garda Síochána.

Gardner, H. (1985). *Frames of mind: The theory of multiple intelligences.* New York: Basic Books.

Garnets, L., & Kimmel, D. (1991). Lesbian and gay male dimensions in the psychological study of human diversity. In J. Goldchilds (Ed.), *Psychological study of human diversity in America: Master lectures.* Washington, DC: American Psychological Association.

Gay and Lesbian Equality Network (GLEN)/NEXUS Research Cooperative (1995).

Poverty, lesbians and gay men: The economic and social effects of discrimination. Dublin: Combat Poverty Agency.

Gelman, R., & Baillargeon, R. (1983). A review of some Piagetian concepts. In J.H. Flavell & E.M. Markman (Eds.), *Handbook of child psychology* (Vol. 3; pp. 167–230). New York: Wiley.

Geraghty, T., Breakey, C., & Keane, T. (1997). *A sense of belonging.* Belfast: Youth Action Northern Ireland.

Giddens, A. (1991). *Modernity and self identity: Self and society in the late modern age.* Cambridge: Polity Press.

Gilligan, R. (1991). *Irish child care services: Policy, practice and provision.* Dublin: Institute of Public Administration.

Gilligan, R. (1999). Child welfare review 1998. *Administration, 47*(2), 232–56.

Gilligan, R. (2000). Adversity, resilience and young people: The protective value of positive school and spare time experiences. *Children and Society, 14,* 37–47.

Gilligan, C., Lyons, N., & Hanmner, T. (1990). *Making connections: The relational worlds of adolescent girls at Emma Willard school.* Cambridge, MA: Harvard University Press.

Gillis, J.R. (1974). *Youth and history: Tradition and change in European age relations 1770 – present.* New York: Academic Press.

Glaser, R. (1984). Education and thinking: The role of knowledge. *American Psychologist, 39,* 93–104.

Glasser, M. (1977). Homosexuality in adolescence. *British Journal of Medical Psychology, 50,* 217–25.

Glendinning, A., Hendrey, L., & Shucksmith, J. (1995). Lifestyle, health and social class in adolescence. *Social Science & Medicine, 41,* 235–48.

Goggin, M. (1995). Gay and lesbian adolescence. In S. Moore & D. Rosenthal (Eds.), *Sexuality in adolescence.* London: Routledge.

Goosens, L., & Marcoen, L. (1999). Loneliness and positive attitude towards being alone in adolescence: Developmental processes and individual differences. In K. Rotenberg & S. Hymel (Eds.), *Loneliness in childhood and adolescence* (pp. 225–43). New York: Cambridge University Press.

Gorby, S., McCoy, S., & Watson, D. (2006). *2004 Annual School Leavers' Survey of 2002/2003 Leavers.* Dublin: ESRI.

Government of Ireland. (1985). *In partnership with youth: The national youth policy.* Dublin: Stationery Office.

Government of Ireland. (1992) *Education for a changing world (Green Paper).* Dublin: Stationery Office.

Government of Ireland. (1995a). *Charting our education future: White paper on education.* Dublin: Stationery Office.

Government of Ireland. (1995b). *Report of the task force on the Travelling community.* Dublin: Stationery Office.

Government of Ireland. (1999). *Ensuring the future – A strategy for rural development in Ireland (White Paper).* Dublin: Stationery Office.

Government of Ireland. (2000) *Supporting voluntary activity (White Paper).* Dublin: Stationery Office.

Green, E., Hebron, S., & Woodward, D. (1990). *Women's leisure, what leisure?* Basingstoke: Macmillan.

Green, K., Smith, A., & Roberts, K. (2005). Young people and lifelong participation in sport and physical activity: A sociological perspective on contemporary physical education programmes in England and Wales. *Leisure Studies, 24*(1), 27–43.

Greene, S. (1994). Growing–up Irish: Development in context. *Irish Journal of Psychology, 15*(2–3), 354–71.

Greene, S. (1995). Marital breakdown and divorce: The psychological consequences for adults and their children. In M. O'Brien (Ed.), *Divorce? Facing the issues of marital breakdown.* Dublin: Basement Press.

Greene, S. (2006). Child psychology: Taking account of children at last? *Irish Journal of Psychology, 27*(1–2), 8–15.

Greene, S. & Hogan, D. (Eds.). (2005). *Researching children's experience: Approaches and methods.* London: Sage.

Greene, S., & Moane, G. (2000). Growing up Irish: Changing children in a changing society. *Irish Journal of Psychology, 21,* 122–37.

Griffin, C. (1997). Representations of the young. In S. Roche & J. Tucker (Eds.), *Youth in society* (pp. 17–25). London: Sage/Open University Press.

Griffin, A.C., Younger, K.M., & Flynn, M.A. (2004). Assessment of obesity fear of fatness among inner city Dublin school children in a one year follow–up study. *Public Health Nutrition, 7*(6), 729–35.

Griffiths, M.D., Davies, M.N. & Chappell, D. (2004). Online computer gaming: A comparison of adolescent and adult gamers. *Journal of Adolescence, 27,* 87-96.

Grube, J.W., & Morgan, M. (1986). *Smoking, drinking and other drug use among Dublin post–primary pupils.* Dublin: ESRI.

Grunbaum, J.A., Kann, L., Kinchen, S., Ross, J., Hawkins, Lowry, R., Harris, W.A., McManus, T., Chyen, D., & Collins, J. (2004). Youth risk behaviour surveillance – United States, 2003. *MMWR Surveillance Summaries: Morbidity and Mortality Weekly Report Surveillance Summaries/CDC, 53*(2), 1–96.

Haan, N. (1974). The adolescent antecedents of an ego model of coping and defense and comparisons with Q–sorted ideal personalities. *Genetic Psychology Monographs, 89,* 273–306.

Haase, T. (2007). Deprivation and its spatial articulation. In B. Bartley & R. Kitchen (Eds.), *Understanding contemporary Ireland* (pp. 264–78). London: Pluto Press.

Hackett, C. (1997). Young people and political participation. In J. Roche & S. Tucker (Eds.), *Youth in society.* London: Sage/Open University Press.

Hagerty Davis, J., & McCreary Juhasz, A. (1985). The preadolescent/pet bond and psychosocial development. *Marriage and Family Review, 8,* 5–10.

Hall, G.S. (1904). *Adolescence: Its psychology and its relations to physiology, anthropology, sociology, sex, crime, religion and education.* New York: Appleton Press.

Hall, S., & Jefferson, T. (Eds.). (1975). *Resistance through rituals: Youth subcultures in postwar Britain.* London: Hutchinson.

Hall, S., Jefferson, T., & Clarke, T. (1976). Youth: A stage of life? *Youth in Society, 17.*

Halpenny, A. (2004). Children's perceptions of closeness and security in relationships with parents following parental separation. Unpublished PhD thesis, Trinity College, Dublin.

Halpenny, A.M., Keogh, A.F., & Gilligan, R. (2002). *A place for children?: Children in families living in emergency accommodation*. Dublin: Homeless Agency.

Hamilton, C. (2005). Child abuse, the United Nations Convention on the Rights of the Child and the criminal law. *Irish Law Times, 23*.

Hamilton, C. & Seymour, M. (2006). ASBOs and behaviour orders: Institutionalised intolerance of youth? *Youth Studies Ireland, 1*(1), 61–76.

Hammen, C.L., & Peters, S.D. (1977). Differential responses to male and female depressive reactions. *Journal of Consulting and Clinical Psychology, 45*, 994–1001.

Hanafin, S., & Brooks, A.M. (2005). *Report on the development of a national set of child well-being indicators in Ireland*. Dublin: National Children's Office.

Hanna, J.L. (1988). *Dance and stress. Resistance, reduction and euphoria*. New York: AMS Press Inc.

Hannan, D., & Ó Riain, S.F. (1993). *Pathways to adulthood in Ireland: Causes and consequences of success and failure in transitions amongst Irish youth*. Dublin: ESRI, General Research Series, Paper no. 161.

Hannan, D., Smyth, E., McCullagh, J., O'Leary, R., & McMahon, D. (1996). *Coeducation and gender equality. Exam performance, stress and personal development*. Dublin: Oaktree Press/ESRI.

Hanrahan, O. (2002). Illegal sales of cigarettes to children in Cork City. *Irish Medical Journal*, March, 95 (3).

Hart, D., & Fegley, S. (1995). Prosocial behaviour and caring in adolescence: Relations to self-understanding and social judgement. *Child Development, 22*, 157–62.

Harter, S. (1985). *The self-perception profile for children. Revision of the perceived competence scale for children*. Denver, CO: University of Denver.

Hartog, J. (1981). Loneliness and the adolescent. In J. Hartog, J.R. Audy, & Y.A. Cohen (Eds.), *The anatomy of loneliness*. New York: International Universities Press.

Hartup, W., & Stevens, N. (1999). Friendships and adaptation across the life–span. *Current Directions in Psychological Science, 8*, 76–9.

Hastings, J., MacGinn, M., Twomey, M., & Groeger, M. (2004). Mental health Ireland: Mental health promotion programmes in schools and with young people. In S. Saxena & P.J. Garrison (Eds.), *Mental health promotion case studies from countries* (pp. 47–9). Geneva: WHO.

Haughton, J. (1998). The dynamics of economic change. In W. Crotty & D. Schmitt (Eds.), *Ireland and politics of change*. London: Longman.

Havighurst, R.J. (1953). *Human development and education*. New York: Davis McKay.

Hayes, N. (2002). *Children's rights – Whose right? A review of child policy development in Ireland*. Dublin: Policy Institute, TCD.

Hayes, N. (2004). Children's rights in Ireland – Participation in policy development. In D. Crimmens & A. West (Eds.), *Having their say: Young people and participation: European experiences* (pp. 47–58). Lyme Regis: Russell House Publishing.

Haywood, L., Kew, F., Bramham, P., Spink, J., Capenerhurst, J., & Henry, I. (1995). *Understanding leisure* (2nd ed.). Cheltenham: Stanley Thornes.

Health Advisory Service. (1995). *Together we stand: The commissioning, role and management of child and adolescent mental health services*. London: HMSO.

Health Development Agency. (2003). *Teenage pregnancy and parenthood*. London: HDA. www.hda–online.org.uk [accessed September 2006].

Health Services Executive (HSE). (2003). *Health and social wellbeing in the mid-west*. Limerick: HSE.

Health Services Executive, National Suicide Review Group, & Department of Health and Children. (2005). *Reach-out: national strategy for action on suicide prevention 2005–2014*. Dublin: Department of Health and Children.

Heanue, K. (2002). *The missing people: A strategic approach to rural repopulation*. Dublin: Area Development Management.

Heaven, P., Connors, J., & Kellehear, A. (1992). Health locus of control beliefs and attitudes toward people with AIDS. *Australian Psychologist, 27*, 172–5.

Heaven, P.C. (1996). *Adolescent health: The role of individual differences*. London: Routledge.

Heaven, P.C. (2001). *The social psychology of adolescence*. London: Palgrave Macmillan.

Helve, H. & Holm, G. (Eds.). (2005). *Contemporary youth research: Local expressions and global connections*. Aldershot: Ashgate.

Hendick, H. (1990). *Images of youth, age, class and the male youth problem*. Oxford: Clarendon Press.

Hendin, H. (1991). Psychodynamics of suicide, with particular reference to the young. *American Journal of Psychiatry, 148*, 1150–58.

Hendrick, H. (1990). *Images of youth: Age, class and the male youth problem 1880–1920*. Oxford: Oxford University Press.

Hendry, L.B., Shucksmith, J., Love, J.G., & Glendinning, A. (1993). *Young peoples' leisure and lifestyles (YPPL study)*. London: Routledge.

Hendry, L.B., Kloep, M., & Wood, S. (2002). Young people talking about adolescent rural crowds and social settings. *Journal of Youth Studies, 5*(4), 357–74.

Hennessy, E., & Hogan, D. (2000). Twenty–five years of developmental and child psychology in Ireland: An analysis of PsycLit and ERIC databases. *Irish Journal of Psychology, 21*(3–4), 105–121.

Hennessy, E., & Donnelly, M. (2005). *After-school care in disadvantaged areas: The perspectives of children, parents and experts*. Dublin: Combat Poverty Agency [working paper 05/01].

Hetherington, E., & Clingempeel, W. (1992). *Coping with marital transitions* (Monographs of the Society for Research in Child Development, Volume 57, No. 2–3). Chicago: University of Chicago Press.

Hibell, B., Andersson, B., Ahlstrom, S., Balakireva, O., Bjarnasson, T., Kokkevi, A., & Morgan, M. (2000). *The 1999 ESPAD report: Alcohol and other drug use among students in 30 European countries*. Stockholm: Council of Europe, Pompidou Group.

Higgins, K., Percy, A., & McCrystal, P. (2004). Secular trends in substance use: The conflict and young people in Northern Ireland. *Journal of Social Issues, 60*(3), 485–507.

Hodgson, R. & Abbasi, T. (1995). Effective mental health promotion: Literature review. Health Promotion Wales.

Hoffman, B.R., Sussman, S., Unger, J.B., & Valente, T.W. (2006). Peer influences on adolescent cigarette smoking: A theoretical review of the literature. *Substance Use and Misuse, 41*, 103–155.

Hogan, D., & Gilligan, R. (Eds.). (1998). *Researching children's experiences: Qualitative approaches*. Dublin: Children's Research Centre, TCD.

Hogan, D., Halpenny, A., & Greene, S. (2002). *Children's experiences of parental separation*. Dublin: Children's Research Centre, TCD.

Holland, J., Ramazanoglu, C., & Thomson, R. (1996). In the same boat? The gendered (in)experience of first heterosex. In D. Richardson (Ed.), *Theorising heterosexuality* (pp. 143–60). Milton Keynes: Open University Press.

Homeless Agency. (2005). *Counted in – 2005*. Dublin: Homeless Agency.

House, A., Owens, D., & Patchett, L. (1999). Deliberate self–harm. *Quality in Health Care*, 8, 137–43.

Howe, C., Tolmie, A., & Rodgers, C. (1991). Information technology and group work in physics. *Journal of Computer Assisted Learning*, 7, 133–43.

Hughes, C., Graham, C., & Grayson, A. (2004). Executive functions in childhood: Development and disorder. In J. Oates & A. Grayson (Eds.), *Cognitive and language development in children* (pp. 205–230). Milton Keynes: Open University/Blackwell.

Hultsman, W.Z. (1993). The influence of others as a barrier to recreation participation in early adolescence. *Journal of Leisure Research*, 25, 150–64.

Hutchinson, L., Magennis, P., Shepard, J. & Brown A. (1998). The BAOMS United Kingdom survey of facial injuries part 1: Aetiology and the association with alcohol consumption. *British Journal of Oral Maxillofacial Surgery*, 36, 4-14.

Hyde, A., & Howlett, E. (2004). *Understanding teenage sexuality in Ireland*. Dublin: Crisis Pregnancy Agency.

Hyde, A., Lohan, M., & McDonnell, O. (2004). *Sociology for health professionals in Ireland*. Dublin: IPA.

Ikeda, J., & Naworkski, P. (1992). *Am I fat? Helping children accept differences in body size*. Santa Cruz, CA: ETR Associates.

Inhelder, B., & Piaget, J. (1958). *The growth of logical thinking from childhood to adolescence*. New York: Basic Books.

Inglis, T. (1998). *Lessons in Irish sexuality*. Dublin: UCD Press.

Ingledew, D.K., and Sullivan, G., (2002). Effects of body mass and body image on exercise motives in adolescence. *Psychology of Sport and Exercise*, 3(4), 323–38.

Inglehart, R. (1990). *Culture shift in advanced industrial society*. Princeton: Princeton University Press.

Inglehart, R. (2000). Globalization and postmodern values. *Washington Quarterly*, 23(1), 215–28.

International Lesbian and Gay Association–Europe (2000). *Report submitted to the legal affairs and human rights committee (Parliamentary Assembly of the Council of Europe)*. Brussels: European Union.

Ireland. (1937). *Constitution of Ireland*. Dublin: Government Publications.

Irish Association of Young People in Care. (2006). Latest available statistics on young people in care in Ireland. http://www.iaypic.ie/org/demograph.htm [accessed November 2006].

Irish College of Psychiatrists. (2005). *A better future now: Position statement on psychiatric services for children and adolescents in Ireland* (Occasional paper OP60). Dublin: Irish College of Psychiatrists.

Irish Examiner. (2006, July 12). Parents fined €4000 for failing to keep children in school. *Irish Examiner*, p. 10.

Irish Girl Guides. (2005) Personal correspondence.

Irish Independent. (2006, June 22). Truancy drive sees parents of 19 pupils brought to court. *Irish Independent*, p. 6.

Irish National Teachers' Organisation (INTO). (2005). Health and physical education survey. www.into/roi/publications/pressreleases/2005/healthandphysical educationsurvey [accessed November 2005].

Irish Nutrition and Dietetic Institute. (1990). *Irish National Nutrition Survey*. Dublin: INDI.

Irish Society for the Prevention of Cruelty to Children. (2006). *2005 Annual call statistics.* www.ispcc.ie/pr clstats06.htm [accessed June 2006].

Irish Sports Council. (2000). *Code of ethics: Good practice for children's sport.* Dublin: Irish Sports Council.

Irish Sports Council. (2003). *'Sport for life'; The*
Irish Sports Council statement of strategy 2003–2005. Dublin: Stationery Office.

Irwin, A. (2006). *Stall anoishe! Minceirs whiden (Stop here! Travellers talking).* Galway: Galway Travellers' Movement.

Jackson, A. (2005) Ask the experts: Travellers in Ireland and issues of social care. In P. Share & N. McElwee (Eds.), *Applied social care: An introduction for Irish students* (pp. 253–70). Dublin: Gill & Macmillan.

Jackson, E.L. (1997). In the eye of the beholder: A comment on Samdahl and Jekubovich (1997), 'A critique of leisure constraints: Comparative analyses and understandings'. *Journal of Leisure Research, 29*(4), 458–68.

Jackson, L.A., Ervin, K.S., Gardner, P.D., & Schmitt, N. (2001). Gender and the internet: Women communicating and men searching. *Sex Roles, 44,* 363–79.

Jackson, S., & Rodrigues–Tomé, H. (1993). *Adolescence and its social worlds.* Hove: Lawrence Erlbaum Associates.

Jaffe, M.L. (1998). *Adolescence.* New York: Wiley.

James, D.J., Sofroniou, N., & Lawlor, M. (2003). The response of Irish adolescents to bullying. *Irish Journal of Psychology, 24*(1–2), 22–34.

Janeway–Conger, J., & Galambos, N.L. (1997). *Adolescence and youth: Psychological development in a changing world* (5th ed.). New York: Addison–Wesley.

Jarman, N., & Tennant, A. (2003). *An acceptable prejudice? Homophobic violence and harassment in Northern Ireland.* Belfast: Institute for Conflict Research.

Jeffs, T., & Smith, M. (1990). *Young people, inequality and youth work.* London: Macmillan.

Jeffs, T., & Smith, M. (1998/99). The problem of 'youth' for youth work. *Youth & Policy, 62,* 45–66.

Jenkins, R. (1983). *Lads, citizens and ordinary kids: Working class youth lifestyles in Belfast.* London: Routledge & Kegan Paul.

Kahn, R.L. & Antonucci, T.C. (1980). Convoys over the life course: attachment, roles and social support. In P.B. Baltes & O.G. Brim (Eds.) *Life-span Development and Behaviour, vol. 3.* New York: Academic Press.

Karvonen, S., West, P., Sweeting, H., Rahkonen, O., & Young, R. (2001). Lifestyle, social class and health –related behaviour: A cross–cultural comparison of 15 year olds in Glasgow and Helsinki. *Journal of Youth Studies, 4*(4), 393–413.

Kashani, J., Rosenberg, T., & Reid, J. (1989). Developmental perspectives on child and adolescent depressive symptoms in a community sample. *American Journal of Psychiatry, 146*, 871–5.

Katchadourian, H. (1990). Sexuality. In S. Feldman & G.R. Elliott (Eds.), *At the threshold: The developing adolescent* (pp. 330–51). Cambridge, MA: Harvard University Press.

Katz, C. (1998). Disintegrating developments: Global economic restructuring and the eroding ecologies of youth. In T. Skelton & G. Valentine (Eds.), *Cool places: Geographies of youth cultures* (pp. 130–44). London: Routledge.

Keating, D.P. (1990). Adolescent thinking. In S.S. Feldman & G.R. Elliott (Eds.), *At the threshold: The developing adolescent* (pp. 54–88). Cambridge, MA: Harvard University Press.

Kelleher, C., Nic Gabhainn, S., Friel, S., Corrigan, H., Nolan, G., Sixsmith, J., Walsh, O., & Cooke, M. (2003). *The national health and lifestyle surveys: SLAN and HBSC.* Galway: Centre for Health Promotion Studies, NUI Galway.

Kelleher, M.J. (2005). *Suicide and the Irish.* Cork: Mercier Press.

Kelleher, P., Kelleher, C., & Corbett, M. (2000). *Left out on their own: Young people leaving care in Ireland.* Dublin: Oak Tree Press/Focus Ireland.

Kelly, J.R. (1987). *Freedom to be. A new sociology of leisure.* New York: Macmillan.

Kennedy, F. (2001). *Cottage to crèche: Family change in Ireland.* Dublin: Institute of Public Administration.

Kenny, M. (1997). *The routes of resistance: Travellers and second–level schooling.* Aldershot: Ashgate.

Kenny, M., McNeela, E., Shevlin, M., & Daly, T. (2000). *Hidden voices: Young people with disabilities speak about their second level schooling.* Cork: Bradshaw Books/South West Regional Authority.

Kenny, M., McNeela, E., & Shevlin, M. (2003). Living and learning: The school experience of some young people with disabilities In M. Shevlin & R. Rose (Eds.), *Encouraging voices: Respecting the rights of young people who have been marginalised* (pp. 138–58). Dublin: National Disability Authority.

Keogh, A.F., & Whyte, J. (2003). *Getting on: The experiences and aspirations of immigrant students in second level schools linked to the Trinity Access Programmes.* Dublin: Children's Research Centre, Trinity College.

Kerpelman, J., Pittman, J.F., & Lamke, L. (1997). Toward a microprocess perspective on adolescent identity development: An identity control theory approach. *Journal of Adolescent Research, 12*, 141–54.

Kerry Mental Health Association. (2001). *A survey of perceived stress levels and coping responses in 1st year post–primary school students.* Killarney: Kerry Mental Health Association. www.kerrymentalhealth.com/research/school–survey [accessed 15 March 2006].

Kiely, G. (1995). Fathers in families. In I. Colgan McCarthy (Ed.), *Irish Family Studies: Selected papers.* Dublin: Family Studies Centre.

Kiely, G. (2001). The changing role of fathers. In A. Cleary, M. Nic Ghiolla Phádraig, & S. Quin (Eds.), *Understanding children (vol. 2): Changing experiences and family forms.* Cork: Oak Tree Press.

Kiesner, J., Kerr, M., & Stattin, H. (2004). 'Very important persons' in adolescence: Going beyond in-school, single friendships in the study of peer homophily. *Journal of Adolescence, 27*, 545–60.

Kilkelly, U. (2005). *The Children's Court: A children's rights audit.* Cork: Faculty of Law, NUI Cork.

Kilkelly, U. (2006). *Youth justice in Ireland: Tough lives, rough justice.* Dublin: Irish Academic Press.

Kilbarrack Coast Community Project. (2004). A prevalence study of drug use by young people in a mixed suburban area. Dublin: NACD.

Kimberlee, R.H. (2002). Why don't British young people vote at general elections? *Journal of Youth Studies, 5*(1), 85–98.

Kirby, D., (2001). *Emerging answers.* Washington, DC: National Campaign to Prevent Teenage Pregnancy.

Kirchler, E., Palmonari, A., & Pombeni, M.L. (1993). Developmental tasks and adolescent relationships with their peers and their family. In S. Jackson & H. Rodrigues–Tomé (Eds.), *Adolescence and its social worlds* (pp. 145–67). Hove: Lawrence Erlbaum Associates.

Kitchen, R., & Bartley, B. (2007a). Ireland in the twenty–first century. In B. Bartley & R. Kitchen (Eds.), *Understanding contemporary Ireland* (pp. 1–26). London: Pluto Press.

Kitchen, R., & Bartley, B. (2007b). Ireland now and in the future. In B. Bartley & R. Kitchen (Eds.), *Understanding contemporary Ireland* (pp. 301–307). London: Pluto Press.

Kloep, M. (1999). Love is all you need? Focusing on adolescents' life concerns from an ecological point of view. *Journal of Adolescence, 22*, 49–63.

Kochenderfer, B.J., & Ladd, G.W. (1997). Victimized children's responses to peers' aggression: Behaviours associated with reduced versus continued victimization. *Development and Psychopathology, 9*, 59–73.

Kohlberg, L. (1976). Moral stages and moralization: The cognitive–developmental approach. In T. Lickona (Ed.), *Moral development and behaviour.* New York: Hoolt, Rinehart & Winston.

Kowalski, A.P., Crocker, P.R.E., & Kowalski, K.C. (2000). The physical self and physical activity relationships in college women: Does social physique anxiety moderate effects? *Research Quarterly for Exercise and Sport, 3*(1), 55–62.

Kuhn, D., Amsel, E., & O'Loughlin, M. (1988). *The development of scientific thinking skills.* San Diego: Academic Press.

Lacourse, E., Villeneuve, M., & Claes, M. (2003). Theoretical structure of adolescent alienation: A multigroup confirmatory factor analysis. *Adolescence, 38*(152), 639–50.

Lalor, K., O'Regan, C., & Quinlan, S. (2003). Determinants of sexual behaviour. *Irish Journal of Sociology, 12*(2), 121–33.

Lalor, K., & Baird, K. (2006). *Our views – anybody listening? Researching the views and needs of young people in Co. Kildare.* Naas: Kildare Youth Services.

Lalor, K., Ryan, F., Seymour, M., &. Hamilton, C. (Eds.). (2006). Conference proceedings, 'Young people and crime: Research, policy and practice', Croke Park, Dublin, 12–13 September 2005 (www.cser.ie).

Lapsley, D.K., Milstead, M., Quintana, S., Flannery, D., & Buss, R.R. (1986). Adolescent egocentrism and formal operations: Tests of theoretical assumption. *Developmental Psychology, 22,* 800–807.

Larson, R. (1995). Variations of experience in informal and formal sports. *Research Quarterly for Exercise and Sport, 55.*

Larson, R., & Kleiber, D. (1991). Daily experiences of adolescence. In P. Tolan & B. Cohler (Eds.), *Handbook of clinical research and practice with adolescents* (pp. 125–45) New York: Wiley.

Larson R., & Richards, M. (1994). *Divergent realities.* New York: Basic Books.

Law Reform Commission. (2006). *Rights and duties of cohabitants.* (Report LRC–82–2006). Dublin: Law Reform Commission.

Lawlor, M., & James, D. (2000). Prevalence of psychological problems in Irish school going children. *Irish Journal of Psychological Medicine, 17*(4), 117–22.

Layte, R., McGee, H., Quail, A., Rundle, K., Cousins, G., Donnelly, C., Mulcahy, F., & Conroy, R. (2006). *The Irish study of sexual health and relationships.* Dublin: Department of Health and Children and Crisis Pregnancy Agency.

Leccardi, C., & Ruspini, E. (Eds.). (2006). *A new youth?: Young people, generations and family life.* Aldershot: Ashgate.

Lee, J.J. (1989). *Ireland 1912–1985: Politics and society.* Cambridge: Cambridge University Press.

Lee, J.M., & Bell, N.J. (2003). Individual differences in attachment-autonomy configurations: Linkages with substance use and youth competencies. *Journal of Adolescence, 26,* 347–61.

Lempers, J.D., & Clark–Lempers, D.S. (1993). A functional comparison of same-sex and opposite-sex friendships during adolescence. *Journal of Adolescent Research, 8,* 89–108.

Lerner, H.E. (1976). Parental mislabelling of female genitals as a determinant of penis envy and learning inhibitions in women. *Journal of the American Psychoanalytic Association, 24,* 269–84.

Lesovitch, L. (2005). *Roma educational needs in Ireland: Context and challenges.* Dublin: City of Dublin Vocational Education Committee/Pavee Point/Roma Support Group.

Lewko, J.H., & Greendorfer, S.L. (1998). Family influences in sport socialisation of children and adolescents. In F.L. Smoll, R.A. Magill, & M.A. Ash (Eds.), *Children in sport.* Champaign, IL: Human Kinetics Publishers.

Leyser, Y., & Cole, K.B. (2004). Leisure preferences and leisure communication with peers of elementary students with and without disabilities: Educational implications. *Education, 124*(4), 595–605.

Liston, K., & Rush, M. (2006). Social capital and health in Irish sports policy. *Administration, 53*(4), 73–88.

Lodge, A. & Lynch, K. (2003). Young people's equality concerns: The invisibility of diversity. In M. Shevlin & R. Rose (Eds.), *Encouraging voices: Respecting the rights of young people who have been marginalised* (pp. 15–35). Dublin: National Disability Authority.

Lodge, A., & Lynch, K. (2004). *Diversity at school.* Dublin: Equality Authority/Institute of Public Administration.

Lourdes, C. (2003). *Learning to grow-up: Multiple identities of young lesbians, gay men and bisexual people in Northern Ireland.* Belfast: Northern Ireland Human Rights Commission.

Lynch, K. (1998). The status of children and young persons: Educational and related issues. In S. Healy & B. Reynolds (Eds.), *Social policy in Ireland: Principles, practice and problems*. Dublin: Oak Tree Press.

Lynch, K., & Lodge, A. (2002). *Equality and power in schools: Redistribution, recognition and representation*. London: Routledge Falmer.

Lynch, K., & Morgan, V. (1995). Gender and education: North and South. In P. Clancy, S. Drudy, K. Lynch, & L. O'Dowd (Eds.), *Irish society: Sociological perspectives*. Dublin: Institute of Public Administration.

Lynn, R., & Wilson, G. (1993). Sex differences in cognitive abilities among Irish primary and secondary school children. *Irish Journal of Psychology, 14*(2), 293–300.

MacHale, E., & Newell, J. (1997). Sexual behaviour and sex education in Irish school-going teenagers. *International Journal of STD & AIDS, 8*, 196–200.

MacManus, E. (2004). The school-based lives of lesbian, gay, bisexual and transgender (LGBT) youth. University College Dublin: Unpublished MSc Thesis.

MacSharry, R., & White, P. (2000). *The making of the Celtic Tiger*. Cork: Mercier Press.

McAuley, K., & Brattman, M. (2002). *Hearing young voices: Consulting children and young people, including those experiencing poverty or other forms of social exclusion, in relation to public policy development in Ireland*. Dublin: Children's Rights Alliance and National Youth Council of Ireland.

McCann James, C. (2005). Ethnicity and social care: An Irish dilemma. In P. Share & N. McElwee (Eds.), *Applied social care: An introduction for Irish students* (pp. 321–36). Dublin: Gill & Macmillan.

McCann, M., Ó Síocháin, S., & Ruane, J. (1994). *Irish Travellers: Culture and ethnicity*. Belfast: Institute of Irish Studies, Queen's University.

McCauley, A.P., & Salter, C. (1995). Meeting the needs of young adults. *Population Report, Series J, 41*, 1–39.

McCullagh, C. (2006). Juvenile justice in Ireland: Rhetoric and reality. In T. O'Connor & M. Murphy (Eds.), *Social care in Ireland: Theory, policy and practice*. Cork: CIT Press.

McDonnell, I., & Wegimont, L. (2000). *Trends in Irish youth opinion on development and justice issues: A comparative analysis of representative samples 1995–1999*. Dublin: Development Education for Youth.

McElwee, N., & Monaghan, G. (2005). *Darkness on the edge of town: An exploratory study of heroin misuse in Athlone and Portlaoise*. Athlone: Athlone Institute of Technology/ Midland Regional Drugs Strategic Taskforce.

McGee, R., Williams, S., Howden-Chapman, P., Martin, J., & Kawachi, I. (2005). Participation in clubs and groups from childhood to adolescence and its effects on attachment and self-esteem. *Journal of Adolescence, 29*, 1–17.

McGrath, D., O'Keeffe, S., & Smith, M. (2005). *Crisis Pregnancy Agency statistics report 2005: Fertility and crisis pregnancy indices*. Dublin: Crisis Pregnancy Agency.

McHale, E., & Newell, J. (1997). Sexual behaviour and sex education in Irish school-going teenagers. *International Journal of STD and AIDS, 8*, 196–200.

McKenna-McElwee, S., & Brown, T. (2005). Community Childcare. In P. Share & N. McElwee (Eds.), *Applied social care: An introduction for Irish students*. Dublin: Gill & Macmillan.

McKeown, K. (2001a). Fathers and families: Research and reflection on key questions – a policy paper prepared for Springboard. Unpublished report to the Department of Health and Children.

McKeown, K. (2001b). Families and single fathers in Ireland. *Administration*, 49(1), 3–24.

McKeown, K., & Sweeney, J. (2001). *Family well-being and family policy. A review of research on benefits and costs.* Dublin: Government Publications.

McKeown, K., Pratschke, J., & Haase, T. (2003). Family well-being: what makes a difference? Report to the Ceifin Centre, Co. Clare. www.welfare.ie/publications/famwelloct03.pdf [accessed July 2006].

McLoughlin, M. (2003). Why young people don't vote. *Irish Youth Work Scene*, Issue 39, July.

McMullan, M., McShane, L., & Grattan, A. (2006). *It's always in the back of your mind: Newry and Armagh area based strategy (developing children and young people).* Belfast: Youth Action Northern Ireland.

McMurray, R.G., Harrel, J.S., Deng, S., Bradley, C.B., Cox, L.M., & Bangdiwala, S.I. (2000). The influence of physical activity, socio-economic status and ethnicity on the weight status of adolescents. *Obesity Research*, 8, 130–139.

McPhail, A., Kirk, D., & Eley, D. (2003). Listening to young people's voices: Youth sport leaders' advice on facilitating participation in sport. *European Physical Education Review*, 9(1), 57–73.

McPhillips, S. (2005). *Dublin children court: A pilot research project.* Dublin: Irish Association for the Study of Delinquency.

McRea, N. (2003). *Steps towards inclusion: Developing youth work with separated children.* Dublin: National Youth Council of Ireland.

McRobbie, A. & Nava, M. (Eds.) (1984). *Gender and generation.* London: Macmillan.

McShane, I. (2004). The youth of Ireland. In M. MacLachlan (Ed.), *Binge drinking and youth culture: Alternative perspectives* (pp. 103–112). Dublin: Liffey Press.

McVerry, P. (2006). Rehabilitation: Are we for real? *Working notes: Facts and analysis of social and economic issues.* Jesuit Centre for Faith and Justice, Issue 53.

Macionis, J.J., & Plummer, K. (2005). *Sociology: A global introduction* (3rd ed.). Harlow: Pearson/Prentice Hall.

Mahoney, J.L. (2000). School extracurricular activity participation as a moderator in the development of antisocial patterns. *Child Development*, 71, 502–516.

Malesevic, V. (2003). Demonic or divine? Attitudes towards sex and sexuality among Galway university students. *Irish Journal of Sociology*, 12(2), 107–120.

Marcia, J.E. (1980). Identity in adolescence. In J. Adelson (Ed.), *Handbook of adolescent psychology.* New York: Wiley.

Marcoen, A., & Goosens, L. (1993). Loneliness, attitude towards aloneness and solitude: Age differences and developmental significance during adolescence. In S. Jackson & H. Rodreguez–Tomé (Eds.), *Adolescence and its social worlds* (pp. 197–227). Hove: Erlbaum.

Marcoen, A., & Goossens, L. (1999). Cited in K.L. Rotenberg & S. Hymel, *Loneliness in childhood and adolescence.* Cambridge: Cambridge University Press.

Martin, K.A. (1996). *Puberty, sexuality and the self: Boys and girls at adolescence.* London: Routledge.

Martin, F. (2000). *The politics of children's rights*. Cork: Cork University Press.

Martino, W. (2001). Boys and reading: Investigating the impact of masculinities on boys' reading preferences and involvement in literacy. *Australian Journal of Language and Literacy*, 24(1), 61–71.

Mathas, E.W., Adams, H.E., & Davis, R.M. (1985). Jealousy: Loss of relationship rewards, loss of self-esteem, depression, anxiety and anger. *Journal of Personality and Social Psychology*, 48, 1552–61.

Mayock, P. (2000). *Choosers or losers? Influences on young people's choices about drugs in inner city Dublin*. Dublin: Children's Research Centre, TCD.

Mayock, P. (2004). Binge drinking and the consumption of pleasure. In M. MacLachlan (Ed.), *Binge drinking and youth culture: Alternative perspectives* (pp. 113–41). Dublin: Liffey Press.

Mayock, P. (2005). 'Scripting' risk: Young people and the construction of drug journeys. *Drugs: Education, Prevention and Policy*, 12(5), 349–68.

Mayock, P., & Byrne, T. (2004). *A study of sexual health issues, attitudes and behaviours: The views of early school leavers*. Dublin: Crisis Pregnancy Agency.

Mayock, P., & Vekic, K. (2006). *Understanding youth homelessness in Dublin city: Key findings from the first phase of a longitudinal cohort study*. Dublin: Stationery Office.

Mayock, P., Kitching, K., & Morgan, M. (2007). *RSE in the context of SPHE: An assessment of the challenges to full implementation of the programme in post-primary schools*. Dublin: Crisis Pregnancy Agency/Department of Education and Science.

Mead, G.H. (1934). *Mind, self and society*. Chicago: University of Chicago Press.

Merten, D. (1996). Visibility and vulnerability: Responses to rejection by non-aggressive junior high-school boys. *Journal of Early Adolescence*, 16, 5–26.

Miles, S. (2000). *Youth lifestyles in a changing world*. Buckingham: Open University Press.

Mills, C., Guerin, S., Lynch, F., Daly, I., & Fitzpatrick, C. (2004). The relationship between bullying, depression and suicidal thoughts/behaviour in Irish adolescents. *Irish Journal of Psychological Medicine*, 21(4), 112–16.

Modell, J., & Goodman, M. (1990). Historical perspectives. In S.S. Feldman & G.R. Elliott (Eds.), *At the threshold: The developing adolescent*. Cambridge, MA: Harvard University Press.

Morgan, M. (2000a). *Relationships and sexuality education: An evaluation and review of implementation*. Dublin: Department of Education and Science.

Morgan, M. (2000b). *Schools and part-time work in Dublin. The facts*. Dublin: Employment Pact, Policy Paper No. 4.

Morgan, M., & Grube, J. (1987). Consequences of maternal employment for adolescent behaviour and attitudes. *Irish Journal of Psychology*, 3(2), 85–98.

Morgan, M., & Grube, J.W. (1991). Closeness and peer influence. *British Journal of Social Psychology*, 30, 159–69.

Morgan, M., & Grube, J. (1994). Lifestyle changes: A social psychological perspective with reference to cigarette smoking among adolescents. *Irish Journal of Psychology*, (1), 179–90.

O.T. (2001). Adolescents and political conflict in Northern Ireland (Letter). *Conflict and Survival*, 18, 102–104.

Muldoon, O.T., & Wilson, K. (2001). Ideological commitment, experience of conflict and adjustment in Northern Irish adolescents. Medicine, Conflict and Survival, 17(2), 112–24.

Muldoon, O.T., Trew, K., & Kilpatrick, R. (2000). The legacy of the troubles on the development of young people. Youth and Society, 32(1), 6–28.

Mullan, E., & NicGabhainn, S. (2002). Self-esteem and health-risk behaviours: Is there a link? Irish Journal of Psychology, 23(1–2), 27–36.

Murray, P. (2002). Hello! Are you listening? Disabled teenagers' experience of access to inclusive leisure. York: Joseph Rowntree Foundation/York Publishing Services.

Murphy, J., & Gilligan, C. (1980). Moral development in late adolescence and adulthood: A critique and reconstruction of Kohlberg's theory. Human Development, 23, 77–104.

Naidoo, J., & Wills, J. (1994). Health promotion – foundations for practice. London: Baillere Tindall.

National Children's Office. (2005a). United Nations Convention on the Rights of the Child: Ireland's second report to the UN Committee on the Rights of the Child. Dublin: National Children's Office.

National Children's Office. (2005b). Second level student councils in Ireland: A study of enablers, barriers and supports. Dublin: National Children's Office.

National Children's Office, the Children's Rights Alliance and the National Youth Council of Ireland. (2005). Young voices: Guidelines on how to involve children and young people in your work. Dublin: Authors.

National Conjoint Child Health Committee. (2001). Best health for adolescents – get connected. Developing an adolescent friendly health service. Ireland: National Conjoint Health Committee.

National Crime Council. (2001). Crime in Ireland: Trends and patterns, 1950 to 1998. Dublin: National Crime Council.

National Disability Authority. (2002). Disability related research in Ireland 1996–2001. Dublin: National Disability Authority.

National Disability Authority (2004). Disability agenda, 1/04. Dublin: National Disability Authority.

National Disability Authority. (2005a). Disability agenda, issue 2.2, August. Dublin: National Disability Authority.

National Disability Authority. (2005b). Disability and sexual orientation. Dublin: National Disability Authority.

National Education Convention Secretariat. (1994). Report on the National Education Convention. Dublin: National Education Convention Secretariat.

National Education Welfare Board. (2006). Analysis of school attendance data at primary and post primary levels for 2004/2005. Dublin: National Education Welfare Board.

National Heart Alliance. (2001). Position paper on physical activity for children and young people. Dublin: National Heart Alliance.

National Suicide Research Foundation. (2003). National parasuicide registry annual report. Cork: NSRF.

National Suicide Research Foundation. (2004). National parasuicide registry annual report. Cork: NSRF.

National Youth Council of Ireland. (1998). *Get your facts right*. Dublin: National Youth Council of Ireland.

National Youth Council of Ireland. (2000). *Share it with the rest of the class*. Dublin: National Youth Council of Ireland.

National Youth Council of Ireland. (2004a) *Sense & sexuality: A support pack for addressing the issue of sexual health with young people in youth work settings*. Dublin: NYCI.

National Youth Council of Ireland. (2004b). *Good habits of mind: A mental health promotion initiative for those working with young people in out-of-school settings*. Health Service Executive Northern Area.

National Youth Council of Ireland. (2006a). Youth work – An introduction. www.youth.ie [accessed September 2006].

National Youth Council of Ireland. (2006b). What is youth work? (information leaflet).

National Youth Federation (2003). *Policy framework for the delivery of youth services*. Dublin: Irish Youthwork Press.

National Youth Health Programme. (2004). *Good habits of mind: A mental health promotion initiative for those working with young people in out-of-school settings*. Dublin.

National Youth Policy Committee. (1984). *Final report* ('Costello Report'). Dublin: Stationery Office.

NCB Stockbrokers. (2006). *2020 vision: Ireland's demographic dividend*. Dublin: NCB.

Nic Gabhainn, S., & Mullan, E. (2003). Self-esteem norms for Irish young people. *Psychological Reports, 92*, 829–30.

Nic Gabhainn, S., & Sixsmith, J. (2005). *Children's understanding of well-being*. Dublin: National Children's Office.

Nieman, D. (1998). *The exercise-health connection*. Champaign, IL: Human Kinetics.

Nilan, P., & Feixa, C. (Eds.). (2006). *Global youth: Hybrid identities, plural worlds*. London: Routledge.

Nixon, L., Greene, S., & Hogan, D. (2006). Concepts of family among children and young people in Ireland. *Irish Journal of Psychology, 27*(1–2), 79–87.

Noble, K. (2003). Personal reflection on experiences of special and mainstream education. In M. Shevlin & R. Rose (Eds.), *Encouraging voices: Respecting the rights of young people who have been marginalised* (pp. 58–66). Dublin: National Disability Authority.

Nolan, B., O'Connell, P., & Whelan, C. (Eds.). (2000). *Bust to boom? The Irish experience of growth and inequality*. Dublin: IPA.

Nolan, B., Layte, R., Whelan, C.T., & Maitre, B. (2006). *Day in, day out: Understanding the dynamics of child poverty*. Dublin: Institute of Public Administration/Combat Poverty Agency.

North Western Health Board. (2004a). *A little bit of respect. Sexual health: A consultation with young people, parents and professionals in the north–west*. Sligo: North Western Health Board.

North Western Health Board. (2004b). *Consultations with teenage girls on being and getting active*. Sligo: Health Promotion Department.

Nurmi, J.E., Poole, M.E., & Kalakoski, V. (1996). Age differences in adolescent identity exploration and commitment in urban and rural environments. *Journal of Adolescence, 19*, 443–52.

O'Boyle, N. (2006). Addressing youth and being young: The bias of youth in Irish advertising. *Youth Studies Ireland*, *1*(1), 40–60.

O'Brien, C. (2006a, June 7). 250 children have disappeared from care in five years. *The Irish Times*.

O'Brien, C. (2006b, August 15). State failing to provide adequate family support. *The Irish Times*.

O'Brien, C. (2006c, August 29). Number of homeless children rises to nearly 500. *The Irish Times*.

O'Brien, C. (2006d, May 23). The greying of Ireland: The weight of age. *The Irish Times* (supplement on population).

O'Connell, H., Chin, A. & Lawlor, B. (2003). Alcohol use in Ireland – can we hold our drink? *Irish Journal of Psychological Medicine*, *20*(4): 109-110.

O'Connell, P., Clancy, D., & McCoy, S. (2006). *Who went to college in 2004? A national survey of new entrants to higher education.* Dublin: Higher Education Authority.

O'Connor, P. (2005). Local embeddedness in a global world: Young people's accounts. *YOUNG: Nordic Journal of Youth Research*, *13*(1), 9–26.

O'Donnell, M. (2003). Transfer from special to mainstream: The voice of the pupil. In M. Shevlin & R. Rose (Eds.), *Encouraging voices: Respecting the rights of young people who have been marginalised* (pp. 228–53). Dublin: National Disability Authority.

O'Dwyer, A. (2001). *In from the cold: Towards a strategy for rural youth work in the Kerry diocese.* Kerry Diocesan Youth Service.

O'Dwyer, K. (2006). Garda restorative justice programme – highlights and insights. In Lalor, K., Ryan, F., Seymour, M., &. Hamilton, C. (Eds.), Conference proceedings, 'Young people and crime: Research, policy and practice', Croke Park, Dublin, 12–13 September 2005 (www.cser.ie).

O'Higgins, S. (2002). *Through the looking glass: Young people's perceptions of the words happy and healthy.* Galway: Department of Health Promotion, NUI Galway.

O'Moore, M., & Minton, S.J. (2003). The hidden voice of bullying. In M. Shevlin & R. Rose (Eds.), *Encouraging voices: Respecting the insights of young people who have been marginalized* (pp. 67–88). Dublin: National Disability Authority.

O'Moore, A.M., Kirkham, C., & Smith, M. (1997). Bullying behaviour in Irish schools. *Aggressive Behaviour*, *26*, 99–111.

O'Shea, C., & Williams, J. (2001). *Issues in the employment of early school leavers.* Dublin: ESRI.

O'Toole, J. (2005). Gender, sexuality and social care. In P. Share & N. McElwee (Eds.), *Applied social care* (pp. 93–107). Dublin: Gill & Macmillan.

OECD (Organisation for Economic and Social Development). (2000). *Literacy in the information age: Final report of the International Adult Literacy Survey.* Paris: OECD.

OECD. (2002). *Society at a glance: OECD social indicators.* Paris: OECD.

OECD. (2004). *Review of higher education in Ireland.* Paris: OECD.

OECD. (2005). *Education at a glance: OECD indicators 2005, executive summary.* Paris: OECD.

OECD. (2006). *Education at a glance 2006: highlights.* Paris: OECD.

Offer, D., Ostrov, E., Howard, K., & Atkinson, R. (1988). *The teenage world: Adolescents' self-image in ten countries.* New York: Plenum Medical Book Company.

Office for Social Inclusion. (no date). *The national action plan against poverty and social exclusion, 2003–2005*. Dublin: Author.

Office of the Minister for Children. (2006). Teenagers seek the development of a national website for information/exchange about youth activities (press release), 25 March.

Office of Tobacco Control. (2006). *Children, youth and tobacco: Behaviour, perceptions and public attitudes*. Naas: Office of Tobacco Control/TNS mrbi.

Ógra Chorcaí (2005). Personal communication.

Olausson, P.O., Haglund, B., Weitoft, G., & Cnattingius (2001). Teenage childbearing and long-term socio-economic consequences: A case study in Sweden. *Family Planning Perspectives, 33*(2), 70–74.

Oldenburg, R. (1999). *The great good place: Cafés, coffee shops, bookstores, bars, hair salons, and other hangouts at the heart of a community*. New York: Marlowe.

Olweus, D. (1993). *Bullying at school. What we know and what we can do*. Oxford: Blackwell.

Ombudsman for Children. (2006). *Report of the Ombudsman for children to the UN Committee on the Rights of the Child on the occasion of the examination of Ireland's second report to the committee*. Dublin: Office of the Ombudsman for Children.

Ottney Cain, A. (1985). Pets as family members. *Marriage and Family Review, 8*, 5–10.

Parker, H., Aldridge, J., & Measham, F. (2005). *Illegal leisure: The normalization of adolescent recreational drug use* (4th ed.). London: Routledge.

Parsons, T. (1972). Age and sex in the social structure of the United States. In P.K. Manning & M. Truzzi (Eds.), *Youth and sociology*. New Jersey: Prentice Hall.

Passer, M., & Smith, R. (2001). *Psychology: Frontiers and applications*. New York: McGraw Hill.

Passmore, A., & French, D. (2001). Development and administration of a measure to assess adolescents' participation in leisure activities. *Adolescence, 36*(141), 67–9.

Pavee Point Travellers' Centre. (2005). *Shadow report: Ireland's first and second report on CERD (Convention on the Elimination of all forms of Racial Discrimination)*. Dublin: Pavee Point.

Percy-Smith, B. (1999). Multiple childhood geographies: Giving voice to young people's experience of place. Unpublished PhD thesis, Centre for Children and Youth, University College Northampton.

Petersen, A.C., & Taylor, B. (1980). The biological approach to adolescence: Biological change and psychological adaptation. In J. Adelson (Ed.), *Handbook of adolescent psychology* (pp. 117–55). New York: Wiley.

Petersen, A.C., Compas, B.E., Brooks–Gunn, J., Stemmler, M., Ey, S., & Grant, K.E. (1993). Depression in adolescence. *American Psychologist, 48*, 155–68.

Phillips, D., & Skinner, A. (1994). *Nothing ever happens round here*. Leicester: Youth Work Press/National Youth Agency.

Phillips, S. (2006). *Report on the needs assessment of separated children seeking asylum and 'aged out' minors*. Dublin: Transition Supports Project.

Phoenix, A. (2005). Young consumers. In S. Ding & K. Littleton (Eds.), *Children's personal and social development* (pp. 221–59). Milton Keynes: Open University/Blackwell.

Physical Education Association of Ireland (PEAI). (2006). *Strategic plan*. www.peai.org/policy/peaistrategicplan/1introduction.html [accessed Sept. 2006].

Piko, B.F., & Vazsonyi, A.T. (2004). Leisure activities and problem behaviours among Hungarian youth. *Journal of Adolescence, 27*(6), 717–30.

Plummer, D. (2006). *Helping adolescents and adults to build self-esteem: a photocopiable resource book.* Gateshead: Athenium Press.

Pobal. (2006). *More than a phase: A resource guide for the inclusion of young lesbian, gay, bisexual and transgender learners.* Dublin: Pobal.

Pollit, E., & Matthews, R. (1998). Breakfast and cognition: An integrative summary. *American Journal of Clinical Nutrition, 67,* 804–813.

Punch, A. (2006, May 23). To infinity and beyond. *The Irish Times* (supplement on population).

Putnam, R. (2000). *Bowling alone: The collapse and revival of American community.* New York: Simon & Schuster.

Ramstedt, M., & Hope, A. (2004). *The Irish drinking culture: Drinking and drink-related harm, a European comparison.* Dublin: Department of Health and Children.

Raymore, L. (2002). Facilitators to leisure. *Journal of Leisure Research, 34*(1), 37–52.

Reilly, J., Muldoon, O.T., & Byrne, C. (2004). Young men as victims and perpetrators of violence in Northern Ireland: A qualitative analysis. *Journal of Social Issues, 60*(3), 469–85.

Remafedi, G. (1987). Homosexual youth: A challenge to contemporary society. *Journal of the American Medical Association, 258,* 222–5.

Roberts, K. (1999). *Leisure in contemporary society.* Wallingford: CABI Publications.

Robins, J. (1980) *The lost children.* Dublin: Institute of Public Administration.

Roche, J.P. (1986). Premarital sex: Attitudes and behaviour by dating stage. *Adolescence, 21,* 107–21.

Rolston, B., Schubotz, D., & Simpson, A. (2004). The first time: Young people and sex in Northern Ireland. *Journal of Youth Studies, 7*(2), 191–207.

Rook, K.S. (1984). Research on social support, loneliness and social isolation. In P. Shaver (Ed.), *Review of personality and social psychology.* Beverly Hills: Sage Publications.

Rowley, J., Ganter, G., & Fitzpatrick, C. (2001). Suicidal thoughts and acts in Irish adolescents. *Irish Journal of Psychological Medicine, 18*(3), 82–6.

Ruddle, K., Leigh, C., McGee, H., & Layte, R. (2004). *Irish contraception and crisis pregnancy study: A survey of the general population.* Dublin: Crisis Pregnancy Agency.

Rural Youth Work Forum. (1999). *Rural youth work in County Wexford.* Wexford: Ferns Diocesan Youth Service/County Wexford Partnership.

Rutter, M. (1979). *Changing youth in a changing society.* London: Nuffield Hospitals Trust.

Rutter, P.A., & Behrendt, A.E. (2004). Adolescent suicide risk: Four psychosocial factors. *Adolescence, 39*(154), 295–303.

Rutter, M., Graham, P., Chadwick, O.F.D., & Yule, W. (1976). Adolescent turmoil: Fact or fiction? *Journal of Child Psychology and Psychiatry, 17,* 35–56.

Ryan, A. (1997). Gender discourses in school social relations. In A. Byrne & M. Leonard (Eds.), *Women and Irish society: A sociological reader.* Belfast: Beyond the Pale.

Ryan, P. (2003). Coming-out, fitting-in: The personal narratives of some Irish gay men. *Irish Journal of Sociology, 12*(2), 68–85.

Sallis, J.F., Simons–Morton, B.J., Stone, E.J., Corbin, C.E., Epstein, L.H., Faucette, N., Iannotti, R.J., Killen, J.D., Klesges, R.C., Petray, C.K., Roland, T.W., & Taylor, W.C.

(1992). Determinants of physical activity and interventions in youth. *Medicine and Science in Sport and Exercise*, 6, 248–257.

Savin-Williams, R.C., & Rodriguez, R.G. (1993). A developmental, clinical perspective on lesbian, gay and bisexual youths. In T.P. Gullotta, G.R. Adams, & R. Montemayor (Eds.), *Adolescent sexuality*. Newbury Park, CA: Sage.

Scheerens, J., & Bosker, R. (1997). *The foundations of educational effectiveness*. Oxford: Pergamon Press.

Schmidtke, A., Bille-Brahe, U., DeLeo, D., Kerkhof, A., Bjerke, T., Crepet, P., Haring, C., Hawton, K., Lönnqvist, J., Michel, K., Pommereau, X., Querejeta, I., Phillipe, I., Salander-Renberg, E., Temesvary, B., Wasserman, D., Fricke, S., Weinacker, B., Sampaio-Faria, J.G. (1996). Attempted suicide in Europe: rates, trends and sociodemographic characteristics of suicide attempters during the period 1989–1992. Results of the WHO/EURO Multicentre Study on Parasuicide. *Acta Psychiatr Scand.*, 93: 327–338.

Schubotz, D., Rolston, B., & Simpson, A. (2003). Researching young people and sex in Northern Ireland. *Irish Journal of Sociology*, 12(2), 5–27.

Seefeld, V., Malina, R.M., & Clark, M.A. (2002). Factors affecting levels of physical activity in adults. *Sports Science*, 12(1), 34–50.

Sex Education Forum. (1992). *An enquiry into sex education: Report of a survey into local education authority support and monitoring of school sex education*. London: Sex Education Forum/National Children's Bureau. www.fpa.org.uk/guide/education/schools.htm [accessed July 2006].

Share, P. & McElwee, N. (Eds.). *Applied Social Care*. Dublin: Gill & Macmillan.

Shiner, M., & Newburn, T. (1996). *Young people, drugs and peer education: An evaluation of the youth awareness programme*. London: Drug prevention Initiative.

Silbereisen, R.K., & Kracke, B. (1990). The impact of maturational timing and parental support. In R.K. Silbereisen & E. Todt (Eds.), *Adolescence in context: The interplay of family, school, peers and work in adjustment*. New York: Springer.

Skegg, K. (2005). Self-harm. *The Lancet*, 366, 1471–83.

Skelton, T., & Valentine, G. (1988). *Cool places: Geographies of youth cultures*. London: Routledge.

Skilbeck, M. (2001). *The university challenged: A review of international trends and issues with particular reference to Ireland*. Dublin: Higher Education Authority.

Skilbeck, M. (2003). *Towards an integrated system of tertiary education: A discussion paper*. Dublin: Dublin Institute of Technology. www.dit.ie/DIT/about/strategic/Skilbeck discussionpaper_march2003.pdf [accessed July 2006].

Skipper, J.K., & Nass, G. (1966). Dating behaviour: A framework for analysis and an illustration. *Journal of Marriage and the Family*, 28, 412–20.

Smith, P.K., Madsen, K.C., & Moody, J.C. (1999). What causes the age decline in reports of being bullied? Towards a developmental analysis of risks of being bullied. *Educational Research*, 41(3), 267–85.

Smyth, C.L. (2000). *Sociocultural factors in Irish adolescent suicide*. Killarney: Kerry Mental Health Association. WWW.kerrymentalhealth.com/articles/sociocultural.htm. [accessed August 2006].

Smyth, C.L., & MacLachlan, M. (2004). The context of suicide: An examination of life circumstances thought to be understandable precursors to youth suicide. *Journal of Mental Health, 13*(1), 83–92.

Smyth, C., MacLachlan, M., & Clare, A. (2003). *Cultivating suicide? Destruction of self in a changing Ireland*. Dublin: Liffey Press.

Smyth, E. (1999). *Do schools differ? Academic and personal development among pupils in the second level sector*. Dublin: Oak Tree Press/ESRI.

Smyth, E. & Hannan, D. (1997). Girls and co-education in the Republic of Ireland. In A. Byrne & M. Leonard (Eds.), *Women and Irish society: A sociological reader*. Belfast: Beyond the Pale.

Smyth, E., & Hannan, D. (2000). Education and inequality. In B. Nolan, P. O'Connell, & C. Whelan (Eds.), *Bust to boom? The Irish experience of growth and inequality*. Dublin: IPA.

Smyth, M. (2006). Initial audit of: demographic, offences, psychological and psychiatric characteristics of girls remanded/committed to a girls' detention school in a two year period. *Special Residential Services Board (SRSB) Bulletin*, Summer 2006.

Social Services Inspectorate. (2004). *Leaving care and aftercare support*. Dublin: SSI. http://www.issi.ie/publications/guidance_notes/leaving_care_and_aftercare_support/ [accessed November 2006].

Soenens, B., Duriez, B., & Goosens, L. (2005). Social-psychological profiles of identity styles: Attitudinal and social-cognitive correlates in late adolescence. *Journal of Adolescence, 28*, 107–25.

Sport England. (2003). Young people and sport in England: Trends in participation 1994–2002. Research study conducted for Sport England by MORI, London.

Steinberg, L. (1993). *Adolescence* (3rd ed.). New York: McGraw–Hill.

Steinberg, L. (2005). Cognitive and affective development in adolescence. *Trends in Cognitive Sciences, 9*(2), 69–74.

Stevenson, C., Doherty, G., Barnett, J., Muldoon, O.T., & Trew, K. (in press). Adolescents' views of food and eating: Identifying barriers to healthy eating. *Journal of Adolescence* [in press; available online May 2006].

Stryker, S. (1987). Identity theory: Developments and extensions. In K. Yardley & T. Honess (Eds.), *Self and identity: Psychosocial perspectives* (pp. 83–101). New York: Wiley.

Sullivan, C., Arensman, E., Keeley, H.S., Corcoran P., & Perry, I.J. (2004). *Young people's mental health: A report of the results from the lifestyle and coping survey*. Cork: National Suicide Research Foundation.

Susman, E., & Dorn, L. (1991). Hormones and behaviour in adolescence. In R. Lerner, A. Petersen, & J. Brooks–Gunn (Eds.), *Encyclopaedia of adolescence, Vol. 1*. New York: Garland Publishing.

Sweeney, J., & Dunne, J. (2003). *Youth in a changing Ireland: A study for Foróige, the national youth development organisation*. Dublin: Foróige.

Sweeting, H., & West, P. (2000). *Teenage health: The West of Scotland 11–16 study*. Glasgow: MRC Social and Public Health Sciences Unit.

Sweeting, H., & West, P. (2003). Young people's leisure and risk-taking behaviours: Changes in gender patterning in the West of Scotland during the 1990s. *Journal of Youth Studies, 6*(4), 391–412.

Tanner, J.M. (1973). Growing up. *Scientific American, 229*, 35–43.

Task Force on Child Care Services. (1980). *Final Report*. Dublin: Stationery Office.

Thompson, K. (1998). *Moral panics*. London & New York: Routledge.

Thurlow, C. (2002). High-schoolers' peer orientation priorities: A snapshot. *Journal of Adolescence, 25*, 341–9.

Tovey, H., & Share, P. (2003). *A sociology of Ireland* (2nd ed.). Dublin: Gill & Macmillan.

Treacy, D. (1992). *A review of youth work practice in community based projects*. Dublin: Stationery Office.

Trent, K., & Crowder, K. (1997). Adolescent birth intentions, social disadvantage and behavioural outcomes. *Journal of Marriage and Family, 59*(3), 523–35.

Trew, K., Barnett, J., Stevenson, C., Muldoon, O., Breakwell, G., Brown, K., Doherty, G., & Clark, C. (2006). *Young people and food – Adolescents' dietary beliefs and understandings*. Dublin: Safefood (Food Safety Promotion Board).

Udry, J.R., Talbert, L., & Morris, N.M. (1988). Biological predispositions and social control in adolescent sexual behavior. *American Sociological Review, 52*, 841–55.

Udry, J., & Billy, J. (1987). Initiation of coitus in early adolescence. *American Sociological Review, 52*, 841–55.

United Nations. (1951). *Convention relating to the status of refugees*. Geneva: United Nations.

United Nations. (1991). *Convention on the Rights of the Child*. New York: United Nations. http://www.unhchr.ch/htm//menu2/6/treaties/crc.htm [accessed March 2006].

United Nations Committee on the Rights of the Child. (2006). *Consideration of reports submitted by States parties under Article 44 of the Convention on the Rights of the Child. Concluding Observations: Ireland*. Geneva: UNCRC, document CRC/C/IRL/CO/2.

Unicef. (2002). *A league table of educational disadvantage in rich nations*. Innocenti Report Card No. 4. Florence: Unicef Innocenti Research Centre.

Ungar, M.T. (2000). The myth of peer pressure. *Adolescence, 35*(137), 167–78.

Valsiner, J. (1993). Culture and human development: A co-constructive perspective. In P. van Geert & L. Mos (Eds.), *Annals of theoretical psychology* (Vol. X). New York: Plenum Press.

Vandewater, E.A., Shim, M., & Caplovitz, A.G. (2004). Linking obesity and activity level with children's television and video game use. *Journal of Adolescence, 27*(1), 71–85.

von Rossberg–Gempton, I.E., Dickinson, J., & Poole, G. (1999). Creative dance: Potentiality for enhancing social functioning in frail seniors and young children. *The Arts in Psychotherapy, 26*(5), 313–27.

van Schooten, E., & de Glopper, K. (2003). The development of literary response in secondary education. *Poetics, 31*, 155–87.

Vazsonyi, A.T., Pickering, L.E., Belliston, L.M., Hessing, D., & Junger, M. (2002). Routine activities and deviant behaviours: American, Dutch, Hungarian and Swiss youth. *Journal of Quantitative Criminology, 18*, 397–422.

Veale, A., Palaudaries, L., & Gibbons, C. (2003). *Separated children seeking asylum in Ireland*. Dublin: Irish Refugee Council.

Verduykt, P. (2002). Summary of the literature on young people, gender and smoking. In M. Lambert, A. Hublet, P. Verduuyckt, L. Maes, & S. Van den Brouke (Eds.), *Gender differences in smoking in young people* (pp. 15–32). Brussels: Flemish Institute for Health Promotion.

Votta, E., & Manion, I. (2004). Suicide, high-risk behaviours and coping style in homeless adolescent males' adjustment. *Journal of Adolescent Health, 34,* 237–43.

Waddell, N., & Cairns, E. (1991). Identity preference in Northern Ireland. *Political Psychology, 12,* 205–13.

Wallace, C., & Kovatcheva, S. (1998). *Youth in society. The construction and deconstruction of youth in East and West Europe.* Basingstoke: Macmillan.

Walsh, D. (2005). *Juvenile justice.* Dublin: Thomson and Roundhall.

Wearing, B., Wearing, S., & Kelly, K. (1994). Adolescent women, identity and smoking: Leisure experience as resistance. *Sociology of Health and Illness,* 16(5), 626–43.

Wegimont, L. (2000). *Development and justice issues: Irish attitudes.* Dublin: Development Education for Youth/Irish Marketing Surveys.

Wegimont, L., & Farrell, D. (1995). *Justice and development issues: An awareness and attitudes survey.* Dublin: Development Education for Youth/Irish Marketing Surveys.

Weissman, M.M., Wolk, S., Goldstein, R.B., Moreau, D., Adams, P., Greenwald, S., Klier, C.M., Ryan, N.D., Dahl, R., & Wickramaratne, R. (1999). Depressed adolescents grown up. *Journal of the American Medical Association,* 281(18), 1707–13.

Weissbourd, R. (1995). *The vulnerable child.* Reading: Addison Wesley.

White, T. (2001). *Investing in people: Higher education in Ireland from 1960 to 2000.* Dublin: IPA.

White, S.D., & DeBlassie, R.R. (1992). Adolescent sexual behaviour. *Adolescence,* 27(105), 183–92.

Whyte, J. (2006). *Research with children with disabilities.* Dublin: National Disability Authority.

Wickham, J. (1998). An intelligent island? In M. Peillon & E. Slater (Eds.), *Encounters with modern Ireland.* Dublin: IPA.

Wilkins-Shurmer, A., O'Callaghan, M.J., Najman, J.M., Bor, W., Williams, G.M., & Anderson, M.J. (2003). Association of bullying with adolescent health–related quality of life. *Journal of Paediatrics and Child Health, 39,* 436–41.

Williamson, H. (1997). *Youth and policy, contexts and consequences: Young men, transition and social exclusion.* Aldershot: Ashgate.

Wolfradt, U., & Doll, J. (2001). Motives of adolescents to use the Internet as a function of personality traits and social factors. *International Journal of Educational Computing Research, 24,* 13–27.

Wood, K., & O'Shea, P. (2003). *Divorce in Ireland: Marital breakdown, answers and alternatives.* Dublin: First Law.

Woods, C., Foley, E., O'Gorman, D., Kearney, J., & Moyna, N. (2004). *The Take PART study: Physical activity for teenagers.* A report for the East Coast Area Health Board by the Centre for Sport Science and Health, Dublin City University.

Working Group on Domestic Partnership. (2006). *Options paper presented to the Tánaiste and Minister for Justice, Equality and Law Reform.* Dublin: Department of Justice, Equality and Law Reform.

World Health Organisation. (1984). Definition of health. In L. Ewles & I. Simnett (1999). *Promoting health - a practical guide.* London: Baillere Tindall.

World Health Organisation. (1986). *Ottawa Charter on health promotion.* Copenhagen: WHO.

World Health Organisation. (2005). *European strategy for child and adolescent health and development*. Geneva: WHO.

Youniss, J., & Smollar, J. (1985). *Adolescent relations with mothers, fathers and friends*. Chicago: University of Chicago Press.

Youth Council for Northern Ireland. (1998). *Benefits of the youth service: A study of the experiences of 14–18 year old members of youth groups in Northern Ireland*. Belfast: Youth Council for Northern Ireland.

Youth Service Liaison Forum. (2005). *Strategy for the delivery of youth work in Northern Ireland*. Belfast: Department of Education for Northern Ireland.

Zani, B. (1993). Dating and interpersonal relationships in adolescence. In S. Jackson and H. Rodrigues–Tomé (Eds.), *Adolescence and its social worlds* (pp. 95–119). Hove: Lawrence Erlbaum Associates.

Zarbatany, L., Hartmann, D., & Rankin, D. (1990). The psychological functions of preadolescent peer activities. *Child Development, 61*, 1067–80.

Zeijl, E., Poel, Y., du Bois–Reymond, M., Ravesloot, J., & Meulman, J. (2003). The role of parents and peers in the leisure activities of young adolescents. *Journal of Leisure Research, 32*, 281–302.

Zimmerman, P. (2004). Attachment representations and characteristics of friendship relations during adolescence. *Journal of Experimental Child Psychology, 88*, 83–101.

Index